THE ROAD TO FREEDOM

FOURTH EDITION

Jill S. Levenson, Ph.D.
& John W. Morin, Ph.D.

Safer Society PRESS
Brandon, Vermont

This workbook is designed to be used as part of a comprehensive treatment program for people who sexually offended. Group therapy is the recommended treatment modality for sex offending. Reading assignments from this book can assist in understanding treatment concepts and can provide material for group discussions.

Published by:
Jill S. Levenson, Ph.D. and John W. Morin, Ph.D.
Oakbrook Counseling Center, P.A.
4804 W. Commercial Blvd.
Tamarac, FL 33319

Produced and Distributed by:
Safer Society Press
P.O. Box 340, Brandon VT 05733
802-247-3132
www.safersocietypress.org

Printed in the United States. August 2025

ISBN # 978-0-578-88529-2

TABLE OF CONTENTS

ACKNOWLEDGEMENTS

This book, like all projects, is the culmination of years of dialogue, brainstorming, and trial-and-error. We first started writing this workbook in 1994, believing that we had something to offer the field and our clients that was different from existing manuals. We wanted to help our clients prevent reoffending by focusing on their strengths as well as their risks, understanding their lives from a wholistic point of view, and empowering them to be their best selves. We self-published RTF for years, and we thank Dave Wood at Wood n Barnes for first distributing the previous edition of the Road to Freedom in 2002. The current workbook represents the evolution of our early ideas after nearly 30 years working with people who abuse.

Thank you to Safer Society Press, David Prescott, Mary Falcon, and Steve Zeoli for their patience and support in this long revision process. We appreciate your belief in the RTF program and your assistance in expanding its reach throughout the U.S. and around the globe. We are honored to be among the esteemed group of scholars and clinicians represented in the product line offered by SSP. Thank you for the opportunity to help make society safer.

We have had many outstanding mentors and collaborators along the way, too many to count, but we are so appreciative for all our ATSA colleagues and our Florida-ATSA friends. We want to give a shout-out to Markyse Bernadin, LCSW, PhD student, and research assistant at Barry University School of Social Work, who painstakingly helped organized the manuscript to get it ready for production. We are eternally grateful to Shelley Kavanagh, LCSW, who is a friend, co-worker, a natural model of trauma-informed practice, and an all-around exceptional person. Shelley, our clients are so lucky to have you as their therapist.

In our 30-year career, we've learned the most from our clients. We thank them for courageously sharing their most personal and painful experiences. We acknowledge their brave journey on their own road to freedom. We believe that people are more than the worst thing they've ever done. We believe that they do not want to harm others again. We thank them for helping us learn how to best help them.

Finally, we would be remiss if we did not acknowledge Jesse the fluffy love-pup, whose presence in our counseling center and in our home is the epitome of the unconditional love and acceptance that we all need and deserve.

We dedicate this book to our five now-adult children and their children, and we hope that they will be able to live in a world that becomes increasingly safer from sexual violence.

— Jill Levenson & John Morin

INTRODUCTION

Welcome to treatment. We're glad you're here, but let's be honest: you're not. Most men start out in treatment wishing they could be anywhere else. That's only natural. You don't know what to expect, and you're afraid you will be judged. You know you will be expected to be open about things you've never talked to anyone about. That's the last thing you want to do. "What good will it do?" you might ask.

Good question. Until now, there wasn't much to be gained from talking about what really happened. The legal and social consequences made it too risky. You may have had some success keeping people off your back simply by denying your crimes. You may have fooled your partner, your family, your co-workers, and maybe even your lawyer. You might have a great story about how you were framed or wrongly convicted. At times you even fool yourself. So why not just stick to your story?

And even if you did do something wrong, does that mean you need treatment? Maybe you were just drunk and not thinking. Maybe your victim seemed to be willing. Maybe you didn't even know that what you were doing was "that bad." So you made a mistake. So what? Everyone makes mistakes. You've learned your lesson. You did the time and now you want to move on with your life. What's the point of dwelling on the past, putting your mistakes under a microscope, and reminding you of how bad you were? It's just more punishment. Just what is this so-called "treatment" supposed to do anyway?

More good questions. But first, let's start with your story. The reason it's such a good story is that parts of it are true. You talk about the police who wouldn't listen to you and pushed you around. Then there were the prosecutors who made you out to be a monster and wanted to put you away for years. Worst of all was your own lawyer, who was always too busy to talk to you, who promised to help, and then told you to plea bargain.

But that is true, you say. Maybe it is. The only problem with that is that it's the wrong story. It's about them, not you. What about you? What's your story? Is your story that you made a mistake and now you've learned your lesson? Well, then, what was the lesson? Was the lesson that you shouldn't have done it? That it was against the law? That you could go to prison? That you were hurting your victim? That people who loved and trusted you would be horrified? That people who don't even know you would hate you?

Well, wait a minute. The truth is that you already knew those things when you offended, didn't you? And still you risked everything for... for what exactly? Do you really even know? You might have an idea of what you got from offending, but not a very clear idea. Because it isn't just about sex. Can sexual excitement really be worth risking *everything* for? One thing is clear: if you are in this program, your behavior was out of control. You chose to let it be out of control. And you chose to pretend it was somehow okay. It's not easy to see yourself as being out of control. It's much easier to find excuses. Before you went to court you probably thought of a good story and your lawyer may have even helped you. You might still believe your story. But aren't stories just ways of avoiding the truth? If you're willing to give treatment a try, you'll find you don't need a story. You can talk openly about yourself and your problems. People will listen to you and understand. And they will respect you.

At this moment, think back in your mind to when you were offending, after an offense and after the excitement had died, when the shame and disgust flooded you and you said to yourself, *"What am I doing?"* Those were the moments when reality came screaming through to you, when you allowed yourself to feel your real feelings. Maybe it's been a long time since you've had those kinds of genuine feelings about what you were doing. Maybe now it feels safer just to say "I've learned my lesson," and brush off treatment with a wave of your hand. But is that the honest truth? Isn't there really a lot more to it than that? You might hate the idea of treatment now, but you could learn a lot about yourself in treatment. It's hard, but it starts with honesty. For the first time ever, there is now more to be gained than lost by being honest about what you've done.

What Should I Expect from Treatment?

This program is specifically designed for people who have committed sex offenses or who feel they are at risk for committing a sex offense. There are many different types of sexual behaviors that are against the law, and everyone has different motivations, patterns, and contributing factors. We want to help you figure out how all those things fit together for YOU. You will learn more about the treatment goals and graduation requirements at the end of this introductory chapter.

In this program you will become more comfortable talking about what happened in a genuine and authentic way. We are committed to making this treatment program a safe and non-judgmental place for you to explore your thoughts and feelings. Your therapists are experienced professionals who have met hundreds (or thousands) of people like you, so they won't be shocked or judgmental, and they won't shame you for what you share.

You will learn about becoming accountable–not just for your offense but in all aspects of your life. You will learn to cope with the consequences of the crime, including the trauma you experienced as a result of your arrest, incarceration, and/or sex offender registration. You will learn about common types of sexual behavior problems, and about the causes beneath them. You will learn about the impact of sexual crimes on victims (and if you think you did not have a victim, we'll explore that too). You will learn about the factors in your early life and family history that have contributed to your personality, sexual development, and relationship skills. You will learn to be more aware of the ways you think about yourself and others. You will learn about sex and intimacy (have you ever really thought about the meaning of sex?). You will learn healthy relationship and communication skills. And you will learn how to prevent your sexual behavior problems from repeating themselves in the future and ruining your life.

What Should I Expect from this Workbook?

We hope that this workbook provides you with a structure you can use on your treatment journey. Your treatment provider might ask you to complete assignments in order, or assign you to read relevant parts when applicable. This workbook provides general information that can help you understand sexual offending, thinking processes, trauma, victim impact, self-regulation skills, and ways to build a healthy lifestyle and prevent reoffending. The exercises will help you apply the information to your own life history and behavior, and give you food for thought in exploring your own strengths, needs, risks, problems, and solutions.

This workbook incorporates the most contemporary research and best clinical practices available. You can find a bibliography at the end with a list of references that inform our approach. But at the start we want to identify a few important points about the field of sex-offense risk assessment and treatment that are built into the principles of this workbook.

Person-first Language

You might be required to register as a sex offender or predator. These are legal terms determined by statutes, and the definitions differ in each state. It is important to remember that despite the label and the stigma it carries with it, "sex offender" is not who you are, it is something you've done. You are a person who has done lots of good things in your life, and you committed an offense that harmed others. In this book, we will not refer to you as a sex offender, but as a person who committed a sex crime. When talking about registration, we will use the acronym RSO to refer to a person *required to register as a sex offender*. But it is important to separate your behavior from your identity. That's hard, we know, especially with public registries. But changing the way you think about yourself is the first step in changing your behavior.

Risks and Strengths

In this book, you will learn about "risk factors." A risk factor is anything that could increase your chances of committing another sex crime. We will help you figure out which risk factors apply to you, and we'll talk about ways to reduce your risk. Not all clients possess the same risk factors, and not all pose the same level of risk for re-offending. Your therapist will probably conduct a "risk assessment" to better understand the risk factors (based on research) that apply to you. This will help your therapist make recommendations about supervision, restrictions, and your treatment needs. Your treatment plan will also consider other needs, such as housing, employment, medical or mental health care, substance abuse, family, and peer relationships. Everyone has strengths too, and we will help you find and use your character strengths to improve your life. Your therapist will help create a treatment plan that is based on overcoming your risk factors and making the most of your strengths.

Understanding Trauma

In this book you will learn about the impact of trauma in your own life, and also how your offense was traumatic for your victim. Trauma occurs when we experience an event that threatens our physical or psychological safety. In the aftermath of such an event we may experience intense fear, helplessness, or horror. When these effects are overwhelming, they can have a lasting impact and can lead to a mental disorder called Post Traumatic Stress Disorder (PTSD). PTSD first came to the attention of the public when it was recognized in men who were returning from war. Traumatic stress can result from a single shocking experience, or it can also result from a series of stressful events or conditions that leave a person feeling overwhelmed, helpless, and fearful.

Many people arrested for violent crimes, including sex offenses, have a history of early trauma —these are called "adverse childhood experiences" (ACEs). These are a particular set of traumas that can interfere with a child's development and produce long-lasting emotional, physical, and social consequences. ACEs include childhood physical and emotional abuse and neglect, as well as sexual abuse. Growing up in a home with drug or alcohol abuse, mental illness, family violence, an absent parent, or people involved in crime are other adverse experiences. ACEs can also include childhood poverty, racial or ethnic discrimination, bullying, community violence, illness, injury, or death of a family member.

Unresolved trauma can alter the way we think. They can challenge our coping skills, change our self-concept, and affect our ability to form healthy relationships. During treatment you will be asked to think about whether you might have experienced trauma in your childhood, and how such trauma might have contributed to your problems—including your offending. You will learn about the long-lasting biological, social, and psychological effects of trauma. Having experienced trauma is never an excuse for abusive or violent behavior. However, by understanding the role of trauma in your own life, you can better understand how it might have contributed to thinking or behaviors that were involved in your offense. Treatment can help you deal with any trauma you experienced that remains "unresolved" (that is, that you never recognized or got treatment for), and can improve your behavioral control and your future relationships.

Self-Regulation and Prevention

You will not be surprised to learn that one of your primary tasks in treatment will be to understand what motivated your offending behavior, and how to keep it from happening again. You will learn that just as everyone's thought patterns are different, and everyone's relationship patterns are different, everyone's motivations for offending are different as well. Some people are motivated by sexually deviant interests, while others use sex as a form of power or control. Some other people are making shockingly misguided efforts to connect intimately with others. Some people who offend are impulsive, entitled, or ignorant of the potential consequences for themselves and others. You'll hear more about self-regulation throughout the workbook, and specific exercises will help you devise your own personal plan for improving your self-management and self-control.

Living a Healthy Life

This book is designed primarily to help you move *away* from the types of thinking and behaving that have led you to commit sex crimes. But it is equally important for you to figure out what you will be moving *toward*—what will make you happy. You will focus on the future and you will create realistic goals. This affirmative approach ("you can do it!") is designed to counter the discouraging and hopeless messages that many of you hear in your homes or communities. We believe in you, and we want to provide hope for a fulfilling future by creating a pathway out of crime and away from problematic sexual behaviors. We want you to feel more in control of your life. This program will help you create a healthy life and build a future that includes satisfying relationships, and that allows you to use your skills in ways that will make you proud. These are goals that are common to all human beings, and we will help you discover how to accomplish them through your *healthy life plan*.

What Is Sexual Assault?

This program is specifically designed for people who have committed sex offenses or think they may be at risk for doing so. Many different types of sexual behaviors are against the law. Sexual assault means *any kind of sexual activity with a child under the age of consent, or with an adult against his or her will.* Notice that this definition does not mention the words "sexual intercourse." Sexual intercourse is only one of many types of sexual activity, all of which can be assaultive. Another way of defining sexual assault is to say that sexual assault involves any sexual activity with any person who does not consent (agree) to it. There are many types of sexual contact (and non-contact) that can be non-consensual, and all of them will violate the other person and can harm them. Sexual offenses involve any sexual activity with any person who does not or cannot *consent* (agree) to it.

Sexual assault is not simply about sexual touching or sexual activity. It is about abusing your power, authority, or trust to manipulate and take from another person the sexual gratification you want. It is taking away that person's right to choose. It is about tricking someone and stealing their privacy, trust, or innocence. It leaves a victim frightened, ashamed, and unable to trust again. It is taking advantage of someone who trusts you and violating that person. It is an act of betrayal. It is about concealing, lying and exploiting. You don't really need legal definitions to describe sexual assault. You know when you're doing it. Sometimes you might know that something is wrong or illegal, but not really grasp or understand why it's harmful. You might think that it really isn't a big deal. Any time you violate another person's rights for your own sexual pleasure, whether the other person knows it or not, you are committing a sexual assault.

For now, know this: *your sexual interests do not make you a bad person.* No one chooses their sexual attractions. We discover them. We simply find ourselves turned on by certain people and certain acts. However, we do choose our behavior. What you can choose, and must choose, is what you do about your attractions. There are people who are sexually attracted to children but choose never to act on that attraction. There are people who are aroused by non-consent, by peeping on others, or by exposing their genitals, but who choose not to act on those attractions.

Does that seem like a heavy burden, to have attractions but not act on them? Well consider this: *everyone* finds themselves attracted to someone they shouldn't have sex with. Married people don't stop being attracted to others, but they stop acting on those attractions if they don't want to live outside their value system, and don't want to hurt someone they love. Is it asking too much of them, to not act on their attractions? Most people don't feel that way. Most people control their sexual behavior. So can you.

Sex offending is something you've done, it's not who you are. *We don't choose our attractions; we choose our actions.*

But I Don't Really Need This...

Therapy is about regaining control of your life—which means regaining your freedom. Some people say, "Well, yeah, maybe I was out of control then, but I haven't even thought about offending since then, so I must be better." Every single person who comes into treatment says, "I won't do that again, I learned my lesson." And they believe it. But, do they understand what caused it in the first place? Will you know how to handle it if a similar situation presents itself in the future? Has anything *inside* you really changed?

Lots of alcoholics go for years without drinking. It's easy for them to convince themselves that they're "cured." They may have done a lot of thinking about their problem and feel they are older and wiser. But if they haven't dealt with the issues that pushed them toward abusing alcohol in the first place, all their wisdom and willpower can quickly evaporate. In time they learn that until they understand what makes them tick, and until they have a real plan to deal with the urge to drink, their periods of not drinking are just a "pretend normal" phase. Nothing has really changed. When a person with alcoholism or a drug addiction loses control, it is sad for them and their families. But when someone sexually re-offends, it is horribly damaging for the victim and for you and your family. Doesn't it make sense to protect yourself if you can?

But I Don't Really Want This...

Some people have a different objection to treatment. They know that really doing treatment will mean giving up something that has brought excitement and pleasure to their lives. You might think, "If I accept that I can never do this again, I wouldn't have anything to look forward to. I know other people don't approve, but I don't think it really hurts anyone, and it's the only thing I have."

It hurts to give up anything that brings pleasure. It hurts like crazy if it's the *only* thing that brings pleasure. But, then, what does it say about your life when only one thing brings you pleasure? It says you've cut yourself off from other possibilities and given up on the things that make other people happy.

The bad news is that you do have to give up victimizing behaviors that are abusive and cause harm to others, and in some cases, this will be a painful loss to you. You have to give it up because no matter what you have been telling yourself, it hurts your victims terribly. *You don't have any right to hurt other people.*

The good news is that offending may have been much more important in your life than it needed to be. You can give it up and have a good life without abusing and despite having attractions that you can't act on. You will free yourself from a lifestyle that crushed your dignity and your self-respect, kept you hiding from others and lying to everyone, and cut off the possibility of achieving real happiness. You will learn to replace offending with other things that make you feel good. In treatment you will learn how and why you have excluded yourself from the good things in life, and you will learn how to create opportunities to get those things back.

But I Wasn't Convicted of a Sex Crime...

If you were lucky enough to plead to a non-registrable offense, count your blessings. You dodged a bullet… No, you dodged a cannonball. Maybe your lawyer negotiated your crime down to a lesser offense, or a non-sex crime that did not require you to register with the "sex offender" label. Sometimes the justice system allows a plea deal because the victim would not be a good witness, or refuses to testify, or because coming to court would cause more trauma to the victim. Sometimes the evidence is weak. But that doesn't mean it didn't happen. You know what happened. Remember, your pre-trial story is just that—a story, even if it resulted in a non-sex crime conviction. You know the real story. Here's your chance to own it, learn from it, and prevent it from happening again. Because next time, you won't get another chance to dodge that cannonball.

If You Think about All You Have Lost...

Most people who have committed sex offenses have lost a great deal through their offenses. Some of the obvious things are:

- Money lost to lawyers
- Homes, property, and good jobs (or even careers) lost as a result of the arrest and conviction
- Relationships with partners, children, family members, and friends destroyed
- Loss of freedom and privacy
- Loss of new job opportunities
- Loss of dignity and respect from others

There are many other less obvious losses. One is the loss of your self-esteem. You may have felt ashamed about what you were doing, even while you were telling yourself it was okay. If you tried to stop but couldn't, you have probably felt powerless and weak because your behavior was out of control. If you ever let yourself think honestly about the harm you were doing to your victims, you felt guilty.

You lost the ability to have honest relationships because you were afraid to let others know you. You lost your ability to be spontaneous: to just be yourself. It is hard to be close to others when you have secrets. You lost out on the chance for real emotional intimacy with others–the very thing you might have been trying to achieve through offending.

Perhaps the biggest loss is the loss of freedom–not just the physical freedom you lost while incarcerated and will lose again if you are re-arrested–but the freedom to choose. Anytime you become a slave to an addiction or a compulsive behavior, you have lost a measure of your personal freedom. Your behavior may seem to take on a power you cannot resist. Some men talk about being so obsessed with sex that they can think of nothing else. These men have let sex completely control their lives. But you do have a choice.

In treatment you will learn to recognize and talk about your losses. Losses can lead to feelings of helplessness, depression, and/or anxiety. These feelings are painful. But you can overcome them the same way other people overcome painful feelings: by talking about them, confronting them, and finding ways to cope with them constructively. Sharing your pain can be a healing experience, especially when you talk to others who have felt the same way. Remembering your losses is a good way to remind yourself of everything your sex offense has cost you.

But Why Me?

Most people convicted of sex crimes ask themselves this question a million times. *Why did I do what I did? How did I get these sexual interests?* There is no simple answer. All humans are different and all people who sexually offend are different. There is no such thing as a "typical" person who commits a sex offense. The stereotypes you see in the media are just that - stereotypes. You will find that every person in your group has a different background, different issues, and a different pattern of offending. Some people's lives are completely dominated by sexual thinking and behavior. Others say their offense seemed to "come out of nowhere" and took them by surprise.

The one thing all offenders have in common is that they chose to offend. *Nothing and no one made you offend. Your offense was a choice.* As you go through treatment you will be examining your life for clues as to how you came to commit your sex offense. Part of any psychotherapy involves learning how significant events and relationships in your life have shaped your personality, your thinking, and your behavior.

The Road to Freedom Takes Courage...

If you are telling yourself that you don't need treatment because you have already learned your lesson, you are simply fooling yourself about the seriousness of what you have done. Something has gone terribly wrong. Sex offenses are very rarely "mistakes." A mistake is when you try to do one thing but do something else accidentally. A sex offense represents a series of decisions you made, even if you didn't fully understand the consequences of them.

It takes courage to admit to yourself the truth of what you have done. It takes courage to admit that you need help. It takes courage to talk openly about your offenses and your problems in your treatment group. If you have never been courageous in the past, now is the time for you to understand that courage isn't something you *have*, it's something you *do*. By *acting* courageously, you can and will become courageous.

You have probably heard frightening things about people convicted of sex crimes: *They can't be cured. They all reoffend.* That simply is not true. We know that, and in time you will too. It is true that some paraphilic (sexually deviant) attractions (if you have them—not everyone does) can't be changed and will remain with you. But you can and will learn to control your behavior and cope with your problems in a constructive way. If you buy into the idea that you can never change and that your life is hopeless, you will see no reason to take the risk of engaging in treatment. If you have tried many times to control your behavior and have not succeeded, you may believe that you can never control yourself. The truth is that anyone who *truly* commits himself to change can change. It takes courage to make that commitment. In treatment you will learn that there are "tools" you can use to stay in control, make better decisions, and improve your life.

Life is a risk. Everything we do in life that is worthwhile involves risk. From the first step we take as an infant, to our first day in school, to our first job, to our first relationship—every time we stretch ourselves, every time we grow, we are taking risks. To be able to have your life back—to be able t*o have a life that makes you feel good, and that you are proud of*, is worth taking a risk for.

The Road to Freedom Starts with Accepting Yourself

Being a labeled as a "sex offender" is not who you are. It is something you've done. It is a choice you have made. You are always free to make other choices, even when it doesn't feel that way. If you are able to see the totality of who you are, to give yourself credit for your good qualities as well as acknowledging your problems, you will recognize that *you have overcome problems in the past and can do it again*. You will understand that treatment is worth the risk and the pain. If you are denying that you have a problem, you are still not accepting yourself fully. You are trying to cut out the part that you don't want to accept.

Right now, you may not know how treatment can really help you. If you have been feeling different from other people for most of your life, it may be hard even to imagine connecting with others in a genuine way. People who have been in prison for a long time sometimes forget what it feels like to be free. It feels good. And treatment can help you find freedom. But only if you let it.

Don't take it from us. Take it from some men who took the risk of engaging in treatment and using it to its fullest. They both successfully completed treatment and *The Road to Freedom*. We asked them to share their experiences with you:

Howard's Story

Howard molested his two nieces, who were living with him, for over two years. When they told their father a few years later, Howard was arrested. When he started treatment, he minimized the extent of his crimes and did not understand the harm he had caused the girls. Today he writes:

> *As an abuser I lived a life of lies and deceit. I used alcohol to hide my feelings and denied the harm I caused the ones I love. Through counseling I began to understand the hurt and lifelong damage I caused the victims of my crimes. I also learned about the cycles of feelings and unmet needs that lead to abuse, and the ways to prevent future abuse. I am now able to cope with life's problems without becoming a threat to my family. Although I have seen extremely difficult times since leaving treatment, and have been tempted at times to bend the truth, I find I can no longer live with dishonesty. For me, to tell any lie feels like I am backsliding and losing control of my life. Having learned how important honesty is to me, the feeling of being dishonest in any way is no longer acceptable to me.*

Jim's Story

> *I was convicted for downloading child pornography (CP) from the dark side of the internet. I felt the court's punishment for my offense was entirely too harsh for the crime. I felt sorry for myself at this injustice and did not think that court-required professional therapy was appropriate. So I entered group therapy with a very negative attitude.*
>
> *The first thing that happened was I began to feel less sorry for myself when compared to some others in the group who had it much worse than I. Secondly, it became easier to confront my situation because the group members and the therapist were not judgmental, making it easier for me to objectively examine my behavior. And finally, the structured approach of the "Road to Freedom" helped me to find a bridge between denial of a problem with my use of CP and the reality of my illegal behavior. Thankfully, I am past that dysfunctional point in my life, and I am enjoying a new freedom from illicit, offensive behavior. I know myself better, and I'm a better person for it.*

John's Story

John had been exposing himself (flashing) for years before he was arrested. He had tried to stop himself but could not. When he first began treatment, he was nervous and unsure of what the program held for him. He wished we would just leave him alone. Today he writes:

> *When I started with the group I felt alone, out of place, embarrassed, and angry. In the end, it changed my life. I learned that I had the power to change my life. I learned it was my choice whether to live my life to the fullest or to become more and more self-destructive. Nobody is jinxed, and there is never a reason to give up hope.*
>
> *It took me quite some time to open up in the group, but once I did they couldn't shut me up. It felt so good to talk about my thoughts and feelings. I learned that I did not offend because I was a bad person,*

but that there were many things that led me down the wrong path. So many of us have low self-esteem and are afraid of rejection. But guess what? If you do not take rejection personally and do not let it affect how you value yourself, your whole attitude changes. People see the difference and respect you for it. Before long, the rejection will diminish.

For me, a major key is communication. With work, improved communication skills can enable you to open so many doors that seemed closed before. I have learned that I am a good person with much worth. I have learned to be proud of myself.

Now you are at the same crossroads I was. I feel strongly about speaking out because I know how you feel. You will choose to either continue going down the self-destructive path that led you here or you will learn from this experience. If you take hold and grab onto your life as hard as you can, you can take charge of your future and choose a different, better path. That is what I did. I can honestly say that because I had the opportunity to go through and graduate from this program, not only am I not reoffending, but every aspect of my life now is better to some degree.

It just takes some work, some courage, and the desire to live your life again. It's not easy, but the rewards are priceless. I promise you.

Here's a different kind of letter from a man who never gave therapy a chance. While he was attending treatment. he never talked about what he was doing outside of meetings, never even mentioned that he was fighting urges.

Jason's Story

I am writing this letter from the county jail where I sit facing forty-seven years in prison. Since I am only thirty years old, I would be around seventy when I come out–if I don't die before then or someone kills me.

Back in 1992, I was locked up for indecent assault on a child under the age of sixteen. I would go to neighborhoods when school let out and follow kids around. I would drive up beside the boys and let them notice me masturbating in the car, exposing my private parts. I would ask some of them if they wanted me to perform oral sex on them. None would say yes and I would go home and finish for myself. The next opportunity I got I would be out there again, doing the same thing over and over. Eventually some kids got my license plate number and turned me in.

Never being in trouble before, I was scared to death. I remember waiting to be finger-printed, booked, and searched. They searched me naked and I was very embarrassed. The jail was nasty and smelled really bad. I had a mattress on the floor, it was noisy, and the lights stayed on all night. I was there for a total of thirty months before I finally went home on house arrest.

When I got out of jail, I was doing good but then slipped back into my old habits, especially after house arrest was over. How could I be so stupid? I was arrested again just thirteen months after getting out of jail. This time I ended up in jail for seven months before being sentenced to thirty years in prison followed by probation. Even while in prison I was sexually active with my roommate who was eighteen but looked younger.

When I was released, I did good for about two months, then decided to check things out just one time. Of course, you can't do it just one time. I was in treatment at the time, denying that I had a problem. I bought a car and eventually started driving around. I started going to the mall on my way to therapy. I would watch kids in the bathroom and masturbate. I would drive around and ask questions to boys and masturbate in front of them. Once again, I got caught with my pants down. Some kids took my tag number and called the police.

So here I am again sitting in the nasty county jail. I have never been so humiliated in my life. I am now waiting to see what will happen to me. Why am I so stupid? I am now miserable. I went to court with cold handcuffs on my arms, tight. I have to be in the same room sometimes when my roommate goes to the bathroom. I have to eat nasty food. I have nothing to do but wait.

This is proof that no matter what you get out of any bad habit it is not worth it one bit. Don't continue on the same path. Stay in therapy and listen to what your therapists tell you. Listen to the rest of the guys in your group and take it from me, get help through therapy and you can be saved from this evil life.

Getting to Work

Psychological treatment is not something that happens to you. It is not something we do to you. Treatment is something *you* do for *you*. Our job is to help you ask the right questions, to help you clarify your answers, and to teach you how to use the tools you will be reading about in this book. The rest is up to you. You will progress in treatment only to the extent that you decide to work at it. The exercises in this book will help you ask yourself important questions. There are no right answers. We don't know the answers to these questions. Only you do.

This program is a demanding one. You might feel overwhelmed when you begin to look at the treatment plan and all the work that is expected of you. There is a lot to learn if you are going to change your behavior. As with any program, if you take it *one step at a time* you will make it manageable. Work at your own pace and do not pressure yourself to complete all the work at once. Do the assignments as you go along and you will begin to make sense out of different issues. Don't be afraid to ask questions in your group or request individual sessions with your therapist if needed.

You are now ready to begin working toward the goals of the program. Following the Treatment Plan, you will see that most of the items have corresponding activities and exercises to help you understand and apply what you learn. You will keep a notebook, and in your notebook, you will complete each assignment in written form. Writing is awkward for a lot of people, but practicing makes it easier. You will be learning so many things about yourself that if you don't write them down, you will never remember them. Don't worry at all about spelling or grammar–your work will not be graded! Your therapist will go over your work to be sure it is complete. There are sample worksheets provided for many of the assignments that you can copy into your notebook. Discuss your progress in your group as you complete assignments. Use group meetings or individual sessions with your therapist to discuss areas of difficulty.

It is best to do the assignments as the group is discussing them. That way you can bring to the group any questions or thoughts you have about yourself. Initially you may be uncomfortable discussing these personal matters with other people, but as time goes by you will learn that you can trust your group. You will hear other people saying things that you have thought, and you will know that you are not alone. You are among people who can help you to make sense of your thoughts, feelings and experiences.

It will take time for you to give up the defenses you have built around your sexual problems. Everyone works at their own pace. If you work slower than some of the other group members, that's okay. Just keep in mind that before you can leave the program you have to graduate.

Graduation

In the beginning you may want to try to get treatment over with as quickly as possible. But it took a long time for you to get to be the person you are, and change takes time too. Treatment is usually a long-term process. Each person completes the work at their own pace, but generally it takes at least a year to fully work through all the exercises and understand yourself and your problems. For many people it takes longer.

Before you can successfully complete treatment, you must complete the exercises and be able to explain to your group what you have learned about yourself and how you have accomplished the treatment goals as they apply to you. Ultimately, *you must create a plan to prevent reoffending*. This is called your Self-Regulation and Healthy Life Plan. By the time you are ready to graduate, you will be able to describe your plan to the group and convince the other members that it will work.

This means that you must be prepared if you are going to graduate. All exercises must be completed and turned in to your therapist for review before beginning the graduation process. Group time during graduation will not be spent working through the assignments.

Once your therapist has reviewed and approved your work, you will present a summary of your knowledge in group. Please be thorough but brief when presenting your work. Your therapist will let you know how much time you will be allotted. The following is a suggested structure for presenting what you have learned to your group:

Accountability	Chapter 1
Understanding Your Sexual Behavior	Chapter 2
Understanding Self-Regulation	Chapter 3
Understanding Yourself, Family, & Life History	Chapter 4
Victim Awareness	Chapter 5
Relationships and Communication Skills	Chapter 6
Relapse Prevention – Thinking	Chapter 7
Relapse Prevention – Risk, Self- Regulation, and your Healthy Life Plan	Chapter 8

On the next page is the *Treatment Plan*. These are the skills that you will learn in treatment and will be expected to demonstrate before you graduate. Each goal is related to a particular chapter. It is your guide for successfully completing the program.

NOTE: For purposes of simplification, this book generally refers to persons who have committed sex crimes as "he." This is done merely for convenience and is not intended to imply that sex offenses are not committed by females. (Females may have different treatment needs and may use a different workbook). Please also note that, in order to avoid using the awkward and distracting objects "him or her," we sometimes use "they," "their" and "them" with singular verbs.

TREATMENT PLAN

Client Name:
Chapter 1: PERSONAL ACCOUNTABILITY: Client will demonstrate personal responsibility for prevention of sexual assault, and accountability in all areas of life. 1. Admit to instant offense and disclose full sexual history. 2. Acknowledge problem and need for treatment. 3. Demonstrate compliance with supervision restrictions and laws. 4. Make some attempt at restitution either directly to victim or indirectly to others. 5. Show acceptance of consequences for own behavior. 6. Model appropriate behavior in treatment group and in community.
Chapter 2: UNDERSTANDING YOUR SEXUAL BEHAVIOR: Client will demonstrate understanding of sexual, emotional, and general self-regulation problems that contributed to sex-offending behavior. 1. Describe sexual interests, patterns, and behaviors that have been problematic. 2. Describe your understanding of your sexual autobiography.
Chapter 3: SELF-REGULATION: Client will demonstrate understanding of sexual, emotional, and general self-regulation problems that contributed to sex-offending behavior. 1. Describe emotional management patterns and behaviors that have been problematic. 2. Describe general self-management patterns and behaviors that have been problematic. 3. Describe sexual self-management patterns and behaviors that have been problematic. 4. Describe Behavior Management Techniques that have been helpful with the self-regulation problems described above.
Chapter 4: UNDERSTANDING YOURSELF: Client will demonstrate understanding of psychosocial, trauma-related, and family factors that contribute to the development of sexual behavior problems. 1. Discuss and describe childhood history, family dynamics, and significant events. 2. Explore and describe how early trauma and adverse childhood experiences (ACEs) have shaped your personality, attachment, and self-regulation. 3. Identify and describe coping strategies throughout your life. 4. Identify and describe relational styles and patterns throughout life. 5. Describe attempts to meet emotional needs through sex and/or sexual assault.
Chapter 5: VICTIM IMPACT: Client will demonstrate the ability to identify the physical, emotional, and interpersonal consequences of sexual assault for past and potential victims. 1. Identify and describe feelings common to victims of sexual assault. 2. Identify and describe why victims may not disclose the offense. 3. Identify and describe common emotional consequences of sexual assault for victims. 4. Identify and describe why sexual assault is harmful to victims. 5. Speculate as to the ways in which sexual assault impacted your own victims.

Chapter 6: RELATIONSHIPS AND COMMUNICATION SKILLS: Client will demonstrate the ability to build healthy relationships and apply effective communication skills. 1. Use assertive communication strategies such as active listening and I statements. 2. Apply problem-solving and decision-making skills and strategies. 3. Use non-violent, appropriate conflict resolution strategies. 4. Demonstrate shared power through use of negotiation, compromise, dialogue, cooperation. 5. Develop and describe healthy relationship and intimacy skills with age appropriate peers.
Chapter 7: CHANGING YOUR THINKING: Client will recognize and restructure thinking errors (cognitive distortions) that represent unhealthy thinking and/or encourage and reinforce sexual assault or boundary violating behavior. 1. Identify own maladaptive thinking (schemas) across different areas of life. 2. Identify thinking errors related to sex offending. 3. Correct cognitive distortions and replace them with thoughts that promote healthy styles of thinking and responsible sexual behavior.
Chapter 8: RELAPSE PREVENTION: RECOGNIZING RISK: Client will recognize decisions and conditions, both internal and external, which create risk for poor self- regulation and re-offense. 1. Identify sexual, emotional, and general self-regulation problems. 2. Describe risk factors and triggers for sex offending. 3. Recognize the relationship between events, thoughts, feelings, and sexual offense behaviors. 4. Identify decision-making and efforts to meet needs through sex or sexual offense behaviors. 5. Identify grooming strategies used to gain access to victims.
Chapter 8: RELAPSE PREVENTION: SELF-REGULATION AND HEALTHY LIFE PLANS: Client will develop and use a range of cognitive and behavioral coping strategies to prevent re-offense. 1. Use cognitive, behavioral, and relational techniques for sexual, emotional, and general self-regulation. 2. Use anger management techniques to contain aggression. 3. Has a support system that supports responsible sexual behaviors and non-criminal lifestyle. 4. Has developed self-regulation skills for healthy boundaries and sexuality. 5. Has developed a relapse prevention plan for a variety of potential risky situations. 6. Has developed a safety plan for contact with children or other potential victims, and for safe internet use. 7. Has developed and implemented strategies for meeting emotional needs in healthy, non-victimizing ways. 8. Has developed and implemented strategies for de-escalation, impulse control, and sexualized coping.
My individual treatment goals based on personal strengths and needs:

CHAPTER 1

ACCEPTING RESPONSIBILITY

In this chapter, we will discuss reducing denial and increasing accountability. Some degree of denial is ordinarily observed in people who have offended, ranging from absolute denial about the facts of the case, to minimization or rationalization of the offense, to blaming the victim or others for the offense or its consequences, to denying that you need help. The goal here is to help you become more accountable to yourself and others in all areas of your life. This means that accountability is more than just offense culpability. Accountability goes beyond offense admission and in this program will focus more generally on helping you live a life consistent with your values and your view of the person you want to be.

Everyone understands denial because everyone does it. So no one is surprised when we lie about serious things we have done wrong. Amazingly, our legal system is set up to encourage denial. Anything you say can and will be used against you. The prosecutor tells the court you're guilty and should be punished. As the defendant, you have no choice but to deny. When your defense attorney sat with you and asked, "all right, tell me what happened," she wasn't asking for the true story. She was asking if you have a story that makes you believable. Of course, if you really didn't do anything wrong, you would tell her what really happened. But your denial might be all she needs to get your charge dismissed.

But what if you really did something? Well, your lawyer doesn't want to hear you say that because then she can't defend you at all. She can't knowingly lie in court. So she needs some kind of a story to work with in order to plea bargain for you. She can always question whether the victim was confused or mistaken or high or is exaggerating. She will ask you questions that might throw some doubt on what the victim said. And together you will concoct your court story. But that's still better than nothing, because what she really needs to get you a decent plea bargain is to create some type of doubt.

Before you go to court, one way or another, you have a story. And whether it works in court or not, some part of it works for you, and you want to stick with it. So you bring it home and tell your family and friends (if you think they'll buy it) and you bring it to your treatment program (where you're hoping they'll buy it) because you sure don't want to have to do this "treatment" thing. But here's where your story hurts you, because therapy is different from everything else.

When you come into treatment there are no lawyers, no judge, no jury, and nobody to convince of your innocence. It's just you. And whether you took a plea bargain or you went to trial, you've already been convicted. Your treatment provider is not in a position to undo your conviction. So there's really just one question you need to ask yourself now: "Should I be concerned about my sexual behavior?" If there's any part of you that feels the answer is "yes," you will soon see that you're in the right place.

Denial and Accountability

So let's talk about denial and its opposite: accountability. Almost everyone brings some degree of denial to treatment, ranging from absolute denial of the facts of the case, to minimizations or rationalizations (excuses) for the offense, to blaming the victim or others for the offense, to denying that you need help. But you're going to have to give up your denial if you're going to get anything out of treatment. You kind of already know that, don't you? Our goal is to help you become more accountable to yourself and others in all areas of your life. This means that accountability is more than just taking responsibility for your sex offense. In this program we want to help you learn to live a life that you can talk about openly and honestly. A life that fits your values and your view of the person you want to be.

Accountability is a big concept. It includes acting in a transparent and authentic way, taking responsibility for all your choices. It means finding ways to try to right any wrongs you have done to others. It means being in charge of your decisions and the consequences of those decisions. It involves a willingness to be honest with yourself and others about your weaknesses, mistakes, and character flaws. It means recognizing and admitting the role you have played in creating conflict in unhealthy relationships. Of course it takes strength to admit the need for self-improvement and to acknowledge truths about yourself that are hard to face. But this is a safe place to acknowledge your human flaws (we all have them!). The goal is to help you be the kind of person you want to be.

As you are beginning to see, this program is not just about sex crimes. We want you to use this program to improve in all areas of your life. In this program, you will learn to live a life of accountability.

One man in treatment eloquently shared his feelings about accountability:

True change for the offender requires a detailed examination of the effects of the trauma they caused. This 'body count,' however unpleasant, must be taken. The truth usually hurts. For an offender, justification and rationalization are like the blinders worn by a horse. Just as they keep the wagon train moving forward by warding off sights that might distract the horses, they allow the offender to continue moving forward, living a bearable life. As the offender opens himself up to the realization of the harm he caused, these blinders are torn away. The offender is forced to take on the truth, and with it, a bit of everyone's trauma. That owning, that realization, that combining of all the facets of the trauma into one, ultimately leads us to a healing place. A healing place based on a nurturing foundation of truth, rather than a calloused-over story used as justification for the abuse. The offender must begin to see.

Take a look at Figure 1.1, and think about how these principles of accountability apply to you, and how you can use them as tools in everything you do.

Figure 1.1: The Language of Accountability

Natural consequences of one's own decisions	• This outcome is a result of my choice
Focus on the behavior, not the person	• I did a bad thing. I am not a bad person
Develop an Internal Focus of Control	Serenity Prayer: • What are the things I can change or control? • Accepting things we cannot change
Ownership and Empowerment	• If I own it, I can change it (vs. if things happen TO me, there is nothing I can do about them)
Posibility of Redemption	• When I act with respect and responsibility others respond to me differently
Be a role model as a flawed human	• Everyone makes mistakes! And it is OK to apologize!

Exercise 1.1: Applying the Language of Accountability in Your Life.

Using Figure 1.1, keep an ongoing list in your notebook about all the ways you can use each item from the Language of Accountability chart in your own life.

Making a Commitment to Treatment

Most programs for people who have sexually offended include group therapy. Being a group member is a responsibility. Weekly attendance at meetings is mandatory not just because your court order requires it, but because you have a responsibility to your group. Once you get to know the other members and they get to know you, you will become more comfortable discussing personal matters with each other. When group members attend every week and show a commitment to treatment, they develop trust in one another. Of course, sometimes emergencies arise but it is always your responsibility to be in communication with your therapist any time you miss a session.

Group Rules:

1. Arrive on time and put your phone away. It shows respect for everyone when we are ready to go at start-time and avoid the disruptions of people coming in late. When your phone is away, you can pay attention to what is going on in the room. When people are looking at their phones, it says to others: "something else is going on that is more important to me than you are."

2. Confidentiality. Your privacy is very important. Please do not speak about anyone in your group to others outside of group. In order for group members to trust each other, everyone must be committed to the principle: "what is said in this room stays in this room."
3. Speak for Yourself. Don't talk about what other group members think or believe; instead talk about what you think and believe, and what's on your mind.
4. Use "I" Statements. Tell others how you feel about what they've said and how it affects you, such as "I feel that ..." or "when you say that, I feel ..." When you use "I" statements, you avoid telling others how they should feel, you avoid bossing them around or telling them they're wrong, and you get away from assuming that your ideas are the only ideas or the best ideas. Using "I" statements makes you concentrate on how you think, and how you say what you think. Your use of "I" statements shows respect for other group members who think and feel differently than you do.
5. Speak Respectfully. When you say something in a calm way using respectful language, others are more likely to hear you and your message. Sometimes you might feel mad or disagree with something that is said in group. This is fine, but please share your thoughts without raising your voice, cursing, or criticizing others.
6. Model the behavior you want to see in others. Think about what makes a group session feel safe and comfortable for you... Don't interrupt, ask questions instead of always telling others what YOU think, validate and support others when appropriate, and give positive feedback, as well as respectful constructive feedback.
7. What other group rules would help you feel safe sharing in the group?

Group members frequently begin treatment feeling resentful, especially when they feel that the victim, the court, or society has treated them unfairly. If you feel resentful at the beginning, that's okay. As you listen to people who have been in treatment a while, you will learn that others started out feeling angry or misunderstood too. But they have learned that important things happen in the treatment group, and being angry only gets in the way of those things. They came to understand that personal growth is more important than holding onto feelings of being victimized. Your group and therapist will help you work through your anger. You will be asked to share in your group when you feel comfortable doing so.

Denial in the Treatment Group

What is **denial**? Denial is a psychological *defense mechanism*, which means it is a way of avoiding realities that are obvious to others. It is a way of protecting ourselves from facing things about ourselves we don't want to accept—things that are too painful, too embarrassing, or too threatening. There is no question that our society has placed enormous shame and stigma on sex crimes. That makes these types of behaviors among the hardest things to admit honestly. You think, "What does it say about *me* that I've done this to someone? How am I the sort of person who rapes? Or abuses children? Or watches child pornography? What does this mean about who I am?"

In treatment men will hold on to denial until they recognize that it's safe to let it go. Until they understand that there is more to be gained by admitting than denying. Here, honesty will be rewarded rather than punished.

The first step in treatment is to talk about your sex crimes and begin to acknowledge your problem. For many people, this is the most difficult task they face in treatment. The idea of giving up your denial might be terrifying. But you will find that as soon as you begin to speak honestly about what you have done, you will feel an immediate sense of relief. You will even gain a feeling of control *just by making the decision to allow treatment to help you.*

Why is denial so hard to give up? Because it has become a centerpiece of your lifestyle. You have used it to try to protect yourself from the legal consequences of your offending, and from the shame, stigma, and relationship consequences of offending. Chances are you were using denial long before you were arrested. Denial is almost a part of your identity, isn't it? Think back to the first times you lied about your sexual behavior. Does it seem that you have been lying about your sexual behavior for a long time? How many people do you think you have lied to about sex? You pushed some people away and closed them out of your life because of your sexual secrets. Some of those people loved you and cared about you. Some of those people wanted to get to know you. Maybe they would have loved you.

And now, what? Here you are in treatment, armed with your best stories. You might feel so sure that others can't see through you, that they can't prove anything. Only you know the real story.

But wait… what if you were in a place where you told the truth and the people said, "okay, whatever." And if you told a lie and the people said, "okay, whatever." What would you do? At first you might lie just because it feels safer. But wouldn't it start to feel silly after a while? What do you think it would feel like to tell the truth and have other people not only accept you, but also value your thoughts and opinions? To hear others say, "yeah, me too." That would be a different experience, wouldn't it? Think about this: there is nothing to be gained by lying in treatment. And think about this too: lying takes energy. It's complicated, because lies have to make some kind of sense. Lying makes you anxious because you know you can always be called out on your lies. And lying keeps you locked in your own world. Your treatment group is a place where you can try something different. *For the first time, there really is more to be gained than lost by being honest about your sexual behavior.*

Sex offending occurs and thrives in secrecy. Letting go of your secrets is the first step toward ending the cycle you have been caught up in. At first, everyone in treatment feels embarrassed and ashamed talking about their sex crimes, which is why they have kept them a secret. But you now have the opportunity to share your secrets with others who will understand you and not judge you, because they know what it is like to have shameful secrets of their own.

People can do hurtful, unlawful, or victimizing things—and still be fundamentally good people. No one is all good or all bad, and no one should be defined solely by the single worst thing they've ever done. You are a human being with a wide and complex range of emotions and behaviors. Here, you will learn to see yourself more realistically and embrace the idea that change is possible. By understanding how your past experiences shaped your current thinking and behavior, you can identify areas for personal growth. The message here is "Sex offending is something you've done; it's not who you are." Behavior can be changed. You already know that because you've changed your behavior many times over the course of your life.

After a While, Denial Isn't Fair to Other Group Members

You may not be allowed to continue in your treatment program if, after a period of time, you are still denying that you have committed any sex offense. Talk to your therapist about the policy regarding how long you can remain in treatment while you are in denial. If you haven't committed any sex offense and don't have a problem with your sexual behavior, then you don't have a problem that this program can help you with, right? You're saying you don't belong here, and you're holding yourself apart from the other group members. It is very difficult for group members who are committed to treatment to talk openly in front of men who say they don't have a similar problem. "Deniers" make it harder for all group members to honestly work toward their recovery.

If you keep an open mind you will soon find that there are good guys in your group. Plenty of good people have done bad things. And lots of good people have serious problems. When a man doesn't care about the harm he has caused and doesn't even try to change, then he has to take a hard look at himself in the mirror and ask what kind of person he is. But when he accepts that he has been out of control and decides to do whatever it takes to get back into control, then he deserves respect. In this program you will get respect.

Treatment represents an opportunity; it is a fork in the road of your life. One path leads to a chance at the kind of life you always wished you could have. The other path leads to more secrecy, more shame, more fear... and, ultimately, for some people, prison. Take this opportunity and use it.

It is important to understand that denial doesn't end with simply admitting that you committed the crime for which you were convicted. There are different types of denial and different stages of denial, and people move through these stages at different paces. The more quickly you move through the stages, the more quickly you can start to work on your problem and benefit from therapy. And the more quickly you can complete the program and graduate!

The Range of Denial

The following descriptions of denial were modified with permission from the conceptual foundation regarding denial of facts, awareness, impact, and responsibility. The descriptions were originally published by Terry Trepper, Ph.D. and Mary Jo Barrett, M.S.W. in their 1989 book *Systemic Treatment of Incest, a Therapeutic Handbook*, (pages 110-116).

The first and most obvious type of denial is **Denial of the Facts**. This occurs when you tell others that you never committed a sex offense. Maybe denial of the facts was the way you survived for a long time. Maybe you used it to get away with offending, then, to defend yourself against criminal charges or a child welfare investigation, and now, finally, to avoid the difficult and uncomfortable task of being in therapy. The truth is that up until now you haven't had much to gain by admitting your offenses. *Talking about your offenses in therapy cannot be used against you.* But not talking will keep you from getting anything out of treatment.

Your therapist and the other group members understand how hard it is to speak openly about what happened. That's why you'll be given time to simply observe what happens in group meetings, and figure out what this program might have to offer you.

Most people in society have negative and stigmatizing views about people who committed sex crimes, and that can make it all the more difficult for you to admit what you have done. Keep in mind that society has always sensationalized people's problems and judged them. Not too long ago, people addicted to alcohol or drugs were considered hopeless lowlifes. Today everyone knows that people who abuse alcohol and drugs can recover if they want to, and if they work at it, can go on to live fulfilling lives. The first step is acknowledging the problem and addressing it.

At first you may want to "limit the damage" by admitting only what you were caught for. Over time you will realize that this approach is not going to help you understand the underlying thoughts and feelings that drove you toward your offense. If your victim was a child it will not be easy to admit that you were thinking about him or her in a sexual way, or maybe that you had been tickling her or wrestling with him for weeks (this is called grooming). If you introduce yourself to your group saying it was "a one-time thing," when it had been going on for a while, you are hiding from yourself and your group. Hiding and isolating are not going to allow the group to help you put important pieces together to help you make sense of what you did.

The next type of denial is **Denial of Intent**. Some men say they didn't know that what they were doing was against the law. The truth is that most people knew that what they were doing was against the law, and everyone who commits a sex crime knows that it is wrong. It may be true that you did not fully grasp the harmfulness of what you were doing, or know how serious the consequences would be. Some men say they didn't know how old a victim was. If you didn't know, it was because you didn't want to know. You didn't ask. If a fourteen-year-old told you he was eighteen, you wanted to believe it so you did. Be honest with yourself about what you really knew or should have known, and about what you intended.

Another way of denying your intent to offend is to say it "just happened." You didn't give it any thought; you didn't plan anything; it just happened. How could it really even be your fault if it "just happened?" Except that nothing a person does ever just happens. Sometimes we do things without even thinking about it as we do it, but that doesn't mean there wasn't a plan. It just means the plan was already known. Most offenses were planned in some way.

Next is **Denial of the Impact** on the victims. Do you really believe your victims weren't hurt by what you did, or that it wasn't as bad as everyone made it out to be? Many people begin treatment holding on to beliefs that if they didn't penetrate a victim then they didn't really hurt him or her, or that exposing oneself "isn't showing them something they haven't already seen," or that date rape is not so bad because the victim has had sex with other people, or that looking at CP isn't the same as touching a child. The truth is that any type of sexual assault is harmful to victims in many different ways. You will learn more about these harmful effects when you get to the chapter on Victim Impact. You knew that what you were doing was wrong, but you convinced yourself (and maybe your victim) that it was okay.

Denial of Responsibility is when you say that it *wasn't your fault.* Some people admit what they've done but say that their crimes occurred while they were drunk or high on drugs and they didn't know what they were doing. "*It wasn't me; it was the cocaine.*" Being drunk or stoned may lower your *inhibitions* (resistance) to doing certain things, or make you care less about the consequences, but it didn't put the idea into your head. And you made yourself drunk, didn't you? Whose fault is that? You might say that your wife or girlfriend drove you to it by not having sex with you or by cheating on you. Many people feel that their partner isn't meeting their sexual needs. But that hardly gives anyone the right to sexually assault someone else.

Or maybe you have been telling yourself that your offense was a child's fault because the child "came on to you." Maybe a teenager flirted with you online, and maybe she didn't resist your advances. The truth is that minors are usually willing to go along with anything adults suggest because they have been taught to respect and obey adults. Children trust that adults know right from wrong and will do the right thing. We all know that sometimes teenagers are in a hurry to grow up and experiment with sex. Do we take advantage of those teenagers or should we—as adults—caution them to slow down? Minors are not capable of true *consent* because they don't understand the consequences of those decisions. Because adults *do* know right from wrong, it is always the adult's responsibility to steer minors away from wrong behavior.

In chapter 5, you will be asked to think about your own childhood experiences, not to blame your parents or your family, but to understand the effects of the things that happened to you when you were young. If you were abused, neglected, or had trauma in your childhood, that is important to understand, though it doesn't excuse or condone offending. The reality is that you were always free to make your own choices and you chose to offend. No one else ever made you commit a sex crime, and you are the only one who is responsible for what you did.

Another common type of denial is **Denial of the Need for Treatment**. This could also be called "Denial of the Possibility of Committing a New Offense." Many people come to treatment insisting they've learned their lesson and do not need help. They say they don't use drugs any more, they would never risk going back to prison, or they don't have access to children or other victims anymore. They say they "can't believe how stupid" they were, but they are smarter now. They say they have found the Lord and He will keep them away from deviant sex. The reality is that each of these factors can help you to stay away from offending. But none will prevent you from reoffending. Preventing reoffense is much more complicated than that.

Many people feel ashamed about needing help in their lives. Maybe their experiences with seeking help in the past have been belittling, shaming, or unsuccessful. For individuals who have minor-attractions, shame and fear often prevented them from seeking help due to the fear of being judged, the worry about getting into trouble, or the concerns that no one would understand them. And they don't know where to go for help. Some fear that once they open the door to their inner thoughts and feelings, they won't be able to close it if things get too uncomfortable. These are real concerns and dealing with them is a part of treatment. Anyone can understand the fear of having your life turned into an open book.

So yes, there will be times when treatment is uncomfortable. If you talk about these uncomfortable feelings in your group, you will find that other guys have them too. Men who have been in the program for a while can help by talking about how they have dealt with the feelings. They will help you see that what the program offers is worth going through some discomfort for. Everything worthwhile has a price, doesn't it? In the end, if you let it, treatment will be one of the most worthwhile things you ever do. For now just remember this: you tried to control yourself before but it didn't work. You do need help learning to control your behavior. Treatment offers that help.

There is a range of examples of the different types of denial:

DENIAL OF THE FACTS	"It never happened." "Her mother made it up to get me." "My hand went there by accident." "I have no idea how those pictures got on my phone." "I pled no contest for convenience."
DENIAL OF INTENT	"I was drunk." "I didn't know it was against the law." "If it happened, I don't remember it." "She looked like she was eighteen."
DENIAL OF IMPACT	"I'm the victim. She's doing fine." "I didn't hurt him at all." "Other men do worse things." "I didn't penetrate her." "I just looked at pictures, I didn't touch a child."
DENIAL OF RESPONSIBILITY	"He was chatting with me and knew what he wanted." "She came on to me" "He should have told me to stop." "My wife drove me to it." "It was the drugs, it wasn't me."
DENIAL OF THE NEED FOR TREATMEMT	"It will never happen again." "I learned my lesson." "I don't have those thoughts anymore." "It only happened once. I'm not a pervert."

There are also different types of denial defense mechanisms:

RATIONALIZATION	Attempting to explain or justify behaviors or an attitude with logical reasons, even if these are not appropriate.
JUSTIFICATION	Trying to show the reasons behind something as right or reasonable.
MINIMALIZATION	Reducing something to the least possible amount or degree or position, or trying to make something seem less important.
PLAUSIBLE DENIABILITY	Refers to circumstances where an act of wrong-doing cannot be proved true or untrue due to a lack of evidence about the allegation. In these situations someone can "plausibly deny" an allegation even though it may be true.

Exercise 1.2: Define in Your Own Words the Different Types of Denial. Using Your Own Words, Explain Each Type of Denial.

Denial of the Facts:

Denial of Intent:

Denial of Impact:

Denial of Responsibility:

Denial of the Need for Treatment:

Rationalization:

Justification:

Minimization:

Plausible Deniability:

Exercise 1.3: Identifying Denial

Red the following two scenarios. Then, using the charts provided, explain each of the types of denial you observed in each of them.

Scenario 1:

Angel's mother Gloria never recovered from depression after her husband left her. By the time she was four, Angel knew not to disturb her mother when she was sleeping (which seemed to be all the time). Angel learned to hide in her room when Gloria was in a rage. Gloria lost jobs frequently and turned to her older brother, Fred, to help pay the bills when her money ran out. As time went by and Gloria never got a grip on her life, Fred sometimes lost his patience with her. Still, he felt obligated to help her, and he always felt sorry for Angel, who seemed lost and alone.

When Gloria showed up at Fred's door one day saying she had lost her apartment, Fred offered to let her and Angel stay with him. Fred had recently been divorced himself and felt the company might be good for him. He quickly saw that Gloria had no time or patience for Angel. He found himself protecting and defending Angel and trying to be the parent she didn't have. Angel quickly fell in love with him, and they began spending a lot of time together. Fred was proud that the sad little girl he had always known was full of smiles and giggles around him.

Whe Angel started climbing into his bed at night saying she was afraid and didn't want to be alone, Fred at first tried to take her back to her own bed. When Angel would cling hard to him and plead with him to let her into his bed, though, he couldn't turn her away. Angel would hold onto him as they slept and sometimes crawl on top of him to be as close to him as she could. One night when Fred found himself with an erection in bed, he moved Angel's hand to it and showed her how to move it up and down. After he had ejaculated, he felt a little guilty, but he knew that Angel liked to feel close to him in this way. Soon she was touching him regularly to excite an erection, and she obviously enjoyed masturbating him. He knew he wasn't hurting her, and in fact she seemed to like it. Angel seemed so happy lately. Fred found he could not say no. He told himself he would never try to have real sex with her and he kept his word.

This activity went on for four months, until one day Gloria walked in on them. Fred was arrested and spent nineteen months in prison. After prison he was sent to a treatment program. He had pleaded no contest to the charge and was too ashamed to admit to what he had done in front of other men. He told them that Gloria was drunk and misunderstood what she saw. He said that she was ungrateful and jealous that Angel liked spending time with him more than with her mother. Even though he knew in his heart that he did do it, he also knew he would never do it again.

Exercise 1.3 (continued): Using the Following Chart, Give Examples of Each of the Types of Denial You Observed in Scenario 1.

Denial of Facts:

Denial of Intent:

Denial of Impact:

Denial of Responsibility:

Denial of the Need for Treatment:

Rationalization:

Justification:

Minimization:

Plausible Deniability:

Exercise 1.3 (continued):

Scenario 2:

Kevin worked hard during the week. He liked to unwind at a dance club on Friday nights with his buddies. He'd go home, shower, dress up, and get ready for a wild time. He loved to dance, and always found some hot girls who liked to have a good time.

Kevin had downed about four beers when Carrie came up to him and put her arm around him. He'd seen her at the club a few times. He admired her short black leather skirt and lacy white top, noticing that she already seemed tipsy. She obviously liked him and was trying to let him know it by caressing his back.

A few hours and a few more drinks later, Carrie and Kevin were slow dancing. He kissed her and she responded. She wrapped her arms around his neck, playing with his hair. He asked her if she wanted a ride home. Kevin and Carrie left the club together. Everyone saw her leave with him, kissing him and holding his hand. All his buddies could see Kevin was going to get lucky.

When they pulled up at Carrie's house, they made out in the car for a while. "Aren't you going to invite me in?" Kevin asked. Carrie hesitated for a minute, snuggling up closer to him. "I'd better not," she responded, "but call me, maybe we can get together this week." Kevin found himself getting angry. She was teasing him, coming on to him, and then brushing him off. He kissed her harder. "You know you want me," he said. Carrie responded to his kiss but then pushed him away. She reached for the door handle, smiling at him.

Kevin pulled her back in and maneuvered around to lie on top of her. She began to push him, but he knew that girls always try to play hard to get. He continued to touch her, figuring when she got turned off enough she'd change her mind. When she said "No!" he told himself they always say no when they mean yes. He wasn't doing anything wrong, he thought; she had come on to him. The way she dressed, and the way she hung on him all night, letting him drive her home—she was looking for action. Anyway, even if she really didn't want to, she'd get over it. She'd probably had sex with plenty of guys already. There was nothing wrong with having sex with someone you were dating.

Exercise 1.3 (continued): Using the Following Chart, Give examples of Each of the Types of Denial You Observed in Scenario 2.

Denial of Facts:

Denial of Intent:

Denial of Impact:

Denial of Responsibility:

Denial of the Need for Treatment:

Rationalization:

Justification:

Minimization:

Plausible Deniability:

Exercise 1.4: Identifying Your Own Denial

Thinking about your own offenses, use the chart below to give an example of each of the types of denial you have used in the past. Describe how you acted, what you though, and what you said.

Denial of Facts: ______________________________

____

____

Denial of Intent: ______________________________

____

____

Denial of Impact: ______________________________

____

____

Denial of Responsibility: ______________________________

____

____

Denial of the Need for Treatment: ______________________________

____

____

Rationalization: ______________________________

____

____

Justification: ______________________________

____

____

Minimization: ______________________________

____

____

Plausible Deniability: ______________________________

____

Giving Up Denial

Most men report feeling tremendous relief once they finally admit their offenses. It feels like a burden has been lifted off their shoulders. It takes a lot of energy to present a false self to the world. Finally being able to be honest and be yourself feels much better.

Does your family still think you were falsely accused? That it was all a big mistake or misunderstanding? That it sounds worse than it actually was? Talking honestly with people in your life can be really hard. You might be afraid of losing the people you care about. You may worry about what they would think if they knew the truth.

At first, when you begin to talk honestly and openly about what you have done, you may feel naked. As you disclose your crimes, you may want to backtrack and change your mind. Don't let your honesty scare you. You are taking the risk of doing the right thing. You are giving up the denial, which has protected you since you started offending. You don't know what will happen next. Fear of the unknown is natural.

In the early 1990s psychologists Prochaska and DiClemente described how people in recovery from substance abuse go through predictable stages of change. When someone is in the *pre-contemplation* phase, they have no intention of changing their behavior and may not even be aware that a problem exists. *Contemplation* is when the person acknowledges a problem but makes no commitment to change. *Preparation* is a shifting point where someone starts to believe they have a problem and that change is possible, and begin to take some action to correct the problem. *Action* is where the person is actively making progress modifying thoughts and behaviors. *Maintenance* is sustained change, with new behaviors and thoughts replacing old ones. Sometimes people lapse or relapse, which means falling back into old patterns of thinking or behavior. Usually, each time a person goes through a setback, they can learn from it and better prevent it from happening again. As you go through the treatment process, compare where you are at with these stages to watch yourself progress.

Figure 1.2: Stages of Change

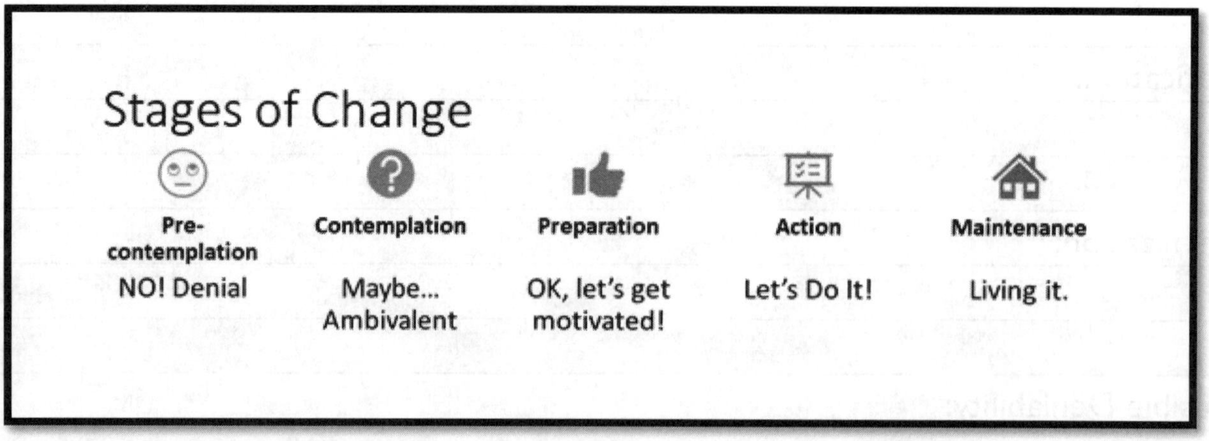

Prochaska and DiClemente (1983)

When you begin treatment you will naturally want to limit your admission only to the offense you were arrested for (this is called the "Tip of the Iceberg" syndrome). But many men in treatment have engaged in other sexually abusive or unlawful behaviors besides those for which they were arrested. If you are going to truly understand and change your behavior, you are going to have to be honest with yourself and others about all the inappropriate sexual things you have done and thought in your life. This will not be easy. This, too, involves emotional risk. Figure 1.3 displays this idea as a tree, with leaves visible to others, but with hidden roots that no one can see.

Figure 1.3: Looking Below the Surface

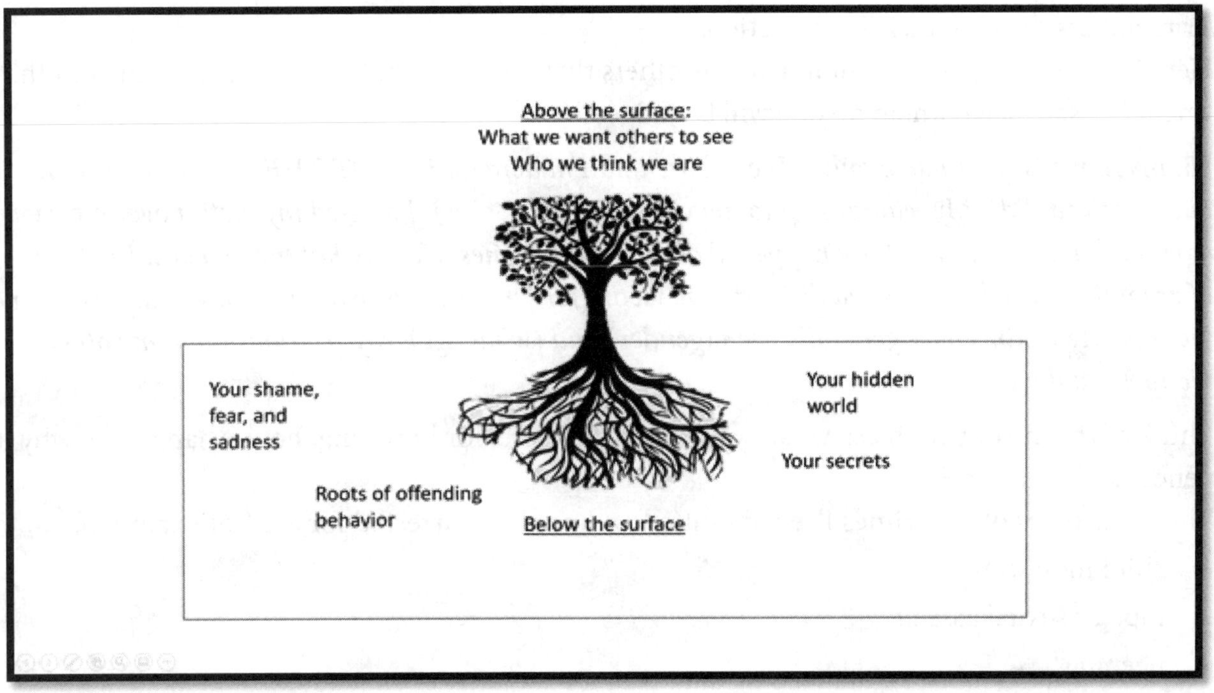

Only by talking about all your offenses (or thoughts of offending) together will you be able to see the *patterns* of your thinking and behavior. You will see how your thoughts and fantasies are "triggered" by certain types of events, how you respond to them, how you planned your offenses, and so forth. When you understand your patterns, you can then develop strategies to change them. If you are only looking at the one thing for which you were arrested, you will not be able to recognize your patterns. Before you can graduate you will have to address the totality of your problem. This takes work and it takes courage.

It is always difficult to admit to other offenses, but it might be more difficult if you fear that something you say will put you at risk for being re-arrested. If this is your fear, talk to your counselor about it. Ask for clarification of the confidentiality laws. The laws of every state respect the confidentiality of psychological treatment because without confidentiality there can be no honesty, and without honesty treatment can't work. At the same time there are certain circumstances in which your counselor is required to report offenses of children, or threat of future harm to someone. You need to understand these circumstances.

Introducing Yourself to Your Treatment Group

One measure of your progress in treatment is what you say when you introduce yourself in group meetings. Introductions may be a regular part of your meetings, not because you don't know each other, but to remind yourselves and each other why you are there. What you say when you introduce yourself tells your therapist and the other group members whether you are genuinely engaging in treatment. What does it tell you when a long-time group member continues to introduce himself by describing only the "tip of the iceberg"? Long-term group members can be great role models for newer members through their introductions.

Here is the kind of introduction that tells others that you are here to work on yourself, and that treatment is a safe place where no one will be judged:

Hi, my name is (first name only). The offense that I'm here for is (NOT THE LEGAL CHARGE, but what you did). My relationship to my victim was (   ). I abused my victim over a period of (time frame), and the abuse happened about (   ) times. Here's what happened... The type of grooming I used was... In addition to the victim for whom I was arrested, I have had (#) other victims. My victims have generally been (gender) and (what age). My relationship to my other victims usually was...

Think of the introduction as: what, who, when & where, for how long, how it happened, why it happened, and what else?

The other types of sex crimes I've committed and not been arrested for are (for example):

- child molesting
- rape or sexual assault
- peeping
- exposing my private parts or masturbating in front of someone
- viewing child pornography (child sexual abuse material: CSAM)
- using the Internet to view or share CSAM
- using the Internet to chat with minors or make contact with victims
- making obscene phone calls

Some other types of sexual behavior that I have had problems with are (for example):

- calling 900 numbers or sexting
- prostitutes
- masturbating too much
- looking at or sharing pornography
- adult bookstores
- going to strip clubs
- dressing in women's clothes or underwear
- using the Internet for sexual purposes
- I am so easily aroused that I can't concentrate sometimes

Talking out loud about your sexual behaviors is important for a lot of reasons. First, it is consistent with your goal of living an accountable lifestyle in all areas of your life. Second, when someone denies their offense, they are also denying the victim's reality. It's like calling your victim a liar even though you know that it really happened. This is re-victimization. Third, it allows you to begin to problem-solve and understand your behavior so that it doesn't happen again.

Figure 1.4 From Externalizing Blame to Personal Accountability

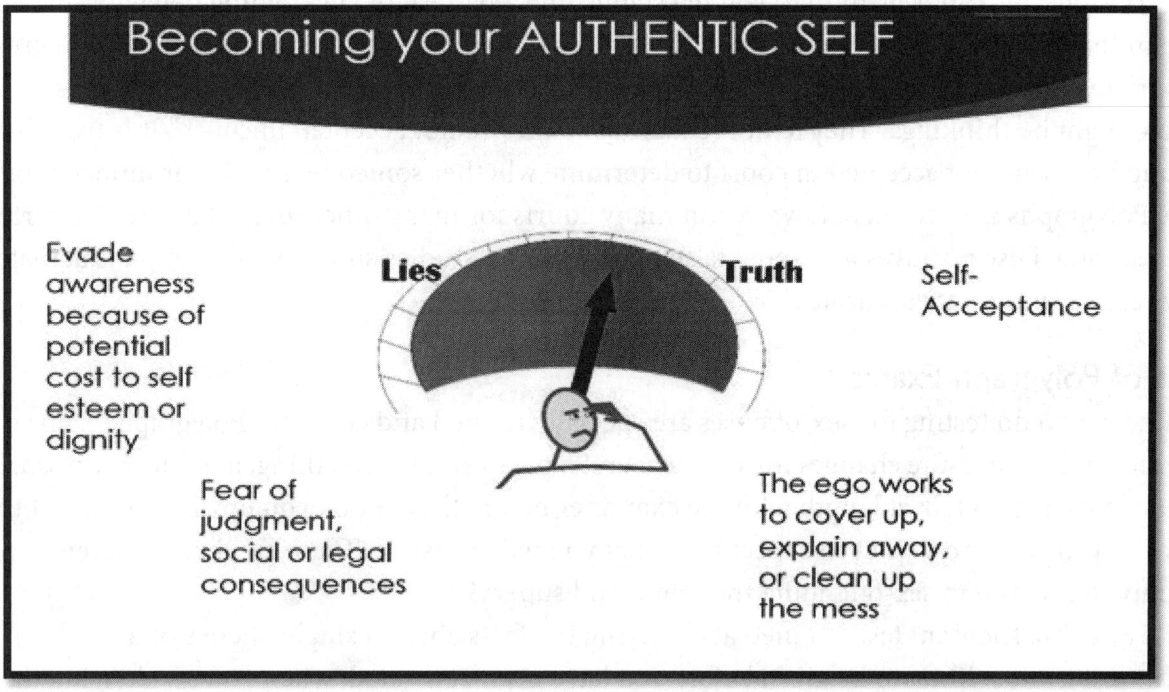

Polygraphs

If the idea of voluntarily reporting sex offenses you were never caught for in the past is difficult for you to imagine, you're not alone. Let's face it; nobody wants to talk about things they got away with. That's human nature. But we talked above about why it's important to your treatment for you to talk about the full scope of your sexual behaviors. In order to best understand how to help you, many programs use polygraph exams (also called "lie-detector tests"). Your program or your parole or probation may require you to be polygraphed. It should go without saying that you will be expected to be truthful on your polygraph exams.

The idea of polygraphs makes most people super nervous, especially if you want to avoid being truthful because you are ashamed of things you've done. We know you also might be worried about possible self-incrimination. Talk to your therapist about your concerns, and how to share honestly without providing identifying information that could get you in trouble. The goal of the polygraph is to help your therapist (and you) to better understand your past patterns and current treatment needs. But it is scary to think about not beingable to hide any longer having your secrets exposed.

Well, when we talk about giving up your denial and fully accepting responsibility for your offenses, that means talking about the secret stuff, doesn't it? If you're not honest, treatment can't help you. As much as you resent having to be polygraphed, it can help you to be honest. And after you've started being honest, you might feel relieved at being able to talk about stuff for the first time.

Polygraphs can help you no matter what your situation is. If your offense was really a one-time event and not part of a larger pattern, it will help your therapist tailor your treatment plan accordingly. If you can produce a truthful polygraph indicating no other victims or sexually unlawful behaviors, then your therapist can feel much more confident communicating with the courts about your low risk. If you can produce truthful polygraphs indicating that you are following all your rules of supervision, this can be helpful to you in establishing a pattern of law-abiding behavior. In this program the polygraph is used to gather important information to assess your problems and create an appropriate treatment plan.

You might be thinking: "They're not reliable" or "They're not accepted in court." It is true that polygraph tests are not accepted in court to determine whether someone is guilty or innocent of a crime. Polygraphs are accepted, however, in many courts for many other uses. They are not perfect and have some false positives and some false negatives. But studies show the polygraph is actually pretty reliable and pretty accurate.

Types of Polygraph Exams

Examiners who do testing for sex-offenses are specially trained and certified. Polygraph exams don't read minds; they measure changes in your heart rate, perspiration, breathing, and blood pressure. You will have a chance to talk at length with the examiner before they "hook you up". By the end of the interview, you will know what to expect and what you will be asked. There are three different types of polygraph tests used in sex-offending treatment and supervision:

1) The **Specific Incident** test is aimed at clarifying the facts about a single offense or a single victim. This test is most likely to be given before you have been convicted, when you are denying the allegations and one of the lawyers wants to try to determine who is telling the truth. The examiner will ask specific questions such as, "Did you ever place (the victim's) hand on your penis?" or "Did you ever have any sexual contact with (the alleged victim)?" This type of test might also be given if you enter into treatment denying that you have committed a sex crime.
2) The **Full Disclosure** or **Full Sexual History** test is aimed at uncovering your full sexual history up to the time of your most recent arrest. Before you take your full-disclosure exam you will need to prepare by combing through your memory to discover all your sexual encounters, sexual behavior problems, and victims. Before the test, in preparation, you may be asked to list all your offenses and all your victims and to present this history to your therapist and your group. You will not be asked to provide incriminating information—only first names or initials of victims—talk to your therapist ahead of time to clarify how to describe victims. Sometimes you won't be able to remember how many times you offended and the examiner will ask you for an estimate (a high estimate, to be sure you've covered all your offenses). Then the examiner will ask you to go over the offenses with him in detail to be sure he fully understands everything. On the exam itself he is likely to ask you something like, "Besides what you have already told me today, have you had any other victims?"

3) The **Monitoring** or **Maintenance** test is designed to find out if you are following the rules of your probation and your treatment program. In the pretest interview the examiner may ask you about any contact with your victims or with anyone else you're not supposed to be having contact with (such as minors). He will ask if you have committed any new offenses since you have come on probation or parole. He will ask if you are using the Internet for sexual purposes. He may ask what kinds of fantasies or material you have masturbated to. He may ask if you have been using drugs or alcohol and how much. He may ask if you have been fully following all the rules of your probation, even rules that aren't directly about sex offending (for example, breaking your curfew or leaving the county). This test is a way for your probation officer and your therapist to confirm that you are committed to a law-abiding lifestyle.

There Is Only One Way to Pass a Polygraph Exam

And that's by being honest. If you try to withhold anything from the polygraph examiner, you will be found "deceptive" (untruthful). Sometimes a person might disclose a great deal, but still try to hold back some parts of it. Usually this is due to shame or fear. Maybe they think they can fool it (after all, they've always fooled everybody else). Or they tell themselves "I've told the important parts; this one thing won't matter." Or maybe there is something unrelated to offending that they are very ashamed or worried about revealing, such as homosexual activity, an extramarital affair, a fetish, or some other type of unlawful activity. If you are not clear about the consequences for a deceptive test, ask your therapist to discuss them in group. And before you go for your exam, make up your mind that you are going to lay your cards on the table—*all of them*—because this is what will help you pass the exam.

The following exercise can help you prepare for your full-history polygraph exam. It will also help you self-reflect on your own sexual behaviors, so you can work with your counselor to develop a treatment plan that makes sense for you. Remember: your therapist is on your side. He or she wants to help you understand and change behaviors that have harmed others and yourself.

Exercise 1.5: Disclose Crimes and Victims

Check off all the activities listed below that you have engaged in. Add any other offenses you have engaged in that are not listed. It is important to include all the sexually abusive or unlawful acts you have committed during your life, even if the victim never knew it happened (such as when you peeped, or masturbated in your car while watching someone walking down the street, or touched a small child in a way they didn't realize was sexual).

☐ I kissed a child under eighteen in a sexual way.

☐ I touched a child under eighteen in a sexual way.

☐ I asked a child under eighteen to touch me in a sexual way.

☐ I allowed a child under eighteen to see my genitals for my sexual arousal.

☐ I watched a child under eighteen when they were not dressed for my sexual arousal.

☐ I performed oral sex on a child under eighteen.

- ☐ A child under eighteen performed oral sex on me.
- ☐ I had intercourse with a child under eighteen.
- ☐ I have spoken with a child under eighteen in a way that was sexually arousing.
- ☐ When I was under eighteen, I engaged in any of the above activities with a child who was 4 or more years younger than me or who I took advantage of.
- ☐ I have engaged or attempted to engage in "chats" with children under eighteen online or through apps for my sexual arousal.
- ☐ I have arranged or attempted to arrange meetings with children under eighteen over the Internet.
- ☐ I have watched others undressing or using the bathroom when they have not been aware I was watching.
- ☐ I have watched others having sex when they have not been aware I was watching.
- ☐ I have exposed myself to other adults without their consent.
- ☐ I have forced others to have sexual contact with me against their will.
- ☐ I have intimidated or manipulated others into having sex by letting them know I would be angry if they did not have sex with me.
- ☐ I have taken advantage of someone who was so intoxicated they went along with something sexual that they would probably not have consented to if they were sober.
- ☐ I had sexual contact with someone who said no, but I pretended they meant yes.
- ☐ I have sent sexual texts to someone without their consent.
- ☐ I have used my position of authority to make sexual advances to someone at work.
- ☐ I have rubbed up against someone in a crowd for sexual pleasure.
- ☐ I have collected or downloaded child pornography (CSAM).
- ☐ I have sent CSAM to someone else.
- ☐ I have taken photos or videos of a child in a sexual pose or act.
- ☐ I have sent, shared, sold, or traded CSAM.

Exercise 1.5 (continued):

Now look at the list below and ask yourself about the other types of sexual behaviors you have engaged in outside of healthy relationships. These acts are not usually illegal. However, if you have engaged in these behaviors and you think they might have contributed to your sexual problems, you may need to address them in this program and cut them out of your life. They are all about unhealthy sex– sex that is anonymous, unfeeling, exploitative, or excessive. All of these behaviors can keep you from having healthy intimacy. Sometimes sexual behaviors become repetitive (sometimes referred to as compulsive or addictive) and can interfere with your life in ways such as: coming between you and a partner; costing you more money than you can afford; taking up time you should be spending on your job or your other responsibilities; keeping you preoccupied with sex so you can't concentrate on anything else; hurting your partner or others in your life; making you neglect other responsibilities.

☐ I have called commercial sex lines or used apps to engage in phone sex.

☐ I have used the Internet or apps to search for sexual experiences.

☐ I have gone online to manipulate others to satisfy my sexual needs.

☐ I have had sexual contact with animals.

☐ I have used appliances for sex.

☐ I have paid people (or traded something in exchange) for sexual acts with me.

☐ I have masturbated to pictures/videos of children that weren't necessarily sexual pictures.

☐ I have used pornographic books, magazines, websites and/or videos, including mainstream porn, that is degrading or violent.

☐ I have frequently used non-deviant pornography.

☐ I have masturbated more than I should have.

☐ I have gone to strip clubs and nude bars frequently.

☐ I have frequently engaged in fetish behaviors using objects or items of clothing for sexual arousal.

☐ I am easily sexually aroused and at times I can't think about anything but sex.

☐ I get sexually excited by "rough" sex.

☐ I get sexually excited by humiliating, degrading, or causing pain to another person.

☐ Other?

In time you will understand that continuing with these types of behaviors can undermine healthy sexuality and relationships. It's not a moral judgment. It just requires you to ask yourself "does this seem like a healthy way to get what I need?" In treatment your ultimate goals will be both to remove unhealthy sex from your life and to learn how to have fulfilling relationships that include healthy sexuality.

Exercise 1.6: Preparing for Your Full-Disclosure Polygraph Exam.

You can make a list describing all your victims:

1. The name of the victim (initials only—avoid identifying information)
2. Your age at the time of the offense
3. The victim's age at the time of the offense
4. Your relationship to the victim, and how you met and set up the offense
5. The number of times you sexually assaulted this victim
6. The length of time you sexually assaulted this victim
7. All of the different types of sex acts that you committed with this victim

Accountability

Accountability means more than just admitting that you were responsible for a sexual offense. Accountability is about taking a full and complete inventory of your behavior. Accountability is a process (see Figure 1.5). There are six steps to accountability, and they are described below.

1. Admission: Admitting to your offenses is just the first step. As we've discussed, most offenders begin by admitting only to the crimes for which they were caught. Accountability is not just about admitting to your crime, but also talking about *the extent of your problem* so you can show that you are serious about stopping all types of harmful sexual behavior in the future. It is scary to admit to things you've never been caught for, because you might be afraid of consequences. You might also be ashamed and wonder what others will think. Talk about all of these feelings in your group. You might be surprised that others feel the same way! Until you get everything out in the open, you cannot hold yourself accountable for your behavior. You will also not be able to get support from others if you don't share.
2. Acceptance of Consequences: There is perhaps no worse feeling than the fear of being caught and punished for crimes you've done. But true accountability includes accepting that when you do something wrong there are consequences of those choices. Obviously this is easier said than done. No one wants to go to prison, lose their children or job, or face the scorn of friends and family. But these consequences provide powerful reminders of how damaging sex offenses are. The person you sexually victimized will face lifelong consequences as well.
3. Restitution: Restitution means trying to right the wrongs that you did. The court might make you pay restitution costs, for example, to help your identified victim get therapy. The true spirit of restitution, however, is about willingly offering to do whatever you can to help ease the loss and pain you have caused your victims. Think about other ways to help your victims, or others, and ease the burden caused by sexually harmful behavior. Even if the court hasn't ordered it, for example, you could make a charitable donation to an agency that serves victims. You could donate items to a shelter for victims or offer to do some public speaking to educate your community about sexual assault. What else can you think of?
4. Supervision: You're probably already under the supervision of the probation department or corrections system. Who else do you trust to help you supervise your behavior? Someone in your family who knows the truth about your sexual behavior problems? A co-worker? A friend? Your treatment group? You need as many people as possible to be your "support system," to alert you when your behavior or mood seems to be different or negative, and to help you question your own motives. Let's face it, the more people who are helping you, the less able you will be to put yourself in risky situations, right?
5. Prevention: Certainly the main point of being in treatment is to change and learn how to prevent sexual assault in the future. That means recognizing your risk factors and learning what situations place you at risk for self-control problems, and staying away from those situations. This is your responsibility. Your therapist and your group can help you, but only when you let them. Don't resist when your group suggests that you are entering a risk zone! Listen to them. Don't make

excuses or insist that everything is under control. We all know it is easier to spot trouble in others than in ourselves. Some group members offer valuable feedback to others, but when it comes to themselves, they become defensive. Take what others say about you seriously and make the necessary changes. Also, point out to others in your group the risk factors you see for them. You will be helping them the same way they are helping you.

6. Modeling: Modeling means setting an example. If you are truly showing accountability, you will set an example for others in treatment. What can you do to be a role model for the newest members of your treatment group?

Talking with Your Loved Ones

It might be really hard for you to talk honestly with your family members about what happened, and that's understandable. They may know your "story" but not the real story. Do they still think you were falsely accused, wrongly convicted, or misunderstood? It may be difficult to come clean with them, especially after you and your family have been so invested in your "story" for so long. And you may rightly fear that they will feel betrayed that you lied to them for so long.

In fact, family members often are in their own denial. They may deny, minimize, justify or blame the victim. They may be very angry (rightly so) about the consequences of your arrest, conviction and/or registration status and its impact on them. But it may be easier for them to direct their anger at the "system" or the victim than at you. And this allows you and your family to bond over your common "enemy." You and your loved ones might have come to an unspoken "don't ask, don't tell" agreement.

You might have a lot of fear about what your family members would think if they knew the truth. Would they be angry at you, disappointed, shocked, freaked out? Are you afraid they would judge you, leave you, or punish you? It's pretty scary to think about sharing the truth with people you love because you are afraid of losing them. They are scared too, because if they really knew, they'd have to come to terms with their own blind spots and their doubts about themselves, wondering "how did I miss this?" If your victim was a family member, other family members might have guilt about not preventing harm. Or, they may feel a loyalty conflict, because it seems that if they believe you, they betray the victim, and if they believe the victim, they betray you. Dealing with sexual abuse is incredibly difficult for families. So instead, they focus on the injustice of the system or the unfairness of registries.

On the other hand, having a support system who knows the real story means they can support you in your treatment and be part of your safety plans. They become your accountability partners.

Exercise 1.7: Accountability with Family Members.

Think about the types of denial you learned about, and see if you can identify how they might show up with your family members. Then, write about your fears or concerns about being honest with your loved ones about what happened.

My Family's Denial	**What I'm Afraid Of**
Denial of Facts	What do your loved ones know about the offense?
Denial of Intent	What don't they know?
Denial of Impact	If you haven't been completely honest, why not?
Denial of Responsibility	What are your fears about disclosing to them?
Denial of the Need for Treatment	What are you most worried about?
Rationalization	What would help you share with them?
Justification	What would you like to say to them?
Minimization	How do you think they might react?
Plausible Deniability	What do you think your loved one is afraid to ask you?

Making a Real Commitment to Change

Admitting to past sexual offenses and becoming accountable to yourself and your group are important first steps in treatment. But your ultimate responsibility is to prevent yourself from victimizing any other person ever again. Preventing a new offense will take a full commitment on your part. It will mean you are determined to prevent another sex offense *at all costs*.

Look at Figure 1.5 and you will see what victims need in terms of accountability. Think about the process of going from denial to accountability. Which seems most difficult for you?

Figure 1.5: From Denial to Accountability

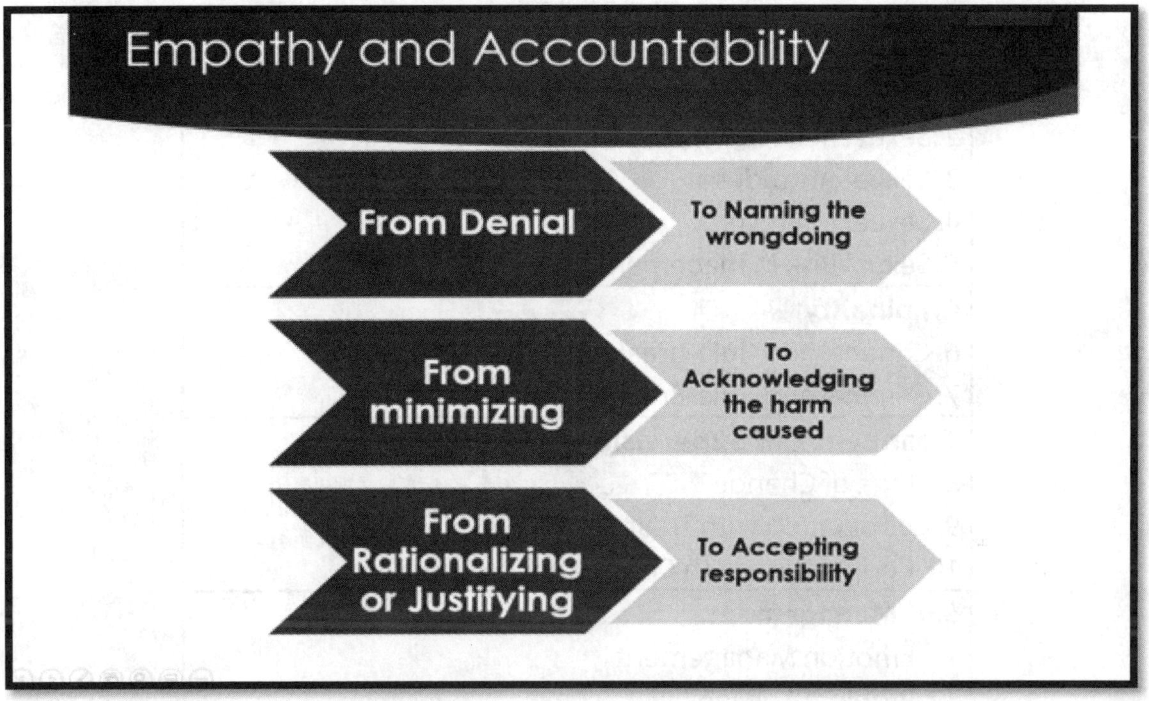

In Figure 1.6, you will see the different risk factors and treatment issues you will work on while in this program. Think about whether you have little or much need for improvement in each area of accountability in your life. A full commitment means making efforts every day to avoid harmful or victimizing behavior. This means identifying risk factors and creating safety plans that are right for you. You will learn to escape or avoid any situations that have put you at risk for offending in the past.

Before you use the Internet, you will discuss setting up a plan for safe internet use with your therapist. You should use the Internet only for legitimate, non-sexual, lawful, non-victimizing purposes. You and your therapist will discuss the circumstances of contact you should have with your own children or other children and you will create an appropriate safety plan.

If you have victimized adults, you should avoid any situation which raises the risk for forced or coercive sex on another person. For some men, pornography reinforces the idea of women (or men) as sex objects. Whatever your offenses have been, you will learn to evaluate risk factors and create safety plans to avoid them.

Accountability means you will talk to your group about your sexual behaviors, relationships, thoughts, and fantasies, and how you handle them. You will find that sharing honestly means you are free to be yourself, and your group will appreciate your authentic participation.

For most men in treatment, using alcohol or drugs is discouraged or prohibited. The use of any intoxicating substance lowers "inhibitions" (our built-in rules that stop us from doing dangerous or stupid things) and impairs judgment. Drugs and alcohol make it more difficult to resist impulses and make good decisions. This might include re-evaluating some prescription drugs (including cannabis) you use, to determine if they lower inhibition or impair judgment.

These conditions may seem like a lot to ask of yourself. However, preventing future sex crimes is your responsibility and yours alone.

Figure 1.6: Treatment Progress: How Much Improvement Do You Need?

Sexuality and Risk Responsibility
1. Sexual Offense Responsibility
2. Sexual Behavior
3. Sexual Attitudes
4. Sexual Interests
5. Sexual Risk Management
Criminality
6. Criminal and Rule-breaking Behavior
7. Criminal and Rule-Breaking Attitudes
Treatment and Supervision Cooperation
8. Stage of Change
9. Cooperation with Treatment
10. Cooperation with Community Supervision
Self-Management
11. Emotion Management
12. Problem Solving
13. Impulsivity
Social Stability and Supports
14. Employment
15. Residence
16. Social Influences

"But You Still Don't Get It – I Just Made A Mistake..."

Who says you really need all this stuff anyway? Maybe your therapist just refuses to understand that you're not like these other guys. Maybe *they* need this commitment stuff. Your therapist means well but you are the only one who *really* knows your situation. You just made a mistake.

You *know* you're not going to do it again! You explain that over and over but no one's listening. You think, "I'm stuck in this program for people who have a real problem when I just made a mistake. No one understands me… ."

It might be comforting to say these kinds of things to yourself. If you did make a mistake, you should still take this opportunity to learn how it happened so you can prevent it from happening again. Keep in mind that most people who have reoffended said at one time: "I learned my lesson; it won't ever happen again." Maybe you are different. Maybe you are at low risk for reoffending. But maybe this program will be beneficial for you even so.

If you recognize that you are attracted to children or turned on by forced sex or by exposing yourself—that can be hard to admit. You didn't *choose* your attractions. Attractions don't make you a bad person. *But you are responsible for your behavior*. You choose your behaviors. You are responsible for not acting on your harmful attractions. And you *are* responsible if you continue to deny that you have a dangerous attraction and don't protect yourself and future victims from it.

You don't choose your attractions. You *do* choose your actions.

For the most part, your therapist won't ever really know whether you have committed yourself to a new lifestyle or just learned the right things to say. It's not your therapist's job to catch you in a lie or prove the facts of your case. You are in this program for you. If it's the best you can do now, start by listening to others who are committed to change.

Exercise 1.8: Your Personal Treatment Goals

What problems would you like to work on?

What's going on in your life that you'd like to change or improve?

What would you like to better understand about yourself, your offense, or your sexuality?

What do you see as barriers to change for you?

How do you think those barriers could be reduced?

What might be the pros and cons of change?

What are your positive characteristics?

What are the things you do well?

What do people like about you?

How can you use all the strengths you listed above to help you reach your goals?

CHAPTER 2
UNDERSTANDING YOUR SEXUAL BEHAVIOR

In this chapter, we will discuss sexual interests, sexual crimes, and problematic sexual behaviors. First, we will explore different kinds of sexual attractions and the types of victimizing behaviors that can result from them. Then you will learn about hypersexuality, also sometimes called sex "addiction" or "compulsion." The exercises in this chapter will help you reflect on your own sexuality and gain a better understanding of how these ideas might apply to you. Finally, you will be asked to create a sexual autobiography, so you can explore your own sexual history, see important patterns, and think about how your sexual offending behavior might have developed.

Remember that the goals of this program are to help you develop a plan to prevent reoffending, and also to improve your sexual well-being. We start here with discussing and understanding problematic and unlawful sexual behaviors. Specific strategies for improving sexual, general, and emotional self-control (or self-regulation) will be found in chapter 3.

It is well known that some people convicted of sex crimes have also committed many undetected offenses, and some have committed different types of sexually abusive acts. When you first came into treatment you may have wanted to pretend that the crime you were arrested for was the only one you had committed, when in reality it wasn't the only type of sex offense you have committed. When you take your full-disclosure polygraph exam you will need to reveal your other types of offenses. As you read the following sections, think about each section that applies to you, not just the one you were arrested for.

Types of Sexual Offenses

Child sexual abuse or molestation refers to any sexual contact between an adult and a minor (or between two minors where one is 4 or more years older). Minors are never able to consent to sex with adults—no matter what they say or do—because in order to consent to something you must be able to understand and appreciate what you are agreeing to. Developmentally, minors are not capable of fully understanding the consequences of sex acts. Therefore, any sexual act between an adult and a minor is *always* "nonconsensual" and *always* unlawful. (We'll talk more about consent later in this chapter).

It is important to recognize that with children it is not necessary to touch their private parts to sexually abuse them—*any* act you do with a child that is sexually arousing for you (or intended to be sexually arousing) is an assault. This includes not only stroking and fondling, but tickling, wrestling, kissing, or hugging if the purpose is for your own sexual gratification. Intentionally exposing your private parts to a child for sexual reasons is sexual abuse. Placing a child's hand on your private parts or asking a child to touch your genitals are sex offenses. Spying or looking ("peeping") at a child for sexual purposes is sexually abusive behavior. Sexual conversations or swapping sexual photos or videos with any child under eighteen, whether in person, by phone, or over the Internet, is a sexual assault.

Of course, there are occasions when parents tickle or hug their children, see their children naked, touch their children's private parts to clean them, or talk to their children about sex. All of these behaviors are appropriate because they are *not done for sexual reasons.* When adults engage in these sorts of behaviors with a motivation for their own sexual pleasure, it is called "grooming." That means using your position of familiarity, trust, or authority to gain the confidence of a child and/or his or her parents, in order to get access and opportunity to abuse. When you were defending yourself against your criminal charges you may have claimed that what you did was really innocent or misinterpreted, and that you were being prosecuted unfairly. As you progress in treatment you may be surprised to realize how many of the things you did with your child victims were not unintended at all, but were designed to manipulate your victim (or their parents) into trusting you or accepting what you were doing.

Many people who have been convicted for having child pornography say they "had no victim." But child pornography is not a victimless crime. If you possess, view, download, collect, or share child pornography you are participating in the abuse of the children who were victimized in the making of the pornography. The children in the photos or videos were *real children being sexually abused* while someone filmed it. When you look at or pass on child pornography to another person you are re-victimizing those children. If you took photos or videos of children for your own sexual purposes, or shared them with others, or sold them, that is considered child pornography production and/or distribution. In this workbook we will alternate using the term "child pornography" (CP), with the more accurate, but less familiar, "*child sexual abuse material*" (CSAM).

Sexual assault includes any sexual acts with an adult who has not consented to have sexual contact with you. Any sexual touching of a person who has not agreed to being touched (including rubbing up against someone in a crowd—called *frotteurism*) is an assault. Remember that consent involves not only understanding what you are consenting to, but also being aware of what is happening to you. That means that any sexual touching of a person who is intoxicated and "out of it" is a crime. Any sexual activity with a person who is unable to consent to sex because they are unconscious or unable to understand what is happening is an assault. Any sexual activity involving a person who is mentally handicapped or mentally ill and does not fully understand what they are doing is an assault.

Rape involves penetration of the sexual organs. However, sexual assault does not have to involve intercourse or penetration to be a crime or to be harmful. Even within an established relationship or marriage, intimidating or threatening a partner into sex when you know he or she does not want it is violating that person's rights. And that's an important aspect of why someone sexual assaults another person: *sometimes the excitement comes not from the sex itself but from the power involved in having your way with the other person.*

Exposing your sexual organs to any person who has not asked to see them (*Exhibitionism*) is violating that person's rights and is an assault. (People who attend "adult" establishments where nudity occurs are consenting to see the performers' genitals; therefore their rights are not being violated). We want to acknowledge that there are true exhibitionists (those who expose their genitals in public for the sexual excitement they gain from being seen by non-consenting strangers), public masturbators (those who masturbate in public places such as cars without a clear desire to be observed), and compulsive masturbators (those who engage in hypersexual public behavior which would be acceptable if done in private). But to the victims of these crimes, who have been forced to see something they have not consented to, these distinctions are unimportant. They have all been violated and many will be traumatized. Exposing yourself can be an unhealthy way to meet needs for attention, validation, and acknowledgement that manifest in a behavior that metaphorically cries "look at me!" and "notice me!"

Watching or spying on a person who is undressed or engaging in sex, who does not know you are there and has not consented to being watched (*Voyeurism*) is also violating that person and is an assault. (People who take off their clothes in sexually oriented entertainment establishments are consenting to be watched). Speaking sexually to anyone who has not consented to sexual talk, whether in person, by phone, by text, or over the Internet, is a sexual assault.

Although the behaviors described above are the most common acts that lead to arrests and bring people into treatment, there are many other ways to violate another person's sexual boundaries. *Sexual harassment* means using a position of power or authority (usually, but not always, in a work situation) to make someone feel intimidated or uncomfortable in a sexual way. As a result of the #MeToo movement, public awareness of sexual harassment has increased and victims are increasingly speaking up and reporting harassment. There are generally two types of sexual harassment that occur between superiors and subordinates in the context of employment: (1) *quid pro quo* ("you do *this* for me and I do *that* for you") means threatening or bribing an employee or other subordinate in exchange for sexual favors. This could include promising rewards (like a raise) or threatening a punishment (like denying a promotion). (2) Creating a hostile environment—a tense, offensive vibe that interferes with a person's ability to feel comfortable at work—is caused by behaviors such as touching, grabbing, telling sexual jokes, sexual talk, gender bias, showing sexual pictures, or sexual gestures. Sexual harassment is not always easy to spot because it includes many behaviors that in the past were normalized in our society and called "locker room talk" or excused by saying "boys will be boys."

Sexual talk, such as commenting on someone's body or asking about their sex life, are other examples of sexual harassment when they occur in an inappropriate setting and/or make someone uncomfortable. Talking about your own private parts or your sexual exploits with a person who has not consented to hearing such talk, or showing sexually oriented pictures to someone who has not asked to see them, can also be ways to gain sexual excitement and power by pushing yourself on another person and violating their boundaries.

Other ways that sex can be used in an abuse of power include sexual assaults and boundary violations that occur in the course of a professional's relationship with non-employees. This is called *Professional Sexual Misconduct*. It is probably pretty clear that when a clergy abuses a child from his church it is child abuse. But what about a clergy who has an "affair" with an adult parishioner? Or a teacher who has "consensual" sex with a college student? Or a doctor who has sexual contact with a patient? What about correctional officers and prisoners? Or police and someone they are investigating? There is a growing concern regarding sexual boundary issues among health and other professionals who interact inappropriately with patients, clients, customers, detainees, or other persons in a position of vulnerability. For instance, although it is under-reported, it is estimated that as many as 10% of health professionals have crossed sexual boundaries with their patients.

Professional boundaries are established to avoid developing unethical, confusing or conflicting relationships. Professional boundaries are important because of the imbalance between the professional's power and the other person's vulnerability. The power differential comes from the professional's position of authority and his/her access to personal information known by the professional about the other individual.

Crossing boundaries of professional behavior can be accidental, thoughtless, or purposeful. Some boundary violations involve an intentional attempt to misuse one's power over another for personal gain or sexual gratification. Such boundary crossings can cause discomfort or distress for the other person but might not be reported because the victim likes and respects the professional, wonders if it was their own fault, second-guesses whether or how it happened, or doesn't want the professional to get in trouble. Victims sometimes worry that others won't believe them, they may not want to "make a mountain out of a molehill," or they feel too embarrassed to tell anyone.

What Is Sexual Deviance and Why Do People Sexually Offend?

The word "deviant" simply means differing from what is "normal." Some people who offend are considered to have *sexually deviant attractions* and have persistent deviant sexual interests. Such people may meet criteria for a mental disorder called a *Paraphilic Disorder*. Paraphilic disorders are described in the diagnostic manual (DSM-5) of the American Psychiatric Association as "recurrent, intense, sexually arousing fantasies, urges, or behaviors that cause distress and/or impairment, and that involve inanimate objects, children or nonconsenting adults, or the suffering or humiliation of oneself or a partner with the potential to cause harm." There are many different types of paraphilic disorders.

Pedophilia is a primary or exclusive sexual attraction to pre-pubescent (undeveloped) children (typically under age 13), and involves a pattern of recurrent fantasies, urges, or behaviors that persists over a period of at least six months. Though not listed as an official diagnosis, some people have *hebephilia*—sexual attractions to pubescent (developing) young teens (usually age 11-14). Others are attracted to older, more physically mature teens under the age of consent (age 15-17). These sexual interests can be exclusive (attracted only to minors) or not (also attracted to adults). Some people who recognize that they have a sexual interest in minors refer to themselves as *minor-attracted persons* (MAPs).

Importantly, not all individuals who have abused a child meet criteria for Pedophilia. If the crime truly was an isolated incident and not part of a persistent and ongoing pattern, the abuser usually would not be diagnosed. Also important to note is that not all people with pedophilia abuse children. In fact, there are MAPs who refer to themselves as "virtuous pedophiles" and do not act on their attractions because they understand how harmful child sexual abuse (CSA) is to kids. Some MAPs might look at child pornography (CP or CSAM). If they collect child pornography, that might be an indication that they are Pedophilic. You have to be honest with yourself about whether you fit into any of these categories.

The term <u>*emotional congruence with children*</u> is used to describe person who feels more comfortable with minors than with adults. Kids and teens can seem less threatening than adults, and their innocence and acceptance sometimes make a person feel special, looked up to, and important. Some people struggle with intimacy (emotional closeness) with other adults, and this struggle can be related to early trauma, family dysfunction, or disrupted attachments with others. (We will be exploring these subjects in chapter 4).

Other paraphilic disorders that can lead to unlawful behaviors include:

Exhibitionism (exposure of sex organs to someone who has not consented to see them), *Voyeurism* ("peeping" at people who are undressed or engaged in sexual activities), and *Frotteurism* (touching or rubbing up against a nonconsenting person).

Some people have a paraphilic interest in forced or non-consensual sex (not officially listed in the diagnostic manual but sometimes referred to as "*Paraphilic Coercive Disorder*") which involves arousal to rape and non-consenting sexual activities. If you have this disorder you might notice that you are more turned on by violent or "extreme" porn, "rough sex," or when you are using force or intimidation with a resistant "partner." You might find that loving, affectionate sex lacks the same excitement.

Some paraphilic sexual interests are not unlawful if they involve consensual adult partners. Fetishism (using objects for sexual pleasure, or specific arousal to a certain body part, like feet, for example), sexual masochism (arousal from being humiliated or forced to suffer pain), sexual sadism (inflicting humiliation or suffering on a consenting partner), BDSM (bondage, discipline, sadism, masochism), and transvestic disorder (sexually arousing cross-dressing) are paraphilic but not necessarily harmful or unlawful. There are also many other paraphilias, such as those involving sexual arousal to urine, feces, or obscene talk. Sometimes these interests or behaviors are referred to as "kink." Notice that engaging in "kinky" sexual activities is not considered a disorder unless it causes you significant distress or it interferes with your life. Kink is not considered a crime unless it involves force or non-consent. We will not address kinky activities in this book.

Other people have what is called *hypersexuality*. These people tell themselves they just have a "high sex drive." But sometimes their sex drive is so high they think about sex all the time, or their sexual behaviors feel "compulsive"—that is, they're not able to stop even when they know they should. Hypersexuality often includes spending too much time thinking about, planning, or engaging in sex, watching pornography, or masturbating. It sometimes involves engaging in risky sexual behaviors that could have negative consequences (legal, financial, or health consequences). Some hypersexual people cheat on their partners over and over again, risking the relationship. Sometimes hypersexual people are so busy thinking about sex or engaging in sexual behaviors that sex interferes with their ability to function in a job, school, or other role, such as parenting.

Some people develop sexually problematic behaviors to protect themselves from the vulnerability of real relationships. Sexual behavior patterns involving online sex with strangers, prostitutes, or excessive pornography use can be indicators of what are called "intimacy deficits." When people feel socially awkward or have low self-esteem, they might avoid real relationships with other adults to protect themselves from being hurt. "Long-distance" sex with people who will never get to really know them seems less threatening.

Some people might adopt *sexualized coping strategies* to combat emotional pain or to compensate for feelings of loneliness. Sex can be used like drugs or alcohol to "self-medicate" in a misguided attempt to meet emotional needs for attention, affection, validation, or closeness. *Sexualized coping* is also used to combat boredom or stress, or just to have something to look forward to.

Some people who end up in a program like this are more *opportunistic* than paraphilic. They might take advantage of opportunities for sexual gratification despite the possible consequences to themselves and their victims. They might have a sense of *entitlement* (I deserve what I want when I want it). They might be impulsive and have trouble controlling their behavior because they don't think through the consequences of their decisions in a particular moment. They might have difficulty understanding social signals like body language (common when someone has an *Autism Spectrum Disorder*). They might be compulsive risk-takers, who are always looking for an adrenaline rush. Entitlement, impulsivity, autism, or risk-taking might also be part of a larger pattern of behaviors in other areas in their life. It will be important for you to ask yourself if any of these factors played a role in your offending.

As you can see, people commit sexual offenses for a lot of different reasons that aren't just about deviant sexual interests. Your behavior doesn't really need to be labeled; the most important thing is for you to be honest about what you're into so we can talk about it and help you with it. This program will offer a safe place for you to talk about things that are usually very difficult to talk about.

More About Child Sexual Abuse (CSA)

Children need a lot of care, nurturing, and attention and when they get it, they respond with love and affection. Children look up to adults. They depend on adults. They believe that adults know everything. Children need to feel valued, loved, seen, heard, and protected. When they receive this from an adult, they bond with that adult. A bond with a child can make an adult feel smart, appreciated, and special because to a child, adults are important in their lives.

If there was a child in your life who made you feel this way, you probably felt close to her or him, which is normal. But sometimes feelings of closeness and affection can become mixed up with sex. Maybe you spent a lot of time with the child, got a lot of positive feelings when you were with the child, and physical affection like hugging and kissing became sexualized. Maybe at first you really didn't know how aroused you would be.

Maybe there was an older child or teenager in your life who you felt you could talk to about your problems. Or many you felt like you could listen to and help this teen or child, who didn't have another adult to trust. Maybe this child seemed like the only one who understood you or respected you. By talking with the child you came to feel close to them and this closeness and intimacy began to feel romantic or sexualized.

Maybe your abuse of a child was more opportunistic or impulsive. A situation presented itself and you took advantage of it. Whatever the situation, CSA is about taking advantage of a relationship with a child and using it to meet your sexual needs. Because sexuality is closely tied with emotional needs, this relationship may have felt like it met psychological needs in you that weren't being satisfied in your adult relationships.

CSA can make the offender feel powerful and in control. Children will usually go along with adults because they have been taught to obey them. Children want to please adults. Maybe you convinced your victim that if she went along with you, she would get special privileges. This put you in control of the relationship, and you used that parental or adult power to get the child to act sexually with you. This is called *grooming*. Grooming can also include caring for younger children and taking advantage of the opportunity to "clean" or "check" the children. You may have tested the waters by exposing yourself or touching children "by accident," rubbing against them and "copping a feel."

Children believe that adults know right from wrong. Because the child you abused knew you and trusted you, she or he believed you when you told them what you were doing was okay. At the same time, they might have known that it wasn't exactly right, because they had been told not to let anyone touch them in private places. They wanted to be special, they wanted you to love them, and they wanted to be close to you. They were confused and torn between your attention and wanting to do the right thing. You knew all of this and took advantage of it, which is also part of grooming.

You may have convinced yourself that what you were doing wasn't wrong because your relationship with your victim was "special" and you really loved them. These types of distorted thoughts allowed you to justify your behavior so you don't feel guilty.

Sometimes, people who abuse children blame their victims by pointing out that the victim really did know about sex or initiated it. Or they point out that the victim was "sexually active" with other adults or older children. What this might really mean is that the victim had already been sexually abused by someone else and you thought that made it okay for you to re-abuse the victim. The fact that a child knows about sexual acts does not mean the child understands those acts or can consent to them. In fact, if a child is acting sexually, shouldn't an adult think, "that's not quite normal, I wonder why they are doing that? I should make sure they are safe."

The fact that a child wants to touch you or wants you to touch her does not mean she has "grown up fast" or is more mature than other children. It may mean that the child is naturally curious and needs adults to help them understand proper boundaries. Sometimes it means that another person has taken advantage of the child's loneliness or lack of self-esteem and taught them that they can get attention by acting sexually.

Often children don't tell about CSA, even if they know it is wrong, because they are afraid of what will happen if they tell. They are afraid of losing your love. They are afraid of getting you in trouble. They are afraid of their parents getting mad at them because it feels like *they* did something wrong. They are afraid of you or them being taken out of the home. Maybe they worry that they betrayed their mother by having sex with her partner. You may have helped them to believe all these things by pointing out to them that they were guilty by going along with you. Children are easy to manipulate and convince that they will get in trouble if the abuse becomes known. Sometimes there is no need to threaten a child (though you might have done this), because the grooming has created a natural bond with you, which sealed their loyalty. Or, maybe being abused instilled fear of punishment.

For all the same reasons, sexually abused children sometimes take back their accusations of abuse (recant) at some point after they have told. They may feel overwhelmed by the pressure on them to talk to social services investigators, police, prosecutors and defense attorneys. When they learn that you might go to prison, they may want to protect you. They may want to protect other people from losing you. They may want others to not be mad at them. Whatever their reason for recanting, it doesn't change what you did and it is not relevant in treatment. All that it really means is that the child was confused and frightened and had mixed feelings about telling.

Sometimes children tell but aren't believed. Sometimes their stories are confused, or change over time because they don't have the language to describe what has happened to them. Sometimes adults don't recognize a CSA disclosure for what it is and miss an opportunity to intervene. Sometimes adults don't want to believe that someone they know, love, and trust could abuse a child, so they convince themselves that the child is confused or mistaken.

The word incest is used to describe sexual contact that occurs in any family-type situation and can include any children living in the home, such as siblings, stepchildren or the children of a live-in partner. If you are in treatment because you made sexual contact with a child in your family or in your home, you might think back to whether you had sexual contact with any members of your family as a child. CSA is sometimes learned in families where it is tolerated or "normalized" and no one talks about the fact that it is wrong. In treatment we are usually talking about an adult having sex with a younger, less powerful person. But sometime older teens abuse younger kids in the same family, or in another relationship.

Sometimes when a person who abused minors looks back over their marriage or relationships with adults, they see that for some reason those relationships were not emotionally satisfying. Maybe the couple could not communicate well about what they wanted out of the relationship. Maybe you felt inadequate or unable to satisfy your partner in sexual, financial, or emotional ways. Maybe your partner did not meet your needs but you felt you could not talk to them about your frustration and hurt.

You might want to blame your partner for not meeting your needs. You might want to blame the minor for going along with the abuse or even seeming to initiate it. You might want to blame society for taking this all too seriously and not understanding that you "didn't mean to hurt anyone." But at some point, you need to be able to be honest with yourself about who was really to blame. You may have felt out of control and told yourself you were powerless to stop. But in your heart, you knew that manipulating and abusing a minor was not the way to meet your needs.

In chapters 3 and 8 you will learn how to manage risk factors, improve self-regulation, and prevent CSA from happening again. In chapter 5 you will learn more about how sexual abuse affects victims. In chapter 6 you will learn how to improve your relationship and communication skills so that your relationships with adults will be more fulfilling and satisfying, and you won't feel the need to turn to a vulnerable minor. In chapter 7 you will learn about the distorted thinking that serves to justify the abuse and allow it to continue.

What If My Primary Sexual Attraction Is to Minors?

You might have never said those words out loud to anyone. But if you are asking yourself that question right now, it's great that you recognize that it might pertain to you. It can be really scary to talk about these things that you've never shared before. Research tells us that many minor-attracted persons (MAPs) have been too ashamed or afraid to seek help before their arrest. MAPs experience a lot of loneliness and negative beliefs about themselves due to the stigma and public perceptions about pedophilia. In fact, if you did seek help, you may have had discouraging experiences with therapists who were judgmental, shaming, or not very compassionate, or who simply did not know how to help you. In this program, expect your therapist to create a safe space for you to discuss minor-attraction.

If your primary sexual attraction is to children, one of the dilemmas you face is the loss of your main sexual pleasure. Obviously, this is difficult for many people with pedophilia to accept. Giving up your primary sexual pleasure feels like giving up a part of yourself. We are all sexual beings, and we all seek sexual gratification. But if your main source of sexual pleasure is children, what choice do you have but to give it up? You probably don't want to spend your life hurting children and living in fear of being found out, and you definitely don't want to go to prison (again). Accepting and dealing with minor attraction can be very painful, lonely, and can create feelings of shame, loss, and hopelessness.

Everyone needs love, intimacy, romance, and a sexual outlet. If you are primarily or exclusively attracted to minors, it may be really painful, and even seem unbearable at times, to think about not being able to have the kind of intimate relationship that most everyone wants. We will help you grieve this loss, accept it, and cope with it. Can it be done? Yes! Most people would not choose to give up sex completely. But most people do have sexual desires that they choose not to act on. For example, when someone gets married, they don't stop being attracted to others, but they might stop acting on it because they are committed to their partner and don't want to hurt them. Some other people choose to live a life of total abstinence, usually for religious reasons.

Along with CSA prevention, we also want to focus on your emotional well-being. MAPs have told us (and other researchers) that they need therapists to help them improve their self-esteem and decrease their isolation. They have to deal with the stigma of minor-attraction and figure out how to live a genuine and authentic life despite this attraction. They need to make sense of their sexuality. They need to feel less depressed and more content with their lives. Many persons with minor-attraction say they experience deep distress, and suicidal thoughts are common. MAPs commonly describe fears of rejection, hopelessness, and anxiety about the future.

This program is designed to help you with the following goals associated with primary or exclusive minor-attraction: *self-acceptance* (dealing with stigma, shame, identity confusion); *cognitive reframing and restructuring* (changing the way you think about yourself and the meaning you've attached to your minor-attraction); *alleviation of mental health symptoms* (depression, anxiety, suicidality); *relationship and intimacy issues* (sexual and non-sexual intimacy; secrecy can be very isolating); *future hopes, dreams, and goals* (wanting to have what others have: marriage, family, close relationships); *living an authentic life* (figuring out how to surround oneself with safe and supportive others in order to have genuine, close relationships). And, of course, let your therapist know about other concerns or issues that are unique to your own experience and recovery.

Some offenders have confusion about their *sexual orientation*. Sexual orientation is another way of describing who you are sexually and/or romantically attracted to. If you are attracted to adults of the opposite gender, this is called *heterosexual*. If you are attracted to adults of the same gender, it's called *homosexual or gay*. If you are attracted to both (even if not equally), you are considered bi-sexual. If you are attracted primarily to minors, you may have a *pedophilic* (attracted to pre-pubescent children), *hebephilic* (attracted to young teens), or *ephebephilic* (attracted to older teens) sexual orientation.

There is a lot of controversy about sexual orientation change efforts—sometimes referred to as "conversion therapy" when referring to gay/lesbian orientation. Conversion therapy is now unethical in most states and according to professional guidelines for psychologists, counselors, and social workers. Sex-offending treatment used to emphasize what was called aversion therapy to change someone's attraction to kids. By using behavioral conditioning like bad smells, therapists tried to reduce the arousal to children by associating it with something distasteful, like a whiff of ammonia. A previous version of this book used odor aversion. But most research indicates that changing attractions isn't really possible for most people, and so a more realistic goal is to accept the attraction (but not act on it). This book will help you find ways to accept yourself, experience your sexuality, and manage your sexual interests to minors without engaging in harmful or unlawful behavior.

Some men report being attracted to both adults and to children. Some are attracted to adults of one gender and minors of the other. This apparent contradiction can be very confusing. If you are attracted to teenage boys but not adult males, are you gay? If you are attracted to women as well as boys, are you bi-sexual? There are no easy answers to these questions, but labels are less important than understanding and accepting your sexuality. Sexual interests seem to be mostly pre-determined before birth but can be shaped by experiences, including trauma. Sometimes sexual attractions are influenced when first sexual experiences occur that are outside of one's primary orientation.

Having been sexually abused in your childhood can confuse your sexual orientation. The feelings you feel in your first sexual experiences can stay with you and shape both your understanding of sex and your expectations of what sex will be like in the future. The body responds to sexual touch (even abusive touch) and victims might be very confused by this. At the same time, they also feel manipulated, used, ashamed, or pulled into something they don't understand. Sexual abuse is usually confusing and frightening for children, even if they don't label the experience as "abuse" (and even if they think they're getting "lucky" with an older person). If you were sexually abused as a minor, you might find that sex with adults brings back feelings of fear, shame or being out of control. As adults, some formerly abused children may associate sex with other adults with feelings of being small and afraid. But with children they don't have to feel vulnerable or powerless. With children they can feel powerful and in control. This can lead to sexual abuse of kids.

If you have *any* attraction to adults, male or female, you can nurture that attraction and find sexual pleasure in relationships with other adults. It will still create a loss to give up sex with minors but if you have a sexual interest in adults, it can be exciting and satisfying. If your intimate relationships with adults have been few, in treatment you should explore the reasons why, and discuss your feelings with your group.

Some men believe they can walk a tightrope of sexual abuse by choosing partners that are legally of age but remind them of the children they are primarily attracted to ("barely legal"). This is a dangerous game. If you continue to choose to have sex with teenagers or young adults, even if they are eighteen or older, you may be reinforcing paraphilic sexual interests. This can be a risk factor for reoffending. Are you reinforcing your interest in minors by choosing partners who look really young? It may be legal, but is it safe? Is this consistent with your treatment goals? How does this choice help you change your lifestyle? Is this kind of sex emotionally satisfying? Is it healthy to continue to seek out partners with whom you have an age gap, and who are at a very different stage of life development? This may keep you from experiencing true emotional intimacy with an adult partner you can genuinely be close to.

If you are primarily or exclusively attracted to minors, you might have asked yourself: Am I a bad person? Why am I like this? Who can I talk to? Should I disclose this to people close to me? If so, who? What? Where? When? How? Why? (more about this in Chapter 6).

- ☑ WHO? Who do you trust to share your authentic self?
- ☑ WHY? You are looking for support, understanding and direction from this person.
- ☑ WHAT and HOW? Understand that your disclosure may be shocking and/or overwhelming to others, so be prepared to slow it down by asking, "may I continue?" Understand that what you say may result in acceptance or rejection.
- ☑ WHEN? When it feels right for you – the right place, the right time, the right circumstances.
- ☑ WHERE? Where neither of you feels trapped.

Remember, your attractions do not make you a bad person. We do not choose our attractions; we choose our actions. If you have internet access, you can go online to learn more about minor-attraction and talk to other MAPs who are committed to a non-offending lifestyle. You can also find a list of links to easily click on from your device at https://safersocietypress.org/rtf4-resources.

Link 2.1 – Help Wanted Prevention
https://www.helpwantedprevention.org/

Link 2.2 – B4UACT
https://www.b4uact.org/attracted-to-minors/

Link 2.3 – VIRPED (Virtuous Pedophliles)
https://www.virped.org/

Link 2.4 – Stop It Now!
https://www.stopitnow.org/

Link 2.5 – The Global Prevention Project
http://theglobalpreventionproject.org/

Link 2.6 – The Prostasia Foundation
https://prostasia.org/blog/an-introduction-to-map-support-club/

Link 2.7 – Troubled Desire
https://troubled-desire.com/en/

Link 2.8 – This American Life
https://www.thisamericanlife.org/522/tarred-and-feathered

Non-Contact Offenses

You may have engaged in what are called "non-contact offenses": *exhibitionism, voyeurism, or obscene phone calls or sexting.* Exhibitionism means exposing your genitals (private parts) to others who don't want to see it, and frequently involves masturbating in public places. Another word for exhibitionism is "flashing." Voyeurism means watching others who don't know they are being watched while they are nude, bathing, having sex, or getting undressed. Another word for voyeurism is "peeping," which involves looking in the windows of someone's home, or somehow viewing others who don't consent to it.

Exposing or voyeuring can also be done electronically, through video chats or apps that allow you to show yourself or see someone in a sexual way. When these activities are done without someone's consent, they are unlawful. Sometime voyeuring is done by placing a camera device in a place where someone is unaware, to photograph or record them. Sexting occurs when you text about sex or use sexual language, or send photos or videos of a sexual nature. Just as exposing yourself without consent is violating another's rights by forcing them to see something they don't want to see, sexual calling or sexting forces others to listen to or see something they didn't ask for.

In today's day and age, young adults have grown up in an electronic world where boundaries are confusing and less obvious than at other times in history. Social media allows people to have "friends" they've never met, connect in intimate ways online, and say things they wouldn't have the guts to say if someone was right in front of them. We share stories, photos, videos and ideas in ways never possible before the 21st century. This means that the online rules of social engagement and communication are often unclear, inconsistent with conventional social norms, and sometimes easily misunderstood.

It isn't unusual to engage in non-contact offenses prior to a rape or sexual molestation. Sometimes these offenses are part of a grooming process. For instance, before touching a child, a person may prepare the child for sexual contact by walking around naked in front of him or her, showering together, watching the child bathe or get undressed, or even masturbating in front of the child. A person who rapes may watch his victim, stalk her, or call her before the actual assault.

Engaging in flashing or peeping or sexting with a non-consenting person is unlawful and harmful even if you never actually touch a victim in a sexual way. This type of offense is often used to gain the feelings of power and control through these distant ways of forcing himself on someone else. Some people flash because they are self-conscious about their looks, their body, or their penis, and are looking for acceptance and validation.

People who offend in these ways usually have difficulty with intimacy in relationships—not just sexual intimacy, but *emotional intimacy*. It is difficult for these people to truly be close to others and to find satisfaction in sharing themselves with another person. Though many of them are married or in relationships, they don't *feel* close to their partners and may fear getting hurt in close relationships. At the same time, they want to be noticed and they need attention because they feel they don't get the recognition or validation they deserve. Often the flashing or peeping is an attempt to have a long-distance sexual "relationship" with another person without the fear of rejection or the risky complications of trying to communicate.

As one exhibitionist (flasher) explained,

> *I could control when it started, when it stopped, and how it happened. While I was doing it, I was definitely getting her attention. For a few minutes I wasn't a nobody: I was somebody. When I was done, it was over, and I didn't have to try to talk to her. I saw my victims as objects, not as people. If the victim talked to me or made eye contact, I couldn't do it. Suddenly the victim would become a real person, not just an object I could use to achieve sexual gratification.*

Other flashers do want their victim to respond to them. Usually they're hoping for a positive response. One flasher stated that if the victim seemed interested or talked to him nicely, this was enormously exciting. This response only happened once or twice—out of *hundreds* of times that he flashed—but those few times provided the fuel for his fantasy that it could happen again. Each time he flashed he was hoping for that "perfect" response. When he didn't get it, he would feel the urge to flash again and again, always seeking the response and convincing himself that eventually it would come. Other flashers want their victim to be shocked and scared. For them, these reactions feel like respect. For just that moment they feel powerful. They may feel humiliated if a victim acts bored or laughs at them. But still they keep searching for their "perfect" victim.

As children, some non-contact offenders were involved in experiences that were sexually or emotionally inappropriate. For example, some report that they were exposed to pornography at a young age by an older person. Some report loose sexual *boundaries* in their homes. For instance, some non-contact offenders say that in their homes there was excessive nudity, or adults having sex within sight or hearing of the children. Others talk about adults making sexual comments that were confusing to them. In homes where divorced parents are themselves lonely or confused, they sometimes treat their children like "buddies," and talk to them about their sex lives. All of these experiences can be confusing—and at the same time stimulating—to children. Some offenders say they had no privacy; they were bathed by parents long past the age of being able to do so themselves, or they were not allowed to close or lock bathroom and bedroom doors. Some had no *emotional* privacy; their parents read their messages, went through their personal belongings, or listened in on their conversations.

As adults, these men may have problems establishing appropriate boundaries in their relationships. These problems can appear in several ways, such as failing to respect other people's personal space or privacy, or (at the other extreme) not being able to be open at all with a partner. They may have poor sexual relationships because they are afraid to talk to their partner about their wants and needs. They may fear being close to others at the same time that they need to connect with them.

Some non-contact offenders report having felt neglected as children. Sometimes their parents worked a lot and left them at home to fend for themselves. Their parents may not have paid attention to them or didn't have time for them, and they felt un-noticed, unloved or unlovable. As children they desperately needed emotional contact with the adults around them, but when they attempted to get their needs met, they were pushed away or told, "don't bother me!" They may have grown up believing that it was dangerous to express love or get close to others because they would be rejected.

Sometimes it is a combination of emotional neglect or abuse and confusing sexual boundaries in the home that lead to confusion about the link between sex and emotional closeness (intimacy). They may resolve this confusion by achieving sexual gratification through a distant (and therefore emotionally *safe*) sexual act. In this way they can be sexual without getting close to anyone emotionally and risk getting hurt.

Contrary to popular jokes, victims of non-contact offenses are rarely amused or entertained. They are frightened and repulsed. They don't know what the offender will do next. Masturbating in public or peeping seem like bizarre things to most victims, and they see the offender as out of control and capable of doing anything. As with all deviant fantasies, the fantasy of what the other person is feeling can become so distorted that it has *no connection with reality*. Consider this fantasy:

I have carefully orchestrated the scene in the restroom. I place a wad of paper in the door so it stays open and I can see out. I have a perfect vantage point when I turn the garbage can over so I can stand on it. Looking out, I have a clear view of anyone entering the bathroom. I watch as man after man passes by.

After a while I see this gorgeous guy coming. Please, please, please, let him be the one! The feeling grips me as I see him approaching. That wonderful, tingling feeling in the pit of my stomach. As he gets closer it becomes obvious he's coming in and I begin to get harder. I quickly get into position, deciding in a flash whether I want him to actually see me or just hear the sounds of my moaning. I decide that I want him to see me so I run to the urinal and pull my pants below my butt. My heart begins to race as I imagine the look on his face when he finally sees me. I hear him enter the restroom, his footsteps lightly sounding on the tiled floor. I lean against the urinal and start to moan loudly. I time it so that he rounds the corner just as I spill my juice. My ears are tingling and I open my eyes to see him staring, wide-eyed in amusement and disbelief. The look in his eyes envelops me like the soft embrace of a lover. I feel wanted. I feel appreciated. I feel that without actually uttering a sound, I have been heard. I smile to myself as he regains his composure and enters a stall. I exit quickly, wondering if he will be doing the same thing.

In reality, of course, it is hard to imagine this flasher's victim feeling "wonder" or "amuse-ment." Most people would be horrified, scared, and disgusted. But when you have come to believe your distorted fantasies, it is easy to convince yourself of anything. Consider how this voyeur convinced himself he could get away with the most bizarre behavior and risked everything that was important to him:

As time went on, I delved more and more into the world of voyeurism, using a digital video camera to spy between the legs of an unsuspecting co-worker. I stayed at the office late one night and cut a hole in the shelf in front of her desk. Another time, I tried to prop my phone in such a way as to look up the skirts of girl students as they came to the front table to collect their materials. It wasn't long after this that I was forced to resign my position of fourteen years. I later turned myself in. I lost my wife and my two-year-old daughter. Public humiliation soon followed, as the details of my offenses were all over the television and the newspapers.

Was this offender really after pictures of women's panties? Of course not. He could find pictures of women in panties in countless ways online or even in magazine ads. It was the sexual assault that turned him on—the taking from an unsuspecting victim something she had not consented to give him. And it is the assaultive nature of non-contact offenses that is most frightening and most hurtful to victims. They know they have been violated. They don't understand why, and question what have they done to you? They feel confused and vulnerable.

Many victims of these offenses report that the experience was so traumatic they became with-drawn and frightened of any new person or situation. These feelings change victims' lives, limiting their ability to feel safe and to function with other people.

Exhibitionism has been described as a *courtship disorder* in which the exhibitionist's exposure of his genitals represents a misguided attempt to initiate intimate interaction prior to appropriately establishing a relationship. In clinical settings, it is not uncommon for exhibitionists to describe their behavior not as a prelude to an interaction, but rather as a complete sexual act in and of itself. The behavior is usually repetitive and habitual, and most exhibitionists have engaged in the act hundreds of times.

An important component of assessing exhibitionism is to distinguish between true exhibitionists (whose fantasies, urges and behaviors involve exposing their genitals expressly for the sexual excitement they derive from being seen), public masturbators (who masturbate in public places with the possibility of being seen but without a clear desire to be observed), and compulsive masturbators (those whose hypersexual behavior—no matter how excessive or disruptive to their lives—is usually kept within the bounds of law and social acceptability). Furthermore, sexual acting out with others (mutual masturbation in public places or phone sex) may sometimes involve exhibitionistic behavior but might be more characteristic of compulsive or hypersexual behavior.

Researchers have suggested that some hypersexual individuals engage in a wide range of unconventional sexual behaviors characterized by excessive sexual appetite, sexual preoccupation, and repetitive impulsive enactment that leads to adverse consequences and/or a failure to fulfill roles or obligations. These symptoms can include excessive masturbation, promiscuity, pornography use, cybersex, or sexting— behaviors that when practiced in private and in moderation with consenting adults are generally socially acceptable and not unlawful. The practice of engaging in sexual encounters with strangers can indicate a fear of intimacy and a desire to keep others at a distance in an effort to avoid becoming emotionally vulnerable.

Repeatedly engaging in conduct that can lead to adverse consequences is a key indicator of compulsive or addictive behavior. In other words, the need for immediate gratification becomes paramount and overrides rational consideration of consequences to self or others.

Rape and Other Sexual Assaults

Rape means forcing someone to have vaginal, oral, or anal sex against his or her will. Sexual battery includes these offenses and any other unwanted sexual touching. Rape is an act of violence. People who rape are using sex to gain power and control over another person. Sex is just the mechanism for dominating the victim.

Despite what you might have heard or read, women *do not* want to be raped. In fact, rape is one of the most traumatic experiences a person can suffer. Women do not ask to be raped by the way they dress or act. Sometimes women (and men) want attention and want to be seen as attractive and sexy, so they wear sexy clothing. Everyone has the right to try to make themselves attractive. A woman's appearance never makes it okay to force sex on her.

Men are rarely falsely accused of sexual assault; research suggests that 2-8% of cases involve false allegations. Women are much more likely not to be believed than to fabricate an allegation. Men are more likely to not be prosecuted for a real offense. Women press sexual assault charges because they feel violated. They believe they were forced to have sexual contact against their will. Men deny their crimes and blame the victim to avoid taking responsibility and suffering consequences. People who sexually assault others may have distorted beliefs about dating, sex, and intimacy. The truth: *People don't say no when they mean yes.*

Sometimes women (and men) do have mixed feelings about a sexual encounter as it is happening, and want to change their mind about going ahead with it. *Everyone has the right to stop sex at any point along the way.* When a person says no, the other person has no right to continue. Pushing your partner into sex is rape. Appropriate sex stops as soon as either partner becomes uncomfortable with what is happening and says no either verbally or nonverbally (by pulling away, pushing you away, turning away from you).

The truth is, you know when someone doesn't want to have sex with you. You don't have to use physical force to be committing a rape. If you frighten or intimidate someone into going along with sex when they don't want to you are committing a rape. If you have sexual contact with someone who cannot consent to it either because they are too intoxicated to know what they are doing or because they are intellectually limited and cannot understand what sex means, you are raping them. If you continue to try to "persuade" someone to go further sexually then they want to, that is a sexual assault.

Some rapes are fueled by raw anger. Anger can be a result of feeling powerless in many areas of your life. Rape can be a way of attempting to regain a sense of control over your life by making someone else helpless. Rape can also be about entitlement. Some people feel they are entitled to get what they want. Being told "no" can trigger a feeling of being deprived. A person who rapes might feel that he is entitled to punish the person who "is making him angry" by depriving him of the sex he wants.

An angry rapist may be impulsive, acting on an opportunity that presents itself suddenly. They may abuse drugs or alcohol, both of which interfere with their thinking and self-control. A man may be angry with a woman in his life, and feel entitled to take out his hostility on any woman who crosses his path. Rape can involve physical violence, but sometimes involves intimidation without physical aggression. But it is usually not the victim who is the actual source of his anger. As with many intense feelings, it is often past experiences that are at the root of the feelings. The victim has only triggered old, unresolved feelings.

Other rapists are also motivated by a need to feel powerful but are not angry with their victims. A "power" rapist may carefully plan their crimes, stalking their victim and watching his or her routines before attacking. They may not physically injure their victims in a non-sexual way, using only as much force as necessary to gain compliance. Often, they need only to threaten a victim to frighten them into submitting to the assault. In their "perfect" fantasies this rapist may imagine that his victims enjoy being violated and even climax. They may be hoping to feel respected and wanted by their victims. They are afraid of not feeling respected or wanted by others in general.

A third type of rapist is very different. This is a person who is sexually excited by seeing people suffer. This "sadistic" rapist wants to see their victims suffer as much as possible because the more pain, humiliation, or degradation their victim suffers the more they are turned on. They may torture a victim or trick a victim into a dangerous situation with a "con" approach.

As noted earlier, some people are turned on by rough sex, or "bondage and discipline." Doing this with other truly consenting adults is not unlawful or wrong. However, if you are turned on by coercive sex (or if you like to role-play with someone who is resisting and is afraid), you may have a paraphilic interest that can put you at risk to victimize non-consenting persons.

Some people who commit rape do so because they have hostility toward women. These feelings are sometimes connected to past experiences with women. They may also grow out of beliefs about women, gender roles, and power. Feelings of contempt for women can be reinforced by the normalization of gender-based violence in the culture. But coercive sex is never acceptable. Some people commit rape as part of a general pattern of violence and aggression. These patterns may seem normal and acceptable to those with a criminal mindset.

Hostility, criminality, and aggression can also develop as defensive measures, since violence can seem like a necessary survival skill to people from dangerous families or communities. Some people have seen hostility and violence all around them their whole lives. Sometimes, abusing others feels empowering in ways that seem to compensate for the pain of living in poverty, discrimination, or community violence. Not having the things other people have can breed resentment. Out of that resentment can come entitlement, leading you to feel justified abusing or exploiting others. If you never saw people respecting each other's boundaries in childhood, you might not realize how important boundaries are. You might think it is acceptable to misuse power to get what you want.

If you have ever forced someone to have sexual contact against their will, treatment will be a place for you to explore the roots of your anger, your need to dominate others, your feelings of entitlement, or your belief that you can never be satisfied by consensual sex. To understand your motivations is to understand your needs. Later we will talk about meeting your needs in healthy ways.

Consent and Power Differentials

True consent involves the ability to make decisions that are well thought out. In order to truly consent, a person must have the ability to understand the consequences of their decisions, weigh the pros and cons, and make an independent, non-forced choice. Adults with cognitive (intellectual) impairment, people who are intoxicated, and people with mental disturbances are not able to consent. Some minor teens may seem mature, but they don't have fully developed brains. They make decisions based on what feels good in the moment without recognizing the longer-term consequences. This is why the law protects them from themselves.

- *Consent* occurs when one person voluntarily gives agreement to the proposal or desires of another, fully understanding the potential risks and benefits and their right to say no (sex between two competent adults who agree to a sexual encounter or relationship with no hidden agenda).
- *Cooperation* means working together in a joint action that requires active engagement from both people (could be a minor teen who seems to be willingly engaging in consensual sex but who doesn't have the maturity to make a fully informed and consensual decision).
- *Compliance* is the act or process of going along in order to please someone else's desire, demand, proposal, or wishes; or due to worries about retaliation if they don't go along (example: sex workers, who are seemingly engaging in a business transaction, but who are often brought into "the life" by pimps or human traffickers who exploit their vulnerability, poverty, drug dependence, or homelessness (often teen runaways and former foster children).
- *Coercion* is persuading someone to do something they don't really want to do by putting pressure on them, manipulating them, making them feel guilty, or using intimidation, or threats, which can be stated or unstated (implied).

Figure 2.1: Consent

EVERYDAY CONSENT

PEOPLE OFTEN THINK CONSENT IS ONLY IMPORTANT WHEN IT COMES TO SEX.
Really, consent is about always choosing to respect personal and emotional boundaries.
By practicing consent in everyday situations, you show that you value the choices of others.

ASK FOR CONSENT WHEN TOUCHING

- It's important to ask for consent before hugging, tickling, or other kinds of touch.
- Ask sincerely so others understand it's okay to say no.
- For people who have experienced sexual abuse, any unexpected touch can be scary and traumatic. Others may just prefer more personal space.

For example: "Is it okay if I put my arm around you?" or, "Want to hug or wave goodbye?"

RESPECT PRIVACY

- Everyone has boundaries. Some people like to keep things about themselves private, while others are more open.
- If someone shares personal information with you, it's important to ask what their boundaries are.

For example: "My cousin was assaulted and is afraid they will never feel okay again. Is it okay if I tell them that you're a survivor, too? It's all right if you're not comfortable with that."

ASK PERMISSION

- Just like everyone has different boundaries about touch, everyone has different levels of comfort about sharing things online, like photos.
- It is important to always ask before posting or tagging photos of someone on social media.

For example: "This is a great photo of all of us! Is it okay if I share it online, or should I take another one without the kids in it? I know you don't often post photos of them."

SEX AND CONSENT

- Sex without consent isn't sex. It's sexual assault.
- Consent must be freely given. A person must understand what they are agreeing to, and they can change their mind at any time.
- Consent needs to be clear and enthusiastic. The absence of "no" or silence does not mean "yes."
- Past consent does not mean current or future consent.
- When drugs and alcohol are involved, clear consent is not possible. A person who is intoxicated or impaired cannot give consent.

HOW TO HANDLE THE "NO"

- Whenever you're asking for someone's consent, they could say "no."
- Accept the answer and move on. Don't pressure someone to change their mind.
- It's okay to feel disappointed with a "no" answer. But always remember that respecting boundaries is the right thing to do.

NSVRC national sexual violence resource center

Sexual Assault Awareness Month

WWW.NSVRC.ORG/SAAM #SAAM

Power differentials can occur between people in many ways, and the more powerful person is always in a position to exploit the other. Power differences can come from differences in age, size, status, financial resources, position of authority, or by having some type of control over outcomes in someone else's life.

A person may submit to unwanted sexual advances for many reasons, including a desire to please someone in authority, to feel important, or to avoid a perceived threat. A power differential always challenges the legitimacy of the consent.

In a truly equal and consensual sexual relationship, each partner explicitly knows the purpose of the sexual relationship, the possible negative and positive outcomes of such a relationship, and the limits of the relationship. Each person feels they have the right to refuse or withdraw agreement and to weigh the pros and cons of the decision. Victims of sexualized power and boundary violations are faced with the stress of a potential range of threats or benefits depending on their positive or negative response to the advances. This stress may interfere with their ability to make a sensible decision or to assert themselves.

Any situation in which one person holds the power and another person is expected to go along with them creates the potential for exploitation. A victim may feel powerless to resist sexual advances or they might not believe they have the right to say no. They may fear retaliation and go along with the seduction out of fear. In a majority of, victims avoid confronting the perpetrator or reporting the incident.

Can an individual who is dependent on another truly and freely decline to participate in some aspect of a relationship? Or does the dependency, by definition, negate the ability to equally participate in relationship decisions? What appears to be consent may actually be, in many cases, compliance—going along. Sexual boundary violations rarely involve violence or overt force and the person in power may not need to threaten or bribe the other person to attain compliance. The dynamics of most sexually exploitative encounters are more subtle and can create a false illusion of consent. Because exploitative sexual relationships are usually kept secret, they isolate the victim and limit social support that could help them cope with this traumatic experience. See the website below for is a thoughtful and provocative essay about the complexities of consent:

Link 2.9 – JoDS

https://jods.mitpress.mit.edu/pub/hqglqga6/release/1

Figure 2.2: How Does Power Impact Consent

I Ask How Power Impacts Consent

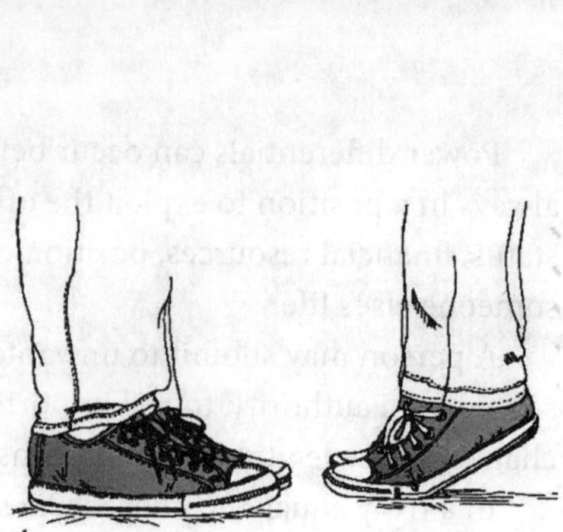

Consent can be complicated when one partner holds more power than the other. By being mindful of the ways power imbalances may impact consent, you can take steps to ensure your partner feels comfortable communicating their needs.

What Is Power?

- Power is the ability to influence the actions and choices of others.
- Power can be obvious, like in the case of a supervisor or mentor, or it can be less apparent like when there's a difference in sexual experience.

Imbalances of Power

- Relationships have a power imbalance when one person has the power to influence things like money, a place to live, a job, or a reputation.
- Having power over someone can influence how comfortable they feel saying no to sex – someone may fear negative consequences for not consenting.
- When someone abuses power over a partner, they may use verbal threats or not. Either way, consent is never possible when someone feels they don't have a choice.

Examples of Imbalances of Power

- **Age differences and sexual experience:** An older or more sexually experienced adult may make a younger or less experienced adult feel they need to "prove" that they are mature or experienced.
- **Level of ability:** Some adults who have physical or intellectual disabilities, older adults, or those who need assistance from a caregiver may rely on their partner in some areas of life, but their decision-making in other areas should still be respected.
- **Position in society:** Someone may have more social privilege than their partner – through their education, job, wealth, citizenship, or other factors.
- **Privilege:** White privilege, male privilege, and other unearned advantages are part of the power some of us bring to relationships.

Checking In

- Before asking for consent, consider how holding a position of power might influence the situation.

Ask yourself: "Would this person say yes if I didn't have power/authority over them?"

Make Consent Clear

- If there's a difference in power between you and your partner, your partner may feel less able to tell you their needs.
- Let them know they can tell you when they're not interested in doing something.
- Ask questions in a way that communicates you're okay with their answer – no matter what it is.

For example, "I hope you know you can tell me how you're really feeling - saying 'no' is always okay."

NSVRC national sexual violence resource center   Sexual Assault Awareness Month

www.nsvrc.org/saam   #SAAM   #IAsk

Exercise 2.1: Think About Consent

Can you describe them in terms of the characteristics of consent, cooperation, compliance, and coercion? What power differentials existed? Use the questions listed below to think about these complicated issues.

Understanding consent definitely begins with a simple idea: **YES means YES and everything else means NO**. But it can be more complicated than that. Understanding consent requires consideration of the many complex motivations, thoughts, feelings, substance impairments, and relationships of the people involved. Like other issues, consent is also impacted by social and cultural context.[*]

a. Do you agree that unwanted sexual contact through force or threat is non-consensual and illegal? Why or why not?

b. Let's think about the ability of someone to safely decline a sexual encounter: Women historically have been socialized and expected to give in to male demands and desires, and some women will feel less secure declining advances than other, more empowered women. Other factors may play a role: A man making advances when three of his buddies stand beside him; a man making advances when a woman is in his apartment alone at 3AM. How would you know whether someone is truly consenting, complying, or being coerced?

c. Level of drug or alcohol induced impairment: How do you know if someone is too intoxicated to consent? What would you look for? How much intoxication is too much, and how would you know when true consent is not possible?

d. Relationship status: Sometimes behavior which indicates consent within marriage clearly does not mean consent on a first date. The ways of communicating consent are different for established vs. less acquainted partners. But even in established relationships all situations are not so clear. Can non-consensual acts can still occur in a marriage or long-term relationship? Why or why not? What are the factors that might be confusing for you?

e. Time after the act to reflect and consider: Is consent or non-consent established at the moment an event occurs? Was something consensual if later in time it is reflected upon as non-consensual? Is it possible for someone to not recognize until after the fact that he/she felt coerced?

f. Laws: To what extent does the legal climate contribute to the sense of consensual sexual behavior? Can certain types of illegal sex be consensual—with sex workers or sex between teens? What's the difference between legal and consensual?

g. Social context: If intoxicated Jane hooks up with Kevin at a party, and in one case her friends applaud her ability to land the captain of the lacrosse team, and in the other case they frown at how he manipulated her and used his social status to seduce her, how might she see the situation differently? What if her friends call her a "slut" afterwards? If certain behaviors seem to be "normalized" how does that raise the risk for victimization and perpetration?

h. The person who initiates the sexual encounter may also fall in the category of legally unable to consent (minors and intoxicated people, for instance). Whose responsibility is it to determine age of consent, or intoxication level, and how should this be done? What is the responsibility of the other person to determine whether engaging in the sexual encounter is right or wrong?

---

* Modified with permission; posted by Dan Rosen on the ATSA list-serve 3/8/19.

Grooming

"Grooming" is about setting up an offense plan. First, the offender gains the trust not only of the victim, but also of others in the victim's circle, like friends, a child's parents, or other family members. Once familiarity, authority, or trust is established, the offender moves on to creating opportunities to be alone with the victim, and then manipulates or forces the victim into sexual activity. Grooming can involve manipulating physical space to ensure being alone with a victim, tricking the victim into a vulnerable place or position, or even keeping the victim from being able to "escape." Predatory sexual perpetrators become skilled at identifying and preying on vulnerable victims, including those who may be naïve, passive, or unlikely to resist.

With child victims, grooming usually involves keeping the child's loyalty after the offending has begun by making the child feel important and special. Children are easily manipulated by adults because they are eager to please adults, trust adults, are taught to obey adults, and they depend on adults to take care of them.

Sometimes an abuser singles out their future victim for special attention even though, in their distorted way of thinking, they may deny their attraction or their intention to abuse the child. After the offender has been caught, those who saw what was happening may look back and recognize how the offender manipulated everyone by giving the victim special attention, special privileges, or buying things for the child. They may say, "We thought he was so good, so concerned, so caring."

Playing, hugging, tickling, and wrestling with the child can get the child used to being touched, and at the same time provide an opportunity for the offender to test how comfortable the child is with touching. The child, being sexually naïve, is completely unaware of where the touching is leading. The touching progressively becomes more intimate or sexual (i.e. tickling to hugging to kissing to fondling to mutual sexual touching). By the time the child realizes that something is wrong, he or she might have strong feelings of affection for the abuser. And because they have encouraged the abuser's attention and affection, victims often feel they have played a role in their own victimization. Grooming leads the child to blame him or herself for the abuse. As a result, the child suffers even more from the abuse.

Physical proximity, non-threatening touch, compliments, and other "courtship" or dating rituals may be part of grooming of adult victims.

Think about the times you have done any of the things in the list of grooming examples in order to get a child to like or trust you. If you molested a child, you engaged in some grooming behaviors. Recognizing these behaviors will help you learn what to avoid in the future as you develop your relapse prevention plan.

Some Examples of Child Grooming:

- Befriending a child and engaging in activities that the child likes.
- Spending a great deal of time with a child, making her/him feel special.
- Giving a child gifts or privileges.
- Taking the child to fun places.
- Letting a child sleep over or sleep in your bed.
- Getting the child's parent to trust you and like you.
- Talking to a child about her/his problems and helping her/him solve those problems.
- Talking to a child about your own problems.
- Engaging a child in "intimate" talk, including opening up about his feelings. The child may feel privileged to be included in such grown up matters.
- Allowing a child to do grown-up things she/he would not ordinarily be allowed to do such as drink alcohol, smoke cigarettes or drive a car.
- Showing a child pornography.
- Hugging or kissing a child more than you usually would.
- Lying with a child, and rubbing her/his back or buttocks.
- Bathing or showering with a child.
- Undressing or being naked in front of the child.
- Talking with a child about personal things online or through texting or apps
- Using your relationship to gain a child's trust

Some Things Offenders Tell Children:

- It's our special secret
- No one will believe you.
- Your mom will be mad at you.
- If you love me you'll do it
- They will think it's your fault.
- We might get in trouble.
- They'll send you away.
- They'll put me in jail.
- No one would understand our special relationship.
- I'll kill your dog if you tell.
- I'll do it to your sister.
- Someone else did it with me, so it's ok.

Exercise 2.2: Grooming

If you sexually assaulted an adult victim, you may also have engaged in grooming. Sometimes exhibitionists engage in conversation to get the victim's attention prior to exposing (like calling someone over to your car to ask for directions). A person who has raped may buy a woman (or man) drinks, flirt with her, make her feel safe, gain her trust, or even date her. You may have befriended someone in your workplace in order to later request sexual favors from him or her. If you have, you have "groomed" them for sexual purposes. List some examples of your grooming behavior.

Things I *Did* to Gain a Victim's Trust	Things I *Said* to Gain a Victim's Trust

Here are some good documentaries to watch that will help you understand grooming, the power dynamics of sexual assault, and why victims often don't tell or aren't believed:

- Leaving Neverland (HBO)
- Surviving R Kelly (Lifetime; also on Netflix)
- The Keepers (Netflix)
- What Haunts Us (Starz, or Amazon)
- Rape on the Night Shift (Frontline)
- I am Evidence (HBO)
- The Hunting Ground (CNN or Amazon)
- Audrie and Daisy (Netflix)
- The Invisible War (Amazon)
- Filthy Rich: Jeffrey Epstein Documentary (Netflix or Hulu)
- Athlete A (Netflix)

Internet Offenses*

Some of you have been arrested for crimes you committed by using the Internet. As you now know, Internet offenses are real crimes with serious consequences.

Researchers have spent the past 25 years studying and understanding the many different aspects of online sex-offending and the wide range of problematic online sexual behaviors. By talking to many hundreds of people arrested for online offenses, they've contributed much to our knowledge and ways of thinking about these complex behaviors. This section will help you explore many aspects of your online behavior to assess where the main problems might be for you.

We will describe different categories (sometimes called "typologies") of online offending to help you determine where you fit in to the wide range of behaviors and motivations. Remember – you know the answers. We don't. We might speculate based on the facts of your case, but it's up to you to be honest with yourself and your therapist so you can get a handle on understanding yourself and managing your behavior.

The Internet can contribute to sexual behavior problems for many people, but not all. We will talk here about Internet offenses and other types of problematic online sexual behavior. For starters, you can use the Internet Sex Screening Test tool on Link 2.10 to assess yourself and your online habits. If you don't have Internet access now, but you've had trouble with online behavior, you can ask your therapist to download it for you.

Link 2.10 - Internet Sex Screening Test

https://www.tarcrecovery.com/test/internet-sex

Online sexual behavior that is *fantasy-driven* usually involves cybersex, exposing genitals or watching others via webcam or video chat apps. Often these activities are motivated by a need for a quick orgasm, which can cause someone to be indiscriminate (not really caring what they see or who is on the other end). Fantasy-driven activities are about looking and sometimes interacting online, but the purpose is to maintain emotional and physical distance from real relationships and real intimacy.

For others, the online behavior is *contact-driven*, meaning you were using digital grooming with a goal to engage someone in offline contact. You might have chatted with the other person for a while, shared information, asked about them, and sent or received photos. Your ultimate goal was to hook up in person. People who groom teens and children and arrange to meet them are often called "Travelers."

The most common types of Internet offenses include the following:

Child Sexual Abuse Material (CSAM): Some people are convicted for viewing, possessing, or downloading CSAM (also called child pornography but that term sort of implies that the children were consenting to be involved. Let's call it what it is—sexual abuse of children being captured in photos or videos). Some people have also looked at child models, Anime (animated art), or read sexual stories involving CSA or incest.

---

* Some of the material in this section has been borrowed and/or modified with permission from Elizabeth Griffin and David Delmonico: Digital Deviance Presentation at the FATSA Conference 2019, and supporting materials.

There are different ways that people obtain CSAM. Some have downloaded this type of material from peer-to-peer networks. Others use other types of social media. Sometimes people say they downloaded CSAM by accident. In almost all cases, this isn't really true. You might want to ask yourself the following questions:

- If you saw it accidentally, what was your initial reaction to it?
- What did you do with it after you realized what it was?
- Did you keep it? Why?
- What search terms were you using?
- How tech-savvy are you?
- Did you erase searches? Clear cache? Use software that camouflaged what you were doing?
- Save files with new names that seemed innocent?
- Did you organize your photos, videos, or other CSAM materials so you could easily find them later?
- What was the ratio of your CSAM compared to adult porn?
- Did you repeatedly look at certain material?
- Did you hide what you were doing from others? Why?
- Did you feel like you had a secret online sexual life?

What have you learned about yourself after answering those questions? Was your crime more complicated than just an accidental download? It's really important to be honest with yourself and your therapist so you can better understand why and how your behavior happened, and how to create a safe and healthy online plan.

A final note: some people use Lolicon, Shotacon, or Manga to view sexually suggestive art that may depict youthful images of what appear to be minors. According to the U.S. federal PROTECT Act, obscene art can be treated in much the same way as child pornography under federal law if it would be illegal to depict a real child in that way, and if the depiction is also judged obscene: that it is patently offensive and that it lacks serious redeeming social value. If you look at material like this online, you should speak with your therapist about that behavior, and explore whether it fits with your healthy sexuality plan. If you are looking at such artwork for sexual stimulation to characters who appear to be minors, this might reinforce problematic sexual interests and interfere with your efforts to develop a healthier sexuality and lifestyle.

CSAM Production or Distribution involves the taking of photos or videos, and sharing them with others for trade or profit.

Do you recognize yourself in any of these categories?

Accidental	• I truly stumbled upon CSAM without trying to. (Then what did you do with it? Why did you keep it?)
Curiosity	• I Searched for… • I saw it, I was intrigued, I wanted to see more • I was testing boundaries
Indiscriminate	• I like a variety of visual sexual materials (porn) • Some of my porn interests are atypical • My hypersexual behavior leads me to experiment with new and different sexual material.
Collector	• I collect material I have a paraphilic interest in (like what?) • I had large collections of lots of digital material (for instance?) • I like to organize files and documents into categories • Sometimes I feel like I engaged in digital "hoarding"
Commercial	• I took pictures or videos, produced, shared, traded, and/or sold CSAM for money or other material goods. • I think I was drawn to doing this because…

Online Solicitation: Some people are arrested for speaking sexually with a minor through text, chat, or video, traveling to meet a minor for sexual purposes, or communicating with other adults for the purpose of finding a child for sexual activity. In some cases, the minor was a real child, and in other cases, police agents were acting in a sting operation. In sting cases, the assumption is that you believed you were communicating with a real minor.

Some offenders who have arranged meetings with children are arrested, but they claim they were not planning any sexual activity. For a small fortune lawyers will claim the same thing. Only you know what your real intent was, and it is important to be honest with yourself and with your therapist so you can better understand your behavior.

Sexting: Talking sexually to someone online can be very exciting for a lot of people. Teenagers who are just learning how exciting sex is can become obsessed with it. They want to talk about it all the time. But they may not be ready to talk to someone in person, which can be awkward, especially when they're not sure what to say or how the other will receive it. Texting about sex (sexting) seems a perfect solution, and many teens sext with each other. As long as both parties in a sext are about the same age and are both consenting, sexting can be looked at as a form of flirting or engaging in foreplay.

Problems arise when one of the parties has not consented to sexual talk (or photos or videos). Texting sexual material to someone who hasn't asked for it is imposing yourself on the other person sexually and is a form of sexual assault. Do you think it is less assaultive to *type* the words than to speak them? Why would it be? And if you are an adult and you're typing sexual words to a minor—

whether or not you think the child is "consenting" to the sexual talk—how is that different from talking dirty to a child in person?

You are an adult. How did you become engaged in sexual chats with teens or kids? Did you look online to connect with people who were underage? Did you ignore signs of their true age? Did you meet a minor through your adult role as a parent, teacher, coach, relative, clergy, babysitter, or other caretaking role?

A lot of people arrested for online offenses or sexting were convinced that minors "wanted" to talk dirty to them. Interestingly, though, almost none of these offenders had presented themselves honestly in their profiles. They had pretended to be much younger than they were. And none could give examples of the teens *starting* the dirty talk. So what does it mean if you approach a teenager pretending to be another teenager and talk dirty to him or her and you get a response? Does that mean the resulting "cybersex" is consensual? Remember no one can consent to something they don't understand and are not capable of understanding, and that's why we have laws protecting children from sex with adults. Why would cyber-sex with children be consensual if real-life sex is not? It wouldn't be. It's not. *It's a violation of that child and a sex offense.*

Cybersex and Digital Disinhibition*

John Suler, a professor at Rider University wrote the following about the psychology of cyberspace:

> *It's well known that people say and do things in cyberspace that they wouldn't ordinarily say or do in the face-to-face world. They loosen up, feel more uninhibited, and express themselves more openly. It's a double-edged sword. Sometimes people share very personal things about themselves. They reveal secret emotions, fears, wishes, or they show unusual acts of kindness and generosity. On the other hand, the disinhibition effect may not be so benign where individuals explore the dark underworld of the Internet, places of pornography and violence, places where they would never visit in the real world.*

Suler called this phenomenon the "Online Disinhibition Effect" and the elements include:

You Don't Know Me—This factor is fueled by the layer of anonymity the Internet offers users. When individuals feel anonymous, they are more inclined to engage in behaviors they would have otherwise never considered. The very nature of the Internet creates a sense of anonymity for the user.

You Can't See Me—Although related to anonymity, this factor refers to the feeling of invisibility that Internet users often experience. Individuals feel as if they are invisible and therefore believe they can neither cause nor receive consequences as a result of their online behavior. The opportunity to be physically invisible amplifies the disinhibition effect.

See You Later—The Internet provides a time delay where individuals can be more thoughtful about their communication, sometimes leading to a deeper expression of thought and feeling. Although this is not necessarily a negative effect, it is a disinhibited one nonetheless. Another dimension of the "See You Later" concept is the fact that when online interactions create discomfort, you can easily escape such situations by exiting the conversation or deleting the text, almost as if it never existed. "Click and move on."

---

* Modified with permission from Elizabeth Griffin and David Delmonico: © 2017 Internet Behavior Consulting, LLC Permission Granted for Client Use

It's All in My Head—This concept relates to the idea of projection. In the absence of sensory and non-verbal cues, individuals may assign personal attributes to the unknown virtual partner. The line between our projected fantasy and reality is blurred allowing individuals to say and do things they would not consider in the real world. At that moment, reality is one's imagination.

It's Just a Game—Individuals often see the virtual world as one in which the rules and norms of everyday offline living are not applicable. Once they turn off the computer and return to their daily routine, they believe they can leave the online game and their online game-identity behind. Internet users may feel they should not be held responsible for what happens in the make-believe, play world that in their mind has nothing to do with reality.

We're Equals—A person's status is unknown to others online and may not have the same impact as it does in the face-to-face world. Everyone, regardless of status, wealth, race, gender, age, etc., starts off on a level playing field. This lack of hierarchy on the Internet has its advantages; however, hierarchies play an important role in our society, including the division between adults and children, which can be easily downplayed in the online world.

Think about the ways that digital disinhibition might have applied to you:

Anonymity	I can do what I want online and no one will know. No one has to know the real me.
Fantasy	I can explore things I'd never do in the real world. There are no real-life consequences online.
E-personality	The "virtual Me" -- I can be whomever I want online. I can engage with others in ways I would never do in real life. I can pretend I'm different.
Escape	I can click and move on. I don't have to risk real intimacy, commitment, or rejection. I'm in charge of where I go, who I am, and when it ends when I'm online.
Familiarity	I have a million "friends" I feel like I know people and they know me in ways that aren't true in real life. The social boundaries and hierarchies are very different online.

In addition to Online Disinhibition, way back in 2001, researchers Delmonico, Griffin, and Moriarity discussed six different aspects of the Internet that they envision as parts of a hexagon (see figure 2.3). These *cyberhex* factors make the Internet more seductive than any other medium.

Figure 2.3: Cybersex Effects

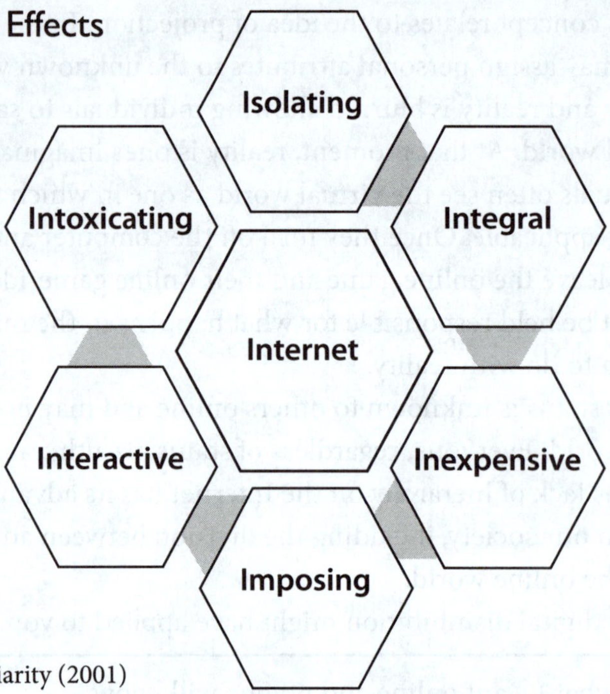

Delmonico, Griffin, and Moriarity (2001)

Isolating—Technology is isolating. Even though interpersonal relationships are abundant online, these relationships do not require the same level of social skills or honest interactions that real life behaviors require. Cyberspace becomes a world unto itself where it becomes easy to lose track of time, consequences, and real relationships. The isolation and anonymity of the Internet provide the illusion of an escape from the real world. While everyone wants short escapes (that's what vacations are for!), cyberspace can become the "drug of choice" that is just as powerful, and just as isolating, as any other drug.

Integral—The Internet has become almost essential in our lives and it is nearly impossible to avoid. Even if an individual decided to never use technology again, that boundary would be almost impossible to maintain, since the majority of people need the Internet for work, banking, job hunting, etc. Technology has become a necessary part of our daily routines.

Inexpensive—For a relatively small fee, or for no fee at all, one can access an immense amount of material (sexual and non-sexual) using the Internet. In the offline world, such information is not as easily obtainable and could be expensive. Technology allows affordable access to an infinite amount of information and material (the world at our fingertips).

Imposing—The amount of general information found through technology is staggering. This is true of sexual material as well. The Internet provides an endless supply of sexual material 7 days per week, 365 days per year. The amount of information and the imposing nature of sexual information on the Internet contribute to being drawn into the world of cybersex and problematic online sexual behavior.

Interactive—While isolating in nature, technology also "hooks" individuals into forming pseudo-relationships. These pseudo-relationships often approximate reality without running the risk of real relationships—emotional and physical vulnerability and intimacy. This close approximation to reality can be fuel for the fantasy life that can lead to problems with online sexual behavior.

Intoxicating—This is the phenomenon that occurs when you add together the first five elements of the CyberHex. This combination makes for an intoxicating brew that can be difficult for many to resist. It can become compulsive and can feel addictive. This intoxication of technology is multiplied when cybersex is involved, since behaviors are reinforced with one of the most powerful rewards—sexuality.

In Chapter 3 you will identify treatment targets to help you create a healthy online activity plan for acceptable Internet use in the future. If you are allowed to access the Internet now, or if you need to be given permission from the court or your therapist, you will need a plan for accountability outlining what you *need* to do online versus what you want to do. In the meantime, you can think about which of these areas seem to apply to you and contributed to any problematic online behavior you've engaged in:

- Emotional regulation (sexualized coping)
- Social skills, intimacy deficits, social anxiety
- Deviant or indiscriminate sexual interest
- Hypersexuality
- Sensation seeking (saturation)
- Problematic technology use in general (shopping, gambling, screen addiction)
- Poor boundaries or poor victim awareness
- Boredom/Loneliness

How Pornography and the Internet Affect Relationships

Before we move on, let's take just a moment to talk about pornography. Some sex offenders deny using pornography because they are embarrassed to admit that they masturbate. Others say, hey, what's the harm? It's legal, it's accepted, it must be okay. By now you should be starting to understand that some things that might be acceptable for other people are dangerous for you. For you to say, "It's okay, it's only pornography" might be like an alcoholic saying, "It's okay, it's only beer." It's not okay for an alcoholic to drink beer and it might not be okay for you to use pornography.

We realize it is not easy to avoid being exposed to pornography. Just as the alcoholic must deal with sitting through endless beer ads if he wants to watch a football game, you must deal with the fact that pornography sometimes seems to be everywhere nowadays. In some ways it is downright confusing. On TV girls are everywhere dancing suggestively, society is more sexualized than ever, and the Internet…well, that's just like a kid in a candy store. What, you might well ask, is going on? Why can't I be interested in the same things other people are so interested in?

The answer is simple: you're not like other people. You ended up here. Other people may be able to look at fantasy sex and not act on what they see. Yes, there is pornography that is not deviant and that portrays sex as consensual. But even this pornography objectifies the people in it. All pornography makes it appear that the models exist only for the purpose of sex, that they are not real human beings but just objects for you to fantasize over. This idea, that other people are objects that exist only for your sexual pleasure, is at the heart of sexual offending. It is exactly the idea that allowed you to convince yourself that it was okay to use your victims for your sexual pleasure. Do you think continuing to masturbate to pornography will help in your recovery? Is it going to help you understand how to relate to real people so you can have real relationships? What do you think?

But let's be honest about what we're really talking about. You know full well that the day of the Playboy centerfold with big breasts is long gone. Today's pornography is not really about sex at all. It is about defiling and degrading the people in it. It says, "Look at what people will do! They'll do anything! We can do anything we want to them and they don't care!" The excitement this pornography sells is about taking advantage of someone and stealing something from them. Today's pornography is a direct assault on the human dignity and respect, and true romantic intimacy.

Is this a positive thing? We don't think so. Do you? What do you think children and teens exposed to this material are learning about sex? About relationships? About pleasuring a partner?

Is it fair to you that this material is so easily available? Does it give you an excuse to sneak online and indulge your cravings? Well, let's see… is it fair to recovering alcoholics that drinking is everywhere? Is it fair to diabetics that candy and doughnuts are available everywhere? You could say it's not fair if you wanted to, but you'd really just be saying that life is not fair. So if something seems unfair to you that's just the reality you have to deal with. Deal with it. Don't fight it, just accept it. Using pornography can feed your deviant fantasies and increase your risk of reoffending.

Porn can become repetitive, with someone always searching the bottomless supply for visuals that are different and more exciting. Very frequent masturbation can then lead to "saturation," where more exciting material is needed for arousal, or where it takes much longer to get excited or to achieve orgasm. Excessive porn use can also lead to unrealistic expectations of one's partner, in terms of what the partner should look like or be willing to do sexually. Depictions of sex in porn videos are usually one-sided and seldom display mutual, nurturing relationships. It is important to know that what you see in heterosexual porn is rarely a good indicator of what feels physically pleasurable and arousing to a female partner.

During the COVID-19 quarantine of 2020, pornography use surged!

Figure 2.4: Porn Viewing Increased During The COVID-Quarantine in Spring of 2020

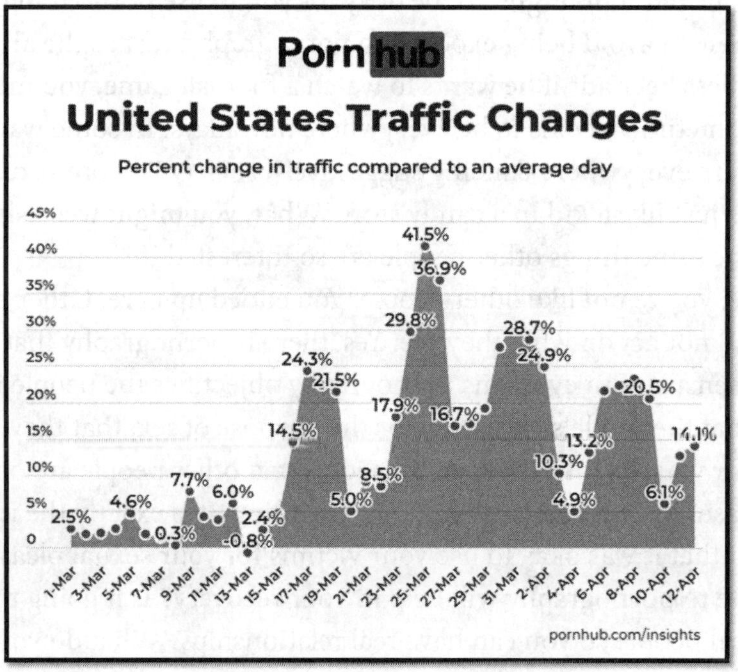

Here is a resource to learn more about Pornography:

Link 2.11 – Fight The New Drug

https://fightthenewdrug.org/
(An interesting non-religious, non-political website exploring the impacts of pornography on the brain, on relationships, and on societal norms and expectations)

Many people who are in relationships have found the Internet destructive to their relationship. Why? Because the Internet offers the opportunity for fantasy relationships and allows a person to forget about real life and *pretend*. Real life is hard. It's complicated. It involves risks. In real relationships you can have disagreements, misunderstandings, and hurt feelings. Sometimes you need to talk when you'd rather not talk.

On the Internet there's no need to worry about real people or real feelings because no one knows who you are. You can make up a new identity and be someone else. You can be young and in-shape and attractive and successful—just by saying you are! In the real world you can lie about what you do and what you're after. But you can't tell people you're six-four when you're really five-five, and you can't say you're fourteen when you're really forty-eight.

Let's look at what the Internet really offers in the way of relationships. Let's assume, for the moment, that you don't have any deviant intentions in going online; that you're going to play it straight and just check out the scene. The first thing you'll notice is lots and lots of people. You can choose anyone you want to "chat" with. And if they don't immediately respond the way you'd like, click, they're gone, and you're on to the next person. What that means is that it's a perfect setup for *contacting* people but not really *connecting* with them. Isn't that what unhealthy relationships are about? Looking for people who aren't really people but objects for fantasies?

Here's what one compulsive Internet user said: "People were void of emotions. I became desensitized. There were so many people online that it didn't matter what you said to someone, there were plenty of other people to communicate with."

But there's much more to it than that. One expert wrote: "What the Internet offers is the instant gratification of a fantasy without the vulnerability and personal exposure of a real relationship. You don't have to grow up to have sex on the Internet." We have been talking about throughout this book about instant gratification, fantasies, and the avoidance of taking the risks involved in real relationships. Isn't refusing to grow up and deal with real relationships what kept you stuck in your old lifestyle? How will you maintain a new, healthy lifestyle?

Researchers have found that as people spend more time online, they decrease the amount of time they spend with the important people in their real lives. That makes sense, doesn't it? And the studies show that increased Internet use leads to *increased loneliness and depression*. Listen to this person who offended talking about his computer—a machine: "*My computer was my soulmate. I did not have to love it back or nourish it. It never let me down. It never stopped being there for me.*" Notice how online sexual behavior can impact relationships: "*I turned to the Internet for sexual pleasures because of the great sensation I got from it. I could have 'sex' with other men while my wife was sleeping. The computer brings sex to you. You don't have to leave your house to engage in the most bizarre sex ever.*" Or how this guy described the impact of online porn on his marriage: "*I had a wife who cared for me. She did not deserve the disrespect I so often showed her by going online instead of spending time with her.*"

For some sexually compulsive men, the Internet literally takes over their lives. And how could any relationship survive when one of the partners is spending lots of time looking for someone else to have fantasy sex with? Many couples have lost their relationships as a direct result of the Internet. It is likely that some of those relationships were not strong in the first place. But when one partner gets it into his head that he can "cheat" with others anytime he wants–or all the time, in some cases–there is little hope for *any* relationship. For some people the question becomes this: will you stick with a real relationship that is not perfect but at least involves *real* people and *real* caring? Or will you sacrifice that relationship in the hope of fulfilling a fantasy, looking for "perfect" sex with a "perfect" partner—or a perfect victim?

Some people who are not in relationships believe the Internet will help them find a partner. After all, isn't social media filled with lonely people looking to meet someone? It is possible you could meet someone online. But knowing how difficult it has been for you to find and maintain a healthy relationship in the past, and knowing how easy it is to distort and manipulate online, is it realistic to think you will find an honest, full relationship on social media? In reality, being online takes time and energy away from working on real intimacy and reinforces the problems that interfere with intimacy. Looking for sex online can lead down a rabbit hole to deviant behavior.

Here's what another guy describes: *After my wife and I separated I found that I had a lot more free time and I started to use the computer more and more. Being separated from my wife kind of put me in a shell and I felt safer in the cyber world. I started using chat apps. The one I visited most frequently was 'Black women who love white men.' Most of my chatting was casual talk but as I started feeling more comfortable, I engaged in cybersex and sexting. I checked out a room called 'Older men for younger women.' One girl entered the room and was asked to leave because she was under eighteen. I checked her screen name and later noticed she was in another room called 'Daddy/daughter sex.' I am not sure why that intrigued me, but I started spending a lot of time in that room, engaging in cybersex and phone sex.*

Hypersexuality

Maybe the easiest way to describe "hypersexuality" is just to say "obsessed with sex." Hypersexuality is characterized by an excessive sexual appetite, sexual preoccupation, and repetitive, impulsive sexual behaviors despite the risks of negative consequences. Sexual behavior that is out of control can persist indefinitely (even when it's not that pleasurable!) and escalate. What is excessive? It's hard to define a normal amount of sex or masturbation, but if you are doing it more than you think you should, or than other people seem to, that's important to think about.

Hypersexuality leads people to spend enormous amounts of time engaged in sexual activity, planning sexual activity, or trying to arrange opportunities for sex. It can create a cycle of distorted beliefs, impaired thinking, and seemingly uncontrollable behavior, followed by guilt, despair, and remorse. Some people are so obsessed with sex that it leads them to risk their freedom, relationships, health, finances, and safety. Sexual preoccupation interferes with their ability to live within their value system. There is some research to suggest that sex releases endorphins in the brain, which leads to a type of "high." This chemical reaction may increase the addictive power of sex for some people. Medications have been found to help in some cases.

The causes of hypersexuality or "sex addiction" are different for everyone, but there can be a link to a person's general mood state. Sometimes, a person with bipolar disorder will have manic episodes that involve reckless, excessive, impulsive sexual behaviors. For other people it just feels like an obsession, something they feel they can't stop thinking about or doing. Or sex can simply be a way of seeking relief from painful moods, like depression or anxiety. For some people, hypersexuality is a way of avoiding the emotional vulnerability of true intimacy: if they do it with everyone, they don't risk being close to anyone.

Compulsive masturbation is one of the most common hypersexual behaviors (others include promiscuity, infidelity, pornography addiction, or cybersex). In the past 25 years, the increasing availability, volume and variety of pornography online has contributed to problems of hypersexuality. This means that a whole generation of youngsters were (and continue to be) exposed very early and frequently to porn, often without any meaningful guidance from adults to offer other perspectives or information.

Some people struggling with hypersexuality spend large amounts of time (and money) on pornography, Internet sex sites, chat apps, sexting, prostitutes, strip clubs, adult bookstores, bars and clubs, sexual fantasies, and masturbation. One client described:

> *Strip clubs are the main place for me to avoid. I used to go a lot because I felt noticed and important when a girl came and flirted with me or wanted to give me a lap dance. I felt like she liked me and that I was attractive. Now I see that I wanted instant gratification of having an attractive member of the opposite sex sit and talk to me, but she was only pretending to be into me, so that only furthers my depression once I leave. Clubs are not good for me because I do not need to be consuming alcohol with all that temptation. Also, I spent too much money there that I do not need to be spending! But mostly I want someone to like me and be attracted to me for real, not because I'm paying them to act that way.*

Not all hypersexual behavior is illegal; many of these behaviors, no matter how excessive or disruptive, are within the bounds of the law and social acceptability. But be honest with yourself as you think about what parts of your sex life have been out of control and what parts are healthy.

Do you feel like you have always had control of your sexual behavior? Or have there been periods of sexual acting out? If so, how or when was it out of control? Ask yourself:

- "Am I able to stop myself when I know I should?"
- "Is my behavior rational (reasonable and sensible) or irrational (unreasonable and foolhardy)?"
- "Is my behavior interfering with my life?"
- "Am I living outside my values?"

If you are not sure if hypersexuality applies to you, use this checklist to see:

Hypersexuality questionnaire	While Offending	Now
I spend a great deal of time each day thinking about sex or fantasizing about sex or planning sex or engaging in sex. (How much?)		
I spend much time, energy and/or expense to gain access to sexual activities or materials. (For example…)		
I feel empty or angry if a day passes without sex. (How often?)		
Sometimes thinking about sex interferes with my concentration on other things. (How often?)		
Sometimes I neglect work or other responsibilities because I am too busy with something sexual. (How often?)		
I sometimes masturbate more than once a day. (How often?)		
I sometimes masturbate to the point where it loses its pleasure or even becomes painful. (How often?)		
Sometimes I would rather masturbate than be with a partner. (How often?)		
In relationships I am so focused on sex that my partner complains. (How many times?)		
I am always on the lookout for new sexual things to try. (For example…)		
I spend money that I can't really afford on sex. (How much?)		
I tell myself "I'm going to stop doing this," only to find myself doing it again. (How many times has this happened?)		
I continue to engage in sex acts despite negative consequences in my life, such as: tension (or breakup) in a relationship, arrest, debt, job loss, health or safety risk, etc. (For example…)		
I lie about my sexual behavior to others. (Who?)		
I find it hard to be faithful to my partner when I'm in a relationship.		
I seek out lots of partners but often feel empty and lonely.		
My sexual behavior has affected or hurt someone else in some way. (Who?)		

Another online resource for assessing your own hypersexuality can be found at:

Link 2.13 – Trauma and Addiction Recovery
https://www.tarcrecovery.com/

Sexualized Coping

Sexualized coping can be a way of soothing distress and/or meeting needs for attention, power, or control. It is sometimes used to compensate for feelings of loneliness or powerlessness. Some people talk about using sex or masturbation to relieve stress or boredom, or to relax and fall asleep. For some people, it's the only thing they feel like they have to look forward to. For others, anytime they have negative feelings, they tend to turn to sex to feel better.

Most people have probably used sex at one time or another to try to soothe or relax themselves. When sex is used regularly for these purposes, however, it can become the "solution" for all of one's negative feeling. It can then become like a drug. And like any drug, it can be abused. Abusing sex means removing it from its natural function of expressing affection and intimacy. Instead of fostering connection between people, it can become a "band-aid" for all of life's upsets. As it is increasingly overused it can turn into hypersexuality.

Sexualized coping also means that you might not be practicing other methods for soothing yourself, coping with uncomfortable feelings, dealing with boredom, or dealing with your underlying issues. When you practice using an expanded range of coping skills, you will get better at all of them and won't have to rely so much on sexualized coping. In chapter 3 you will learn about many coping strategies – you might be surprised that there are so many to choose from!

Addictions and Compulsions

Anytime we speak of behavior that is out of control the words *addictive* and *compulsive* come up. These words mean roughly the same thing, but usually we use the word "addiction" to refer to using substances, like alcohol or drugs, and "compulsion" to refer to behaviors, like gambling or sexual activities. Compulsions and addictions are similar because the person caught in them is only interested in the *right now* ("immediate gratification"). He wants to feel good right now so much so that not much thought is given to the consequences of his behavior. You might be saying to yourself about your offense: "I was just stupid then. I'm smarter now." That sounds like an explanation and a solution, but is it really? Were you really just "stupid?" When smart people do stupid things, something powerful is at work…

Compulsions and addictions sometimes come out of a need to alter one's mood state–to make us feel different from how we are feeling; to make us *feel better right now*. Compulsive behaviors are often the result of trying to escape from the emptiness of depression or reduce feelings of anxiety.

Lots of things can make us feel better: alcohol, drugs, food, cigarettes, gambling, and sex are obvious ones. Working, exercising, praying, being around other people, competing, and shopping are less obvious ones. *Anything that can make us feel better has the potential to become repetitive and problematic.* Whenever we start to use something outside of ourselves to escape from something inside that feels bad, we are setting ourselves up to become addicted to that substance or activity.

Aaron has been lonely all his life finally finds a woman to marry. He feels like the happiest guy in the world because he had believed no woman could love him and his need to feel loved is strong. Later he learns that his wife is having an affair and is planning to leave him. He finds that all his old fears and self-doubts are suddenly stronger than ever: his wife's betrayal proves that he is unlovable. His pain feels overwhelming. But instead of dealing with it—going for professional help or finding someone else he can open up to and talk with about his pain—he throws himself into his work, because that's the one thing that makes him feel good about himself. Soon he finds that whenever he's not at work, he feels bad. He has not done anything either to heal the pain inside him or to meet his need for love and companionship. All he's done is escape from his feelings through his work. Eventually he finds himself working eighty hours a week and looking for more work to do on weekends. He is no longer free not to work: Work has become a compulsive activity for him. He is a "workaholic."

Why does sex become compulsive? For a lot of reasons. It's exciting. It feels good. Just thinking about it—fantasizing—feels good. Sex can be an immediate relief from stress. Masturbation can become compulsive as well because it's comforting. Sex also meets many emotional needs. It makes people feel powerful, desired, and special. It makes people think they can be close to others. Sex makes you feel you're getting the attention and affection you need but can't get otherwise.

After you have completed your sexual autobiography you will know what needs you have tried to meet through sex. The bottom line is that we use sex to try to make ourselves feel good in a number of ways. And anything that feels good can become something we can't do without if we are using it to avoid or escape from painful feelings. Understanding why sex is such a powerful compulsion is not so hard. *It feels great, and it temporarily makes you feel better.*

Addictions and compulsions are often *progressive* in nature. That means they become stronger over time, leading to more frequent and more serious out-of-control behaviors. A compulsion may begin with a relatively harmless behavior, such as social drinking or occasional masturbation. But when a person begins using the behavior to rid themselves of negative feelings--especially when they have only that one thing to make them feel good--they turn more and more to that behavior. Excessive behaviors can also create changes in the brain that further reinforce the repetitive loop of addictive behavior.

As the behavior becomes more frequent and begins to interfere with the person's life, it becomes a compulsion, meaning the person feels like they can't NOT do it. This progression can be slow and gradual or rapid and intense. At first the behavior is highly pleasurable, but as it becomes more and more frequent the enjoyment lessens because anything done too often loses some of its pleasure. The person is "wearing out" the behavior. If they have to continue to somehow escape from the pain inside and they have no other way to do it, they may find themselves *escalating* the behavior—trying more extreme behaviors, more frequently and more seriously, and feeling unable to stop.

When we asked people in treatment who were arrested for online offenses to write about their experiences, most mentioned the addictive nature of the Internet.

> *A whole new, perverse world opened up to me as I sat in my office. It became a drug that I could indulge without having to worry about being seen or breaking any laws. It was intoxicating trying to see how far I could go and what I could get to. I was hooked by being in a world I had never seen. It brought something exciting into my life of boredom and failure. It really became the focal point of my day. The high I felt must be like a drug because I could feel my skin tingle every time I went online.*
>
> *Getting and staying online became an obsession. It was just as addictive as any other vice out there–drugs, alcohol, gambling. I found myself constantly getting online and staying online for hours. It was a cycle, like any other addiction, that was hard to break.*

One offender talked about the likelihood of breaking his Internet addiction without help:

Until my computer was confiscated my fantasy world of deviant sex dominated my life. The addiction is so great that at times I was up all night and almost late for work. Believe me, it would have continued had I not been stopped. Internet addiction has no "patch," no twelve-step program to help you stop. It takes therapy and the lack of Internet access to break out of the addiction.

Treatment is about learning to control your behavior.

It is very difficult to curb one's appetite for a favorite food or activity. It has been so with my addiction to the Internet. The techniques I've learned in treatment, as well as lessons learned during the three most devastating years of my life, have helped me return to life as a normal person. My interest in child porn has lessened, but I still fight to abstain from all types of porn.

The dangerous and insidious thing about going online is that every barrier has been removed. For someone who already has an established obsession with deviant sex the breaking down of all barriers is that much swifter and easier. An individual no longer has to leave his home to receive and look at porn. A simple click of a button is all it takes. Unfortunately, that is also how quick and simple it is to spiral into disaster by sending or receiving child porn or trying to set up a sexual liaison with someone that is underage.

Cravings, Urges, and the "PIG" (Problem of Immediate Gratification)

Anyone who has ever had a problem with a compulsive behavior knows all about cravings and urges. Cravings and urges are what you *feel* when you have a compulsion or addiction. Technically, a *craving* is a *desire* for the pleasure you get from your compulsion. It is a state of arousal. Cravings can start either from a bad feeling that you want to escape, like anger or depression, or they can come from something that reminds you of pleasure you have gotten in the past. An *urge* is an *intention* to do a specific thing—a behavior—that will satisfy the craving.

Taken together, the experience of a strong craving and the urge to relieve the craving through a behavior like offending are known as the **PIG**—the **P**roblem of **I**mmediate **G**ratification. The PIG can drive you to find a way to satisfy your desire without giving any thought to the consequences. In the presence of the PIG, you don't want to stop yourself from offending because *it feels like the only important thing is to satisfy your desire*. If you let it, the PIG will take over your common sense and you will start lying to yourself about how it will be "just this once," or "I deserve it," or "I'm not really hurting anyone." (We call these thoughts "*distorted thinking*" and we will be talking about distorted thinking more in Chapters 6 & 7.) Then, if you do act on your urge, the negative feelings you experience after offending (shame, disgust, hopelessness) can trigger *more* cravings, beginning a new cycle of cravings, urges, distorted thoughts, and offending. *Once fed, the PIG becomes hungry for more*!

One of the most important things you will learn in this program is how to recognize and avoid the PIG *before* it grabs you and leads you to disaster. It is also important to accept that cravings for sexual activity (including inappropriate or deviant activity) will continue to be part of your life, although they will become less frequent and less intense over time.

Let's look at a simple, everyday example of the PIG in action. Let's say you're on a diet, and you've been very good. But because you've been very good you have a bad feeling: hunger. That bad feeling *triggers a craving* for something sweet. If you allow yourself to think about your craving, before long you have an image of ice cream in your mind (we also call this image a fantasy). Then, if you allow yourself to think about ice cream, in no time at all you have an urge to satisfy your craving–an intention to eat ice cream. You are in the grip of the PIG. You want ice cream and you intend to get it.

"But wait," a little voice says, "what about the diet?" "Oh, I'll just have a few bites," another voice says, "I've been so good a few bites won't hurt. I deserve a reward." Which voice wins? Well, if the first voice had spoken up sooner it might have had a chance. But by now you've already let your mind dwell on your craving, and worse, your fantasy. *By letting yourself enjoy these thoughts, to a large extent you have already made your decision.* And because you've already made your decision, the second voice doesn't even have to be logical or realistic to win the debate. Even distorted, completely unrealistic thoughts will seem perfectly reasonable.

So you move on to *planning* how to get the ice cream. Now, if you had to get in your car and go and buy some, that might weaken the hold the PIG has on you by distracting you, giving your reasonable voice a chance to speak up again. But it just so happens that earlier, when you were shopping, you picked up your favorite flavor of ice cream–not for yourself, mind you, but just in case someone else came by who might want some of your favorite flavor. Thanks to this *seemingly irrelevant decision*, you're fully prepared to just open your freezer and dig in. Will you? Well, let's see…you've got this hunger that feels awful, you know exactly what it will take to make you feel better, you've pictured the ice cream so you can almost taste it. You've given yourself permission to have just a few bites, and, best of all, the ice cream happens to be right there in front of you. You haven't given yourself much of a chance to say no, have you? In fact, you've set yourself up to fail by creating what's called a *high-risk situation*. So you give in.

Now what? It tastes so good at first, doesn't it? But it isn't long before you begin to feel bad because you've let yourself down. You were having such a good day, you suddenly remember. You tell yourself you have no willpower and will always be fat. Now you feel terrible. Worse, you feel hopeless. So what difference does it make what you do? You might as well enjoy yourself and eat even more. (This type of distorted thinking is so common it even has a name: it's called the "abstinence violation effect.") So you open the bag of Oreo® cookies you also happened to buy (for guests).

Blowing your diet isn't usually a serious problem. But acting on deviant sexual urges is. Most of what you will be learning in this program is about controlling the PIG, which means staying in control of your behaviors. Later, in the chapter on Relapse Prevention, we'll be talking more about the various steps along the road from having a craving to losing control—the *triggers*, the *seemingly irrelevant decisions*, the *distorted thoughts* and the *high risk situations*.

With the PIG around it is very difficult to distance yourself from a high-risk situation and cope with it. In fact, it's hard to think clearly at all. The problem of immediate gratification means that you feel like you *need* what you want *now*, and that you cannot delay the pleasure or do without it.

The reason the PIG stays with us all is that one of the things your brain does best is to remember the things that have brought you intense excitement or pleasure. So don't be surprised when a memory flashes back to you of offending, or a person you meet grabs your attention and you find yourself attracted. Remember, attractions can happen without your wanting them. Attractions happen to everyone and are just a part of life. It is what you do when you feel an attraction that is important. Like everyone else, you are always responsible for your behaviors.

Right now, we're going to look at one piece of the offense "chain" that is so important it can't wait until later. Remember we said that once you had let yourself imagine the taste of the ice cream you had pretty much made your decision? We call that "fantasizing." For many people in treatment, fantasizing is the most dangerous thing you can do. The sooner you understand the power of your fantasies, the sooner you can start making important changes in your life.

Fantasies

A fantasy is a scene that we imagine and play out in our mind. A fantasy can be based on a memory or we can make it up. Everyone fantasizes and fantasies can serve positive functions. They can be inspiring and exciting and fun. But fantasies can also be dangerous. When we repeatedly indulge in distorted fantasies that are exciting and pleasurable, we can convince ourselves they are true even though our experience tells us otherwise. When we believe in fantasies just because they make us feel good, we risk losing touch with reality. Fantasies are only healthy when they lead us in positive directions and when we don't let them blind us to reality. Unrealistic, unhealthy fantasies keep people stuck in destructive behavior patterns.

Compulsions and addictions are often fueled by particular fantasies. Often the fantasies of the compulsive person are based on memories of the best experiences they ever had with their compulsive behavior—the highest highs or the most exciting offenses. Or the compulsive person makes up the fantasy, imagining what the ultimate high or the most exciting sex offense would be. Either way, the fantasized behavior is *always perfect*. In real life, only once in a while—if ever—is the behavior as exciting as it always is in the fantasy. Once in a while a cigarette is really "satisfying." Once in a while a gambler gets hot and the adrenaline flows and the excitement is supreme. Once in a while a sex offense happens just the way he imagined it. But most of the time the compulsive person's real-world experiences are not anything like what they had imagined. Like a drug addict chasing that first high, they continue with their compulsive behaviors because their fantasy is always perfect and always exciting. And their fantasy tells them, "Next time, it's going to be perfect."

In their heart, compulsive people know that what they are doing is not paying off. But they don't want to think about that because reality seems depressing to them. They don't see a way to satisfy their needs in the real world. In their fantasy world they can have the perfect high; the ultimate orgasm. Sadly, the more the compulsive person sinks into endless repetition of their compulsive behavior, looking for that perfect high, the less frequent are the payoffs. Only when they are willing to compare their reality with their fantasy do they recognize how they have fooled themselves. Usually this only happens in treatment.

Deviant Fantasies

Deviant sexual fantasies are especially destructive because they are more distorted than other fantasies. In the molester's fantasy the child feels loved, wants to be touched, knows what she is doing and understands that what you are doing is because of how much you "love" her. In order to keep it going you have to completely blot out reality, so you don't let yourself think about what the child is really feeling: fear, confusion, revulsion, shame, disgust, and self-blame.

When you linger on your fantasy and let it play in your mind, it's almost as good as the real thing, isn't it? And when you masturbate to a "perfect" fantasy your orgasm might be as powerful as if you really committed the offense. In fact, sometimes a fantasy offense can be even better than a real encounter with a real person.

Many men swear they don't fantasize about deviant sex. Some of these men are simply trying to deny their problem, but others really aren't aware of their fantasies. Some of you know that you would not be here if you didn't have that fantasy. Fantasies often reveal what you hoped to get out of offending, what emotional needs you were trying to meet. Other men believe that fantasizing is okay because they "aren't hurting anyone." In fact, you might believe that fantasizing and masturbating to abusive acts is better than acting out and abusing a real person. This is somewhat true, but the problem is that each time you reinforce the deviant fantasy with an orgasm, you keep it going and even strengthen it.

Prior to getting online I would say I most definitely had a pornography problem. I had been viewing, renting and purchasing all sorts of different pornographic subjects for a long time. When I first started to go online I thought it was absolutely the greatest thing, the novelty and the technology and all. Of course, having a weakness for porn, there was a rapid progression to having sexual conversations in the chat rooms and ultimately receiving pornographic pictures including child porn images.

Think about this. If you go someplace where you've heard there's deviant stuff, and sure enough when you arrive there's deviant stuff, what are the chances you're going to resist it?

Curiosity was my fuel. I had already had my fill of regular porn and the young girls' freshness and innocence intrigued me. I knew very well that it was morally wrong as well as against the law. But I developed a knack for shutting out thoughts that held me back (kind of like turning a deaf ear to the little angel on my shoulder). This ability to ignore my conscience turned out to be what brought me down.

I knew it was wrong but I didn't think it was illegal just to look at it. I didn't think that looking at it was the same as possessing it. After all, how would anyone know? I was in my own home.

When they're trying to defend themselves in court, some people claim that porn they didn't want was sent to them without their knowledge or consent. But by now everyone knows that if you go into certain chat apps or online groups, you're going to be sent a certain kind of porn. One person who raped a woman was upfront about who was responsible for the violent and sadistic porn he collected: "*Once or twice I was surprised by something I was sent, but pretty soon I knew exactly which social media groups would produce what I was after.*"

And it's not just the porn that's deviant, is it? The chats are pretty exciting too: "*Yes, I enjoyed the pictures. Momentary perks to masturbate to. But at my age verbal stimulation, fantasy 'action,' is what addicted me to the Internet. I could go online and talk to anybody about anything, without being embarrassed, because they didn't know who I was.*"

An older offender reported that he used to expose himself but hadn't done it for several years. He said he hadn't even been thinking deviant thoughts before he discovered the Internet. The net helped him reawaken his deviant desires. "*In my case, when 'old' age made the thrill of exposing myself less gratifying, the computer ended up filling the void. I could angle the camera… I could do more in a fantasy than I could in my car. Soon my deviant fantasies were back big time. I didn't have to worry about whether or not others saw me as attractive, either, because they couldn't see me at all.*"

The point here is simple. Thinking about things that turn you on, being around things that turn you on, having pictures of things that turn you on, reminding yourself of things that turn you on—is likely to lead to your wanting to *do* the things that turn you on. *Is there anything surprising about that*? If what turns you on is sexually deviant, and you choose to go to the fantasyland of deviant sex, the risk is obvious. Next to admitting your offenses and your problem, the most important thing you will do in treatment is to stop fantasizing about unlawful or abusive sex. However hard it is for you to accept, reinforcing them can put you at risk for reoffending. We will be returning later to the subject of fantasies to be sure you understand what they mean and how you can stop them.

This can be a dilemma. If you are exclusively minor-attracted, talk with your therapist about how to experience your sexuality without breaking the law or harming anyone.

Assessing the Strength of Your Sexual Interests

One factor that differs from offender to offender is the strength of different attractions. If you are attracted to children, for example, you should ask how strong this attraction is compared to your attraction to adults. Where do you fall on this continuum?

Exclusively attracted to minors — Exlusively attracted to adults

Exclusively attracted to females — Exlusively attracted to males

When you answer the next questions, you can roughly place yourself on the continuum below. If you are about equally attracted to adults and minors, you will fall in the middle of the line. If your attraction to adults is stronger than your attraction to minors, you will fall on the right side of the line. You might be most attracted to young adults (barely legal); if so, note that. Some men say they are sexually attracted to "anything that moves." Think about your attractions to males and females (some people are attracted, for instance, to female adults and male minors).

A little — A lot

- How often do I fantasize about children or teens?
- How often do I notice their attractiveness?
- How much time and effort do I spend placing myself near them?
- How much do I sexually fantasize about adults?
- How often do I notice their attractiveness?
- How much effort do I put into being in relationships with adults?
- How often have I had sex with adults?
- Has it been arousing?
- Have I fantasized about a minor when I was with an adult to make it more arousing?

What If I Was Arrested for a Sex Crime with an Adult?

You can test the strength of your attractions by asking the same questions as above, only substituting "consenting partners" for "adults" and "non-consenting partners" for "children."

- How much time do I spend fantasizing about forcible sex compared to consenting sex?
- How often have I had consenting sex?
- Has it been arousing?
- While having consensual sex, I sometimes fantasize that it was non-consensual to make it more arousing?
- When I use pornography do I look for violent, degrading materials or materials about consenting sex?

What If I've Never Physically Touched a Victim?

If your offenses have been primarily exhibitionistic, voyeuristic or online-related, you will ask yourself how much time you spend fantasizing and pursuing deviant activities versus pursuing normal, healthy, sexual relations.

- Have I had healthy sexual relations with appropriate adult partners?
- Has healthy sex been as arousing as flashing, peeping, or masturbating to pornography?
- Have I sometimes passed up opportunities for sex with an appropriate partner to pursue deviant sex?

We know how hard it is for you to be honest with yourself about these questions. But remember what we said at the beginning: a healthy lifestyle begins with accepting yourself fully. You need to be honest about who you are to begin with if you are going to take control of your life.

Don't ignore other deviant attractions you have just because you haven't been arrested for them. The time for hiding stuff and pretending is over. The exercises and tools described in Chapter 3 will help you understand self-regulation and manage your behavior.

Understanding Sexual Functioning

We all talk about sex, read about it, and think about it because it is an essential part of what it means to be human. You may have thought it to be odd that in this book we have talked so little about sex. Well this book is not about sex itself but about how sex gets used in destructive ways. If you have always felt a little confused about sex (as lots of people do) but haven't known where to look to learn more about it, there are many good books and websites on the topic. It is important to learn how to create a healthy sexual relationship in your life, and to feel confident that you know how to please a partner sexually as well as get your own needs met. A helpful website to learn more about sexuality, sexual functioning, and sexual health can be found at:

Link 2.14 – ASHA (American Sexual Health Association)
https://www.ashasexualhealth.org/

Exercise 2.3: Sexual Autobiography Timeline

Now, you can begin to work on your sexual autobiography to understand the development of your sexual behavior problems. It's helpful to start with a timeline and identify significant events or experiences in your life history from early childhood until now that might have influenced your sexual development. Do a thorough job on this exercise and it will help you later with many of the other exercises. You will do part 2 of your sexual autobiography at the end of chapter 4.

Remembering all of your sexual experiences is important because they shaped your expectations and ideas about sex in the future.

1. Describe your early sexual memories and experiences.
   How did you learn about sex? Did you overhear someone talking about sex or having sex? Did you walk in on someone? Did a friend tell you about it? Include any education about sex. What were the myths you heard as a kid? How were your beliefs about sex influenced by family, friends, teachers, church, community, social media, TV, movies, gaming, Internet, etc.
2. Describe any sexual experiences you had as a child.
   Include any experiences with other children, adults, siblings, other relatives; describe your age at the time, the other participants' age and relation to you, and the type of activity. Include sexual experiences that didn't involve actual physical contact, like exposure to nudity or pornography, etc.
3. Masturbation.
   Describe your masturbation habits during your childhood and teenage years and your recent past. How did you learn about or discover masturbation? Describe what you are feeling before you decide to masturbate and describe the fantasy that is coming to you. What were you taught about masturbation as a youngster?
4. Describe any and all sexual contact you've had at any time throughout your life. Start with your first memory of sexual contact and work through your life chronologically.
   Include child-to-child contact, adult to child contact, and adult-to-adult contact.
5. Pornography.
   Reading materials, with or without pictures, magazines, videos, websites, apps, chat forums, P2P networks, dark web, and adult TV channels. Was porn exciting to you? What types? What did you hope to find? What are you drawn to? Why? How often? For how long? For what purpose?
6. Dating/Courtship/Marriage.
   Begin with your initial experiences. Begin with your first crush, whether you pursued him/her or not. When did you first have physical contact of any kind, including kissing, touching, and intercourse? How did your experiences compare with your friends? Did you talk to your friends about your experiences? Did you compete with them? Examine how you chose your partners and your patterns of partners. How often did you have sex just because you could? How were those experiences? Describe experiences that were memorable or significant, either for being positive or negative. Comment on any cheating on your part or by a trusted partner. Did you usually want to be faithful or did you want to cheat? If there were issues with your sexual functioning or satisfaction, talk about them. Describe the significant romantic relationships you've had. How old were you the first time you fell in love? Discuss how these relationships worked out. Describe your level of

satisfaction in them, including your sexual satisfaction. How did you talk to your partners about sex? About what you each wanted or liked? Describe the times you were hurt or when your heart was broken.

7. Outlets.

   Outlets are sexually related behaviors people use INSTEAD of intimacy and sexual closeness with an appropriate partner. Describe any experiences you have had using the following outlets:

   - STRIP CLUBS
   - PROSTITUTION
   - PORNOGRAPHY
   - RAPE OR SEXUAL ABUSE
   - FETISHISM (USE OF AN OBJECT FOR PLEASURE)
   - EXHIBITIONISM (EXPOSING GENITALS)
   - VOYEURISM (PEEPING)
   - FROTTAGE (TOUCHING A STRANGER IN A SEXUAL MANNER)
   - SEXTING, VIRTUAL SEX, VIDEO CHAT, ONLINE SEXUAL BEHAVIOR
   - BESTIALITY (SEX WITH ANIMALS)
   - MASSAGE PARLORS
   - ANONYMOUS OR PROMISCUOUS SEX

For each outlet, discuss when it began, how the outlet developed, how often you used it, and your thoughts about using the outlet. How did it feel? Were you trying to achieve something? Power, control, intimacy, importance, attention, or some other result? Think about how it felt and talk about it. You will come back to this exercise at the end of Chapter 4 (Sexual Autobiography, Part 2).

CHAPTER 3
MANAGING YOUR BEHAVIOR

Self-regulation is the ability to monitor your thoughts, feelings, and behaviors, and to make decisions that further your goals. Self-regulation involves controlling your temper, being able to calm yourself down, conforming to social norms, and being aware of the perceptions of others. Everyone is different, and our unique biological make-up, along with our life experiences and role models, affect how we control our thoughts, feelings, and behaviors. Not surprisingly, stressors in daily life can produce feelings that seem hard to deal with, and this chapter will help you take effective action when such feelings and thoughts arise in all areas of daily life.

Self-regulation means that you have the ability to:

1. Control your impulses and stop doing something, if needed
2. Do something (even if you don't want to) because it is needed.
3. Calm yourself down when you feel agitated or upset.

We learn how to behave and think by watching others around us, including, primarily, those we live with when we're young (our families!). But everyone has natural abilities or challenges (for example, intelligence, ADHD, behavioral health disorders, or learning differences) that can strengthen or weaken our ability to respond to situations and make decisions in the best ways. Drugs and alcohol can also impair our decision-making ability

General, Sexual, and Emotional Regulation

In this chapter, we will explore general, sexual, and emotional self-regulation. Here are some examples of self-regulation challenges in different areas. Think about which ones seem to apply to you, and discuss them with your therapist and your group (ask for more information about any you don't understand):

General	Sexual	Emotional
✓ Impulsivity ✓ Poor decision-making ✓ Poor judgment ✓ Difficulty delaying gratification ✓ Inability to create structure, routine and planning in your life ✓ Entitlement ✓ Poor coping strategies ✓ Financial budgeting	✓ Preoccupation with sex ✓ Excessive sexual appetite ✓ Sexual compulsions ✓ Sexualized coping ✓ Deviant or atypical sexual interests ✓ Poor sexual boundaries ✓ Being promiscuous ✓ Being unfaithful to partners ✓ Consumer sex (paying for sex services)	✓ Chip on your shoulder ✓ Over-react to things ✓ Quick to anger ✓ Trouble tolerating distress, frustration, or disappointment ✓ Intense emotions ✓ Difficulty relaxing ✓ Mood instability ✓ Self-medication with drugs or alcohol ✓ Can't calm down ✓ Feeling hyper-alert or anxious a lot ✓ Negative thoughts or excessive worries

General Self-Regulation

How many times have you thought to yourself: "What was I thinking?!" "Why didn't I see that coming?" "When will I ever learn my lesson?" "How many times does that have to happen before I change my ways?" "I just have no common sense." Do you sometimes seem to keep engaging in the same behaviors despite negative consequences and sometimes without any seemingly rational reason? Have others (parents, friends, partners, probation officers, therapists) sometimes viewed your behavior as willful rebellion, disobedience, or rejection of values everyone else agrees on? The truth is that self-regulation requires a complex set of skills that come naturally to some people but are more difficult for others.

Self-regulation involves external controls and internal controls. *External controls* are rules, rewards, and punishments that are imposed by others or society to help us know what's expected of us. *Internal controls* are the methods we use for controlling ourselves and managing our behavior within the rules of society and our own value system.

Some children did not get a lot of instruction or see good examples of how to be organized, set goals, structure their time, or plan ahead. Without a chance to learn those skills and practice them early on, their adult lives may take on the chaos that is familiar from their childhood. They may not have had adult caretakers who created external controls to curb the urge to act impulsively--that is, without thinking. You might not have learned a process for decision-making. Good decision-making involves exploring alternatives and weighing the pros and cons of possible outcomes in order to make a well-reasoned choice.

Sometimes children raised in deprived environments don't learn to delay gratification. They learn to take what they can get when it's available. Sometimes their very survival depends on taking advantage of opportunities as they present themselves. Although this attitude may make perfect sense in their home, later, out in the world, it can lead to an attitude of *entitlement*: "I deserve whatever I want and I'm tired of the unfairness of not having what I want."

The truth is that life-management skills that seem very simple and obvious to some people but can be like a foreign language to others. You don't know what you don't know. Navigating the adult world can be pretty tricky, and lack of self-regulation skills can interfere with your overall success. Some sex offenses occur in part because people have not learned to resist the urge for immediate gratification, respect the boundaries of others, or read cues about what's acceptable or appropriate. It is always a good idea to associate yourself with others who display good general self-management on a consistent basis in various areas of life. This helps you observe and conform.

Sexual Self-Regulation

Some people end up in programs like this one because they have unusual sexual interests that lead them to seek sexual contact in ways that are unlawful. Some sexual attractions—such as those to children or to forced sex—are inherently victimizing because they involve a non-consenting "partner." We call such attractions *paraphilic* (see chapter 2). Other sex offenses occur because a person has a sexual *preoccupation* – that is, they can't seem to stop thinking about sex. When you think about sex all the time it can lead you to engage in inappropriate or repetitive sexual behaviors despite the risk of negative consequences. Both paraphilias and sexual preoccupation can interfere with a person's ability to live within their value system.

Sexualized coping can be a way of soothing distress. Many people use masturbation to comfort their feelings of stress, anxiety, loneliness, boredom, or depression. For the most part masturbation is harmless. But when masturbation is the primary or even the sole comfort a person has, it can take on a life of its own. Some people are looking at pornography or masturbating for most of the day, swiping their phones to watch porn constantly, and neglecting their work or their family members. When masturbation occurs outside of the home—such as at work or in your car—it can lead to serious problems. For example, if a child happens to see a person masturbating in their car, it can lead to the same type of felony charge as if the person had intentionally targeted the child or sexually abused the child.

Other sexual self-regulation problems arise when people use sex to meet needs for attention, power or control. This may be especially true for clients with a childhood history of abuse. Molestation in childhood can contribute to sexually abusive behavior in different ways: compensation for feelings of powerlessness, repeating their own abuser's behavior and distorted thinking, or associating sexual arousal with adult-child sexual activity. Witnessing violence in the childhood home can also contribute to unhealthy power dynamics in relationships. Men without healthy role models as children can grow up with inaccurate ideas about gender roles, male privilege, respect, and consent.

For still others, sexualized acting out can be a way of creating emotional distance from other people to avoid the vulnerability of true intimacy. Having sex with many people often means being close to no one. Even though everyone needs affection and intimacy in their lives, true intimacy is risky business. It means allowing yourself to be truly known by another. That means being emotionally open, and that openness carries with it the risk of rejection.

Jason, in treatment for exhibitionism, grew up in a family in which frequent bouts of verbal abuse and name-calling violated both generational and emotional boundaries. The home environment lacked examples of appropriate emotional regulation, and as a young teen, masturbation quickly became something Jason looked forward to as way to cope with his anxiety and emotional distress. At the same time, his parents, as a part of their affluent lifestyle, reinforced his entitlement and need for instant gratification by buying material things.

With confused boundaries and limited strategies for managing his emotions, Jason spent 20 years exposing himself hoping to receive a positive reaction from the women who saw him. He accidentally discovered that public masturbation seemed to meet his emotional needs for self-soothing, validation, and acknowledgement. It seemed to be a way to say "Look at me! Notice me!" Let me know I'm OK!" At the same time, because his victims never knew him, he kept a safe distance from any real intimacy. He said he had thousands of victims. That means he felt entitled to impose himself on all those women. His own immediate gratification took priority over the violation all those women endured.

Emotional Self-Regulation

Learning to regulate one's own emotions occurs throughout childhood as we develop the ability to control our responses to all the demands of our environment and other people. Ideally, we have the opportunity to observe others around us behaving in a manner that is socially acceptable, which helps us to witness a range of skills flexible enough to adapt to different situations.

Emotional *dysregulation* can show up as a tendency to over-react in ways that are out of proportion to a situation. Or it can appear in the form of detachment from emotions. Your early experiences interact with your personality and temperament to create your emotional style. Emotional regulation requires the ability to tolerate uncertainty, to have a range of different coping skills to use when things go wrong, and permission for yourself (and others) to make mistakes and learn and grow from them.

Here are some important features of emotional regulation:

1. *Emotional Knowledge*: The ability to identify emotions, recognize their purpose, identify the links between feelings, thoughts, and behaviors, and to recognize helpful and unhelpful reactions to situations.
2. *Flexible Thinking*: Being willing to see things from another perspective, being aware that we sometimes interpret things in flawed ways based on past experiences, and accepting that others have different points of view (even if you don't always agree with them).
3. *Acceptance*: of yourself, of others, of your feelings. Be compassionate to yourself. Give yourself permission for trial and error, to not be perfect, and to learn from mistakes.
4. *Tolerating distress*: Just accept that sometimes you have uncomfortable thoughts, feelings, and body signals. You don't have to "fix" your feelings by engaging in unhelpful behaviors. You can learn a set of coping tools for mental distraction and healthy self-soothing behaviors.
5. *Self-awareness* of your personal goals, values, identity, and strengths. Stay aware of what truly motivates you.

When Smith felt angry, sad, or hurt, he usually looked at online pornography and masturbated. He was seeking a quick fix with something that feels good and is easily attainable. Looking back, he recalled that when he was 12 years old, his father died suddenly of a heart attack.

This event shifted his world into a frightening place where unpredictable things happened. To make matters worse, his mother, in her own grief, was not emotionally available to him. He remembered blaming himself for his father's death, because he was a "mischievous child" who "gave my father stress." In those early years, food gave him something to look forward to and he became obese. Masturbation later became a desirable alternative to relationships, because he saw himself as unattractive, unlovable, and perhaps even deadly to those he loved. Later, compulsive gambling also became a way of trying to feel better in the absence of other satisfying situations in his life. Talking online to teenagers allowed him to be whoever he wanted to be without having to reveal his real (and, to him, fatally flawed) self. Not knowing what to do instead to manage his feelings of loneliness and self-hate, he sank into a dangerous online world of sexual excitement.

Risk Factors for Reoffending

Now that you've learned a little bit about self-regulation, let's discuss risk, so you can assess your own future risk for reoffending. Researchers have identified a number of "risk factors," which just means anything that increases the likelihood of reoffending. Not all risk factors apply to everyone, but generally speaking, the more you have, the higher your risk. We'll talk about three types of risk factors: (1) general criminality risk factors; (2) static (unchangeable) risk factors for sexual reoffense; and (3) dynamic (changeable) risk factors for sexual reoffense. Once you are familiar with these ideas, and have identified which ones apply to you, we will move on to thinking about how to translate the risk factors into treatment "targets" or goals for your own recovery.

Criminality Risk Factors (called the "Big Eight" by researchers Andrews & Bonta)

Researchers Andrews and Bonta identified eight factors that seem to predict future criminal behavior for people who have been arrested for a crime. We call future arrests after a first arrest "recidivism," which simply means reoffending, or repeating criminal behavior. The word "antisocial" is a fancy word for "criminality." It means "against society," and is characterized by a dismissal of rules or norms, feeling like rules don't apply to oneself, and a disregard for the way one's behaviors impacts others. As you can see, having antisocial beliefs, behaviors, and peers can lead the way for repeated criminal acts of all different sorts. Other factors, like having a dysfunctional family, abusing drugs or alcohol, having difficulty maintaining stable work, housing, or employment, and a lack of positive activities or goals are all factors that increase risk for engaging in crime. Take a look at the chart below, and honestly see which ones might apply to you. Which ones did you engage in before your arrest, and which ones do you think still apply to you?

Figure 3.1: "Big 8" Risk Factors for Criminal Behavior

Antisocial attitudes, beliefs and values	Distorted thoughts, resentments, and defiance that are supportive of crime
Antisocial Behavior patterns	Early and continuing involvement in a variety of criminal behaviors
Antisocial Personality or Temperament	Pleasure seeking, low self-control, aggression, entitlement, disregard for others
Antisocial Associations	Criminal peers and environments, relatively few pro-social supports
Family Stressors	Lack of nurturing/caring support; lack of accountability
Substance Abuse	Use of substances that impair judgment and decrease inhibitions
Lifestyle Instability	Low levels of performance and stability in work or school; Housing, employment, or relationship instability
Lack of pro-social activities	Low level of involvement and satisfaction in non-criminal leisure activities

(Andrews & Bonta)

Static Risk Factors for Sexual Reoffense

These risk factors are used to estimate your risk of reoffense by adding up the points you get for each factor to see if you fall into a low, medium, or high-risk category. This is determined by looking at your past criminal history, types of victims, your age, and your relationship patterns. People with more risk factors are at higher risk for a future arrest for a new sex crime, according to research tracking convicted persons over long periods of time. These risk factors don't really change because they reflect circumstances related to your prior offenses. Think about these risk factors at the time of your release for your most recent sex crime.

Risk assessment can't predict whether you WILL commit a new offense. However, it gives you a starting place to see how you might compare to other people who have been convicted for a sexual crime. Your car insurance company can't know for sure that you'll have an accident, but they charge you a higher premium if you have risk factors like previous accidents, young age, or speeding tickets. They charge more because research shows that people with those risk factors are more likely to get into accidents than older people who don't speed or have accidents.

Exercise 3.1: Which Static Risk FactorsAapply to You?

Static Risk Factors	Check if YES
▶ Criminal history (# of prior arrests, charges, and convictions)	☐
• Sexual (how many?)	☐
• Non-sexual (how many?)	☐
• Violent (how many?)	☐
▶ Age under 35 at time of SO arrest (risk decreases as people get older)	☐
▶ Never married or in a long-term relationship for at least 2 years	☐
▶ Any male victims	☐
▶ Victims outside the family (unrelated to you by blood or marriage)	☐
▶ Stranger victims (you offended within 24 hours of meeting the person)	☐
▶ Non-contact offenses (exposing, voyeuring, computer offenses)	☐
▶ Victims under 12	☐
▶ Multiple victims	☐
Note: Researchers Seto and Lalumiere identified victim under 12 years old, and multiple victims, as risk factors for pedophilic interest and behaviors.	

How many checks do you have? 0-2 is lower risk, 3-4 is moderate risk, and 5 or more is high risk.

Dynamic Risk Factors for Sexual Reoffense

Dynamic factors can change with time and/or circumstances. Risk can change depending on your mood, your coping skills, your attitudes, your lifestyle choices, and your ability to form healthy relationships. They can also change with treatment progress, so the ones you check are things to work on in treatment. Which ones apply to you?

Exercise 3.2: Which Dynamic Risk Factors Apply to You?

Dynamic Risk Factors	Check if YES
▶ Sexual preoccupation (thinking about sex a lot)	☐
▶ Deviant fantasies (thinking about kids, or other non-consensual sex)	☐
▶ Sexualized coping (using sex to calm down or deal with distress)	☐
▶ Emotional identification with minors (relating to kids more than adults)	☐
▶ Hostility toward women or toxic-masculinity	☐
▶ Accepting of tolerant attitudes of sexual assault, or victim-blaming	☐
▶ Lack of emotional intimacy with others	☐
▶ Relationship instability	☐
▶ Social rejection, interpersonal conflicts	☐
▶ Impulsivity and self-regulation problems	☐
▶ Poor problem-solving skills	☐
▶ Resistance to rules or rule-breaking behavior	☐
▶ Grievance thinking (feeling wronged, blaming others, feelings of unfairness)	☐
▶ Negative moods (depressed, anxious, obsessive thoughts, loneliness, shame)	☐
▶ Anger/hostility, agitation	☐
▶ Negative peer influences	☐
▶ Substance abuse	☐
▶ Lifestyle instability (unstable housing or employment)	☐

Protective Factors

Researchers have also identified protective factors -- characteristics that lower the risk of reoffending. These can include positive internal (psychological) traits, as well as external (environment or circumstances) features of an individual's life situation. Think about which apply to you, and which ones you can work on increasing if they don't apply to you right now.

Exercise 3.3: Which Protective Factors Apply to You?

Protective Factors	Check if YES
▶ Positive social supports and connections	☐
▶ Housing stability	☐
▶ Employment stability	☐
▶ Empathy for others	☐
▶ Good coping and problem-solving skills	☐
▶ Demonstrate self-control	☐
▶ Positive and law-abiding hobbies and leisure activities	☐
▶ Motivation for treatment	☐
▶ Positive life goals	☐
▶ Respect for authority	☐

Strategies for Self-Regulation

Now that you've given some thought to which risk and protective factors apply to you, here are some suggested strategies for improving your coping skills, reducing dysfunctional or upsetting thoughts, and managing your behavior. You should ask your therapist and group to help you with the ones that seem to relate to you.

Self-regulation and accountability start with transparency. If you are behaving in ways that you keep secret from others, step back and ask yourself about why you do that. You can stop and ask yourself: What would my probation officer say if he knew I was doing this? What would my group or my therapist think? What would my spouse say? Could I get in any trouble for doing this if someone knew? If I got in trouble for doing this would it be worth it? Why am I hiding it?

Managing the PIG

Remember the PIG? (see chapter 2) The Problem of Immediate Gratification? You know that indulging unhealthy fantasies and deviant desires only feeds the PIG. The longer you let the PIG build the harder it will be to break away from it. It is important to remember that having a craving never means you *must* give in to it. People who are in control of themselves have learned that if they can tolerate a craving for just a few minutes and not give in to it, the intense feeling starts to fade and soon goes away.

Some people describe waiting out their urges as "riding it out," and picture themselves on a surfboard, heading for the beach. They know that the wave of craving they are feeling will soon crash on the beach and be gone. And they know that in place of the craving will come the proud feeling of being in control.

Notice that we are talking about how you think. As soon as you start tuning into your thoughts on a regular basis, you will see how automatic most of them are and how easy it is for distorted thoughts to influence your behavior. It seems like there are automatic thoughts that go along with the PIG, thoughts like, "I can't stand it! I must give in!" and "I can't think of anything else." These thoughts are actually false. The truth is that you can stand it and you can think of something else. You can think of how clear it is to you now that your offense pattern unfolds in a predictable way: with a trigger stimulating a desire, followed by a flood of distorted thoughts telling you that you must act on that desire. Identifying those thoughts and recognizing them is the key to breaking the hold the PIG has had on you in the past. Below you will find strategies for self-control.

Thought Suppression: ABCD (Modified from Dr. Robert McGrath)

Awareness	Recognize when you are having inappropriate thoughts.
Be Accepting	Do not judge yourself. Thoughts do not make you a bad person. Thoughts come and go. You can always choose not to act. Thoughts are just thoughts.
Commitment	Make a conscious decision to change what you are thinking about.
Distraction	Do some other activity, call a support person, or use another coping strategy.

Exercise 3.4: Thought suppression—try it! give an example of how you used it.

Awareness	
Be Accepting	
Commitment	
Distraction	

Some other strategies that people find to be successful in managing intrusive thoughts:

1. Breathing deeply: Breathe in deeply for a count of 4, hold it in for another count of 4, then breathe out slowly for a count of 4. Deep breathing slows your heart rate and blood pressure, relaxing the body and reducing mental agitation.
2. Use a Mindfulness App: You can download many free mindfulness apps that will help you be mindful instead of having your mind full. These apps, like 1 Giant Mind, or the Mindfulness App, or the Calm app, will help you practice breathing and relaxation.
3. Physical Movement: Get up, move around, do push-ups, exercise, take a walk. Physical movement re-focuses your brain on a new goal, releasing chemicals that help your mind get away from obsessive thinking.
4. Creativity: Listen to music, hum a song in your mind, or draw what you are feeling. Using the creative parts of your brain takes your focus away from sex and changes the processing of thoughts and feelings.
5. Visualization: Visualize something like a scene from nature, or an animal, that symbolizes your ability to feel in control of your thoughts and actions. For instance, imagine yourself in the ocean, with waves crashing around you. If you try to fight the powerful waves, you will get knocked down and captured by them. But if you roll with the waves, allowing yourself to move through them, you will get past the waves and into calmer waters.

Managing Objectification

Sexual objectification means viewing someone primarily as an object of your sexual desire, rather than as a whole person. The person is viewed solely as existing for the purpose of your sexual gratification. This has the effect of dehumanizing that person because you are not seeing them as a whole person, with emotions and characteristics beyond their body or their role in a sexual encounter. Objectification justifies offending.

Sexualization and objectification of women are prevalent in our society, and can be seen in advertising, movies and TV, and social media. Women being openly evaluated or judged (like "catcalls") in public spaces are examples of the objectification of women. Pornography, and the occupations of stripping and prostitution, involve the total sexual objectification of the performers. Men and children can be sexualized and objectified too.

Objectification can create a justification for victimization. After all, if you see someone only as an object for your sexual needs, you lose your empathy for them as a human being. When you find yourself sexually objectifying someone, you can:

1. Remember that they really are a person and wonder about their personality.
2. Ask yourself, what would I like to get to know about this person?
3. Remember that he/she is someone's child, parent, sibling, or partner.
4. What would it be like for you to think that someone else was objectifying or sexualizing someone you love and care about?

Exercise 3.5: Avoiding Objectification—Give an Example of How You Used it

Using the strategies described above, write down a recent time you found yourself objectifying another person.

How did you remind yourself that they really are a whole person with <u>thoughts & feelings</u>?	
What would you like to get to know about this person?	
How did you remember that he/she is someone's child, parent, sibling, or partner?	
How did you gain empathy by imagining someone objectifying a person you love?	

Managing Your Fantasies

Some people can stop themselves from fantasizing just by turning their attention to something else. But others need to work at minimizing the excitement their fantasies bring before the fantasies will stay away. If you have recurring fantasies about unlawful or abusive sexual acts, the best way to deal with fantasies that keep returning is to use the Covert Conditioning exercise that is described in the next section. As you will discover, this exercise is not fun. But it works. If you really want to stop abusive fantasies, you will use it—not just once or twice, not just when you feel like it—but until you don't have deviant fantasies anymore. If you find that no matter what you do you cannot escape from thoughts of sex, talk to your counselor about seeing a psychiatrist for medication. There are medications available that are effective at breaking obsessive thoughts and freeing your mind to think of other things.

"Conditioning" is a form of learning. Some things we learn by being taught; other things we learn *directly from our experiences.* Our experiences "condition" us. Frequently we forget the things we have been taught, but the lessons we learn from our experiences stay with us. Without knowing it, we learn through conditioning all the time. Conditioning happens in primarily in three ways: (1) associating one thing with another, (2) reinforcers such as rewards or consequences, and (3) observing others—this is called "social learning."

Association by conditioning is about learning *what things go together*. Simply through the experience of living we come to expect certain things to be associated with each other. We may never actually say to ourselves, for example, "when I hear raised voices, I know there is a conflict coming." But over time, because we learn by experience that people tend to raise their voices when they are getting angry or upset, whenever we hear a raised voice, we *automatically* get ready for a confrontation or a conflict. We associate the raised voice with conflict.

Some conditioning takes place instantly, especially when an experience is painful. For example, once you've been stung by a bee, every time you see one you will notice it and want to move away from it. You associate the bee with pain. Notice that you can tell children over and over to stay away from bees, but until they've been stung, they don't pay much attention. Experience is a much better teacher than simply being told something.

Other types of conditioning experiences work slower but they still shape our thinking and expectations. We all have many connections, or *associations*, that we learned through experience over time. If, in our families, good times were associated with the smell of a barbecue or going fishing, even as adults we will still have a good feeling when we smell food on a grill or we take the fishing pole out of the closet. All kinds of feelings become associated with people or events in our lives. For some people, every time they hear the words "school principal," they will always feel a little fear. Or, every time you smell a particular perfume, it may make you think of a particular person you knew who wore that scent. You might hear a song on the radio that always reminds you of a particular time in your life.

When abusive fantasies become associated with sexual pleasure, a counter-conditioning technique can be designed to create new, unpleasant ("aversive") *associations* with deviant or inappropriate sexual thoughts. Covert conditioning helps you control your arousal by linking your inappropriate sexual thoughts with images (pictures in your mind) and feelings of some of the terrible consequences of sex offending. In this exercise you will write three types of scenes: *arousal* scenes, *aversive* scenes, and *escape* scenes. Don't worry, the scenes are all short and will take only a few minutes to write. You will then picture them, and practice thinking about them to prepare yourself in advance for the next time you find yourself having inappropriate thoughts. The idea is to get in the habit of pairing the deviant or inappropriate thoughts or fantasies with an immediate thought of the negative consequences (instead of thinking about what's enticing or pleasurable).

One final note about conditioning techniques: because the purpose is to create new, automatic associations in your mind, conditioning exercises must be done in advance of when you might need them. Remember the PIG—the "Problem of Immediate Gratification"? When the PIG grabs you, when you're already excited and tunnel vision sets in and your common sense flies out the window, *it's too late* then to think about reducing your sexual arousal. The last thing you'll want to do then is think about this program; all you know when the PIG gets you is that you want what you want and you want it now. The conditioning technique you are about to learn will *help protect you from the PIG* by taking the arousal out of your deviant thoughts. But remember, they can only help if you have done them before you need them.

One nice thing about covert conditioning is that it is easy to learn because *everyone uses a process like it already* without even realizing it. You have probably been in a store, for example, looking at something you really want–let's say, a new pair of expensive sneakers. What happens?

1) You *fantasize* for a second or two about how cool they'd look on your feet and how comfortable they'd be. Then 2) You begin to think of the *negative consequences* that would occur if you spent your money on the sneakers: Your rent would be late. You then have a brief picture in your mind, an image of your landlord scowling and saying something nasty to you. Finally, 3) You say, "Nah, I can't really afford them now." You make a decision not to buy the sneakers based on your negative (aversive) thoughts. You pass on the *immediate gratification* you would get from having the sneakers because

you know you will feel bad later. This is just common sense in action, right?

The effect of this process of wanting something but then picturing the negative consequences of having it is that *you change your mind and change your behavior*. We all do it. Maybe you've gotten a speeding ticket on a certain road. What happens? The next time you drive on that road, you can picture those blue lights in your rear-view mirror. You slow down because you automatically associate the road with the memory of what happened before, right?

It you're going to be prepared to resist the PIG, you need to change something inside yourself *ahead of time*. That's what conditioning is about. By practicing picturing the disastrous consequences *ahead of time*, you will train your mind to automatically associate negative consequences any time you have a deviant thought. By creating these associations ahead of time — now—you won't have to choose to think about negative consequences when you start having deviant thoughts. They will come to you **automatically**. These thoughts of disaster will lessen the excitement and give you the strength to remove yourself from the situation, *escaping the PIG*.

Exercise 3.6: Covert Conditioning

The idea of covert sensitization is to associate different kinds of scenes with each other. You will be writing short scenes of situations that could lead you to risky thoughts or feelings and/or offending if you were in them, and then alternate these scenes with short scenes describing some of the worst consequences of offending. Like a movie that flashes from scene to scene, you will be flashing back and forth between the risky scenes and the punishment (aversive) scenes.

1. Start by writing a description of an offense situation that would be exciting for you. You can work from memories of actual offenses, or fantasies, or a combination of both real events and made up events. Let's call this the "*risky*" scene, you will not actually write anything arousing. You are only describing a situation that *could lead* to risky thoughts, feelings, or offending. This description will be easy because it will be short, and you will only write one scene because you will be using the same scene over and over.
2. Next, you will write your *aversive* scene. think of what for you would be the *worst* consequences to sexual offending. These consequences could include: having the police storm into your home while your family sleeps, being arrested, being humiliated by having your picture on TV, being thrown into a smelly, scary jail cell, going to court, facing the parents of your victim in court, waiting for the judge to sentence you, trying to explain to your family members what you've done (again!), or being in prison. When it comes to the awful consequences of sex offending, you should already have plenty of material to work with. No doubt you have very clear memories of some of these events that have happened to you. Now is a time that you can actually make positive use of the *worst things* that have happened to you. Or you can imagine even worse things. You will write short but detailed descriptions of what it would be like for you if these events, or events like them, were to happen again. These scenes will take a little more time because you will need several of them for the exercise.

Your descriptions will be of scenes in which you are participating in the here and now. An example of an aversive scene: "I'm at work when two police officers walk into the store. They approach my boss and start talking. I can't hear what they are saying, but suddenly my boss turns and points to me. I freeze in fear. I know what they're here for. As they start to walk toward me, I can't breathe. I feel so weak I can hardly stand up. It's all happening again and I caused it. I feel like dying."

Each of your aversive scenes should be detailed so that you can really picture the negative consequence and *feel the feelings* you would feel. Include details about what things look like, hear like, smell like, sound like, and especially what they feel like. The more detailed your scene, the more real it seems, the more powerful the conditioning will be.

Now you are going to order your scenes. Start with your risky scene. Like,

A. "It's a Saturday and I'm visiting my sister. It's a sunny day and I'm swimming in the pool at my sister's apartment complex. I start to notice that this young teen girl in the pool keeps swimming right up next to me. It occurs to me that I could probably touch her and she wouldn't even notice. I start to get thoughts of this and get excited." Here write: **STOP**!

Now begin your aversive scenes. Something like:

B. "I'm at the jail waiting to be finger-printed. It's crowded and noisy. The cops keep me standing and waiting while they chat. I can overhear them talking about the "scumbag" they've nabbed. I can't believe I'm here again! It feels like a nightmare. I think about calling my sister but I don't think I can face her, even on the phone. I don't know if she'll even accept my call." Here write: **SWITCH**

Now go back to the risky scene. Same scene, same place. Write **STOP**!

Now, back to the aversive scene:

B. "I'm holding the phone, trying to think of what to say to my sister. She trusted me. How can I tell her what I've done? The fat cop is staring at me, telling me to hurry up. I have to call her. I am terrified that she'll just hang up on me." **SWITCH**

Back to the risky scene: **A**. Write **STOP**!

Now:

B. "I'm back in the holding cell now. It's crowded with loud, scary guys. One guy with long, dirty hair and tattoos all over him starts bumping into me like he wants to start something. Others stare at me as if wondering what my story is. God, I hope they don't find out! My sister said forget bail. I'm alone! I'm in this stinking nightmare place. I'm so scared I'm shaking. I can't get out. I may never get out! This is my life from now on." **SWITCH**

Back and forth. Risky to aversive to risky to aversive. Your complete script will include at least five repetitions of the risky scene and five different aversive scenes. That means you will have five **STOP**!s and five **SWITCH**es. Notice that the **STOP** brings you out of the risky scene and into the aversive scene, and the **SWITCH** brings you out of the aversive and into the risky scene.

At the end of your script, you will add a final scene. First, *repeat the risky scene*. Then you will add an "***escape scene***," which is an image of yourself getting away from the risky situation instead of offending. The escape scene will include 1) a **specific plan** about where you will go and who you will talk to about what happened, and 2) a **reward** for yourself for maintaining control. The reward should be something real and something good. First, think of how you will *congratulate yourself* for being the new you. Then think of a fun activity you could do or thing you could buy for yourself that you would really enjoy. Be specific. You're probably not in the habit of treating yourself to good things. But you deserve good things. Learn how to treat yourself right. *Rewards for doing the right thing are the most important element in shaping and reinforcing your positive behavior.*

Now the end of your script looks like this:

"It's a Saturday and I'm visiting my sister. It's a sunny day and I'm swimming in the pool at my sister's apartment complex. I start to notice that this young teen girl in the pool keeps swimming right up next to me. It occurs to me that I could probably touch her and she wouldn't even notice. I start to get excited." Here write: **STOP**!

C. "I realize immediately the danger of this situation. This is exactly the kind of unexpected temptation that could cost me everything I have worked so hard for. I swim to the side of the pool and dry off. I immediately return to my sister's apartment and tell her what happened. She is a good listener and understands what I go through. There is a good college football game coming on in a few minutes that will be fun to watch. I decide to spend the rest of the afternoon watching the game and then throw a steak on the grill. I congratulate myself for being the new person I have become—someone who won't hurt a child and won't hurt myself or my family."

This is the end of the script. Notice that we have labeled the risky scenes "**A**," the aversive scenes "**B**," and the escape scene "**C**." Now, when it is all put together, the sequence looks like this: **ABABABABABAC**. All that remains to this exercise is to read over what you've written until it's clear in your mind. Keep it and read it over again whenever you find your mind wandering into risky thoughts.

Journaling

Impulsivity, sexualized coping, sexual preoccupation, and hypersexuality can be factors in sex offending. You already know if one of these applies to you. Journaling is a strategy used to intentionally pay attention to your thoughts and emotions throughout a day. You write down times when you notice yourself thinking sexually, wanting to act on impulse, feeling anxious, or tempted to engage in unhealthy behaviors. By monitoring your thoughts and feelings, and the situations that seem to trigger them, you can begin to see patterns and then speak with your therapist about how to devise strategies for coping and changing your reactions.

Trauma can also play a role in problems with self-regulation (more on this in chapter 4). Sometimes a person with a history of trauma can have difficulties within current relationships or other daily life experiences. For example, a routine occurrence for some people, such as being criticized by a supervisor at work or cut off on the highway, might be enough to re-activate old feelings of fear, helplessness, or anger that can overwhelm the person's ability to cope. Then, the person may act before they fully explore their options.

You can journal the events of a day, with a focus on which events activated various responses, what you thought and felt, what actions you took, and what you could do differently in the future. As you think about your current experiences by turning your attention inward, you can make some connections between current and past events.

The first step is to just write about your daily experiences. Choose significant experiences that make you feel something. Then, think about the thoughts that you had in response to the situation.

- What does the current situation remind you of?
- When do you remember thinking or feeling this way before?
- How do you think your reactions might be "automatic" from past experiences?
- What do you wish you could have done differently, or think differently about it now?

Self-Monitoring and De-escalation Skills

Here are some helpful tips you can try the next time you need to calm down. Our brain responds to a perceived threat in the environment. Sometimes we misinterpret our experiences (or other people) as threatening because we associate certain environmental conditions with old traumas. Just because a situation feels threatening real doesn't mean the threat is real.

When we feel anxious or threatened, our brain goes into fight or flight mode. You might notice that you heart races, your fists clench, your stomach hurts, and you feel either like fighting, running, or disappearing (fight, flight, or freeze).

1. What do you notice about your body? (breathing, heart rate, tension areas)
2. Breathe. ... in for a count of 4, hold it for a count of 4, out for a count of 4. Repeat 4 times.
3. Admit and accept that you're anxious or angry.
4. Examine your thoughts. Challenge them.
5. Release the anxiety or anger by consciously relaxing and untensing your muscles.
6. Visualize yourself calm.
7. Think it through.
8. Listen to music, draw, watch something that distracts your mind.
9. Change your focus.
10. Progress, not Perfection!

Managing Post-Conviction Traumatic Stress

Post-Conviction Traumatic Stress (PCTS) is a concept developed by Dr. Jill Levenson and Dr. Danielle Harris which describes the experience of community re-entry following a conviction or incarceration for a sexual crime. Having a criminal record is generally full of challenges, but the many additional obstacles and restrictions faced by RSOs complicates their experience and creates additional stress. We introduced the idea of PCTS to describe the specific set of cognitive-emotional symptoms experienced by RSOs, which are related to post-conviction circumstances and characterized by the four DSM-5 criteria for Post-traumatic Stress Disorder (PTSD):

(1) <u>Intrusive thoughts or imagery</u>: This includes flashbacks in which the person acts or feels as if the event is recurring; nightmares, repetitive and distressing intrusive images or memories, and thoughts that seem "obsessive" and uncontrollable.

(2) <u>Avoidance of triggers and reminders</u>: These reminders include people, places, situations or circumstances resembling or associated with the event. You try to avoid thinking or talking about it in detail, particularly about its worst moments, and might avoid people, places and things that remind you of the distressing event and trigger anxiety.

(3) <u>Negative thoughts and feelings</u>: After a traumatic event people may find themselves in a negative mood (anger, fear, depression). They might feel irritable, fearful, or want to isolate themselves from others. Or, you might feel numb.

(4) Hypervigilance: Symptoms of hyperarousal include scanning the environment for perceived danger, exaggerated startle responses, irritability, difficulty concentrating, and sleep problems. Trauma can interfere with emotional and behavioral regulation; you may over-react to things, feel like you have a chip on your shoulder, or become obsessed with worry about the future.

You can read more about understanding the impact of trauma and PTSD) at:

Link 3.1 – Understanding the Impact of Trauma
(National Center for Biotechnology Information / SAMHSA)
https://www.ncbi.nlm.nih.gov/books/NBK207191/

The experience of every stage of one's passage through the criminal justice system is traumatic. This doesn't mean that punishment and accountability aren't appropriate. It just means that we recognize the fear and stigma you face in the re-entry process and we know it is real.

Upon release from custody, most RSOs face many social and practical barriers. The stigma of a felony label makes it harder to obtain and keep employment, housing stability, and access to social supports. These obstacles can create disempowerment, fear, anxiety, social isolation, hopelessness, and shame. Negative labels like RSO, predator, pervert, molester, deviant, or offender can even lead people to adopt or resume behaviors that create self-fulfilling prophecies. In the U.S., sex offender registration policy often labels individuals for life (sometimes because of a single and isolated incident) in ways that negate any positive aspect of their character and behavior. Facing significant barriers to safe community re-entry, many registrants describe deep desperation and despair, along with the constant and crippling fear and anxiety we refer to as PCTS.

You might notice that seeing a police officer, visiting your parole agent, or driving past the courthouse can trigger anxiety because you are associating these things with your arrest. You feel at the mercy of authorities, and fear that you could lose your freedom again. You worry that you might violate your probation with a mistake you didn't even know you made, like changing your phone number and not knowing you had to report that. A knock at the door might take you back to the night of your arrest. A phone call from your officer might create panic that you are in trouble.

These are PCTS reactions and they are normal, but they are uncomfortable. A trigger in the environment causes your automatic "survival" response to go into full gear, as stress chemicals like cortisol surge through your body. It isn't a cognitive or logical response; it is a physiological response. You can use the de-escalation, mindfulness, and self-monitoring skills described on the previous pages to help you with these symptoms, and talk to your therapist and group about them as well.

Mindfulness and Mind-Body Interventions

There is definitely a mind-body connection. Current stress and past trauma can impact your body's response system and ability to calm down. You might benefit from yoga. The benefits of yoga are physical as well as emotional. For instance, physical benefits include increased flexibility, strength and muscle tone, improved respiration, energy, metabolism and blood circulation. Emotionally, yoga can reduce anxiety, depression, and chronic pain, and improve sleep patterns. You can take a yoga class or learn to do it yourself watching YouTube videos or downloading some free yoga apps. Practicing even simple stretching can keep your mind in touch with your body.

Mindfulness is a fancy way of saying, "calm your mind and stay in the present moment." It comes out of Zen Buddhism. Mindfulness exercises begin with simply slowing down and feeling the ground beneath your feet on the floor, and noticing the position or tension of your hips and shoulders. This can be followed by breathing in and out, deeply and slowly, while orienting yourself to your current surroundings (what can you hear? See? Feel?). Your mind might wander, and that's ok. Simply bring your mind back to focusing on your breathing and your senses here and now. There are many free mindfulness apps that can help you develop skills in the areas of self-observation, calming, and relaxing. Here are some great ones:

Link 3.2a – The Mindfulness App
https://themindfulnessapp.com/

Link 3.2b – Calm Breathing YouTube video
https://www.youtube.com/watch?v=gLbK0o9Bk7Q

Exercise 3.7: Your Emotional Regulation Plan

Emotional management is a skill that you can improve (with help from your therapist and support system). It starts with noticing and identifying your feelings. Most people never notice or identify their feelings, so these are skills that will feel clumsy at first and will require practicing. But they get easier with time. You will find a "feeling list" in Chapter 4 that can help with your practice.

	Notice	**PLAN for change**
WHAT	People, places, situations. How do I react to things? List different kinds of feelings that I commonly feel in the situations I identified above.	
HOW	Look at my list of feelings, and write down how I typically express these emotions? How do my feelings connect with my thoughts and behaviors?	
WHO	Are there certain people who seem to "bring out" certain emotions in me? Who are they and how do I respond to them?	

WHERE	Internal—what are the things I feel inside of my body when I feel upset, angry, anxious, or agitated? External—how do the people around me (family and friends), social situations, peer pressure, cultural messages impact my feelings and thoughts?	
WHEN	When does my emotion seem unregulated? How long does it usually last? Is it truly situational, or part of a "strategy" I usually use to cope with difficulties?	
WHY	What are my motivations to better manage my emotions? What do I have to gain? What do I have to lose? Can I identify both conscious and unconscious goals?	

Here is a great website describing ERIC (Emotional Regulation and Impulse Control)

Link 3.3 – Emotional Regulation and Impulse Control
https://blogs.deakin.edu.au/eric/what-does-eric-target/

Decision-Making skills

Good decision-making is a skill that takes practice. Sometimes it is hard to stay focused on goals when you have strong emotions about something, or strong urges or cravings. Do you remember taking multiple-choice tests as a kid? There were always one or two obviously bad answers, and other choices that might work and might not. The skill is to evaluate each choice, find the reasons why it fits or does not exactly fit, and then choose the best answer. Similar strategies exist for decision-making, which takes practice. You can implement a plan to solve problems. This can help you make decisions that are in line with your personal values, and with how you want your life to go. You first need to stop, slow down, and ask yourself some questions to come to the best decision.

Exercise 3.8: Your Decision-Making Strategies

Name a current problem. Let's look for a solution!

What is my goal?	
What are all my options and alternatives?	
What are the pros and cons of each choice?	
What do I think might happen as a result of each choice?	
How can I rule out the bad options and narrow down the best option?	

Medications

The use of psychotropic medications can be an important consideration. Some medications can have a direct effect on sexual, emotional, and behavioral self-regulation by reducing sex drive and stabilizing moods. Others can have an indirect effect on general self-regulation by assisting with attention deficit, depression, obsessive-compulsive conditions, or anxiety symptoms so that it is easier for you to practice the skills you are learning in therapy. You and your therapist can decide together if a referral to a medical doctor (psychiatrist) will be helpful in your treatment plan.

12-step Programs

The 12 Steps were created by the founders of Alcoholics Anonymous to help people overcome addiction to alcohol. The program gained success over many years by providing support groups for people addicted to drugs or alcohol. In fact, there are many 12-step programs for various addictions and compulsive behaviors, including Cocaine Anonymous, Eaters Anonymous, Gamblers Anonymous, and Sex Addicts Anonymous—all using similar 12-Step methods and principles, which can be adapted to one's own needs. AA is a spiritual program, not a religious program, so if you are not sure if you believe in God, or if you have your own ideas of a "higher power," that's OK. The idea is that you are part of a greater universe, and that sometimes you have to surrender your belief that you alone can control everything.

In 12-step programs, they say the "Serenity Prayer" which is brilliant in its simplicity:

"Grant me the serenity to accept the things I cannot change, the Courage to change the things I can, and wisdom to know the difference."

The most important piece of the 12-Step model is that through a "fellowship" (support group), you receive support, encouragement, and accountability from other people who also genuinely want to overcome their addiction. People come together to share their experience, strength, and hope. By listening to others, you learn about yourself and about ways to cope. You learn that hope for the future is possible, even when you feel like you've reached your lowest low. More experienced members "sponsor" newer members by providing leadership and mentoring, based on their own trial and error and success. The sponsorship model as well as regular meeting times encourage the kind of social support that has helped countless people stay "clean and sober." In most metropolitan areas, there are hundreds of meetings each week to choose from, in churches, community centers, hospitals, and other places. Meetings are free.

Sex Addicts Anonymous (SAA) meetings can be especially helpful for some people in treatment who are struggling to contain their hypersexuality. Talking with others (and listening to others) who are working on various types of sexual self-regulation can be very enlightening.

Here are the 12 Steps as defined by Sex Addicts Anonymous (modified from the 12-steps of Alcoholics Anonymous):

1. We admitted we were powerless over addictive sexual behavior –that our lives had become unmanageable.
2. Came to believe that a Power greater than ourselves could restore us to sanity.
3. Made a decision to turn our will and our lives over to the care of God as we understood Him.
4. Made a searching and fearless moral inventory of ourselves.
5. Admitted to God, to ourselves and to another human being the exact nature of our wrongs.
6. Were entirely ready to remove all these defects of character
7. Humbly asked Him to remove our shortcomings
8. Made a list of persons we had harmed and became willing to make amends to them all.
9. Made direct amends to such people wherever possible, except when to do so would injure them or others.
10. Continue to take personal inventory and when we are wrong, promptly admit it.
11. Sought through prayer and meditation to improve our conscious contact with God as we understood Him, praying only for knowledge of His will for us and the power to carry that out.
12. Having had a spiritual awakening as the result of these steps, we tried to carry this message to other sex addicts and to practice these principles in all our affairs (through service to others).

Here are some websites where you can learn more about 12-step programs:

Link 3.4 – SAA Recovery
https://saa-recovery.org/

Link 3.5 – Al Anon
https://al-anon.org/

SMART Recovery Programs

Another program geared toward Self-Management and Recovery Training (SMART) is the Smart Recovery Program. SMART is seen as an alternative to AA or other 12-step programs, and uses a 4-point set of cognitive behavioral principles to help people gain control of all kinds of problematic or addictive behaviors. The four principles are: (1) Building and maintaining the motivation to change. (2) Coping with urges to use. (3) Managing thoughts, feelings, and behaviors in an effective way without addictive behaviors. (4) Living a balanced, positive, and healthy life.

SMART recovery has a website with lots of free resources and videos, and you can find free support group meetings in most metropolitan areas. Online support groups are available too, and so are support groups for family members and loved ones impacted by your behavior. Check out this website, which provides information about how SMART recovery can supplement your treatment program.

Link 3.6 – Smart Recovery
https://www.smartrecovery.org/

Creating Your Personal Vision of Sexual Health

Now it's time for you to think about creating your very own plan for healthy sexuality. Let's start with some general brainstorming questions. Ponder them yourself, with your group and therapist, or with other support persons in your life, like a friend, family member, or romantic partner. Begin with what, who, where, when, how, and why questions about your behaviors.

You might also need a healthy online sexuality plan. On the following pages, you will also have a chance to develop an internet safety plan for your online boundaries and behavior.

Exercise 3.9: Your Healthy Sexuality Plan

1. WHAT kinds of sexual activities are healthy for you to engage in? (what kinds are not?)
2. WHO should you be engaging in sexual activity with (or who not to engage with?—think about age, power differentials, marital status, etc.)
3. WHERE are the appropriate places for you to engage in sexual activities (and where not to engage?)
4. WHEN are the appropriate times for you to engage in sexual activity? (times of day or times when you are supposed to be focusing on other things, or timing in terms of sexualized coping).
5. HOW should you structure your lifestyle to encourage your healthy sexuality?
6. WHY should you be motivated to develop a healthy sexuality plan? (What are the positive reasons for change, or the negative consequences that could happen if you don't get healthier?)

Healthy Sexuality Worksheet

	To Do	**To Not Do**
WHAT		
WHO		
WHERE		
WHEN		
HOW		
WHY		

Exercise 3.10: Your Healthy Online / Technology Plan

1. TIME—How much time should you spend online, how often, and for how long?
2. NEED VERSUS WANT—What websites or applications MUST you use for legitimate non-sexual purposes, and which ones should you avoid?
3. POSITIVE VERSUS NEGATIVE ONLINE ACTIVITIES—Which types of activities reinforce isolation, poor boundaries, hypersexuality, or other problematic behaviors (gambling, shopping, excessive gaming, etc.)
4. ONLINE BOUNDARIES—What are the healthy online boundaries you want to maintain?
5. ACCOUNTABILITY and SUPPORT—What safety and accountability plans can you put in place?

	Plan
TIME	Create a schedule for online activities. This might include a routine for checking email, paying bills, reading news, or doing online research – when (after work each night? First thing in the morning with your coffee?) and for how long? You might also devise a plan for "unplugging" from your phone or device (for example, not sleeping with your phone near you). When should you NOT be using your device?
NEED VS. WANT	What websites or apps must you absolutely have? Make a list of all the legitimate non-sexual activities that require internet access.
POSITIVE VS. NEGATIVE	What types of online activities are healthy for you? What types are unhealthy? Why? What should you avoid?
ONLINE BOUNDARIES	Make a list of the online boundaries you want to maintain (this could include time limits, spending limits, social media, who you "friend" or who you meet). This might include making tough decisions about owning or using certain devices (smart phone, computer, tablet). Importantly -- How do you set boundaries with your phone, which you probably have with you all the time? Will you be accessing the Internet on a phone, pad, computer, other device? Why or why not?
ACCOUNTABILITY	Do you need to set parental controls on your device? Who can you trust to help you put those in place? Should you plan to use your device only in a public location in your home where others can see you? Do you need a software monitoring program like NetNanny? Who will monitor your online usage?

Coping with and Understanding Anger

Anger is a problem for many people who have committed sex crimes. If you find yourself feeling angry much of the time, an important task for you in treatment will be to identify the underlying source of your anger. Usually anger is about feeling that something is unfair and feeling powerless to make it fair. We feel angry with others when we are needy but can't depend on them to meet our needs. We also feel angry at ourselves when we are out of control.

"Rage" is extreme, long-lasting anger. For some people, rage can be so intense they are afraid they will hurt someone. Sometimes people feel as if they could explode from rage. If you think about the things that make you feel this way, you will find that usually they are things that you can't control or change. For many people, feeling powerless reminds them of when they were little and really were powerless. When we feel small and childlike, sometimes we act in childish ways.

Maybe you are stuck in a situation at work in which you get no recognition for your efforts, no reward, no raise. Perhaps you have a boss who criticizes you all the time and demands overtime from you with no respect for your schedule. This might feel like a helpless situation because there seems to be nothing you can do to change it. You need the job, so you can't risk making waves.

Anger is often the flip side of powerlessness. When we feel powerless, anger can be an empowering response. Anger can make us feel stronger and compensate for a lack of control. Any situation that leaves you feeling powerless puts you at risk to reoffend. You may never consciously say to yourself, "I'm mad so I'll go offend and take it out on someone else." On the contrary: You may believe whole-heartedly that you will not reoffend and that you are in control. But if you are in a situation that has you feeling out of control, or if many things in your life leave you feeling angry or helpless, eventually you will find yourself seeking or drifting into situations in which you can regain that sense of control and power. You will begin making decisions that lead you in the direction of opportunities to feel some power. That opportunity may be getting into a fist fight or it could be seeking a relationship or encounter in which you can be in control. *It may come in the form of manipulating a minor or adult into sexual activity, or by engaging in other sexual violations that make you feel more empowered.*

Anger can be a comfortable feeling because it makes us feel powerful. Underneath anger, however, are often other feelings of vulnerability:

- Sadness
- Shame
- Fear
- Helplessness

These feelings are less comfortable because they make us feel unsafe, or weak. Sometimes it is way easier to get in touch with the anger than the vulnerable feelings. It is also easier to focus on the people or situation who seem to "cause" your anger than the underlying feelings. As you think about exploring your anger, think about what other feelings are under the anger. Do you know who or what made you feel powerless and angry in the past? If you think about it you will know.

- ► What kinds of things make you angry?
- ► What do you think is the underlying feeling?
- ► Symbols and Metaphors (e.g.: do you wear a "coat of armor" to keep from being hurt? Do you feel like a "bee" who tries to fly away but stings sometimes?)

- Can you imagine the powerless experience with a different ending?

You might ask yourself:

(1) What meaning am I attaching to this situation?
(2) What do I think it means about me?
(3) What do I think it means about others?
(4) As I think about those things, what other feelings come to mind, besides anger?

Anger Management

Anger management is the process of learning to understand your anger and learning to control your expression of anger. It is made up of three distinct parts:

1. Awareness of Anger
2. Taking Responsibility for Anger
3. Changing Destructive or Unhealthy Patterns of Expressing Anger into Healthy Communication

In the next several pages, you will become aware of some specific tools you can use to help you manage your anger. Later in this book, when you identify your "triggers" for sex offending, you may learn that controlling your anger will be central to keeping you away from offending.*

Clayton, a client on the autism spectrum, sniffles loudly every minute or so in group therapy sessions. He seems unaware that this behavior is bothersome to others. Jerry was raised by parents were violent and drug addicted. His earliest memory is of his father, in an alcoholic rage, throwing the Christmas tree and all the gifts into the fireplace. Now, Jerry aggressively says to Clayton, "Hey man, use a fucking tissue and blow your nose!" The therapist observes that Jerry seems angry. "Yeah man, he's disgusting," answers Jerry. The therapist wonders out loud whether that is the way Jerry's father talked to him, and then prompts Jerry to try to share his reaction to Clayton's sniffling in a less hostile manner. This opens up a group discussion about how easily anger can be triggered, and how to express one's reactions in a way that is more consistent with how we all want to be treated by others.

Dominick explores his anger:

One night in therapy, a group member said something that Dom didn't agree with. He reacted by yelling at the other guy, then jumped up from his chair and began to storm out of the room. The therapist validated what she saw: "Dom - I can see that you are very upset right now, and very angry. Can you please come sit down and tell us what is bothering you?" "No!" Dom yelled, red-faced. "I need to leave before I do something I'll regret." The therapist tried one more time. "I really want to understand what's happening for you. I'm not going to let you do anything you'll regret. This is a safe place, and we'll just talk about what's happening. No one will get hurt by talking."

Dom reluctantly turned around and sat back down, crossing his arms and looking defiant. The therapist gently probed for information, in a calm and soothing voice, and asked Dom to tell the

---

* Note: The following anger management tools have been modified from Sexually Abusive Behavior: Evaluation and Recovery (SABER), presented by Michael Scolatti, Ph.D. at the 14th Annual ATSA Research and Treatment Conference, 1995, New Orleans, LA.

other member what made him so angry. It seemed that Dom was triggered by some statements that he perceived as disrespectful or argumentative. Sensing that conflict was brewing, he had gone on the offensive and his anger quickly escalated.

As the group discussed the incident, Dom calmed down and was able to see that perhaps he over-reacted to an interaction that reminded him of his father, who was a real bully. Dom felt very disrespected and belittled by his father growing up. His father called him stupid a lot. Dom couldn't talk back to his father or he'd get punished. As he got older and bigger, when he didn't like what others said or did, he bullied them, just like his father did to him.

After the anger subsided, the therapist thanked him for being willing to talk it out, and observed: "I bet I'm not the first person to tell you that you're kind of scary when you're mad." Dom laughed sheepishly, saying, "Yeah, I hear that a lot from my mom and my girlfriend." The therapist then asked, "What's in that for you? Do you want to be the kind of person that people are afraid of?" After pondering this question, he realized that his angry demeanor usually results in people giving in to what he wants, and also it gets people to "come after him" when he storms out of a room, which makes him feel like they care about him. After he got some insight into this pattern, he was able to think about how he could respond differently, and how he could get his needs for respect and love met in other, more healthy ways.

Awareness of Anger

Controlling anger starts with becoming aware of it. Many people feel some level of anger several times a day. Until you recognize and write down your angry experiences you may not really be aware of how often, or how intensely, you feel angry. You can use an "Anger Log" to increase your awareness of angry thoughts and feelings by writing them down.

There are four major factors that provoke feelings of anger:

1. Frustrations: occur when you are trying to do something but are prevented, blocked or disappointed in achieving your goal.
2. Irritations and annoyances: are things which get on your nerves: noise, flat tires, pain, careless drivers.
3. Powerlessness: includes all types of encounters or experiences that make you feel like you don't have control over your own life, goals, wants, and needs.
4. Injustice and unfairness: are situations in which you believe you have not been treated fairly.

Exercise 3.11 Part 1: Anger Log

Use an Anger Log to keep track of the things that make you angry and the typical ways you react to them. After writing things down for seven days, use the Anger Worksheet to describe your anger triggers and to develop new anger management strategies.

Exercise 3.11 Part 2: Anger Log Worksheet

1. Write in detail any event that made you angry.
2. Identify which of the four categories (above) the event fell into.
3. Write your emotional reaction to the event.
4. Rate your anger on a scale from 1 (low) to 3 (high).
   - Low (1): Slightly annoyed, irritated or ticked-off. At this level I usually do not react or respond to the person or situation, but just feel tense and upset inside.
   - Moderate (2): Somewhat angry. At this level I might verbally confront the person who is "making" me angry or actively try to change the situation.
   - High (3): Very angry. At this level I might become verbally or physically aggressive with the person who is "making me angry." This might include yelling, cursing, getting intimidating, threatening, moving toward someone, or even pushing, grabbing, hitting, or otherwise violating them.

Write how you reacted or responded to the event. Then write what you could have done differently in the same situation to have a more effective outcome.

Event that made you angry:

Thoughts you had at the time:

Level of anger:

Behavior in response to anger:

More Effective Alternative Behavior:

Exercise 3.12: Anger Autobiography

To better understand your anger, answer the following questions.

1. Who first showed anger to you? How did they show anger?	
2. When have you most intensely felt anger? What are the situations that most commonly trigger anger for you? What has your reaction been? The consequences?	
3. When have you most intensely felt anger? What are the situations that most commonly trigger anger for you? What has your reaction been? The consequences?	
4. How does your behavior show this emotion? How would we know if you were feeling angry? How do people usually react when you show anger? Has your behavior in response to anger frequently caused negative consequences for you?	
5. When was the last time you felt angry? What was the situation? What were the consequences?	
6. Is anger a comfortable feeling for you to feel and show? Do you need better management of your anger?	

Taking Responsibility for Your Anger

Identifying Your Anger Cycle

Angry feelings and behaviors frequently happen in "chains" or "cycles" of events. Once you become familiar with your cycle, you will begin to see that other people never "make" you behave in destructive ways. The ways you choose to think about the actions of others and to express your anger are decisions you make yourself.

Cycles, by definition, go around and around in the same pattern. The last part of a cycle leads back to the first. Everyone's anger is different, of course, so everyone has a different cycle. The following outline will help you see how your own anger cycle comes together. Fill in your own experiences in each phase of the cycle.

Phase One: Precipitating Stress. Write out all the short-term or long-term, intense stressors that you feel contribute to your anger. In this phase, you feel something has gone wrong in your life.

Phase Two: Negative Mood. Usually when a person has a lot of stress, their mood gets worse. They begin to have periods of depression and anger. Anger and depression are often closely related. Depression can be "anger turned inward," which means the person is angry at themselves for something they think they have done wrong or failed at. When something has gone wrong for you, you either blame yourself (depression) or you blame others (anger).

Phase Three: Pre-Assault. You are having consistent angry thoughts. You are physically and mentally preparing yourself for the expression of anger. You select a person or event to be the focus of your anger. You may set someone up for an angry situation. This is a time that can bring you to your "boiling point."

Phase Four: Expression of Anger. In this phase, the "explosion" occurs. Do you use threats or intimidation? Do you use sarcasm or put-downs? Do you become physically aggressive? Do you hit people or break things? Do you withdraw from others, becoming silent, or giving someone "the cold shoulder"? Are you *passive-aggressive*, meaning you express your anger indirectly through procrastination, lateness, slamming doors, forgetting, stubbornness, stealing, vandalizing property, or lying? This is important – because sometimes people think "I don't have an anger problem" because they don't hit, scream, or become violent. Instead, they seethe inside, holding in anger but being reluctant to talk about it. This can make you distant, mean-spirited, or rejecting to others.

Phase Five: Positive and Negative Consequences. What are the positive consequences to your anger? For instance: getting your way, feelings of power, feelings of status, control. What are the negative consequences? For instance: a night in jail, losing relationships, guilt, remorse, self-doubt, and physical injury. Positive and Negative consequences might occur at the same time, resulting in a feeling of conflict inside you.

Phase Six: Defense Mechanisms. You find a way to reduce the psychological pain of negative consequences by getting rid of your feelings of responsibility, guilt, and shame. You do this by rationalizing your behavior. Because you are angry, you tell yourself, you have a right to act in destructive ways. You use distorted thinking to justify your actions. This phase brings you back to a feeling of normalcy, and your rationalizations allow you to fall back into the same patterns the next time you experience Precipitating Stress (Phase One).

Exercise 3.13: Mapping Your Anger Cycle

Using the phases discussed on the previous pages, use two personal examples to outline your anger cycle. Clearly describe what took place during each stage. Use the following chart to complete the assignment.

Phase	Example 1	Example 2
Precipitating Stress		
Negative Mood		
Pre-Assualt		
Experession of Anger		
Negative / Positive Consequences		
Defense Mechanisms		

Changing Your Patterns of Expressing Anger

PACE Yourself: This method will help you to better solve your problems. It is a positive way to deal with angry situations and allows you to anticipate problems and plan for an effective way to react. When you handle situations effectively you get your needs met.

When you solve problems, you don't need to get angry. Talking through a problem situation with another person and working it out is called "conflict resolution." You can resolve conflicts if both people are given a chance to speak, and if each person listens to the other.

PACE stands for:

P = PROBLEM
A = ALTERNATIVES
C = CONSEQUENCES
E = EVALUATE RESULTS

Now use this method to anticipate problems and find solutions. Using the chart on the next page, go through the steps mentioned above in the following manner.

Exercise 3.14: PACE

Problem: Go back to your anger cycle and use the situations that you identified.

Alternatives: List at least five possible ways you could behave in response to each problem. Include some ways you have responded to anger in the past plus some positive alternatives you haven't tried.

Consequences: For each alternative you outline, picture what the positive and negative consequences might be for your behavior.

Evaluate Your Results: For each positive alternative behavior and positive consequence, identify the ways in which you resolved your conflict. What happened? Did you succeed? Give yourself credit for constructive conflict resolution and find a way to reward yourself for it.

PACE	
Problem	
Alternatives	
Consequences	
Evaluate Results	

Finally, Take a Time Out

Like young children, even adults sometimes need a break or a "time out." It's okay to feel angry. It is not okay to hurt someone when you do. When you get mad, try to notice the signs your body is giving you.

What happens to your body when you get angry?

- A tight feeling in your neck, hands, face
- A hot feeling somewhere in your body
- Faster and harder breathing

- Faster heart beat
- Voice gets louder
- Other signals

Before the explosion, take a time out.

- Go for a walk or run
- Leave the room or house
- Take a shower
- Play sports or a musical instrument
- Mow the lawn or some other physical activity

Figure out why you are angry.

- Are you really angry with yourself or someone else?
- Are you taking out your anger on a person close to you?
- Are you really feeling hurt, afraid, sad, disappointed or insecure? Are these feelings coming out as anger?
- Are you suffering from fatigue or stress that is making you irritable?
- Are you exaggerating what is going on? Maybe the situation isn't as serious as you think.

Remember: You are in control of your own behavior. You alone choose how you act. You alone are responsible for the consequences of your behavior.

Figure 3.2: Anger

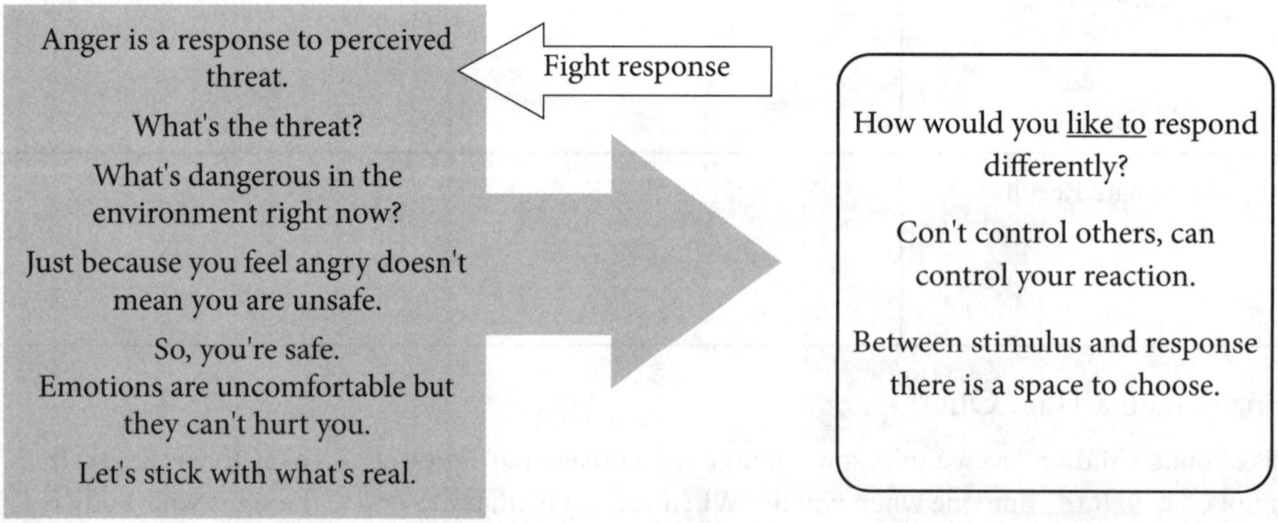

CHAPTER 4

UNDERSTANDING YOURSELF

Changing your behavior and thinking starts with understanding how you came to be you in the first place. In this chapter you will be asked to look back on your whole life to think about how your early experiences shaped the way you feel, think, and behave. You will think about your earliest relationships and experiences, and how they shaped your ideas about yourself, other people, and the world in general. We don't ask: "What's wrong with you?" Instead, we ask: "What happened to you?" Your early life experiences aren't an excuse for your offense but exploring them might help you understand why you did some of the things you did.

Take a deep breath… this chapter can be challenging and painful, but most people find it really enlightening. As you go along, you might want to ask your therapist for some individual sessions to help process some of what you are learning about yourself.

We Believe the Things We Learned in Childhood

Childhood is the period when we learn most of the things we need to know to get through life. As we learn we develop a set of *basic beliefs,* which are simply the things that we know are true. We take a million things for granted. We assume that day follows night, that we can step out of bed without being swallowed by the floor, that water will flow from the faucet, that toothpaste will come out of the tube, and so forth. We never actually think about any of these things. We don't have to. Not having to think about the things we already know is good—it frees our minds to think about new things.

In childhood we didn't just learn about things, we also learned a great deal about *people,* including ourselves. Whoever we grew up with—our parents (or stepparents or grandparents), our brothers and sisters (or step-brothers and sisters)—whoever lived in our house was our *family.* Our childhood relationships with our family members, because they were our earliest relationships, shaped our thinking about ourselves and other people, and the lessons we learned became part of our basic beliefs. In order to understand how these experiences with our families affected us, it is necessary to remember and examine them.

Talking about early experiences will bring up good memories as well as bad ones. Often the worst memories are the ones that push to the surface first, because these are the ones that affected you the most. Things that happened that were particularly bad or disturbing may have traumatized you in ways that changed your life. To this day traumatic events from early childhood may still be affecting you. Talking about trauma is not about blaming your parents, excusing your behavior, or feeling sorry for yourself. It is simply about understanding. By understanding how your past experiences shape your current thinking and behavior, you can identify areas for personal growth.

What We Learned About Ourselves

Perhaps the most important thing we learned in childhood was how to think about ourselves. As babies we have no awareness or understanding of who we are. We have no *identity.* We form our identity, our sense of who we are, from the input we receive from the other people in our lives: our family. Of course, all our family members who were in our lives were important, but the most important were our primary caretakers (usually our mother). If our mother was thrilled to have us in her life, we knew that. When she saw us, her face lit up and she smiled and talked baby-talk to us and hugged us. When that happened, we felt wanted and special and important. We learned to see ourselves as someone who was worthwhile and lovable. After all, what we saw was someone who was crazy about us.

But what if our mother was angry, maybe because she had gotten pregnant by mistake, and saw us as a burden, or as someone who was tying her down and ruining her life? What if she was depressed and therefore could not enjoy her baby? What if every time she looked at us all she could think of was the man who had abandoned her? Her expression, her tone of voice, the way she held us (or refused to hold us)—all these things may have taught us that we were not special, not wanted, or not important. We might have felt that we were unlovable, a nuisance, and not worth affection or respect. We might have developed an identity as a worthless person.

Or what if mother was an alcoholic or a drug user? Some days she might have been feeling good and treated us with love. That would have made us feel good about ourselves. But other days she might have felt frazzled or angry or depressed. On those days she might have seen us as a pain in her butt, and made us feel like nothing but a nuisance. On other days she might have been drunk and might have completely forgotten about us. How would we have felt if we were left crying with no one coming to feed us or change us? We probably would have felt terrified. If mother was different every day -- some days loving, some days angry, and some days nowhere to be found -- over time we would have learned that other people were unpredictable and not to be trusted, and that there was nothing we could do to change that. We probably felt helpless, frightened, and even angry.

We know from research about childhood attachment that interactions with parents must be consistent, nurturing, and responsive to our needs in order for youngsters to learn that the world is a safe place. Children who are exposed to mistreatment and family dysfunction or inconsistent parenting can have trouble developing secure attachments to their parents, and later to others in their lives. Psychologist Erik Erikson said that trust in our earliest relationships with caretakers is necessary to develop a healthy personality. Without learning trust early on, people can have trouble developing their own identity, and later have trouble feeling close to others.

Different children in the same family can experience early life in different ways. Take, for instance, three siblings who respond to domestic violence between their parents very differently:

> *One hides under the bed covering her ears, one tries to intervene by yelling and fighting back, and one attempts to step in and reason with the violent parent. These children are demonstrating diverse methods for dealing with distress. They grow up to interact quite differently in relationships, especially when it comes to resolving conflict and trusting others. The first tried to de-escalate her own fear by withdrawal; she becomes very passive as an adult, avoiding conflict and giving in to the demands of others. The second child tried to manage the intensity of their chaotic family by becoming confrontational; as an adult, his family describes him as a bully who is quick to agitation*

and anger, and who has intense negative responses to any disagreement. Finally, the third child, who attempted to "make peace" and negotiate between her parents, became an attorney; the courtroom is the only place she feels in control and where she successfully uses the skills that were futile in her childhood home.

Remembering Is Part of Understanding

We may not ever really know what happened when we were infants, because we were too young to attach language and understanding to memories. But we can remember much of what came later. Most people have some memories from the age of four or five on. If you don't have any memories from childhood, or certain parts of your early years are missing from your memory, that might be because of trauma. Trauma interferes with the processing and organization of memories. Part of what you will be doing in treatment is remembering whatever you can about what life was like in your family, school, neighborhood, and with your peers. The memories you have will contribute to your understanding of how you came to be the person you are.

You might better understand where you got your positive attitudes toward other people: why you enjoy gatherings, why you have a sense of humor, why you sometimes feel close to other people. You might also understand better why you have trouble relating to people: why you expect people not to like you, why you expect them not to listen to you, why you fear people, why you have trouble trusting people. You will learn why you think and feel about yourself the ways you do: why you believe in yourself in some ways but not in others, why you like yourself or hate yourself, why you feel you are somebody important—or somebody who is worthless and will never amount to anything. *Some people feel angry or afraid or sad all their lives and never know why.* By exploring their childhood and their families they can learn how to make sense of their feelings.

Don't worry if you feel like you can't remember much about your childhood. During the process of treatment you will be surprised at how much comes back to you. You will find that you can search your memory. An easy way to start is to try to picture the house or apartment you lived in as a child. Picture your school, your teachers, your friends. Remember the name of your little league team and what position you played. Remember your first crush. See, it's in there, right? Talking to your parents, your brothers and sisters, even cousins and old friends, can help you remember. Old photos, diaries and yearbooks also help. A visit to your hometown usually brings back lots of memories. Talk to your siblings, old friends, cousins, or other relatives.

If you find that there is a period of time (after age five) about which you really can't remember much, that may mean that something particularly bad or painful was happening at that time. Over the course of treatment, as you learn how to handle your feelings—as you come to understand that you don't have to be afraid of your feelings—you might find some of these memories coming back to you. As you will see, it is important to remember the bad things as well as the good things that happened to you. The bad things helped to shape you just as much as the good things, but in ways that can leave you confused and struggling all your life. You survived. That's the good news. But in an unfortunate twist, it's possible that your survival skills from long ago may now actually be holding you back and interfering with your current goals and relationships.

Understanding Trauma

Trauma results from a direct or witnessed experience that threatens a person's sense of physical or psychological safety. Trauma can take many forms, but usually involves an event that is unexpected and out of a person's control, leaving them feeling physically or psychologically threatened, with a sense of helplessness and fear. It can have a lasting impact on the person's functioning and mental, physical, social, emotional, or spiritual well-being.

Following a traumatic event, people may have difficulty sleeping, eating, or concentrating; they might have nightmares, hyper-arousal to things in the environment, or negative moods. These are common post-traumatic stress symptoms, and can last for a short time or for years following the incident. Examples of trauma include victimization, natural disaster, illness, accident, or an unexpected event that leaves a person feeling distressed and which compromises their typical coping skills.

Acute trauma results from a single incident, while repeated and prolonged exposure is known as *chronic* trauma (such as experiencing or witnessing domestic violence). *Complex* trauma occurs when someone is exposed to multiple traumatic events, accumulating over time, and that often includes interpersonal victimization.

Also, the oppression, discrimination, and marginalization often experienced by poor and minority groups can be traumatic. Poverty and social injustice can create a vicious cycle of hopelessness, helplessness, and lost potential.

Some childhood traumas are pretty obvious, like physical and sexual abuse or witnessing domestic violence. Other experiences like emotional neglect, an absent parent, or a substance abusing caretaker may be harder to identify but can lead to long term impacts. Some people have parents who were well-intentioned but smothering, and they grow up needing to push people away, because being close to others feels like you can't have your own identity. Early losses that cause children to take on adult roles in childhood can promote positive qualities like leadership and confidence but can also mean difficulties asking for or accepting help. Some people may have grown up in families who were warm and loving, but they ran into hurtful social rejection or bullying by peers, causing them to fear that they don't fit in, or will not be accepted by others. Traumatic childhood experiences can lead to lasting dysfunctional patterns of relating to others.

ACEs (Adverse Childhood Experiences)—What are they? And why is it important to talk about them?

Life experiences play a central role in the development of our ability to connect with other people. In fact, we are all best understood as a product of our past experiences. Discussing bad (adverse) childhood experiences isn't about blaming your parents or making excuses for your own behavior. It's simply a way to try to understand your own development, and the family experiences that might have contributed to how you became you. Early developmental trauma –like child abuse or neglect–can make it hard to trust others, limit your ability to bond with others, and interfere with learning effective coping skills later. Sometimes early home life can cause a child to feel extremely threatened and powerless. This can create what is called Post-traumatic Stress Disorder (PTSD): unwanted thoughts, avoidance of things that remind you of bad times, negative moods, and hyperarousal –being wound up and on guard all the time.

ACEs are a particular set of traumas that can produce long-lasting consequences. The name comes from a study by the Centers for Disease Control (CDC), who in the 1990s, surveyed over 17,000 people about their childhood experiences. The ten ACE items include physical and emotional abuse and neglect, as well as sexual abuse. They also include growing up in a home with someone who is a drug or alcohol abuser, or who is mentally ill. Other types of ACEs include violence in the home, an absent parent, or criminality in the family. The study revealed that nearly two-thirds of adults reported at least one form of early adversity in their childhood homes, and 12.5% reported four or more types. We know now that rates of childhood trauma are even higher in people who have been sent to jail, or prison, or are on probation. Harmful childhood experiences are also more common among poor people and minorities. Researchers found that the higher a person's ACE score, the more at risk they are for a bunch of different medical conditions, mental illnesses, and problems later in life (including committing crimes).

Exercise 4.1: What is Your ACE Score?

Look at this list and see how many apply to you. Check each item that happened to you even once before you turned 18. This is your ACE score. Your ACE score can range from 0-10, and higher ACE scores indicate a greater number of adversities in childhood.

While you were growing up, during your first 18 years of life:	**Check if Yes**
1. Did a parent or other adult in the household often or very often swear at you, insult you, put you down, or humiliate you? Or, act in any way that made you afraid that you might be physically hurt?	☐
2. Did a parent or other adult in the household often or very often push, grab, slap, or throw something at you? Or ever hit you so hard that you had marks or were injured?	☐
3. Did an adult or person at least 5 years older than you ever touch or fondle you or have you touch their body in a sexual way? Or attempt or actually have oral, anal, or vaginal intercourse with you?	☐
4. Did you often or very often feel that no one in your family loved you or thought you were important or special? Or your family didn't look out for each other, feel close to each other, or support each other?	☐
5. Did you often or very often feel that you didn't have enough to eat, had to wear dirty clothes, and had no one to protect you? Or your parents were too drunk or high to take care of you or take you to the doctor if you needed it?	☐
6. Were your parents separated or divorced, or not married to one another?	☐

7.	Was your mother or stepmother often or very often pushed, grabbed, slapped, or had something thrown at her? Or sometimes often or very often kicked, bitten, hit with a fist, or hit with something hard? Or ever repeatedly hit at least a few minutes or threatened with a gun or knife?	☐
8.	Did you live with anyone who was a problem drinker or alcoholic or who used street drugs?	☐
9.	Was a household member depressed or mentally ill, or did a household member attempt suicide?	☐
10.	Did a household member go to prison or jail?	☐

After the ACE study, other researchers added questions about other types of common childhood trauma. Did any of these other things happen to you while you were growing up?

- ☐ Bullying or social rejection
- ☐ Living in a dangerous or violent community
- ☐ Poverty – being poor or on public assistance; evicted, or homeless
- ☐ Death or unexpected loss of a family member
- ☐ Exposure to pornography or sexual material or behavior before age 12
- ☐ Arrested or involved in the justice system before age 18
- ☐ A family member seriously ill or injured
- ☐ You were seriously ill or injured
- ☐ Placement in foster care, with relatives, in a group home, or other out-of-home placement
- ☐ Refugee or immigrant from another country
- ☐ House fire
- ☐ Natural disaster and/or home displacement
- ☐ Racial / ethnic / gender discrimination or inequality

Can you think of other early traumas that you would like to share?

When traumatizing things happen in childhood, it is not just the event or experience that is important, but the meaning attached to it. The biggest questions are: What does this experience say about me? About others? Is the world a safe place? Can I depend on others and trust them?

ACEs are also thought of as *relational* trauma, which is caused when kids feel betrayed, not validated, dismissed, invisible, or when their attachments to important people in their lives are disrupted. Relational trauma occurs when caregivers are *needed* and at the same time *dangerous* or *unavailable.* Growing up in a home with chronic abuse, neglect, or other sorts of family chaos can introduce feelings of powerlessness at a young age. Children might feel afraid, alone, unwanted, threatened, or ignored by people they depend on — in the very place that is supposed to feel safest. Over time, any person adapts to their environment and does whatever helps them survive. They may adopt coping strategies that protect them in their home. Unfortunately, those same strategies might be counterproductive in other places. The child might develop a worldview of mistrust or self-blame. Chaotic households often lack good role models for healthy relationships. Some children never get to see what a healthy relationship looks like.

Childhood trauma can disrupt healthy brain development, affecting memory, emotions, thoughts, and impulse control. Trauma can impact a child's ability to make friends and to get along with teachers and other adults. Trauma contributes to difficulties controlling emotions (like anger and sadness). And it can alter one's sense of self and identity. Traumatizing experiences set up negative expectations of others, and these expectations can then interfere with future relationships. A traumatic childhood can lead to behaviors that bring out of other people the very responses that are feared.

Fight, Flight or Freeze

Have you ever heard the expression "fight or flight"? It refers to the changes in our body in response to fear or anxiety. When a threat is detected in the environment, the body automatically releases hormones that give us the power to act quickly to survive. This isn't a cognitive decision process, but rather an automatic kind of primitive response.

Imagine a zebra at the water hole. A lion approaches (yikes!). The zebra doesn't think like we do, but her brain goes on autopilot for survival. She can stand her ground and fight the lion (which might be necessary if she has offspring nearby), run as fast as possible to get away from the lion (flight), or hide and hope the lion doesn't notice her (freeze).

Humans have these responses too. When you feel threatened, your heart pounds, you breathe more heavily, your body tenses up. This is your body getting ready for fight or flight. For some people, anxiety in your body takes on a feeling of faint, dizziness, or numbness in your hands or feet – this is the freeze response. When anxiety occurs frequently, it creates what is called "toxic stress," which takes a toll on your mental and physical health. Because children are relatively helpless, they are especially vulnerable to stress and may easily find themselves overwhelmed by it. Events that leave children feeling confused or scared, especially when they occur repeatedly over a long period of time, can have life-long effects.

The point is that childhood trauma isn't just in your mind. It's in your brain and your body. Toxic stress in childhood creates hyper-arousal (super arousal on a continuing basis), increasing body chemicals that activate automatic fight-flight-freeze responses: Physical or verbal aggression (fight), running away or avoidance (flight), and hide or surrender (freeze).

Some children live in homes or circumstances where they have to constantly be on guard and scan the environment for danger, so they are prepared to react. The constant flow of stress chemicals in the body can actually change the structure of the brain! The automatic response system gets a lot of practice, while other areas of the brain, like decision making and impulse control, do not. People can't think straight or process information effectively when they are in a state of crisis or fear.

For example, when a child is constantly fearful at home, he has trouble concentrating at school and this interferes with academic performance and social skills. A child who can't sit still, stand in line, follow the rules of a game, or wait his turn will constantly get negative feedback from teachers and classmates (Sit down! Be quiet! Stop that! I don't want to play with you!). This feedback feels like social rejection and may make him believe he's dumb. He feels angry, sad, and lonely.

Figure 4.1: This is Your Brain on Trauma

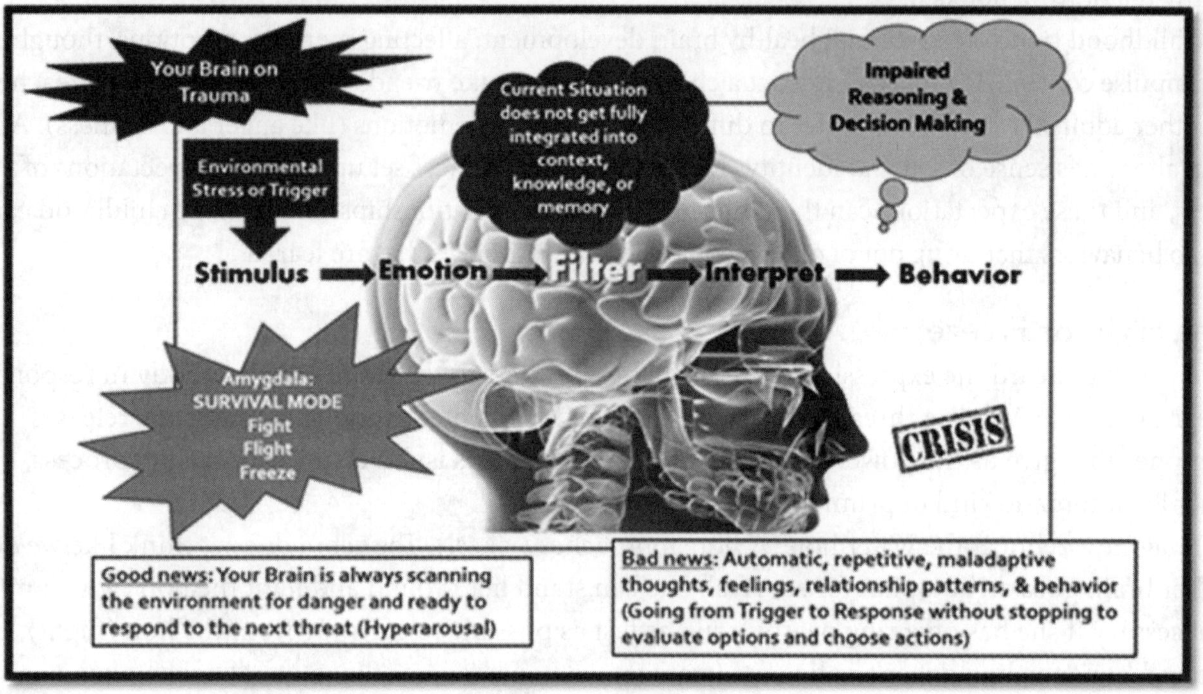

Figure 4.2: How Childhood Trauma can Impact People Throughout Life

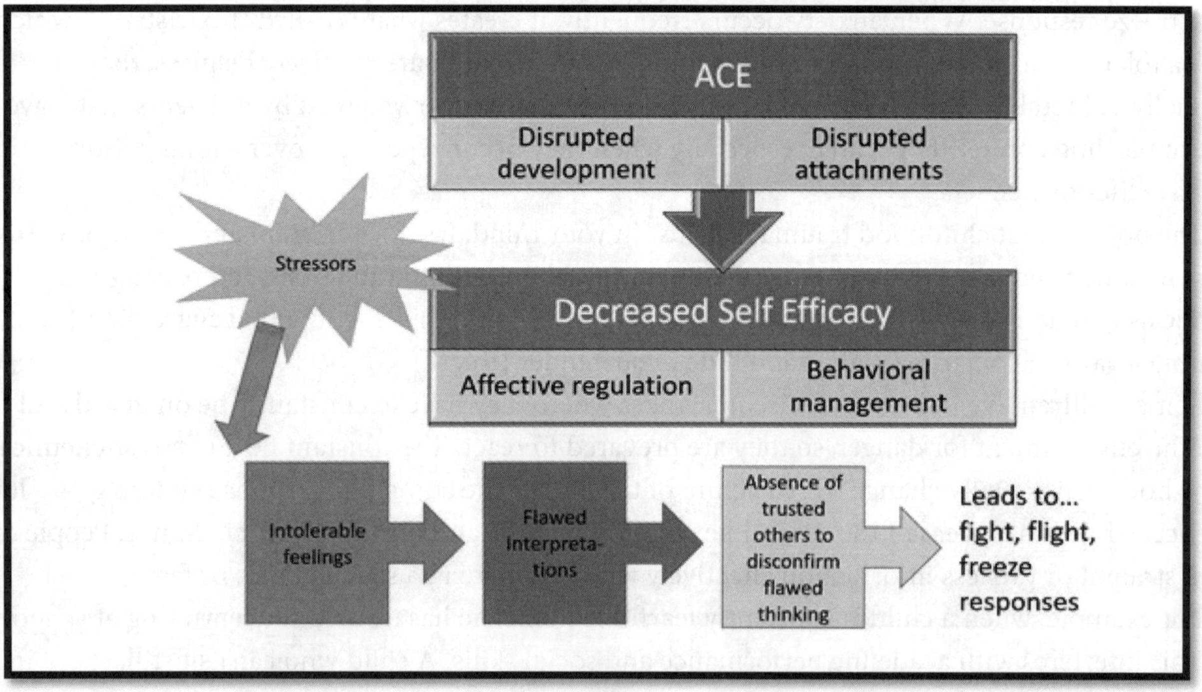

These feelings can increase his risk for joining in with delinquent peers who provide a sense of belonging and acceptance but who draw him into antisocial behavior. When adults with trauma in their backgrounds encounter current stress, they may feel intense and intolerable emotions, and cope

with them through negative behaviors they learned in childhood. Figure 4.2 shows the way that adults impacted by chronic trauma in childhood can develop a flight, flight, or freeze type of "personality" – this is their automatic way of reacting to anything that might feel uncomfortable or threatening. Trauma can also lead to a person mis-interpreting cues in the environment (or people) as threatening, even when they are not. In other words, when something in the present triggers a trauma reaction in your mind or body, you feel unsafe even though you are not actually unsafe.
Take a look at Figure 4.3. Does anything seem to apply to you?

Figure 4.3: Fight, Flight, or Freeze

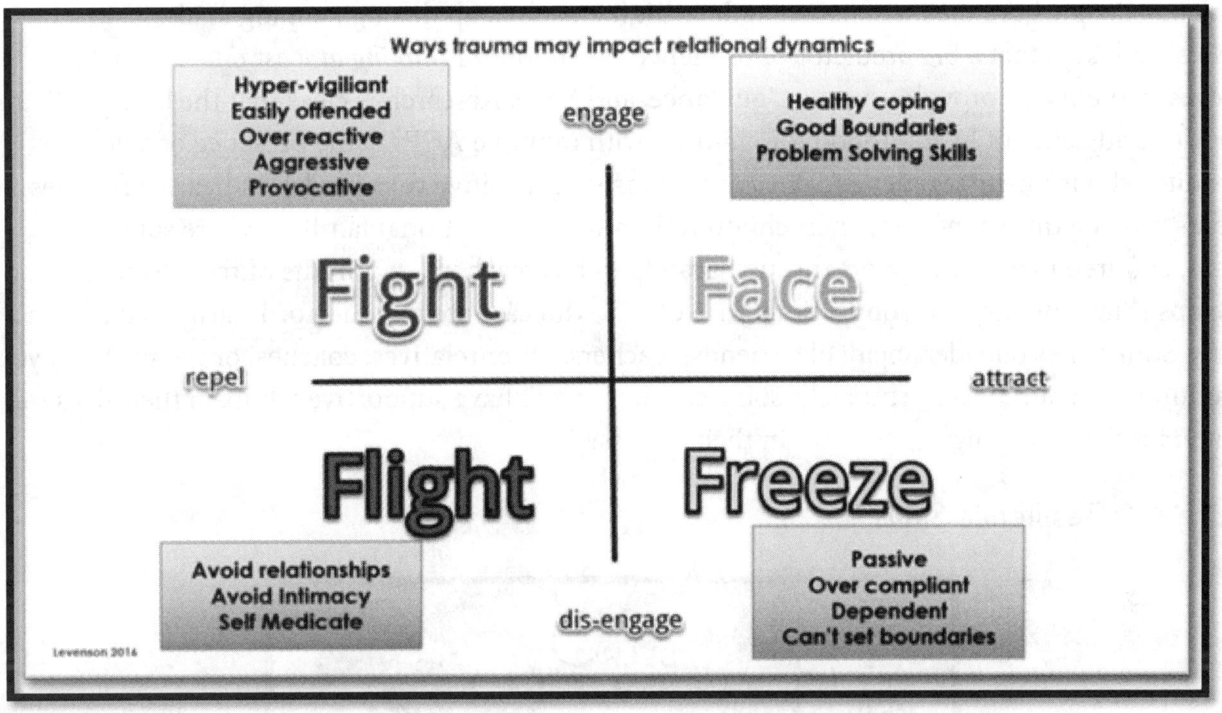

Trauma Can Occur in Adulthood, too.

- ☐ Physical, Emotional, or Sexual Assault / harassment
- ☐ Substance Abuse (or having someone close to you with an addiction)
- ☐ Living in a violent community
- ☐ Discrimination, oppression, racism, marginalization
- ☐ Poverty
- ☐ Domestic Violence
- ☐ Death, accident, injury, illness of self or others
- ☐ Health Problems, hospitalization
- ☐ Divorce
- ☐ Arrest or incarceration of self or loved one
- ☐ Homelessness
- ☐ Other unexpected or traumatic losses
- ☐ Witnessing a traumatic event

Traumatic events in adulthood can produce feelings of fear and powerlessness. PTSD can occur, leading to intrusive images or memories of an event, avoidance of reminders, feeling hyper-aroused (on edge all the time), and having negative thoughts or feelings. These symptoms can persist for a long time, causing distress and interfering with your ability to sleep, work, or relate to others.

Resilience

What can change the outcome for a person who has experienced abuse, mistreatment, losses, or family dysfunction in their life? *Resilience* refers to the ability to bounce back, to recover and move forward. Psychological resilience is a person's ability to effectively manage stress and cope with problems. People have the internal strength to lift themselves up through coping skills.

Research says that a big predictor of resilience for children is *having at least one adult* who believes in them and provides support, guidance, and hope. Research is clear that the best predictor of positive adjustment in adulthood for children with multiple ACEs is the presence of at least one adult who is nurturing, dependable, and a consistent positive role-model. In healthy families, parents provide this support for their children. In more dysfunctional families where support is absent, children may find support through grandparents, teachers, or parents of friends. Resilience develops primarily through connections with others who care about you— ordinarily that is your family. Sometimes outsiders help; like friends, teachers, other relatives, coaches, or people from your community or church. Unfortunately, some children never have supportive adults in their lives to counteract the damaging experiences in their homes.

Figure 4.4: Resilience Skills

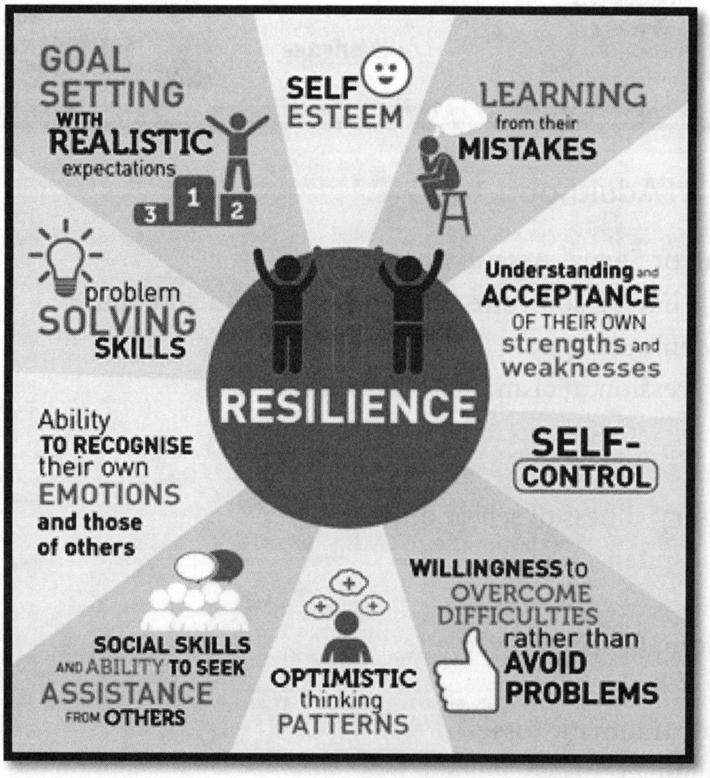

Resilient children learn that sometimes bad things happen but the world is still a safe, predictable, good place. They learn that they can cope with bad things and that hard times will pass. They learn they can rely on others for help when things go wrong. They learn that even after grief or loss, they can still be happy. This is true of resilience in adulthood, too.

It is never too late to build resilience. Through creating and maintaining new, healthy relationships, you can learn to trust. You can establish a network of people you can turn to for company or for help. Over time, as you learn to recognize your strengths, you will increase your hope for the future. You will become more aware of your emotional state and you will learn to regulate your emotions.

Family Dynamics of Child Abuse

Earlier in this chapter you learned about ACEs and the ways childhood trauma can affect people throughout their lives. Here we will talk a little more about child maltreatment, starting with some definitions:

Physical abuse: physical injury caused by an adult caretaker.

Sexual abuse: being asked or forced to do something sexual with an adult or older child.

Neglect: Not being taken care of properly by parents or caretakers.

Emotional abuse: Being put down, ridiculed, humiliated, told you are stupid or bad, forced to accept adult responsibilities as a child, not being supported in your ambitions, not given credit for achievements, not being allowed to express feelings.

Most of us love our parents and feel a loyalty to our families. Most people believe that their parents meant well, were doing the best they could, and didn't mean to hurt them. Usually that is true. Most parents do the best job they can. But children still have feelings about what happened to them. When you focus on things that happened to you and hurt you as a child, what is important are the feelings you were left with that stayed with you—not your ability as an adult to look back and explain why those things happened.

Abuse is any behavior by an adult that causes physical or emotional harm to a child. Harm could be physical: bruises, cuts, welts, burns, broken bones, or internal injuries. Harm can also be emotional: feeling unloved, attacked, abandoned, ignored, dismissed, burdened with responsibility, never good enough, never listened to, blamed for everything. Neglect is the absence of behaviors by adults that can lead to physical or emotional harm to a child. Not watching, not feeding, not listening to, not taking to school are all examples of neglect.

Below is a list of some experiences you may have had.

- ☐ I was frequently physically disciplined as a child beyond normal spanking.
- ☐ As a result of physical discipline, I received bruises, cuts, or welts.
- ☐ As a result of physical discipline, I received burns, broken bones, or internal injuries.
- ☐ I was hit with objects such as a belt, switch, cord, etc.
- ☐ I saw my parents hit each other.
- ☐ I saw my parents hit my sisters or brothers beyond normal spanking.
- ☐ Sometimes I had to protect others in my family from getting hurt.
- ☐ People in my family fought, yelled or screamed a lot, and it scared me.

- ☐ My parents or other family members called me names.
- ☐ My parents told me I was no good and would never amount to anything.
- ☐ My mother or father drank to the point where they were irrational and mean.
- ☐ My mother or father drank to the point where I couldn't talk to them.
- ☐ I was never allowed to speak my mind.
- ☐ I was made to feel I was worthless or bad.
- ☐ I was made to feel stupid.
- ☐ I was punished if I said I was angry or unhappy about something.
- ☐ When I cried they said, "We'll give you something to cry about."
- ☐ When I got hurt someone said I deserved it.
- ☐ I was told I was responsible for the problems in my family.
- ☐ Frequently I didn't have enough to eat.
- ☐ No one ever paid attention to me.
- ☐ My parents didn't care that they were unfair.
- ☐ I was allowed to stay out till all hours, and felt no one cared where I was or what I was doing.
- ☐ I was rarely taken to the doctor when I needed to be.
- ☐ Nobody ever listened to me.
- ☐ I was left alone sometimes as a young child.
- ☐ No parents are perfect… how did your parents let you down?

Any of these experiences might have left you with mixed feelings. Any of them might have hurt and confused you. It is also important to understand that you may have had feelings about things that happened, or didn't happen, that were not a result of bad parenting or bad intentions, but simply unfortunate circumstances. Having a sick family member in your home means that the family's attention is focused on that person. That means the other people, including the children, get less attention. If your father had trouble keeping a job, there may have been constant tension in your home. Your mother might have been so frustrated and so preoccupied with her financial worries that she was always stressed and irritable. If your parents worked long hours, they might have been out of the home a lot, and then too tired to give you attention when they were there. As an adult you can understand why these things would have occurred, but as a child all you know is that no one is paying attention to you. That can feel lonely and scary.

As you got older you may have intentionally isolated yourself from others out of anger and resentment that they weren't there for you and found ways to please yourself. Sex offending may be a way of pleasing yourself that no one can take from you. And it may be a way of getting back at someone who hurt you by rejecting you, not protecting you, or not paying attention to you.

Randy was convicted of raping two colleagues while in the military, and was recently released from prison. In group therapy, at times he adopted a sarcastic attitude which seemed designed to belittle others in a very subtle way. He didn't describe an overtly abusive upbringing, but said that his mother was a police officer and he described her as demanding, rigid, and critical in her approach to parenting her sons. She sometimes verbally abused their father in front of the boys, describing him as a "loser" who didn't make enough money. Randy talked in group about having an "anger problem" which was beginning to surface in his relationship with his new girlfriend.

He began to see that his tendency to respond in a belittling or combative way, especially with women, seemed linked to his relationship with his mother. He explained that her unfair rules, harsh discipline, and dismissive attitude had made him wary of females, whom he viewed as manipulative and controlling. His rape of two women, whom he perceived as "teasing him," was triggered by a desire to overpower women who, in his mind, are trying to deprive him of what he wants, just like his mother did.

Everyone's trauma narrative is different. The point of remembering and talking about experiences of abuse is never to blame anyone else for what you have done or to excuse your offenses. But identifying the things that happened in your childhood is part of understanding how you came to be the person you are. Knowing how you were hurt and expressing that hurt is an equally important part of becoming a whole person. The point is to understand the meaning you attached to your experiences, and what they "taught" you about life, about yourself, and about what to expect from other people.

If you were Sexually Abused as a Child....

Some people who commit sexual crimes were sexually abused as a child or exposed to sexuality early and inappropriately. Again, this abuse does not "explain" or excuse your sexual crimes. It is simply one factor to look at in your attempt to understand your behavior. If you were sexually abused, it is important to understand the ways your past experience of sexual abuse might be related to your crimes.

Many men in treatment say they were not sexually abused. Many, of course, weren't. Some may say they weren't because they are ashamed and have never admitted it to anyone before. Others simply may not remember. There are several reasons why these kinds of experiences are hard to remember. One is that children don't understand sexual abuse well. Anything we don't understand is hard to remember. Another reason is that our mind has a way of protecting us from painful memories by forgetting them.

Some men have been sexually abused but don't even realize it. Many men think of sexual abuse as forced sodomy or oral sex with an older man. Sexual contact with an older girl or a woman may have been seen as "getting lucky." But sexual abuse takes many forms. Even if you weren't raped, forced, penetrated, or physically hurt, you might have been sexually abused. Any sexual contact between an adult and a child, or between or older child and a younger child, is sexual abuse. The older person takes advantage of his or her power over the child to manipulate the child do what he/she wants. The older person uses their position of trust or authority to take advantage of the child's vulnerability, desire to please, and need to feel valued.

If you had any of the following experiences as a child, you were sexually abused:

- ☐ An older person touched me sexually.
- ☐ An older person kissed me sexually.
- ☐ An older person showed me their naked body.
- ☐ An older person asked me to touch them sexually.
- ☐ An older person asked me to perform oral sex.
- ☐ An older person performed oral sex on me.
- ☐ An older person looked at my naked body.
- ☐ I was exposed to pornography at a young age by an older person

Some other experiences that involve boundary violations can shape people's views of sex. These include:

- ☐ People in my family who were older than me walked around naked or semi-naked.
- ☐ Adults around me carelessly had sex within my hearing or sight.
- ☐ I had no privacy in my bedroom or bathroom.
- ☐ People in my family watched me bathe or dress beyond the time I could do those things myself.
- ☐ My parents bathed me even after I could do it myself.
- ☐ I was physically disciplined on my genitals.
- ☐ I was made to stand naked as punishment.
- ☐ Someone in my family made sexual or negative comments about my body.
- ☐ Adults around me told me about their sex life.

How Sexual Abuse Can Affect Child Development

When children are sexually abused, especially during the elementary school years, it throws them off track. Before puberty (usually around age 12), children are not normally thinking about sex. What kids are supposed to be doing is forming relationships with other kids their own age and gender ("peers"). Boys play with boys and girls play with girls. Sexually abused children often find it harder to get along with others their own age. They may feel different, maybe because they are keeping a secret about the abuse. They may avoid playing with other kids.

Children at this age are trying to identify and develop the skills they are good at. They are involved in a lot of activities: sports, lessons, scouts, catching snakes, thinking up ways to annoy their siblings, playing games, riding bikes or skateboards. At this age kids try a lot of different things just to have fun. They are also discovering what they are good at. Being good at something makes children feel good about themself. At the same time, they are focusing educationally on the basic skills they will need to get promoted to the next grade: reading, writing, arithmetic, etc. Children need to focus their energy on learning these skills or they will not succeed in school.

When children this age are being sexually abused, it takes away energy from their developmental tasks (what they are supposed to be doing), and they become focused on the sexual abuse. Maybe they are focusing on the sexual abuse and thinking about it constantly, wondering when it will happen again. Maybe they are focusing on their fear of it happening again. Maybe they think it is their fault and are afraid of getting caught and getting in trouble. Maybe they are confused and anxious, wondering what it is all about, why it is happening to them. They are afraid to talk about it because nobody else does. They feel different from others. They don't have language to describe it.

Feeling different from others and being preoccupied with sex may have kept you from developing the social skills you needed to have good relationships later in life. Maybe you never learned how to be part of a team, or how to do well in school, or even how to be comfortable with other people. Maybe you lost a chance to get really good at some activity because you were busy thinking about the abuse and not knowing what to do about it. And if you felt you had a shameful secret that no one could find out about, you might have pulled back from forming friendships with other kids.
That would have left you feeling isolated, lonely and unacceptable.

Many men who were sexually abused like to tell themselves it didn't affect them. Sometimes they do this because it makes them feel less guilty about the harm they have caused to their victims. Sometimes they just never gave it a thought beyond feeling that they had "gotten lucky." The truth is: If you were sexually abused it probably did affect you in some way, whether you know it or not.

For one thing, it introduced you to sex before you were emotionally ready to handle sex. Maybe it felt good physically, but it was also very confusing. Maybe there were some positive feelings of closeness with the person who abused you. Maybe you wanted to please them. But even these feelings were confusing, because you knew they were involving you in something secretive that you didn't understand. Worse, there were other feelings, bad feelings. Even as a child, when you know you are not supposed to talk about something, you know you are doing something wrong. And when you've participated in any way in something that's a secret or wrong—even by not telling—you feel ashamed.

You may have known you were being abused by the adult but felt helpless to stop it because your abuser was more powerful than you and you were afraid of making him or her angry. If the adult was rough and threatening with you, you may have feared retaliation if you told. Or maybe you didn't want to betray your abuser or hurt their feelings. You may not have felt you could trust anyone else with your secret either. Maybe you tried to hint to your mother or father that something bad was going on, but you weren't sure if they would believe you, weren't sure if they would blame you or the abuser, and weren't sure if they would really protect you.

Feeling helpless in situations of abuse sometimes leaves children determined never to lose control of their lives again. Having once lost control, some children grow up feeling they need to control everything and everyone around them. They might dominate their families like dictators. They intrude into everyone's life, violating family members' boundaries and rights. Sexual abuse can contribute to a controlling, abusive personality style.

It's even more confusing if a part of you liked the attention or affection of your abuser. That wouldn't be surprising, because all children want to be noticed and to feel special, loved, and important. A part of you might have felt you should do something to stop it, but another part of you maybe didn't want it to stop. It might have been the only time someone was nice to you, or that you felt loved. You might have felt loyalty to the abuser and did not want him or her to get in trouble. Sexual abuse can leave a child believing you something wrong, or that you're bad. You may believe today that if anyone else knew about these things, they could never accept you, let alone love you. These are painful feelings.

Sexual abuse may have left you in a kind of emotional time warp, wishing you could stay a child even as you grew older. You may have noticed that you are attracted to children who are about the same age that you were when you were abused. You may associate sexual pleasure with that first sexual experience as a child, or you may feel self-conscious or inadequate with other adults. You may even be afraid of adults. You may notice that you are not able to trust adults as a result of your abuse but can always trust children.

Feeling uncomfortable or sexually unacceptable to other adults would be a natural feeling if you have felt different from other people for many years. Being uncomfortable could also be a result of not developing social skills because you were preoccupied with the early abuse. Through your interactions with others in group therapy, you will have the chance to develop these skills and learn to feel more confident with other adults.

Think about whether you might have experienced sexual abuse as a child, and think about the things you were feeling and thinking while it was happening. This will help you begin to understand how it affected you and how it might have contributed to your sexual offense.

Losses

Loss comes in many forms. The death of a loved one, especially a parent, is the most serious loss a child can face. But other events, such as divorce, moving to a new home, loss of health (either for oneself or for someone in the family), and physical injury can also cause sadness and pain. Any change in a child's life which upsets their sense of stability will shake their feelings of security. Feeling secure means that the world feels like a safe, predictable place and the people around you are consistent, dependable, and non-shaming. If as a child you became insecure due to a loss, that could have been confusing and frightening.

Some other losses are not of the type that are easily identified. For instance, if you were required to take on adult responsibilities at a young age you "lost" part of your childhood (this is sometimes called "pseudo-maturity" or "parentified child"). If you were sick, or overprotected, or were kept out of childhood activities or kept away from friends, you also lost part of your childhood. These losses can hurt. They are real losses and need to be treated as such.

Everyone, whether child or adult, needs to process a loss—that is, to talk about the feelings a loss leaves you with. If you didn't understand your feelings, and no one really explained your loss to you or gave you a chance to talk about how you felt, you couldn't really resolve the loss. That would have left you feeling hurt and confused.

When children lose something or someone important to them, they need to grieve the loss just like adults do. But children need help understanding their grief. If they don't get that help, they can grow up feeling afraid and vulnerable, scared to love or commit for fear of losing someone again and getting hurt again.

Lee described a pretty happy childhood and felt secure in his family until he was 13. Everything changed when his twin brothers, who were 11, were killed in a school bus accident. His parents were so overcome with grief they could barely function. The household became a sad, silent place. His depressed parents were unable to interact with him, perhaps detaching from their surviving son because the pain of losing two children was so great. He was sent to live with his grandparents, who were kind and nurturing, but he felt rejected and abandoned by his parents. He was lonely and sad, but couldn't talk to his grandparents about it because he didn't want to upset them. They already had enough to deal with.

In high school, Lee over-ate because eating was the only thing that gave him pleasure. Because he was so large, girls did not seem to be attracted to him. While babysitting at age 15, a 6-year-old girl sat on his lap and he became aroused. After accidentally discovering this way of sexually pleasing himself, he continued sexually molesting her, and they "bonded" over their secret activities. She looked up to him and made him feel loved.

He didn't really recognize at that point that what he was doing was wrong, because he felt like he was in love with her. As he got older, however, his attractions did not grow older, and he remained attracted to young girls, seeking them out. He found that by taking care of small girls, he could develop a relationship with them, which felt safe, and replaced the connection that was lost with his family after the tragedy.

Some losses you may have never identified include:

☐ I had to take care of my younger sisters or brothers beyond normal babysitting.
☐ I had to take care of my parents as though I were an adult and they were children.
☐ I had responsibilities dumped on me that adults should have handled.
☐ My brothers or sisters got special treatment that I never got.
☐ Sometimes we had nowhere to live.
☐ We moved around a lot.
☐ We moved here from another country.
☐ My parents didn't speak English, and that was embarrassing, and I had to be the "family interpreter"
☐ I had curfews that kept me from having friends.
☐ I had to go to work at a young age and lost my chance to get an education.
☐ My mother or father was sick often and everyone else had to shape their lives around them.
☐ I was sick often as a child and missed out on what other kids did.
☐ I had many hospitalizations and was isolated from people.
☐ When I got hurt no one tried to make me feel better.
☐ I was overprotected by my parents and never allowed to go anywhere.

Exercise 4.2: Identifying Childhood Experiences

Identify and discuss your own childhood experiences of abuse/neglect, loss, or other victimization. Describe any of the experiences discussed on the previous pages that relate to you, or any other similar experiences that you can think of that happened to you.

1. How did you think about these experiences? What do you think they meant about you?
2. How would you define them?
3. How did you deal with losses or significant events in your life?
4. Who helped you by talking to you about your feelings?

Understanding Your Family

Our ways of getting along with others were learned very early in childhood by watching how the people in our lives treated each other and how they treated us. The lessons we learned in our families stay with us and later either help us to form relationships with others or interfere with our ability to form fulfilling relationships. In the exercises at the end of this section you will be asked to describe your family in some detail. Before you can do this, you need to understand what is meant by family rules, *family roles,* and *boundaries.*

Rules

Rules told you what was acceptable in your family. Different families have different rules, some which are spoken and some of which you learn just by watching how people act (unspoken).

Some examples of spoken and unspoken rules might be:

Spoken	Unspoken
Don't hit your sister. Curfew is 11:00 PM. Knock before entering. Come when mother calls you. Don't talk back.	Watch out for dad when he's drinking. Don't complain about anything. Don't bother your mother. Don't talk about family business with outsiders. Don't speak unless spoken to.

Roles

Roles are the "jobs" that family members have—not the kind of "job" you do for money, but the job you do *within* your family. Often these roles are unspoken. Families assign roles to family members. A role creates a type of identity for family members and tells them how they should think about themselves and how others will think about them.

Some examples of spoken and unspoken rules might be:

- Dad is the boss.
- Brother is the "black sheep"
- Big sister is the smart one.
- Little sister is the pretty one.
- Mom is the sickly one.

Children learn that when they act in certain ways—that is, when they conform to their assigned role—their behaviors are accepted and rewarded. When they attempt to create their own identity and reject their role they may be ignored or punished. They learn this by observing the way others treat them. Sometimes these roles are hard to identify because the family members assume them automatically. No one really talks about them; you just come to know what's expected of you. For example, in some families, the boys are expected to be athletes. No one ever says, "You have to be good at basketball." You just know that Dad is going to spend more time with you and treat you with more respect if you get team. If you happen to mention that you won't be playing ball this season because you're joining the science club instead, maybe no one comes right out and says you shouldn't do that, but you might hear a loud silence. So if you really don't care much about basketball but you'd love to learn more about snakes, you're kind of trapped. In some families it doesn't feel like it's okay to be who you really are. So you pretend to be someone else.

Family members' roles define how they are expected to act and how others should react to them. For example, a "bad kid" will always be expected to be bad and may even be blamed for things he didn't do. If your role is to be the bad one, it becomes kind of pointless to try to be good, because no one ever gives you any credit anyway. Why bother to be good? On the contrary, if your role is to be the "perfect" one, that might mean that you're never allowed to express anger or unhappiness, because your parents need you to make them feel they are doing a good job. A family member seen as sickly or "fragile" might be the one that people keep secrets from because that person "wouldn't be able to handle" hearing the truth. The youngest child is sometimes the "baby" all his life, and treated like one. He is pampered with special privileges and overprotected because he is so young and "helpless." This role has some advantages, but what happens when you are growing up and no one takes you seriously? When you come to understand that no one expects you to accomplish anything it can be hard to develop any confidence in yourself.

Families with rigid, fixed roles can cause a great deal of damage. Sometimes one person in the family has a lot of power or control over others. Sometimes another person is the one who really takes care of everyone. There might be one person who always seems to be taken care of. Over time the unspoken roles come to be almost written in stone: Grandmother is in charge; mom takes care of everyone; older sister is the one everyone has to take care of. Here, mom and older sister both suffer: no one ever thinks about what mom needs because she's so "strong," and older sister never learns how to take care of herself because someone else is always doing it for her. Later, when she goes out into the world, she will feel helpless.

As we grow up and leave our families, *we tend to bring our roles along with us.* If we were the one who always kept the peace by stepping into arguments and soothing ruffled feathers, we might bring the skills we developed into our business, where they will benefit us. But if we were the "lost soul" of the family who everyone gave up on because we were "never going anywhere," we may have given up on ourselves. In other cases, the roles are not viewed as negative, but shape how we see ourselves nonetheless.

Santiago was the youngest of five sons and was born years after his next-oldest sibling. When he was 10, his brothers were all out of the house. His father had abandoned the family long ago. His mother, who had been disabled most of her adult life due to a muscular disorder, was confined to a wheelchair. Santiago became her primary caretaker. He loved his mother and accepted the fact that she depended on him for feeding, bathing, and getting around the house. He was kind of lonely, though, because he couldn't socialize with other kids due to his responsibilities at home.

As a teenager, Santiago noticed he was attracted to males. But in the South American country he lived in, being gay was religiously unacceptable, and violent attacks on gay men were common. He suppressed his feelings, and eventually joined the army, where he could be a hero. After the army he married and had children. Later he moved to the U.S.

In his 40s, with his children now young adults, Santiago always had a feeling that something was missing in his life. He felt distant from his wife. He separated from her and moved in with a friend. His friend had a teenage son, and the son's friends often came over to play video games. Santiago found himself drawn to the world of gaming, and to the young teens that surrounded him. He befriended the kids, bought them games, took them places, and allowed them to smoke weed. While playing, he sat close to them, eventually engaging them in sexual touches. He performed oral sex on them, and they seemed to like it. He was shocked when they told an adult and the police came for him.

After his arrest and incarceration, Santiago was in treatment questioning how this all happened. In thinking about his childhood, he realized he'd always been drawn to vulnerable, dependent people. This seemed to come from the identity he developed as a caretaker while he was a youngster taking care of his mom. The caretaker identity was further reinforced by his patriarchal culture, which placed men in the dominant position of providing for women and children. As a natural caretaker, he welcomed the role of "mentor" and "provider" for the teen boys he met while living in his friend's home.

He was also attracted to their boyhood – they seemed to have the teen life that he was denied because he was caring for his mom. He envied them and wanted to "join them" in their teenage activities that he missed out on. At the same time, he was still struggling with the stigma of being gay, leading him to be drawn to "secret" relationships. He couldn't be publicly gay (in his mind), so secret relationships with teen boys seemed like less of a risk of being "outed."

While in treatment, he met a man online while still searching for "secret" gay relationships. He never met the man, but he felt surprisingly close and connected to him. They talked about everything online. After a few months, the man explained that he wanted to start a business and needed money to invest in it. He said they would be business partners. Santiago eagerly began sending him money to help, despite not really knowing who this person was, not seeing a business plan, and not getting reports about the business development and implementation.

His group expressed concern that he was being "catfished." This was a real blow to Santiago and crushed him. When he thought about it, he realized he was repeating his old pattern of "caretaker" – and this time it made him vulnerable to being exploited.

Once he began to talk about and understand the factors in his early life that contributed to his patterns and behavior, he could connect the dots between all these different experiences in his life. He then began to construct a new identity that didn't involve taking care of people. He let go of the shame of being gay, and started to seek relationships with others who wouldn't be dependent and needy, but who could be an equal, mutual partner in a healthy relationship.

Boundaries

Boundaries are unspoken barriers, or limits with regard to one's physical or emotional space. For instance, when a person stands too close to you and you want to back away, you are uncomfortable because the other person is invading your physical boundary. If a guest in your house begins to look through your cupboards, you may also feel that person is invading physical boundaries. If someone you barely know asks you personal questions or tells you personal things about themselves, you may also feel uncomfortable. When you tell that person "it's none of your business," you are protecting your emotional boundaries.

Boundaries define what feels comfortable or acceptable for you. Everyone's sense of boundaries is different; everyone draws a different line around themself. Like an invisible fence, your boundaries are a shield to keep others from intruding where they don't belong. When people don't respect your boundaries, you feel hurt and confused and angry.

Boundary *violations* occur when someone invades your space— physically, sexually, or emotionally. Children don't have the power to protect their boundaries or set limits with others, and so are especially vulnerable to boundary violations. In some families, children aren't allowed to maintain physical boundaries: parents feel free to walk into the bathroom when the door is closed, or walk into their bedrooms when they are changing their clothes. Parents might read a child's personal diary. Even hugging and kissing a child who doesn't want to be hugged or kissed is a boundary violation and can leave that child feeling powerless and resentful.

More commonly, without even realizing it, parents violate children's *emotional boundaries* by not respecting the children's feelings. These violations can be very subtle. For example, when a parent says to a frightened child, "There's nothing to be afraid of, get over it" that parent is trying to be helpful. But part of the message the parent is sending is, "It's not okay to feel the way you do." This usually feels dismissive to a child, and sends them message: Your feelings are wrong, and no one can help you calm down or feel safe. In some families, these violations are more serious. Some parents tell their children, "You'll do what I say and *you'll like it.* If you don't wipe that frown off your face I'll give you something to frown about."

Figure 4.5: Boundaries

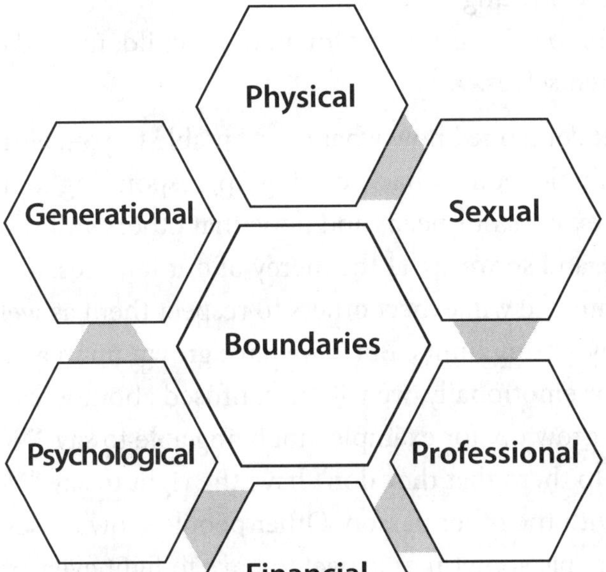

Boundary violations can also occur when generational roles are not clear. Parents and their children live in different emotional worlds. Parents, of course, can place themselves in the child's emotional world because they can understand children. But children cannot simply place themselves in the emotional world of adults. When adults expect a child to behave in ways that are beyond his years, or when a parent expects a child to care for him or her (instead of the other way around), a *generational boundary violation* has occurred. When a parent talks to a child about financial stress, the child worries about something that isn't his problem and that he is powerless to control. When a parent shares with a child about the other parent's infidelity, this is something children should not know about. These are generational boundary violations.

For adults to talk to children about sex to educate them is appropriate. But any time an adult involves a child in their sex life—even by talking about it—or shows a child sexual materials, or asks about the child's sexual experiences, or makes comments about the child's body; these are *generational and sexual boundary violations.* These violations usually leave a child feeling confused and conflicted: on one hand, sexual talk may be exciting. On the other hand, coming from a parent or trusted adult, such talk can leave a child feeling embarrassed, nervous, and even violated. If such violations go on over time a child may feel overwhelmed with fear and confusion, and these feelings may continue to be *associated with sex* in the child's mind as he or she grows up.

Examples of Physical, Emotional, Sexual and Generational Boundary Violations:

- A mother looks through a teenager's phone and reads private messages.
- A child is not allowed to lock the bathroom door for privacy.
- A father watches his teenage daughter shower.
- A mother confides in a child about her husband's infidelity.
- A parent tells a child the details of their sex life.
- A teenage sister walks around the house without a top on
- A father shows porn to his young son.
- A parent always steps in to solve problems for an older child, instead of allowing them to figure it out themselves.

Setting limits is how you let someone know what is acceptable to you, either verbally, by telling them, or non-verbally (for example, pulling back, closing up, responding to intrusive questions with a shrug). As children, we can express our needs and hope that others will respect us, but we don't have much power to set limits, and so we are at the mercy of our families. If we grow up in families that respect our boundaries, later we will expect others to respect them as well—and when they don't, we will demand that they do by setting limits. But if we have grown up in a family that violated our boundaries, either physically or emotionally, we will be confused about what our rights are and how to enforce them. Some people grow up, for example, not being able to say "No" to others without feeling guilty or afraid. It *feels* to them that they don't have the right to say "No"—even when they really don't want to go along with the other person. Other people grow up saying "No" automatically to every request. These people sometimes expect to have to fight everyone to keep from being exploited and violated, and they are ready to do battle. Sometimes they spend their lives fighting battles that never had to be fought—all because they felt violated as children.

In families where boundaries are regularly violated, children grow up with a confused sense of who they are—where they end and others begin. As adults these individuals may display that same boundary confusion with others. We say they show "poor boundaries." Poor boundaries may take the form of either keeping others at a distance (closed, rigid boundaries), or of feeling entitled to be too close to others (open, overly flexible boundaries).

People with closed boundaries don't like to let anyone in: they are afraid if they don't protect themselves other people will move in and "take over." Maybe they grew up with the awful feeling of being controlled, being expected to think and feel as someone else did, and never being allowed to be themselves. They expect others to try to control them and they are not about to let anyone do that again. They often find that their relationships don't really meet their needs—something important is always missing. What's missing is the trust, the closeness, the feeling of really belonging. These are the things that *intimacy* is about. Intimacy is only possible when people really know each other. The closed off person is never completely known by anyone—even their spouse. As a result, no matter how much such a person may love their partner, in their hearts both people are lonely.

People with overly open boundaries have other problems. They don't know where to draw the line with others. When you meet people like this, at first you are impressed with how open and friendly they seem. But then you may start to think, "Well, wait a minute here. I just met you but you're talking like we're old friends. I really don't need to know how much money you make or how you're doing with your cocaine problem. And I definitely don't need to hear about how sick you were last week, when it was 'coming out both ends." You get the uncomfortable feeling that you are being drawn into something you didn't ask for. Part of you might be interested but another part knows something is wrong with this picture.

And there is something wrong, because once this stranger has poured out all this personal information, guess what? It's your turn! Now they want to know all your personal stuff, whether you're comfortable talking about it or not. It's a setup. Now *your boundaries are being violated,* but you feel guilty not spilling the beans, because after all, they told you all their personal stuff. You are being manipulated and controlled by someone whose boundaries were never respected and who doesn't respect anyone else's boundaries. If you don't pull away from people like this, next they'll be doing "favors" for you—favors you haven't asked for and don't even want, and then they will likely expect something from you in return. And then getting mad at you when you don't want to reciprocate!

Sometimes people whose boundaries were violated as children have no clear sense of their own identity and may desperately need the acceptance and approval of others to feel like somebody. They become "people pleasers" because the possibility of rejection puts them in a panic: they will do anything to avoid the emptiness they feel when they can't be close to others. When they feel rejected (and sometimes even the smallest slight can make them feel rejected), it can feel to them like they don't even exist—they are "non-entities," nobodies. Of course, when you are dependent on others for your very sense of existence, you may find yourself being angry a great deal of the time. After all, others have their own lives, and may not understand how needy you are.

A therapist who brought her therapy dog to group sessions noticed that a young male client was holding the dog tightly on his lap while the dog struggled to get free. The counselor casually said, "Barry, I think the dog wants to get down." The client replied, "But I want to hold him." The therapist gently said, "I can see that you are feeling like you need to cuddle with the dog right now, but he seems to need to get down." Another group member observed, "You're violating his boundaries, man!"

This led to an excellent group discussion about how to handle it when you want something, and someone else wants something different. What are the obvious, non-verbal, or other clues that someone is trying to let you know they want something different? How do you get what you need while also respecting the needs of others? Barry was able to see how what he was doing with the dog could be related to sexual violations of others.

Further exploration revealed that Barry's mother, a well-meaning "helicopter parent," frequently crossed his boundaries physically (e.g. going through his belongings, entering his room without knocking) and emotionally (enabling his financial dependence on her by constantly giving him money but then criticizing and demeaning him for not budgeting). The group helped Barry explore how he felt when these things happened, and he was able to conclude that he needed to work on maintaining a healthy separation between himself and his mother, for starters, and practice good boundaries with other people as well.

Sometimes people with confused boundaries have given up on getting their needs met by others. If you have been a loner you might learn something important from trying to figure out why. Were your boundaries violated in your family, or were you able to develop your own identify? Does being alone feel safer than having relationships?

In families where boundary violations occur, children become confused about what proper boundaries are. They may feel that they need and deserve privacy, for example, but if adults are violating this boundary, the children learn they are helpless to enforce the boundary. Any time people feel helpless to change situations that seem unfair they will become angry.

Entitlement

Individuals who grow up angry and confused—maybe because they have felt violated—may try to seize back from others some of the control they feel they were denied. *They may grow up with the idea that it is okay to violate others' boundaries.* In their anger and their need for control, they may convince themselves they have the right to take from their children what they lost in their own childhood. Or they may feel that some people deserve to be violated just because they are too weak to protect their own boundaries.

Of course they are not admitting to themselves what they are doing or why. It just *feels* to them that they have the right to own some part of that other person, to take it for themselves and to ignore the hurt they are causing the other person. Sometimes growing up in a family where your needs weren't met can lead to a sense of entitlement: *"I'll take what I can get when I can get it."* Deprivation can breed entitlement: *"I have to take what I want because no one will give it to me."*

Dr. Alice Boyes described entitlement in a Psychology Today Blog. You can read it at Link 4.1.

She described how entitled people expect that rules that apply to others shouldn't apply to you. That they feel annoyed when others ask for favors, but also expect that others should be willing to do favors for them. They expect others to be interested in them, but see their own interests as much more interesting than others. They may talk a lot about themselves, but have little curiosity about others. The often disregard rules if they feel the rules aren't important to them, or unfair, or shouldn't apply. They might feel okay about taking things from others, like using programs to download movies for free rather than paying for them, or taking credit for someone else's idea. They may inconvenience others without caring about the effects on them. They think it's okay to say or do whatever they want, not caring if it upsets or offends other people. You see people who like to keep the peace as weak. They want to be recognized as right, strong, and smart – expecting to take leadership positions, even when someone else would be better suited.

Exercise 4.3: Entitlement: Do Any of These Characteristics Seem Like You? (check in box if "yes")

Modified from: Links 4.1 & 4.2

	Check if Yes
1. You make demands of your family, children, friends, acquaintances, lovers, employees, and/or employers.	☐
2. You tend to feel sorry for yourself if things don't work out the way you wanted, and let others know this in melodramatic, attention-seeking ways.	☐
3. People have called you a "bully", "manipulative", "ruthless", "egotistical", "vain", or a "liar".	☐
4. You believe that you deserve happiness and go to great lengths to ensure that happens, sometimes at the expense of others.	☐
5. You punish people when they don't give you what you want either passive-aggressively (e.g. silent treatment, spreading rumors) or aggressively (e.g. yelling, verbal or physical abuse).	☐
6. You believe you have the right to do anything that helps you succeed.	☐
7. You see other people as competitors or "threats".	☐
8. You have double-standards in the ways you behave or interact with other people (e.g. I can be late and forget my duties and commitments, but YOU can't; I can disrespect you, but YOU can't disrespect ME.)	☐
9. You tend to take more than you give in friendships and relationships.	☐
10. You feel you have to look out for yourself, your needs, and desires.	☐
11. It's hard for you to compromise or negotiate a solution that works for all people involved.	☐
12. You sometimes request special treatment of some sort.	☐
13. People often seem to be offended or upset by what you do or say.	☐
14. You generally think that you are better, or more important, than other people and that other people should recognize this.	☐
15. You expect admiration and validation.	☐
16. You tend to assert your dominance or superiority over other people	☐

After looking at the entitlement items you checked off, think about when, where and how you tend to behave that way.

- What does that tell you about how other people might view you?
- Think about you? Feel when you are around?
- Why do you think you tend to act this way? (Think about your childhood, your family, and what you learned about boundaries from your life experiences)
- Are these behaviors consistent with how you want to be seen? (why or why not?)
- Are they consistent with the kind of person you want to be? (why or why not?)

Exercise 4.4: Explore and Discuss Your Family of Origin Patterns of Interaction.

Write about your family, including who you lived with growing up, the number of siblings, the education and work-life of family members, and significant events in your life.

- How would you describe your father? How would you describe your mother?
- How would others describe your parents?
- What was your mother's role in the family?
- What was your father's role in the family?
- What was your role in your family?
- Did your siblings have special roles?
- Did family members talk to each other easily?
- How was anger expressed?
- How was love expressed?
- How did your parents get along?
- What role did extended family (grandparents, etc.) play?
- What were the important values in your family?
- How was conflict handled?
- How were you disciplined when you misbehaved?
- How did you get along with your siblings?
- What kinds of attitudes did your family have about outsiders?
- What kinds of things did your family fight about?
- Did anyone in your family have special problems?
- How were these problems handled?
- Who was the boss in your family? How did you know?
- How would you describe your family's boundaries? (physical, sexual, emotional, and generational).
- Were your boundaries violated by anyone? In what way(s)?
- How did you feel when your boundaries were violated?

If Treatment Is About Feeling Better, Why Does It Feel So Bad?

Some men feel that treatment emphasizes negative events in their pasts and ignores the good things. The truth about everyone's childhood, of course, is that there were good and bad experiences. The worst childhood had some happy times, and the best had hard times.

Sometimes people don't want to think about things in their lives that have hurt them. They say: "Why dig up all that bad old stuff? What good will it do? I want to forget that stuff and move on with my life." It is important to understand that to whatever extent you struggle with your feelings now, to whatever extent your life feels out of control and doesn't feel satisfying, it may mean that you never properly dealt with the feelings you had early in your life. You may never have had a chance to talk about them or make sense of them. Understand this: you were not born to be unhappy. If you have not been happy in your life it does not mean that you can't be happy. In fact, whatever you have been through, whatever you believe, there is *never any reason* that you can't start to have a satisfying life as soon as you decide you are no longer going to accept being unhappy. Dealing with painful feelings is the first step toward that new life.

Many children don't have anyone who will listen to them if they are confused or upset. That means they have to keep all their feelings to themselves. That's not only painful, but also means they can't make sense of confusing things in their lives. Those children grow up still confused and afraid of their feelings, because bad feelings that make no sense are too painful to think about. So those feelings get "stuffed." They get "forgotten." Only they don't really get forgotten, because they are still active inside. They can make you depressed or angry or afraid and you never know why you have those feelings. When you don't understand what's going on inside of you, you feel out of control.

Sadness and Depression

We all have a tendency to use the words "sad" and "depressed" as if they mean the same thing. Actually they are very different. Sadness is a feeling that is a response to loss or change or hurt. Sadness is a normal part of everyone's life. It is unavoidable. Anything that can make us happy will make us sad if we lose it.

Depression is not a normal part of life. Depression is not a feeling but the *absence of feelings*. Depression happens when we numb ourselves to feelings. In its extreme form it feels like complete emptiness, hopelessness, and worthlessness. To a depressed person, life is not sad. It is meaningless. Nothing matters. Nothing feels good. There is an absence of joy and hope.

Depression affects everything about a person's life. It affects their feelings: there are none. It affects their thinking: they begin to think there is nothing good about life, nothing good about themselves, and nothing good about their future. It affects their behavior: they find they don't want to do anything. They sleep all the time, or can't sleep at all. Or they spend their time trying to find anything that can make them feel good, even if only for a few minutes: drugs, drink, eating, sex.... As you have seen in the section on addictions and compulsions, turning to something that feels good instead of dealing with the source of bad feelings sets the stage for loss of control and loss of freedom.

Many people carry a form of low-level persistent depression with them all their lives without even realizing it. They may function and they may hold a job, but they get no joy from life. If you have grown up afraid to know what's inside you, afraid to feel your feelings, afraid to be who you are, you probably have been depressed. One thing you will learn in this program is that you don't have to be depressed. You don't have to be afraid of your feelings. You're not a child anymore. Your feelings can't hurt you. When you allow yourself to start feeling your feelings, including your sadness, you start to come alive. Surprisingly, when you can feel sad, you can stop being depressed. Depression is an illness, and when it persists and interferes with your life, sometimes medication is helpful.

Expressing Feelings

Women are fond of saying: "Men never express their feelings." Of course, that's a crock. Men express feelings all the time. A good tackle brings a "Yeah!" (pleasure, enthusiasm). A missed extra point brings moans and groans *(unhappiness, anger, frustration, despair)*. A field goal in the closing seconds that pulls your team ahead seals the emotion-filled day *(happiness, triumph, pride)*. So what are women talking about, anyway? Maybe they just need to be in the right place at the right time to hear men let out their feelings on the really important stuff.

The truth is that most men do fine expressing certain emotions. Some men are terrific at expressing anger. Other men are good with excitement and enthusiasm. What most men aren't very good with is feelings that make them feel weak. Feelings like sadness or fear or pain aren't in the men's handbook. What is in the men's handbook is: *"No one likes a wimp. Grow up. Quit whining and get over it!"*. Everyone knows that real men, like James Bond, or Captain Kirk, are always in control. Right? To be a man is to always give the appearance of being in control. So if you've spent a lifetime being in control, or at least acting like you are, it's not surprising that you would be out of practice talking about the feelings that remind you of when you were small and helpless—when you had no control. But some men have felt helpless and have been hurt by others. It you were hurt as a child, you probably want to just forget about it.

But, ultimately, remembering and talking about those very feelings turns out to be exactly what it takes to get rid of them. That's the catch! Feelings are like a form of energy. When they don't get used—when they don't get expressed in some way, either by talking about them or writing about them or crying about them—they come out in some other way. They don't just disappear.

It's easy to see this with anger. With anger your choices are 1) talk it out, 2) act it out (putting your fist through a wall, say, or shouting at someone), or 3) it eats you up. Lots of people say they just "forget" about things that make them angry. They may not keep those things in their conscious mind, but that doesn't mean they're forgotten. It's energy. It doesn't just go away. It has to go somewhere.

Sometimes we carry our feelings with us for a long time before they come out. Some people believe they sometimes do things for no reason—like blowing up, but a blow up that happens one week, apparently for no reason, might be the expression of anger that has been accumulating for months or even years before it comes out. Nobody blows up for no reason. If you've been forgetting things that bother you; that's a reason to blow up.

It's not easy to see the effects of ignoring the hurts you have suffered. This is why we spend so much time talking about feelings in group sessions. This is why we want you to talk about things you'd rather not think about, never mind talk about. Just like anger, feelings of sadness and hurt have energy that doesn't go away. That energy can take a lot of forms, from feelings of being "not good enough," to confusion, to mistrust, to depression, to drinking and drugging, to sex offending. Feeling out of control is frequently being out of touch with your feelings. Recognizing those feelings and expressing them in the group is an important part of becoming whole and seeing hope instead of hopelessness.

The first step in being able to change your behavior, your thinking, and your life is to acknowledge your feelings and to accept that you have a right to feel them, whatever they are. Sometimes this is not a simple task. If you're not in the habit of focusing on your feelings you might not even be able to identify them. We all have lots of feelings.

Here is a list of some feelings that everyone experiences. Looking at the feeling list can help you identify and put a word to some of the things you feel inside.

Figure 4.6 Feeling List

empty	resentful	excited	relaxed
weird	confused	abandoned	furious
worried	angry	anxious	betrayed
glad	concerned	satisfied	lonely
nervous	deprived	curious	afraid
sad	fearful	frightened	depressed
unhappy	elated	foolish	embarrassed
ashamed	good	rejected	accepted
discouraged	encouraged	joyful	happy
bored	stupid	smart	sexy
love	special	ecstatic	inadequate
insecure	unwanted	undesirable	blamed
different	hate	guilty	victimized
entitled	suicidal	thankful	disgusted
overwhelmed	jealous	suspicious	defiant
hurt	controlled	manipulated	threatened
frustrated	understood	enraged	trapped
tired	degraded	proud	humiliated
powerless	helpless	intimidated	Important
Amused	misunderstood	panicked	shy

Learning to Accept Feelings

Children have many feelings about the things that happen to them. Sometimes their feelings go unnoticed by other family members. Sometimes parents can make children feel as though their feelings are unimportant without even realizing it; for example, by saying, "Oh, don't be silly...." or "That wasn't so bad...." or "There's nothing to be afraid of!" Even when they are said with good intentions, these kinds of statements are boundary violations. They give the message: "I'll tell you how you should feel."

Sometimes when children aren't given an opportunity to have their feelings listened to and understood, they stop trying to express their feelings. Or they begin to express feelings in indirect ways. For example, a child who feels angry at home but can't express it verbally may begin to start fights at school, or steal, or destroy property.

*Your feelings are **always** acceptable.* You can't help how you feel but you can control how you behave and you can change the way you think about things. You have a right to your feelings and others should be willing to try to understand how you feel. If you were never encouraged or supported as a child in expressing your feelings, it is not surprising that you would grow up not being very good at it. You might not feel that you even have a right to express your feelings. Over the years you may have convinced yourself that feelings are not important and that you have no need to express your feelings.

Another common problem with feelings occurs when, as children, we learn that feelings are something we don't want to have. This can happen when the negative feelings are more frequent and more intense than the positive ones. Who needs feelings when they just hurt?

When children have grown up in abusive or neglectful homes, or when they have suffered intense losses and have not had help in resolving those losses (because no one ever talked to them or listened to them), they may have had feelings that were so intense and so painful they simply had to numb themselves. Overwhelming feelings that you have during childhood, when you don't have the power to change the things that are making you feel bad, can leave you feeling helpless and *afraid of your own feelings.* You may have had to escape from these overwhelming feelings by simply *turning them off.* Over the years you may have noticed that you just don't feel much of anything—not happy, not sad, not excited, not afraid—nothing. You may have decided that it's okay to be that way because at least you don't feel pain. Now a part of you believes strongly that reawakening your feelings will be a big mistake. As you have read this book you have said to yourself, "Maybe feelings are important for some people, but I'm just fine the way I am."

While you are in this program no one will judge you for being who you are. The program is about changing your abusive behaviors, and as long as you do that you can succeed. But if all you take with you is how to avoid hurting others, you may be short-changing yourself. Life isn't just about *moving away* from bad stuff. To be worth anything, life has to also be about moving toward something that you want, something that makes life worth living. Being cut off from your feelings and choosing to stay that way is a statement that you expect the bad to always outweigh the good, and that life is only about avoiding pain.

There may be good reasons why you feel this way. You don't have to protect yourself the way you once did. You're not a child anymore. You aren't powerless to change situations that make you feel bad. You can choose your friends and acquaintances. No one can hold you down and abuse you anymore. If you let yourself feel again you will feel pain. But it won't be the same overwhelming pain of childhood; the pain of powerlessness and helplessness. And along with the pain will come other feelings that are worth the price. Should you go through your whole life never feeling joy or pride or love—just because your childhood was painful?

If you are willing to feel your feelings you will start to gain a new, and much clearer, sense of who you are. Maybe for the first time you will start to trust yourself, because your life will make much more sense to you. Even then, though, if you are not expressing your feelings to others you will continue to feel isolated and powerless. Without even being aware of it, you might be in the habit of hiding your feelings. Or you might express feelings in ways that make your life more difficult and more painful (for example, expressing anger through violence). *You might also express feelings in ways that aren't very effective in letting others know what you need from them.*

Notice that the men who have been in treatment for a while and are using the group to improve their lives are more comfortable talking about their feelings. One of the most important reasons for having therapy in groups is to give everyone a chance to talk to others about what is really important in their lives: how they feel. Use this opportunity. If you start to talk about the real you it not only will feel like you are starting to come alive, but it will change the way you look at the future as well. When you know yourself, when you accept yourself, when you can let others know who you are—all things become possible.

Exercise 4.5: Identify and Discuss Feelings About Your Family and Childhood

Think about all the things you described in the last exercise. Answer the following questions and add anything else that seems important to you.

1. What were some of the feelings you had about each experience?
2. What were some of the feelings you had about interacting with your family?
3. How did you express your feelings?
4. How did others react when you expressed your feelings?
5. How would you have liked others to respond to your feelings?
6. Discuss three of the significant childhood events that stick out in your mind.
7. Discuss how you felt about these events.
8. How did others in your family express feelings?
9. How did you know how other people felt?

Learning About Your Needs

"Needs" is a word that takes on a special meaning when we are considering our emotional well-being. Typically when we use the word "need" we mean just that: without it we will die. And, of course, we do have those needs. We call them "survival needs." Everyone can easily recognize the survival needs. But in order to have a life that feels worth living, we must do more than just survive. We also have lots of emotional "needs" that must be met. We won't die if they're not met. But we might as well be dead, because we won't be truly alive. Emotional needs are the driving forces of our lives. Everything we do is an attempt to meet some emotional need—even if we are completely unaware of that need.

Without emotional needs we would not be motivated to do anything. We would have no wants, no desires, and no fantasies. We would be like robots.

Psychologist Abraham Maslow said that all humans have the same basic needs. These needs include survival, physical and psychological safety, social connection, self-esteem, and self-actualization. Maslow arranged these needs into what looks like a pyramid, with the foundation on the bottom and everything else resting on it. The needs are considered hierarchical, which is a fancy way of saying there is an order to them. The needs on the bottom of the pyramid are the most basic and the most urgent, and must be met before we can turn our attention to other, higher level needs. This is easy to see at the bottom-most levels. For example, if you don't have water, you will not be thinking about anything but finding water. If you live in a war zone (where you're feeling unsafe and insecure), you will not be worried about self-esteem. You will want only safety. As we will see, the different needs are related to each other, either directly or indirectly.

Figure 4.7: Maslow's Hierarchy Of Needs

When it comes to emotional needs, we are all surprisingly similar. Our needs vary in intensity from one person to the next. But we are all the same species and we all have the same ***basic needs***. These are general categories of needs. As you think about your own needs, you will find that you have specific needs that fit into one or another of these broad categories. And some of your specific needs can "spill over" into several levels of the hierarchy. For example, you may have needed your mother to recognize your athletic ability. This need for attention and respect would fit into the "Love and Belongingness" level in the hierarchy, but might also have affected your self-esteem. Or you may need your partner to understand that rejecting your sexual advances makes you feel insecure about their commitment to you. Feeling accepted and wanted by your partner is both a love and belongingness need. But since your partner is involved in your sense of security as well, not feeling close to them makes you feel insecure. Let's look more closely at the needs in the figure above.

Survival Needs: Food, water, warmth, shelter from the elements, health, sleep. These are physiological needs. They are the fundamental needs for life, and don't vary from person to person. They are at the bottom of the pyramid because if these needs aren't met, nothing else matters: the individual dies. Even the U.S. and other advanced countries, people can still suffer from homelessness and food insecurity. In fact, many RSOs in some states are prevented from living near schools and parks, and this leads them to become homeless. When you are focused on surviving, you are living in a state of fear.

Notice that sex, although a physiological (bodily) process, is not on this list because a human can survive without having sex. Some people live their entire lives without sex, usually for religious or philosophical reasons.

Safety and Security Needs: These needs are placed on the second level of the hierarchy because, next to the basic needs for life, they are the most urgent needs we have. *Safety,* of course, involves protection from harm or danger. When we feel unsafe, we are fearful. The power of fear is unmistakable. When we are fearful, we will keep watching, hoping to learn how we can stay safe. We must be safe and we must feel safe. We might worry about other people making us unsafe.

Related to safety, but slightly different, is security. Security is about predictability, about a sense that we will remain safe, not only physically, but also economically and emotionally. Security is about a lot of things: reliability, continuity, freedom from want, and freedom from coercion are a few of these things. Privacy and protection from intrusion are others. Security means having a job, having skills that will allow you to find a new job if you lose the one you have, having money in the bank, and having trustworthy people in your life. Security means, having a handle on your life, being able to direct it the way you want it to go, and not fearing it could be torn away from you. When things or people are unpredictable, it makes you uncomfortable because you don't know what to expect. Information and understanding are security needs as well, and so the importance of science and religion are both designed to help us make sense of the world around us.

Love and Belonging Needs: Central to our need for safety and security is the need to belong. Being part of a group (family, neighborhood, church, school) makes us safer and more secure because we have other people we can turn to for help (and protection if necessary). But think about some of the other things we get from other people: acceptance, attention, approval, affection, comfort, companionship, and desire, just to name a few. Other people can make us feel wanted or needed. Only other people can make us feel important or special.

We are social animals. We are not okay being by ourselves for long periods. We need company. If you think about how we fit into the animal world, we are puny and helpless. We have no natural weapons. Only by joining together were we able to survive before we had tools. The same need for connection is what makes our lives meaningful today. We need to feel wanted and secure in our family or group, believing that people care about us. We need to have friends; feel close to others (intimacy), to know and be known by others, to feel valued and accepted by others. Having "status" allows you to feel admired and accepted by others. As we will see in a later section on understanding sex, it is our love and belongingness needs that make sex so powerful. We use sex to try to meet many of these needs.

During the COVID quarantine of 2020 people experienced isolation from one another. When we couldn't go out and socialize, we connected through social media and video chatting. We connected to others through our shared experience and that helped get us through it. But people who lived alone really felt the isolation strongly. And research shows that Pornhub visits surged during the COVID isolation! Why do you think that happened?

<u>Self-Esteem Needs:</u> Having "high" self-esteem means feeling good about yourself and the things you do, believing in yourself, valuing yourself, recognizing your accomplishments and good qualities, feeling competent to deal with life, feeling worthy of being accepted by other people. You will learn more about self-esteem later in this chapter.

<u>Self-Actualization Needs:</u> Realizing your potential, developing your talents and skills to their fullest, understanding and becoming who you were meant to be, contributing to the world and/or to the next generation, and being able to explore and enjoy life fully and take reasonable chances to develop the richest possible life. (Actually, the Army said it best: *"Be all that you can be."*)

You can use Link 4.3 to take the Self-Actualization Quiz:
https://www.scottbarrykaufman.com/characteristics-of-self-actualization-scale/

Exercise 4.6: Identify and Describe Your Needs According to Maslow

Using the chart below, identify and describe your needs according to Maslow's Hierarchy, and how you meet them (or how they might NOT be getting met).

Survival	
Safety and Security	
Love and Belonging	
Self-esteem	
Self-actualization	

Many people go through their entire life without ever stopping for a minute to ask what they really need to be happy. If you don't even know what your needs are, what are your chances of getting them met?

It is important to think about and recognize your needs. Of course, not all needs can be met immediately. We may work a lifetime toward achieving some needs (such as the self-actualization needs). As adults we understand this, and practice what is called *frustration tolerance or delayed gratification,* which means that we can be patient and keep focused on long-term goals instead of expecting rewards for everything we do. If we recognize and respect our needs as valid and important, we will keep focused on working toward meeting them. When things don't go the way we want them to, we can figure out other ways to get the things we need.

Your Needs as a Child

When a child's needs are not met in a consistent, predictable way, he learns not to expect his needs to be met. Of course, this doesn't mean that children should always get everything they want; it means that in a stable, healthy environment, children need to know that they can depend on the adults around them to provide the fundamental things. If this happens consistently, it also means that at isolated times when a child's needs do not get met, this can lead to positive skills: coping with distress, tolerating frustration, delaying gratification, and learning to self-soothe.

Children are completely dependent on adults. They need to know that they will be taken care of. When their fundamental needs are not met, children will begin to feel some of the negative feelings described on the previous pages—especially helplessness, powerlessness, betrayal, distrust, depression and anger. These feelings can stay with a child as they grow up. They may carry these feelings throughout their life. They may not even know that they feel different from other people—they may simply believe that life is about helplessness and anger. Earlier in this chapter you learned about "relational trauma" which is caused when kids feel betrayed, not validated, or when their attachments to important people in their lives are disrupted. Relational trauma occurs when caregivers are needed and at the same time *dangerous or unavailable*. This makes it very hard to trust others and to feel safe.

Children learn to survive in their environments. They learn what they have to do to get some of their needs met. Sometimes these strategies work well in childhood, but become counter-productive in the adult world. Behaviors that worked in a child's family but later interfere with his ability to achieve happiness are called *maladaptive coping behaviors.* Keeping your mouth shut may have protected you from punishment as a child, but when you try to use this strategy with an adult partner who is angry with you, it means that you can't communicate effectively to solve problems together.

Sometimes situations occur in the present, which trigger feelings similar to those that occurred in the past. Especially when something frustrates us, we may feel small and helpless, just as we did as children. Instead of recognizing that we are not helpless children anymore and can act to get our needs met, we react automatically in the same ways we did as children—with anger and hurt. That can lead to lashing out at someone and hurting them. Remember fight, flight, or freeze? Which do you tend to use? Violence can be a product of people feeling helpless and angry, or sometimes people use escape behaviors to avoid feeling the frustration of not being able to meet their needs. They simply shut down, or isolate themselves from others. Or they turn to pleasurable behaviors can take the focus off their painful feelings. Drug or alcohol use, gambling, overeating, or sexual behaviors provide short-term good feelings. As we have seen, when these behaviors are used as substitutes for meeting emotional needs, they can easily end up being destructive.

Sometimes people, without even realizing it, create situations that are similar to old family patterns—even hurtful patterns—because these patterns are familiar to them and they feel like they know what to expect.

Some examples:

A man grew up feeling that he could never please his mother. He felt like a failure and believed that anything he did was never good enough. Later, in his marriage, even though his wife seemed to appreciate him, he always felt as though he was not providing enough for her. He began to believe his wife's loving acceptance of him was phony and pitying. He began to turn to his stepdaughter for affection and sex because he felt he didn't have to prove anything to her. She was always affectionate and unconditionally loving to him. She was easy to please. The sexual abuse helped him meet needs for affection, attention, and importance that were missing in his marriage.

A young boy lives in a home where whenever he talks about what he would like, someone makes him feel that he is being selfish. If he tries to talk about his feelings, no one wants to hear it. If he is unhappy about anything, he is told he's ungrateful. When he's hurt, they tell him to toughen up. As an adult he finds himself in a lousy job, afraid to ask for a raise or promotion, feeling he doesn't deserve any better. He finds himself unable to talk to his wife about his feelings or his innermost thoughts. On the outside the marriage looks okay, but his relationship with her is superficial. The man is so afraid to reveal himself due to fears of rejection that he is unable to have a truly intimate relationship with her. When he peeps into houses, he can get what he wants without having to ask and without risking being denied.

Sometimes one of the hardest things for adults to accept is that you can never get back some of the things you didn't get in childhood. We can learn, however, to get what we need in ways that are appropriate and realistic in adult intimate relationships.

Exercise 4.7: Exploring Your Needs

Explore ways you learned to get your needs met, including ways you have used sex or sexual assault to meet your needs.

1. List some of the things you need from relationships now.
2. List some of needs that went unmet in your childhood.
3. Are there some similarities?
4. How do you feel when your needs are not met?
5. How were your needs met or unmet in your childhood?
6. How do you get your needs met now, in healthy or in unhealthy ways?
7. When your needs are not met, how do you let someone know?
8. What do you say? What do you do?
9. What kinds of non-verbal messages do you send?
10. Can you think of some maladaptive ways you have attempted to get your needs met, and why?
11. Describe some of the negative feelings you sometimes have and identify what kind of needs they create, and what kinds of behaviors you engage in to meet those needs.
12. In what ways has sex, or sexual assault, helped to satisfy some of your needs?

More About Self-Esteem

As we said earlier, *self-esteem* refers to the way we feel about ourselves. If we like ourselves, if we are proud of ourselves and believe in ourselves, we say we have high self-esteem. If we are ashamed, if we feel "not good enough," if we hide from other people because we are sure that if they really knew us they wouldn't like us -- we have low self-esteem.

Low self-esteem underlies many problems. If you don't like yourself then you don't believe you deserve good things. If you don't believe in yourself then you don't stand up for yourself. You don't expect people to listen to you or to think you have anything worthwhile to say. If you don't trust yourself, you can't trust anyone else. In the Introduction to this book we talked about the importance of being willing to take some risks. But if you don't believe in yourself or trust your judgment, you can feel paralyzed. Low self-esteem makes the idea of taking risks seem overwhelming.

Worst of all, if you have low self-esteem you feel unlovable. You can't imagine anyone wanting you for yourself. You may have given up on the idea of finding a loving partner. All the talk in this book about healthy relationships and finding intimacy may seem like empty words to you. If you have bought into the idea that being labeled a felon or a RSO makes you a bad person, you might even believe that no one could possibly love you. What's the point, you might ask, of even thinking about finding a loving partner?

Thinking about making important changes in the direction of your life is what this program is all about. Imagining all the things you would like from life and picturing yourself in that life, a life that is fulfilling and meaningful and worthwhile, are the first steps in moving toward that life. When you can't even imagine having good things in your life because you've never felt worthy of good things, you feel helpless to move toward anything. It may cause you see this program as just about giving up things, avoiding things, and staying away from things that have given you pleasure.

Understand that making changes in your life is not something that some people "can" do and some people "can't." *It doesn't matter where you have come from or what you have done in the past.* You can have the good things other people have. Men and women who have graduated from this program can tell you that. When it comes to creating a better future for yourself the only real questions are: "How much do you want to change?" and "How hard are you willing to work?"

Changing Low Self-Esteem

Improving your self-esteem, like anything that's worthwhile, involves commitment and work. It is not a mystical or mysterious process, and it's not a process that works for some people but not for others. As soon as you decide that you're sick of feeling bad about yourself, you're sick of not standing up for yourself, and you're sick of hiding from other people, you can start to change all that.

There are three steps to the process. The **first step** involves understanding where your low self-esteem came from. The **second step** involves recognizing how your present thoughts connect to the ways of thinking you developed in the past, and changing that thinking. The **third step** is to change the ways you act when you are confronted with a problem. You will learn how to change your distorted, unrealistic thinking to reasonable, realistic thinking. You will learn how to change your behaviors in ways that will create new feelings in you, feelings of liking yourself and respecting yourself. Once you understand how you control your feelings about yourself, whenever you find yourself feeling down on yourself in the future, you will know exactly what to do to change that feeling.

Step One: *Understanding How Your Past Shaped Your Narrative (your "story")*

For most people with low self-esteem, the process began early on. We've talked about the sadness and the pain of not feeling loved or valued in your family, and the ways your self-image and your identity get shaped by such early experiences. Low self-esteem frequently begins with abusive or uncaring parents or caretakers. Physical abuse, emotional abuse, and sexual abuse are all highly destructive to self-esteem. All abuse is humiliating and degrading to children. It leaves them wondering what they did to deserve being treated so badly and how they could be so worthless. This becomes your self-narrative: your "story" of yourself.

We've also talked about families that are not abusive, but are not loving or attentive. The simple fact is that children need love and attention in order to learn to value themselves. When parents treat children as though they are not important, not special, not lovable, the children learn to think of themselves in those ways. In families where the children are required to conform to the needs or expectations of adults (like taking on adult responsibilities), the children learn that their parents' love for them is conditional –"*if* you do this, *then* we will show you attention."

Already, you have done a lot of thinking about your past and are able to identify some of the events and people who originally led you to feel bad about yourself. When you understand how abuse, neglect, boundary violations, and people who could not or did not pay attention to you affected your feelings about yourself, then you understand that the things that originally caused your low self-esteem were never about you in the first place. They were about things that were done to you, or things that were not done for you, by other people.

We have talked a lot in this book about how children are not responsible. That goes for you too. When you were a child you were not responsible for the behavior of the adults in your life. You may still believe that you deserved the abuse or neglect you received because you were "bad." It's time for you to reexamine that belief.

Of course you misbehaved! Of course you disobeyed your parents and got into things you weren't supposed to. All children misbehave. But one of the primary responsibilities of any parent is to discipline their child. Discipline is different from punishment. Discipline should help children to have self-control and learn what the right thing to do is. If your parents weren't able to correct you and help you learn right from wrong without attacking you or making you dislike yourself, then they failed you. And if your parents didn't pay attention to you, even if it was because they were working all the time or they were sick and in the hospital—even if it was because one of them died and the other couldn't cope—then you missed out on what you needed. The point is not to blame them. The point is: it wasn't your fault. In light of what you now know about children, ask yourself if you really were responsible for any of the things that caused you to feel you were worthless or unlovable.

Here is a sad fact: Sometimes parents are unable to love children in the way they need to be loved. Not because there is something wrong with you, but because there was something wrong with them. We might know exactly what went wrong, but we know one thing for sure: It wasn't your fault. You deserved what every child deserves and needs: to feel special, important, loved, and valued.

What we are saying is that by examining your childhood you have already started the process of changing your low self-esteem. If you understand that you really were powerless as a child, then you can realistically reclaim the self-worth that was always rightfully yours—and still is. Understanding where your opinion of yourself comes from makes it possible for you to challenge those opinions and change how they affect you today.

We've talked about the importance of remembering and talking about your early negative experiences as a way to express the sadness and the anger you've carried with you. Another important reason to remember those experiences is to identify the thoughts that you carry with you. Remember, your *basic beliefs* are shaped early on. Your basic beliefs about yourself are a direct product of the messages you were given about yourself when you were a child.

Of course during your childhood you received many, many messages. As you remember your childhood, you will remember the messages that you heard the most. Just because your mother screamed at you one day, "Shut up, you're driving me crazy!" doesn't mean you'll grow up believing you're a person who drives others crazy. But when you hear the same thing over and over, it stays with you. For example, if you were a very active child you probably heard a lot of, "Stop it! Shut up! Sit still!" The message you would you have gotten about yourself would be something like, "I'm too loud. I don't do anything right." Over time, your basic belief about yourself might become: "*I'm annoying.*"

It is important for you to understand that the fact that we heard something frequently as children and believe it now does not make it true. In reality, most of the things we learned early on about ourselves were just one person's opinion. If your father told you, "*You'll never amount to anything,*" as a child you believed him. As an adult you know that everyone has his or her own opinion and you don't have to just accept anyone's opinion as a fact. You look for other evidence, other information, before you decide what to believe. If you have never looked at the things you believe about yourself through your adult eyes—that is, if you have not asked yourself how realistic or sensible those opinions are, or checked them out with other people—you are still thinking as a child. As we know, children think all kinds of distorted and unrealistic things. Your basic beliefs about yourself may be completely unrealistic.

Step Two: *Changing Your Thinking (Changing the Narrative)*

Schema is a fancy word for basic beliefs and worldviews. The basic beliefs that you brought with you from childhood still shape the way you think. For example, if your basic beliefs include: *"I'm not very smart,"* anytime you enter a situation like school or a job where you expect to be challenged, you will automatically be saying things to yourself like, "I can't do this," or "I'm going to look like a fool," or "I better get out of this before they see how dumb I am."

If your basic beliefs include *"I'm boring,"* when you meet someone new you'll be saying to yourself, "They won't listen," or "I better make something up," or "Why even try? She knows lots of people who are more interesting than me."

In the exercise following this section, you will examine your basic beliefs about yourself, or others, or the world. The process of changing your thinking requires you to identify your beliefs and then challenge their reality by asking, *"Is this really true?"* This is actually exactly what scientists do: they test something by looking for evidence that proves or disproves it. You will learn more about "restructuring thinking errors" in Chapter 7.

Here is one quick example of how examining and challenging thoughts leads to new, smarter ways of thinking. Say you have a basic belief of *"I'm boring."* Here is an example of changing that thinking using the four-step formula you will find in Chapter 7. You can think about examples in your own life and challenge your own thinking in this way.

Use the change process when you catch yourself having negative beliefs about yourself. You will end with up with more realistic ways of appreciating your strengths and your limitations.

Internal Dialogue	Thinking Process	What Is True and What is Not True?	Substitute Realistic Thoughts
I'm boring	Over-generalizing Mind Reading Focus on the Negative All-or-Nothing Thinking	<u>True:</u> 1) Some people might find me boring. 2) Sometimes I can't think of anything interesting to say. 3) Some subjects I don't know much about. <u>Not True:</u> 1) Everyone thinks I'm boring 2) I can never think of anything to contribute to a conversation.	Just as I find some people more interesting and some people less interesting, some people will find me more interesting than others. I don't have to know everything or be perfect for people to find me interesting. I certainly know some things and that's really all anyone knows.

Exercise 4.8: Identify and Challenge the Negative Beliefs You Have About Yourself.

1. Describe yourself: Make a list of at least ten things that you believe about yourself. Of course some things will be positive and some negative.
2. Take each of your negative beliefs about yourself and plug them into the formula. In your notebook write out your analysis of each belief, using the four-column approach you see above.
3. Recognize that black-or-white thinking holds you back. Avoid words like always or never, everyone or no one. Then you can create a realistic belief about yourself that will help you take credit where it is due, and change the things that you don't like about yourself.

*Step Three: How You Act Determines How You Feel About Yourself**

When all is said and done, you are what you do. Not what you thought about doing, not what you wanted to do but couldn't find the time, not what you intended to do, not what you said you were

* Many of the ideas in this section are adapted from Bednar, R.L., & Peterson, S. R. (1995). Self-Esteem: Paradoxes and Innovations in Clinical Theory and Practice. American Psychological Association, Washington, D.C.

going to do, not what you wish you had done. And guess what? You already know this! *You judge yourself by what you do or don't do.* And how you judge yourself determines how you feel about yourself.

Some people believe that in order to like and respect themselves, they would have to be "successful." But, surprisingly, there are many successful people who don't like or respect themselves—and many people who would not be considered "successful" who feel quite good about themselves. The reason is that we judge ourselves based not on what we have accomplished or how successful we are but on how we handle ourselves. When we meet our problems head on—*regardless of how successful we are in solving them*—we are proud of and respect ourselves. When we avoid our problems, when we make excuses, when we "wimp out," we don't like ourselves—even if the problems get solved by someone else or go away.

Avoiding: When We Hide Our Heads in The Sand

Have you ever noticed that when you have a tough problem, and you don't know what to do, it's sometimes because you don't want to do what needs to be done? So what do you do? You "forget" the problem. You pretend it's going to take care of itself. You tell yourself it's not really a problem after all. You blame it on someone else. You "live with it." In short, you avoid it.

Some men don't avoid problems they can fix with a hammer or a wrench or muscle power. Some men love those kinds of problems, because they have an obvious solution. *It is the problem that makes us afraid that we avoid—the problem that makes us face who we are.* What are we doing about being stuck in a job that we hate? What are we doing about the empty feeling we have when we recognize that our life doesn't seem to be headed anywhere? Are we doing anything about the anger that seems to take over our body and tie us in a knot? What about not being able to sleep? What can we do about always feeling that we don't belong, even with our "friends"? Are we really happy with the relationship we've been half in and half out of for the past year? Have we ever really been happy in a relationship? Will we ever have a partner we can just be ourselves with, or will we always be putting on some kind of an act? What would we do if we left our present relationship? What about our fear of meeting a partner? What about our fear of not being good enough sexually? What about our fear of falling in love with a person who doesn't love us?

Lots of people would read this list of problems and say, "What's there to be afraid of?" You might think that if you're a fighter, if you can kick butt, you've proved you're not afraid. In your heart you know better. It is emotional pain that we most fear. It is the unknown in ourselves—who are we? What are we?—and the possibility of being found out by others that paralyzes us.

Only you know what your problems are. The point is that when you avoid problems you are telling yourself that you are powerless. Your behavior speaks to you. It tells you that you are not smart enough, not brave, not capable, not lovable, not strong, not good enough. When you avoid problems you don't respect yourself and you don't like yourself.

Lots of people would read this list of problems and say, "What's there to be afraid of?" You might think that if you're a fighter, if you can kick butt, you've proved you're not afraid. In your heart you know better. It is emotional pain that we most fear. It is the unknown in ourselves—who are we? What are we?—and the possibility of being found out by others that paralyzes us.

Only you know what your problems are. The point is that when you avoid problems you are telling yourself that you are powerless. *Your behavior speaks to you.* It tells you that you are not smart enough, not brave, not capable, not lovable, not strong, not good enough. When you avoid problems you don't respect yourself and you don't like yourself.

Coping: When We Face Our Fears

Coping is about facing problems and dealing with them (go back and look at Figure 4.4: Resilience Skills). Coping starts with honestly recognizing problems instead of minimizing or denying them. When you minimize a problem you are excusing yourself from dealing with it. After all, if it's "not that serious," why should you worry about it? When you have decided to do whatever it takes to cope with a problem it's because you have admitted to yourself that it is serious.

The first step is simply *taking responsibility* for your actions. When you are blaming your problems on someone or something else, you are saying you can't do anything about them. When you convince yourself that other people control your life you are telling yourself you are powerless and helpless. How does that help you? Sometimes, it allows you to not have to do anything that will make you uncomfortable or afraid.

When you are ready to start liking yourself you will begin by recognizing that you do have control of everything you do. Your choices, your decisions, your actions are what your life is really made out of.

The simple truth is that if you have a job you hate it is because you chose to apply for the job, you chose to accept the job, and you are now choosing to stay in the job. Sometimes we choose to stay stuck. But we could also choose to take a risk. If you decide to do something different it means you will have to make difficult choices and face new challenges: what kind of job would you like better? What kind of training would you be willing to undertake to get that job? How would you pay for the new training? Are you willing to ask those questions and think about undertaking those challenges?

The point is that even if you choose to stay in your present job, acknowledging to yourself that it is your decision to stay and that you are responsible for everything that decision means will make you feel better about yourself. You are being honest with yourself. You are recognizing that you are in control. You have the power to stay or go. You are not powerless. When you empower yourself, you will respect yourself and like yourself better.

The second step in learning how to cope with your life is *to become willing to take psychological risks.* Sounds like a piece of cake, doesn't it? Easier said than done! Like a lot of people, you may have been afraid of your feelings, afraid to let anyone get close to you, afraid to trust anyone, afraid to be honest in your group. You know when you are avoiding working on these issues, when you are afraid to reveal your authentic self, when you are hiding and hoping the world will just leave you alone. *That's when you don't like yourself.*

Coping with your real problems—the problems that make you afraid—means allowing yourself to know yourself and allowing other people to know you. This is risky business. It makes you uncomfortable at first. You don't know how it's going to turn out. You tell yourself you don't care what other people think of you, but you know that's not true. You could be embarrassed, even humiliated, if you honestly reveal yourself to others. You could be rejected. Those are psychological risks. They are real risks. That can make you feel bad about yourself.

Your group is the perfect place to test what it means to face your fears and take risks. The group is about trying new approaches, letting it all hang out and seeing what happens. Have you tried really being honest in your group? What did it feel like? If you have been fully honest in a group meeting, you know that when you left you felt good about yourself.

Talking honestly in the group means facing fears and coping. Talking openly and honestly with your partner or family members is another way to acknowledge problems and start to deal with them. Talking is a way to begin to address problems. When you talk openly and honestly about your life you respect yourself for having the courage to do that.

The tools for building your self-esteem are right here. You already know people who have picked up those tools and used them. They're the ones in your group who have stopped blaming their victims, their wives, their judge and their probation officer for their problems. By accepting responsibility for their lives and being willing to take the risk of talking about themselves and their problems, they have acted in new ways that earn respect.

Exercise 4.9: Identify Tasks You Have Avoided and Tackle Them.

1. Write down three problem areas which have troubled you and which you have not addressed. The problems could be job-related, family-related or relationship-related. Use real problems and don't be afraid to list the most difficult ones you can think of.
2. Next to each problem write the outcome you would like to see for the problem. What would be the ideal end result? This is your ultimate goal.
3. Now write a list of everything you could do (strategies) that will or could move you in the direction of achieving that goal. Break down any complicated strategies into parts so that each part seems manageable.
4. Now arrange the strategies in the order of how you should try them. If you need more information about the problem start with a list of who or what could provide you with that information. Arrange your information sources in the order of how approachable they seem. If you have a friend or family member who might have information, start with that person. If they don't have the information you need, maybe they know someone who does. Go online. Make the calls. Talk to people. If you have to go to the library or a bookstore, go. Gather the information you need.
5. If your problem involves communicating with another person, read Chapter Six in this book. For more information on effective communication techniques go to the self-help section in any bookstore. You will find material on getting people to listen to you and cooperate with you.
6. Continue moving one step at a time toward your goal. You will head down some dead ends. No problem. Try another path. Don't expect instant success. This is a long-term project. Remind yourself that everyone you have ever envied because they are "more successful" than you has probably engaged in trial and error. Remind yourself that there is no failure, only learning what works and what doesn't work. The only failure is giving up. There are no mistakes – only learning experiences.

7. Report to your group on what your problem is and what your progress is in solving it. Other members will certainly have thoughts about other strategies you could try.
8. Let your group know when you reach your goal. Is it the exact goal you imagined? Maybe not. Is it a realistic, acceptable goal? Only you can judge. Don't settle for something that doesn't meet your needs. If you find that you simply cannot solve the problem in a way that meets your needs–after trying everything you can think of – you may need to accept this outcome. You still will have accomplished your most important objective: facing your fears and overcoming them. If you have learned that you can't do anything about a particular problem, you can stop thinking about it. We needn't be troubled by things that are truly beyond our control.

What Does All This Have To Do With Sex Crimes?

Sex is Never Just About Sex.

We all tend to think of sex as a physical act that is about physical gratification. But if sex were just about the *physical* pleasure, masturbation would be all anyone would need. Think about it. If the physical erection and orgasm you are going to have is exactly the same as the one you have when you masturbate, why go to all the trouble you do to involve another person? Because actually sex is loaded with emotions. It is these emotions that make the sex exciting and rewarding.

Anytime we are sexually involved with another person it brings up feelings in us. At one time or another, virtually all of our feelings get expressed through sex. Even the most casual sex involves lots of feelings. Imagine meeting a person in a club and taking them home for sex. It doesn't get more superficial than this, does it? And yet, think of all the feelings it will involve. Won't it make you feel *desired*? Won't it make you feel *special* (after all, she chose you, didn't she?) And there will be other feelings too: you'll probably feel *wanted, important, powerful,* and *lucky*. And even the most casual sex can meet one of our most fundamental emotional needs—acceptance. If someone is willing to have sex with you, they must want you, right?

Everyone uses sex to meet *emotional needs*. Sex can be a way to feel close to others, or it can be a way to gain a feeling of power. It is likely that you have used sex as a way to meet emotional needs that you haven't even been aware of.

Now that you understand more about your childhood, your family, your needs, and how you have attempted to get your needs met, it is time to explore the role that sex has played in your life. It is important for you to understand how you came to behave sexually in ways that are destructive to all your adult goals.

The single most important question you need to answer about your sex a crime is: What emotional needs were I trying to meet through sex offending? You didn't risk everything for an erection and an orgasm. You don't have to risk anything for an erection and an orgasm. You can have those things anytime you want—no cost, no risk. So what drove you to take such chances?

It is by understanding the emotions surrounding your offending that you will be able to make sense of what you have done. It is our emotional needs that give intensity and power to our desires. This is the question that will help you unlock your behavior, and that will move you through this program toward a new, healthy life.

Exercise 4.10: Your sexual autobiography, part 2

This is one of the most important exercises in this book. A sexual autobiography is an analysis of the personal development of your *sexual self.* The exercise helps you explore the question: "How did I get to this point as a sexual being?" Please reflect on your sexuality development from early childhood, to adolescence, to adulthood, thinking about experiences, relationships, and behaviors. Refer back to your Sexual Autobiography Timeline, which you completed at the end of Chapter 2.

It is important to remember all of your experiences in order to be able to see your overall sexual patterns and explore how you have used sex to meet other non-sexual needs in your life. This exercise helps you think about the meaning of sex throughout your life, what you felt about your experiences; when you felt good about sex and when you felt bad; and how you might have used abusive or unhealthy sex to substitute for healthy relationships.

For instance, if you were sexually abused, from it you might have learned to associate sexual excitement with nervousness, fear, powerlessness, confusion, shame, secretiveness, danger, feeling out of control, or in over your head but couldn't say no. Even if an early sexual experience with an older person felt like "getting lucky," you may have still had other conflicting feelings. These experiences might have confused your boundaries. These feelings might affect the way you would feel about sex in the future—maybe up to today. Here are some things to think about.

Sexual Orientation and Gender Identity.

Sexual orientation is your pattern of romantic or sexual attraction to persons of the opposite sex or gender, the same sex or gender, or to both sexes or more than one gender. Each person uniquely experiences sexuality. Most people begin to notice who they are attracted to in their early teens, but maybe earlier. You might think of yourself as straight, gay, or bisexual, or somewhere else on the spectrum. Some people are attracted to the same sex but uncomfortable being "out" as gay or bisexual because of family or religious messages, or other perceived stigma or shame.

Gender identity is about your personal sense of gender. Do you feel like a male or a female? Gender identity can correlate with assigned sex at birth or can differ from it. Most people feel that their private parts and gender at birth is consistent with how they feel inside. But some people experience gender dysphoria, which is just a fancy way of saying that they don't feel like their body matches their gender identity (born with a penis but feeling inside your mind and heart that you are a female). The word cisgender means a person whose sense of personal identity and gender corresponds with what they were born with.

Gender expression is a person's behavior, mannerisms, dress, and appearance that are associated with femininity or masculinity within a particular cultural context. This can also include gender roles.

LGBTQ+ stands for lesbian, gay, bisexual, transgender, queer, plus other non-conforming sexual or gender minorities. Queer is an umbrella term for sexual and gender minorities who are not heterosexual or are not cisgender.

Think about the development and realization of your sexual attractions and identity. Some good informational websites about LBGTQ+ issues can be found at:

Link 4.4 – LGTBQ Center
https://lgbtq.wfu.edu/resources/guides-brochures/

Link 4.5 – CDC LGBT Health
https://www.cdc.gov/lgbthealth/index.htm

Link 4.6 – APA LGBT
https://www.apa.org/topics/lgbt/

Link 4.7 – LGBT National Help Center
http://www.glnh.org/

Examining the Messages that you received about Sex Growing Up.

Many people receive little information about sex from their parents other than, "we don't talk about that." Were you allowed to ask questions about sex in your family? Who could you ask? Did sex seem like something that had to be secretive or shameful (as opposed to appropriately private?) Sex education in school is often about anatomy, birth control, and STDs. That means you probably learned about real sex mostly from other kids, information on the Internet, or pornography. What messages did you get? Did you ever read or hear anything about sexual values, sex as intimacy, sharing feelings, and feeling close to your partner? How to talk about what feels good with a mutual partner? We live in a sexualized society with a lot of mixed messages, including zero tolerance on the one side, and "locker room talk" on the other. How do these messages shape your feelings and expectations?

Sexual development could be influenced by one's experiences, beliefs, values, attitudes, religious beliefs, peers, family dynamics, cultural influences, TV and movies, video gaming, social media, and societal messages. How do you think each of these shaped your view of sex, sexuality, relationships, gender roles, consent, boundaries, and respectful, acceptable, or healthy sexual behaviors?

Exploring what Sex has meant to you Throughout Your Life.

Has sex ever meant feeling close to another person? Has it meant happiness, sharing, intimacy? Describe those relationships. At other times has it meant power or victory? Has it ever meant anxiety or disgust or shame? What has sex usually meant? Look for the patterns. Have you pulled away from consensual sex with partners your own age? Has the thought of sex brought up fears of not being good enough or of being rejected? Have you been self-conscious or embarrassed about your body or your genitals? Has that made you unsure whether a sexual partner would be attracted to you, love you, reject you? Do you have uncertainty about your sexual orientation (who you are attracted to) or gender identity (male or female)? What does sex mean to you now? How does sex fit into your future?

Exploring What Emotional Needs You Were Trying to Meet Through Sex

Understanding your sexual history will help you do this. Have you hoped sex would make you feel important, acknowledged, noticed, validated, special, or successful? Have you wanted to feel close to your partners? Have you wanted to avoid being close to partners, so you engaged in "long distance sex" using interactive websites, sexting, or hook-up apps, or in detached and impersonal encounters? As you go through your experiences you may find that you tried to meet different needs in different relationships. Or you may find that you have tried to meet the same needs over and over. Either way you will be able to make sense of your choices and your behavior.

Exploring What Emotional Needs You Were Trying to Meet Through Sex Offending.

What were you feeling generally during periods when you were offending? What were you trying to get out of it? How did you feel during the act of offending? What was the excitement about? What were the *specific* things that made offending so much more exciting than just masturbating? Was it the way the victim looked or acted? What the victim said? How you fooled the victim or got the victim to go along with you? Was it the situation? A way to help answer these questions is to ask two other questions:

1) What made a particular offense especially exciting? In other words, describe the perfect offense, whether a real offense or one you only wished for. What are the elements of the most exciting offense you could imagine?
2) What made some offenses not exciting? Describe an unexciting offense. What are the elements that, if you took them out, would make an offense not worth doing? When you identify the things about an offense that make it exciting or not exciting, you know what the offense is really about. You can look at how those things make you feel. *Those feelings are what you were looking for, what made you offend—what you risked so much for.*

***THE MOST IMPORTANT PART OF THIS ASSIGNMENT IS TO THINK ABOUT HOW YOU HAVE USED SEX AND SEXUAL ASSAULT TO MEET YOUR NEEDS.**

Looking back over your sexual history, look for the ways you have used sex or sexual assault to try to meet other non-sexual, emotional needs. Were you looking for power, control, intimacy, importance, attention, affection, emotional distance, safety from vulnerability, validation? What else?

1. What needs do you think you have tried to meet through appropriate sex?
2. What needs have you succeeded in meeting?
3. Which ones have you not succeeded in meeting?
4. What things have made appropriate sex more exciting or less exciting?
5. What needs do you think you have tried to meet through sexual assault, sexual boundary violations, or other sexual offending?
6. What needs do you think you have succeeded in meeting?
7. Which ones have you not succeeded in meeting?
8. What things have made sex offending more exciting or less exciting?
9. In what other ways could you try to meet your needs in healthy ways?
10. What things might interfere with your meeting these needs in healthy ways?

Now that you've done your sexual autobiography and learned more about childhood trauma and family dynamics, what insights have you gained about understanding the development of your problematic sexual behaviors?

CHAPTER 5
VICTIM IMPACT

Now that you understand yourself better, you can begin to better understand your victims. By having more empathy for yourself, you can now have more empathy for your victims. Just as you were able to identify feelings that went unnoticed or unspoken when you felt harmed or violated, your victims have lots of feelings about what has happened to them. This chapter will help you to understand the direct and indirect impacts of sexual abuse on victims.

Most people convicted of sex offenses are prohibited by law from having contact with the person or people they abused. This makes face to face victim/offender sessions impossible in many cases. Since it is not appropriate for you to initiate interaction with those who have been harmed, you must wait for a harmed party to contact you, which may not happen. But we have spoken with hundreds of victims. In this chapter, we offer the voices of real victims and survivors who provide a glimpse into their experience.

What is Empathy?

Empathy is defined as the ability to step into the shoes of another person, to understand their feelings and perspectives, and to use that understanding to guide your responses and actions. Empathy and compassion are about shared humanity—they remind us that we are all people with similar feelings, even though our actual experiences may differ. Empathy helps us bridge human connections, and simply be able to listen, be emotionally present, and accept the perspectives of others.

There is a criminal justice initiative called "Restorative Justice" that allows victims to share their stories with people who perpetrated harm, describe the effects of the crime and the harm it causes, and offer ideas about how to make things right. (You can watch a great TV series on CNN or YouTube with Van Jones called "The Redemption Project." It shows many different cases of victims and survivors speaking with people who were convicted of various types of crimes that harmed them and/or their family member). This process allows for justice that is measured not by the length of a prison sentence, but by conversations about accountability, empathy, amends, remorse, and healing. As survivors express their experiences and feelings, people who have offended can explore ways of making restitution for the harm they have caused. This allows victims to move towards healing and resolution (not "closure").

In order for restorative justice to be effective, Ackerman and Levenson wrote in 2019, a person who offended must see themself as having an obligation to better understand the effects of his crime on his own victim. They must be willing to be held accountable by themself and others. And they must have an interest in feeling and expressing empathy for another person who has been harmed. In this program, most people convicted of a sex crime know that what they've done is wrong and illegal, they might not understand exactly *why* and *how* sexual assault is harmful.

When victims tell their story, they can explain the physical, psychological, emotional, social, and financial impact on their lives. They give voice to the harms caused. To successfully complete your treatment, you must see yourself as having an *obligation* to better understand the effects of your crime on your victim, a desire to be held accountable by yourself and others, and an interest in feeling and expressing empathy for another person who has been harmed. Even at an early stage of treatment you should no longer be denying factual aspects of your crime. You should have some grasp of the impacts of sexual assault on victims across time. Full empathy takes time to develop, because you don't know what you don't know. You begin to know by listening—by wanting to understand the other person's perspective and experience. You should be able to listen to others without judging or becoming defensive, and you need to tolerate emotional discomfort. Remember, empathy is about THEIR feelings, not yours.

Empathy involves being able to understand and imagine another person's feelings. Empathy seems to be a central reason why we usually resist harming others, because we can imagine what it would feel like if it happened to us. A lack of victim empathy can be related to thinking errors about victimization, relationships, gender roles, and entitlement.

An important goal for most survivors is to see the person who hurt them take responsibility and accountability for their behavior by naming the wrongdoing and acknowledging the harm. The person who perpetrated has an obligation to listen, name the harm caused, and acknowledge that they alone are responsible for hurting someone. This is sometimes called the expression of remorse. *Not remorse for getting caught,* but remorse for causing harm and hurt to someone else.

This process can free the survivor from self-blame, doubt and shame they might feel, and place responsibility firmly with the perpetrator of sexual harm. Finally, survivors often have questions for people who offended, and believe the answers can help them make sense of why someone might sexually harm another person, and what might prevent it from happening again.

Here are some common questions victims of sexual abuse have for the person who abused them. What might your victim want to ask you, and how would you answer?

- Why did you do those things to me?
- Why did you pick me?
- Will you do those things to me again?
- Have you done that to anyone else?
- How has counseling helped you? What have you learned? What's different now?
- Did you really love me?
- If you loved me, why did you do this to me?
- How will I know if you are going to hurt me again?
- Should I trust you anymore? Can I trust others?
- What can I do to protect myself?
- How do you feel about my telling and getting you in trouble?
- Did anyone else know when this was happening?
- What would have happened if you hadn't been caught?

How Sexual Abuse Affects Victims

As you learned earlier in this book, sexual assault is any fondling, inappropriate touching, oral-genital contact, rape, exposure, or looking at a child or unwilling adult in a state of undress. Sexual assault is any kind of sexual activity involving a child under 18 or an adult against his or her will, including non-contact behaviors, sexual harassment, or professional sexual misconduct.

Sexual assault victims often experience long-lasting emotional pain from their abuse. They feel hurt, angry, and helpless. Frequently they blame themselves because they feel they should have done something to prevent or stop the assault. Many feel different from other people all their lives and some never learn to have healthy relationships. Many victims struggle with liking and accepting themselves. Nothing crushes a child's self-esteem like being abused.

In most cases, your victim knew you and trusted you. In many cases, a victim feels love for the abuser. Your victims may have appreciated the affection or attention you showed them. They may have acted as though they wanted the sexual contact with you. Maybe your victims at times even initiated the sexual contact with you—or, at least, you believed they did. They probably felt some loyalty to you and may have wanted to protect you from the legal consequences of your actions. Conflicting loyalties is one of the things that makes sexual assault so confusing and damaging—it violates trust in ways that are hard for victims to understand.

At the same time, they probably felt angry and used, confused about why you misled them into thinking it was okay, and deeply hurt that you didn't care enough about them to protect them. They were bewildered and hurt again by the way things changed after they told someone, or maybe even betrayed when the people they trusted to protect them didn't believe them when they tried to tell.

Victims often have a lot of *mixed feelings* about the abuse and the abuser. Think about the feelings you described in previous exercises about abuse you might have endured, as you try to imagine what it was like for your victim to be abused by you.

Victims are Often Re-Victimized

Ironically, we live in an era where #MeToo and zero tolerance co-exist with victim-blaming. This means that laws about sex crimes and people who commit them have gotten harsher, while gender inequality, racial bias, and male privilege continue to leave many victims, especially females, not being believed or validated. Even now, when powerful men are faced with multiple allegations, others will come to his defense, minimizing and dismissing sexual assault as "locker room talk" or "women make these things up" or "boys will be boys." It happens in Hollywood, it happens in every workplace, it happens in politics, it happens at schools, it happens in churches and synagogues, it happens in homes.

When you deny your crime, you are calling your victim a liar. This adds to their trauma. You know the truth, but the burden is on the victim (and the state) to prove it. Sexual assault usually happens in secret. There are rarely witnesses, there is often little or no evidence, and so it comes down to just your word against theirs. Despite the fact that you are here now because you were convicted, the odds are usually in favor of the perpetrator. You are here in this program, but you are part of a small minority. Statistics suggest that less than 10% of sexual crimes are detected, reported, investigated, charged, and prosecuted, and even fewer result in conviction or incarceration.

While you were busy denying your crimes, your victims were feeling like they were being punished. They might have been blamed, doubted, subjected to intrusive medical exams, removed from their home, or even encouraged to protect you. They may have been blamed for the abuse or for reporting it, severely damaging their relationships with friends or other family members. Your denial is another abuse to your victim.

In some cases it is easy for others to discount a victim's story because she didn't yell, run away, or fight back. There are even cases of judges making statements like this in court! Watch any documentary in which survivors describe sexual assault, and you will frequently hear them say: "It was like I left or detached from my body." A study, described online by Catherine Pearson, a reporter from the Huffington Post, reports on this in

Link 5.1 – Huffpost Article

https://m.huffpost.com/us/entry/us_5936f8e7e4b0099e7faff1dc/amp

Here's an excerpt:

"[A] Swedish study, published in a medical journal, shows how normal it is for victims of sexual assault to experience a temporary paralysis that keeps them from fighting back or screaming. The researchers spoke to nearly 300 women who went to an emergency clinic in Stockholm within one month of a rape or attempted rape. Seventy percent of the women said they experienced significant "tonic immobility," or involuntary paralysis, during the attack.

Almost 50% reported extreme paralysis, rendering them almost catatonic and unable to move or fight. "It really confirms that a significant number of women who experience sexual assault do not respond in what we think of as the typical 'fight or flight' pattern; they respond by freezing," Laura Palumbo, communications director for the National Sexual Violence Resource Center, told HuffPost. Palumbo, who did not work on the study, said the findings confirm just how complex the neurobiology of trauma is, and that there is no one-size-fits-all response."

A victim's description in Ackerman and Levenson's book about restorative justice* outlines the many ways that victims are re-victimized, even when a victim immediately reports the crime, is believed, and even when the court case results in a conviction:

Calling out for help and immediately reporting her rape to the police facilitated a quick arrest, but as Alexa articulates, this was not without consequences. She continues, "When I called out for help that night, I did not think about the ramifications of that request for help. If I were completely honest, knowing all that I know now, I would not have come forward." For Alexa, and for many like her, the criminal justice process results in a secondary victimization. The first re-traumatization came from having to retell her story to multiple people. Though some of the details remain fuzzy, Alexa recalls having to tell the police, the emergency room doctor, and the sexual assault nurse examiner (SANE) all on the same night. She had to endure an intrusive medical examination, which included collecting evidence through genital, anal, hair, and fingernail samples, and taking photographs.

Investigators later informed Alexa that the defense had hired a private detective to investigate her. Knowing the defendant was trying to find dirt to use against her in trial was also revictimizing for Alexa.

---

* Ackerman, A. R., & Levenson, J. S. (2019). Healing from sexual violence: The case for vicarious restorative justice. Brandon, VT: Safer Society Press.

As she recalls, "the year and a half leading up to testifying was a horrific period for me," and testifying did not provide the relief she thought it would. Alexa had to recount the details of her assault multiple times to the district attorney (DA). She felt like the DA did not believe her or that she was saying something incorrectly. The whole process leading up to the trial was intimidating and created fear. "I was so scared of the upcoming trial," Alexa continues. "The victim advocate would call me and I refused to call her back. I would go to therapy and insist that I was not going to testify. There was so much pressure on me and I felt pushed into testifying. By the time I testified, I felt like I had sacrificed my sanity for the greater good."

The criminal justice process takes control away from people who have experienced victimization. Alexa's entire life was on hold as she awaited the trial. The trial itself was no different. The district attorney and the victims' advocate made promises to Alexa about how much better she would feel after she testified. They vowed that doing so would feel empowering. Despite rape shield laws that aim to protect rape survivors from experiencing additional trauma on the stand, many defense attorneys still use inappropriate and harmful tactics when questioning victims. This was no different in Alexa's trial. For instance, the defense attorney listed Alexa's parents as witnesses to prevent them from being in the courtroom to support her while she testified. His brazen attitude toward Alexa was apparent while she was on the stand. "The defense attorney was difficult, rude, and just plain offensive," Alexa shares. "It felt humiliating, embarrassing, and stressful. In my initial report to the police, I mentioned that I had walked past the shower stall when I was grabbed, but on the stand, I said bathroom stall. The defense attorney started yelling and questioning how the jury could believe anything I said after that." Visibly rattled, she continues, "When I got off the stand, I ran out of the courtroom and I cried. I didn't feel I was any closer to people believing me."

Two weeks after Alexa testified, the jury returned with a guilty verdict, but as she explains, the verdict did not provide healing, justice or empowerment. "When I got the guilty verdict, I felt good. I felt validated. The jury believed me. They didn't think I was a liar. Still, it wasn't the trial that helped. The victim impact statement was the most liberating part. I could finally say what I wanted to. For the first time I was hopeful that everything would get better." In Alexa's own words, we learn that the trial itself was stressful and traumatizing, though the victim impact statement provided some freedom for her to speak her mind.

What Research Tells Us About the Long-Lasting Effects of Child Sex Abuse

An enormous amount of research about child sexual abuse (CSA) has been accumulating over the past three decades. In 1985, David Finkelhor, one of the world's pioneer experts in violence against children, identified sets of symptoms frequently seen in children who have been sexually abused. These symptoms can be seen shortly after abuse takes place, or they may show up later after a period of time. They often persist into adulthood. In most cases CSA is dramatically damaging for youngsters. Children experience profound betrayal when the very people who were supposed to care for them take advantage of that vulnerability. They feel a sense of powerlessness, fueled by an inability to reach out to other adults for help, due to fear, embarrassment, or loyalty to the abuser.

Being a victim of sexual abuse carries its own stigma. A child often feels blame and shame for the abuse, believing that they were unworthy and deserved what happened. They might think they "participated" in it by somehow inviting the abuse or failing to stop it. Abusers often warn children not to tell, ensnaring the child as a co-conspirator in secret behaviors. The child victim is told that the abuse must be kept from others who "wouldn't understand," might not believe them, or might punish them. This subtle coercion is quite often accomplished with no threat, force, or violence. A child's natural desire to please adults and to be loved and accepted is easily exploited for the abuser's personal gratification. Traumatic sexualization occurs when CSA leads to distorted perceptions of love, trust, and intimacy. For boys abused by men, the stigma might be complicated by wondering if they are gay.

Child sexual abuse hurts not only the victim, but also the victim's family and friends. Relationships are often damaged because the victim has trouble trusting again. The victim may become withdrawn and distant. Loved ones may feel helpless to take away the victim's pain. Even future relationships are affected, because the sexual assault changes the way the victim sees the world and relates to others.

Children who have been sexually assaulted may experience:

- Behavior problems (including sexualized behaviors)
- Anger or aggression
- Withdrawal
- Nightmares
- School problems
- Self-blame
- Isolation/feeling different
- Confusion
- Depression and anxiety

Children who are being abused adapt to their situation. They figure out how to survive in their world of abuse. They may not tell anyone what is happening. They may deny the abuse when asked because they want to protect the perpetrator, who is often someone they know and love. They may deny the abuse because they feel they have done something wrong by "participating" in the abuse. They may be afraid they will get in trouble. Loyalty to caretakers prevents a child from telling the truth and saying what happened. In fact, young children may not even have words to describe the experience or what it felt like for them.

Child Sexual Abuse is highly correlated with teenage pregnancy, drug and alcohol abuse, eating disorders, self-mutilating behavior, depression, and suicide. Unfortunately, these behaviors often result in the victim being seen as "bad" or having "issues" – so they may not be viewed as credible or reliable.

Michelle's Story (CSA)

At six, Michelle was initiated into sexual activity by her cousin Paul, who lived with her family while he attended college. He started by telling her that she was a "princess" and he wished he had had a sister like her. Tickling and playing turned into fondling and then oral sex. The abuse continued for two years until Paul got a girlfriend. Suddenly, he had no time for her and told her to get away from him if she came into his room. She never told anyone because she felt she was to blame for the abuse and for his pulling away.

"I was desperate for any attention from anybody. My father left us when I was a baby and my mother was too busy working and trying to find a new husband to have any time for me. I don't remember ever being held by anyone until Paul came. I would do anything he wanted. When he abandoned me I was crushed. He never would tell me what I had done wrong. By the time I was fourteen I felt completely alone and the only way I knew to be close to people was through sex. I kept thinking someone would love me if I could please them sexually, so I had sex with lots of boys. For a while I thought I was popular because all the boys in school were calling me. It was only later that I found out they were passing my name around and laughing behind my back because I was 'easy.' The girls excluded me from their groups. It was hopeless. I was an outcast. I hated myself. As an adult I've never felt close to anyone. I've had relationships with a couple of men but never could trust that they really accepted me or cared about me. Food has been the only good thing I've had in my life for so long, and I can't bear the thought of not eating even though my weight is completely out of control. And I guess a part of me wants to be fat because I can't stand the thought of a man being attracted to me for my body. All I ever wanted was to be loved, but now I'm thirty-eight and I'm beginning to give up hope that I will ever have anyone in my life to love me."

Some children become shy and withdrawn so as not to draw attention to themselves. They have learned that attention leads to abuse. Other children become seemingly "seductive" and appear to seek out the abuse. For these children the abuse may be the only attention or affection they have ever gotten.

Adults know right from wrong. Children depend on adults to do the right thing. When adults do things that children know are wrong, kids begin to lose trust in the adults that they depend on for their survival. When abusers deny that abuse occurred, victims begin to think they are crazy because their reality is being challenged. When other adults fail to protect them, children begin to believe that they can't count on others and that no one can help them stay safe. These are very scary feelings for a child.

Rosa's Story (Indecent Exposure)

As a child, Rosa was abused by several strangers in Chicago. The first occurred when she was nine, in a children's movie on a Saturday afternoon. A man sat down next to her, put his arm around her, and started feeling her thighs. She complained to her friend, and they got up and left. When she got home and told her parents, her mother didn't know what to say and her father said it was no big deal. They didn't tell her she was right to leave. They didn't explain what happened to her. And she learned never to look to them for help.

Shortly after that, she changed schools. Rosa had to ride a public bus to school. One day she sat across from an old man. He was staring at her, and then she realized that he was exposing himself and masturbating.

"I thought he was crazy and insane. I was afraid that he was going to rape or kill me. In my mind, only a lunatic would do something like that. I never told anyone. I knew it was useless to tell my

parents. Besides, I wanted to keep going to this school. It was an honor to go to this school. At age 20, I started having panic attacks. I'd go to get on a bus, and as soon as the doors would open, I'd have a full-blown attack with all the symptoms, pounding heart, feeling like I couldn't breathe, feeling like I was going to die. Over a period of years, I ended up not being able to ride the bus, then not being able to get in a car, then not being able to take cabs, and then not being able to leave my home."

Some children look for approval from other adults and try to be "extra" good, to make up for their bad feelings from the abuse. Other children misbehave, trying to force adults around them to notice that something is wrong.

Children who are sexually abused can experience strong feelings of powerlessness, shame, mistrust, and alienation (feeling different from others.) Adult survivors of CSA report struggling with issues of shame and trust. If someone was molested as a child, they may have had trouble developing a healthy sense of boundaries. They may not know how to say "no" to people and they find themselves being abused anew as adults. Or they may keep a distance from everybody to protect themselves, and never have any meaningful relationships.

Children often believe that if they went along with the sexual assault, they were responsible for it. If they experienced sexual pleasure during the abuse, this confuses them and they feel even more to blame.

For some victims, events that happen following the physical act of sexual abuse are just as damaging as the abuse itself. These children are doubly traumatized by:

- Telling and not being believed or protected
- Being removed from their home
- Seeing someone they care about arrested or jailed
- Keeping secrets
- Being accused of betraying the family
- Being blamed for the abuse or its consequences
- Being abused again even after telling someone
- Intrusive medical exams
- Having to testify against someone you love

Tom's Story (CSA)

For years Tom was sexually abused by both of his parents. The abuse began when Tom was 3 or 4 years old and continued until he was arrested at 18 for molesting a young boy, for which he went to prison for seven years. At age 11 he was removed from his home by the local child protective service agency, following a report of sexual abuse in his home. He remained in foster care for several months, separated from his brothers and sister. Finally, the police decided they did not have enough evidence to prosecute Tom's stepfather and Tom was returned home, only to have the abuse continue. To make matters worse, now he was forced to have sex with his little brothers. His stepfather reminded him that now no one would believe him if he told. Tom became convinced that no one would ever help him.

"I learned that I was helpless. No one could protect me or stop my father from hurting me. I couldn't trust anyone, not the adults who were supposed to take care of me, or the authorities who were supposed to protect kids."

"I think that I was born to be heterosexual. I know I'm not attracted to men, and I have memories of being attracted to girls when I was a teenager. But the thought of having sex with any adult just makes me afraid. The fear is so great I can't even fantasize about sex with a woman. To me, sex with an adult means being abused. I am attracted to little boys, and every day is a struggle to control my desire. I feel out of control all the time. The thought of having a real relationship with a woman seems impossible for me."

Male victims may have different issues challenging their recovery from sexual abuse. To learn more about male survivors (to understand your victims, or your own early abuse), check out the website https://1in6.org/ at Link 5.2. There is also a whole YouTube channel with videos of male survivors of all kinds of abuse sharing their stories of abuse, challenges, healing, and recovery at

Link 5.3.

https://www.youtube.com/c/1in6org/playlists

Leslie's Story (CSA)

"I am now 15 years old. The first incident was when I was 8. I went on a business trip with my dad. In the car he reached over and started touching my breast, at first through my shirt, and when I didn't stop him he slid his hand under my shirt. In the hotel I was in the shower and my dad came in and had me hold his penis in his hand to see how hard it was. Then we washed each other's bodies. After the shower, I went to bed. He told me to spread my legs. He rubbed me in my private parts. He asked me if it felt good and I am ashamed to say it did. But he was my dad, and I didn't think he'd tell me to do anything wrong. Afterwards we went to sleep.

About two months later I was in my room getting ready for bed and he sneaked up behind me and started to fondle my breasts. It felt good. He rubbed his penis up and down my back. This happened about every week for a year. Then came the first time we had oral sex. He told me to take off my clothes. I did. Then he licked my private area. I feel awful about this because I liked it. This happened about 10 times. Then he asked me to suck his penis. I did not like this too much but he was my dad and I did as I was told. This happened 5 times.

All these incidents happened when my mom was either not home, or asleep. He told me he was doing it so that I would learn about my sexuality. He said my mother should have taught me this stuff but she was too messed up to do it."

Many children blame themselves for the abuse. Since children are told in school that sexual touching by an adult is bad, many children believe that they have done something bad by "letting" an adult touch them. Some feel guilty because they felt physical pleasure. Victims often feel that their bodies betrayed them. Of course, their body was reacting to touch just like it is supposed to. It is the abusive adult who betrayed the child.

If you had a minor victim, think about the ways they might have been harmed by your abuse (even if you don't know for sure).

Exercise 5.1: Think About Your Own Minor Victim(s)

Answer The Following Questions.

☑ Why was your victim unable to consent to the abuse?

Can children really make decisions and understand the consequences?
Can teenagers really understand and truly consent to sex with an older person?
How do children know right from wrong?
What are children taught about the role of adults?
How do children protect themselves?

☑ How do you think your victim(s) felt about themselves after?

☑ Based on your understanding of how child abuse affects victims, how do you think sexual assault impacted your victim?

☑ What problems do you know or think your victim might have now?

(We realize you might not have contact with your victim and might now know anything about their current life. But what can you speculate or imagine about the way your crime impacted them, based on what you've learned so far?)

A Teen Survivor's Letter to The Man Who Assaulted Her

"I was so excited because I was travelling with my friend and her mom downstate to go to a house-warming party at my friend's sister's new home. We were sixteen, and it was super fun to go on a road trip adventure! We got there and the party was in full swing. Swimming, ping pong, and a beer keg. Me and my friend snuck a couple beers. We weren't real drunk or anything, but her mom wasn't watching too closely so we felt like we were part of the grownup activities. You and I didn't talk, but I saw you there, it was a small crowd. They called you "grandpa" because of your gray hair.

It was a fun night, and we barbecued, and played music, and finally I laid down on the pull-out couch in the living room to go to sleep. I didn't even get undressed. I'm not sure what time it was, but I was really tired. Most everyone had gone home and things were quieting down, but a few people were still on the patio talking and drinking. I guess one of them was you. Next thing I know, I'm feeling someone rubbing on me. I start waking up and look at the clock, and it is 2 am. I see you laying there on the couch next to the sofabed, and you are rubbing me up and down and trying to kiss me. I'm thinking, ewww! Grandpa!!! I pushed your hands away but you started to kiss me again, and then you put your hand in my shorts and I'm like "no!" and pushed your hand away and you said, SSSShhhh, calm down.

I kind of froze, I didn't want to make a big deal of it or wake anyone up, so I just kind of kept pushing you away and hoping you would leave. But then when you started to push my head down … Down there, and your thing was out, and you pushed my mouth on it, and I'm like eewwww! No way! Then I got up and ran into the room where my friend and her mom were sleeping, and I woke them up and told them what you were doing and we all went back into the living room and you were leaving. We heard your car start up.

My friend's mom called 911 and the cops came. By this time I was crying and so confused. I wondered if I did something to make you think I was flirting with you? I don't even remember talking with you, but did I look like a slut to you? I told the police what happened and they asked me all these questions like about whether I found you attractive, and what was I wearing, and why didn't I get up and run right away? They asked me how much I drank and asked if I was drunk or high. They wanted to swab my cheek but I told them I already brushed my teeth – I wanted to get your dick taste out of my mouth. They acted like I shouldn't have done that, but I had no idea. They took all my clothes and put them in a bag, and wanted to drive me to the rape center but I said no. I just wanted to go home. I couldn't get it out of my mind.

Then at the deposition, your lawyer made it seem like I came on to you, and said that I kissed you first. That didn't happen! You made me look like a liar. I finally told my prosecutor, who acted like she didn't believe me either, to let you plead to simple assault, no sex charge, because there was no way I was gonna get on a witness stand.

To this day I feel sleazy, and creepy, and wonder if it was my fault, because I don't know why you ever thought I'd want to make out with an old guy like you. I've had trouble sleeping for a long time, waking up in the night feeling like someone might be watching or touching me.

After that, I totally stayed away from parties and boys, because I felt like I couldn't trust myself to stay safe."

After reading the story above, you might be interested to know that the person who abused her used to introduce himself in group by saying: "I was arrested for kissing a 16 year old girl who flirted with me." Makes it sound pretty much like no big deal, doesn't it?

Exercise 5.1B: Think About Your Own Minor Victim(s).

Answer The Following Questions.
Does hearing her point of view surprise you?
After reading her perspective, how might the guy be dismissing the impact on her?
How do you introduce yourself in group?
How do you minimize your responsibility, ignore the possible serious impacts on the victim, and change the narrative to fit what you want people to believe?
How might you change your introduction to reflect the seriousness and harmfulness of what you did, in just a couple sentences?

But I Didn't Touch a Child! It Was Just Pictures...

If you have downloaded, viewed, possessed, or shared photos and videos of minors in sexual acts or poses [child sexual abuse material (CSAM) – see chapter 2], you might feel that your punishment is unfair because you didn't touch anyone. It is important to remember that what you looked at are not "just" photos or videos. They are real children being abused while someone directs them to act sexually and records it. What you are viewing is minors being sexually abused and exploited, and you are seeking it, becoming aroused to it, and possibly sharing it with others. Even if you did not abuse the children or take the photos, you are re-victimizing those minors each time you look. And you create a market for this type of material, because if no one were interested in looking at it, others would be less likely to make these recordings.

As one guy in treatment realized in an "aha!" moment, it is easy to distance yourself from the reality of what is happening onscreen. He said: "I was thinking that I wasn't touching anyone so I wasn't hurting anyone. It was easy to think of them as "models." I wasn't thinking about what was going on behind the camera."

Researchers interviewed 100 CSAM survivors who had been sexually abused and had photos and videos posted online to shed light on the complex experience of these victims.*

> *"I was aware I was being photographed (age 6–8). In order to survive and reduce violence, I had to pretend to enjoy anal penetration while being photographed. She described that psychological evaluations reported that she appeared happy, with no signs of depression... Just as in my "happy" child pornographic pictures, looks can be deceiving." (p. 243)*
>
> *"As I became an adult and learned that child pornography exists and that is what the camera(s) had been used for, my sense of being victimized was compounded." (p. 243)*
>
> *"The molesting or rape eventually stops. But images keep forever and maybe they'll never stop being circulated." (p. 244)*
>
> *"I keep worrying how long these images will remain, who has them, how they use them; feeling like this continues the victimization and I have no control over it." (p. 244)*
>
> *"When a man approaches at a grocery store and tells me that he knows me from somewhere or that he recognizes me, I get so scared that he has seen my images. I don't know how to handle that." (p. 244)*
>
> But one survivor described something positive:
>
> *"I used to think they (the images) were less than other stuff. Now I think they are critically important. They make the abuse undeniable. They prove my experience." (p. 245).*

One man in treatment described how his thinking changed after being in treatment and learning about the impact of CSAM on victims: *"I always thought I didn't do anything to hurt a child. I just looked. Then in treatment I heard stories of CSAM survivors talking about what it was like to know their picture was all over the Internet forever. They never know who's looking at it or what that person is thinking about them. And it occurred to me, DUH! That's how I feel about being registered as a sex offender and having my name, address, and photo on my state's website. And the news articles about me. And the mugshot that*

---

* Gewirtz-Meydan, A., Walsh, W., Wolak, J., & Finkelhor, D. (2018). The complex experience of child pornography survivors. Child Abuse & Neglect, 80, 238-248. doi:https://doi.org/10.1016/j.chiabu.2018.03.031

pops up if someone googles my name. And I thought, wow. They feel the same way, but they didn't even do anything to deserve that, I did. I might hate knowing I'm on that registry forever, and I might always be embarrassed about it. But it's there because of the choice I made to look at CSAM. Those victims didn't choose anything."

Adults can be victims of non-consensual posting of photos as well. To read a chilling account of an adult who found nude photos of herself posted online, see the Medium article at:

Link 5.4.

https://humanparts.medium.com/i-found-naked-pictures-of-myself-on-the-internet-cccb567169be

Other Online Crimes Involving Minors

Some people in this program were arrested for chatting sexually to a minor, traveling to meet a minor, "sexting," or exposing oneself to a minor using photos or videos online. You might be thinking: "There was no victim! It was a police sting!" This might be true, but what if it was a real kid you traveled to meet instead of a police officer? Teens are especially vulnerable to online predatory behavior for many reasons. They want to feel mature, desired, and independent. They can interact online or on their phones in ways that are easily hidden from their parents. They don't understand the possible dangers or long-term consequences of their behavior, or the dangers of "hooking up" with strangers or older persons. This is why they are harmed by your behavior even if it seemed like they "knew what they were doing" and "wanted it." They deal with the complex and often overwhelming emotional issues of sexual relationships in different ways than adults do.

Ashley's Story (Traveling to Meet a Minor)

Ashley was 15 and using social media to post photos of herself. She lived for the "likes" and spent hours making up her face and choosing just the right clothes so she could pose for selfies to post. When her high school friends liked her posts and made positive comments, she felt popular and accepted. One day she was friended by a 24-year-old guy from a town a few hours away. He told her she was beautiful, funny, and sexy. They chatted and texted dozens of times a day for weeks, sharing personal details of their lives, and she felt like she was connected to him in a way she never felt before. Finally, she had a boyfriend who loved her! Someone who was older and more mature than those high school boys. Someone who could see her inner beauty, not the superficial stuff her classmates are focused on. Someone who wanted to have deep conversations about life. He suggested they meet at a hotel. She told her parents she was staying with a friend for the weekend and asked that friend to drive her to meet him. They met, and their online love came to life. They ate dinner, and talked, and then she lost her virginity to him in the hotel room. She'd never felt so happy.

Ashley's mom described what happened later: "I'd noticed that Ashley suddenly became irritable and withdrawn. I didn't know at the time, but after that meeting, he "ghosted" her— just disappeared from social media and stopped talking to her. I pieced it all together later after finding out details from her friends. She'd thought she'd found love. She believed he loved her. She was devastated, hurt, lost, and just crushed. She loved him, but it turned out that to him she was just a hook-up... just another girl, just another night. I kept asking her what was wrong but she wouldn't tell me. When

I walked into the bathroom and found her hanging, I couldn't believe what I was seeing. My happy, sweet girl was dead, and now I know it was because her heart was broken."

Exercise 5.2: Think About Your Own Online Minor Victim(s). (include CSAM)

Answer The Following Questions.

- ☑ Why was your victim unable to consent to the abuse?
  Can minors really make sexual decisions and understand the risks & consequences?
  What might make a minor want to chat, "friend," or sext with an adult?
  Can minors really protect themselves online from predatory behavior?
- ☑ How did you use or manipulate your victim to get sexual contact?
  How did you groom and manipulate your victim online?
  How did you make them feel safe?
  How did the different boundaries online or on apps allow you to groom and manipulate?
- ☑ In what ways do you think that your behavior harmed your victim?
- ☑ How did you justify your sexual interactions with minors, and minimize the wrong you were doing?
- ☑ If you viewed, downloaded, shared, or took pictures/videos of minors online, how did you rationalize that?
- ☑ Knowing what you know now about CSAM, why was this harmful to them?

When Adults are Sexually Victimized

Adult sexual assault victims also feel like their world has become an unpredictable and frightening place. They begin to believe that nothing is what it seems, and that they have lost a sense of control over their life. Closeness, intimacy, and sexual contact often bring flashbacks of the rape. Victims who knew their attacker, and who may have even had contact with him willingly, often feel guilty, ashamed, and blame themselves for the sexual assault.

Trauma is described as an experienced or observed event that threatens one's sense of physical or psychological safety and produces feelings of anxiety and helplessness. Symptoms of post-traumatic stress disorder (PTSD) usually involve re-experiencing the trauma, avoiding triggers or reminders, having intrusive thoughts or images related to the trauma, and suffering persistent negative emotions and fear. Importantly, mental health professionals who wrote the criteria for PTSD in Diagnostic Manual of Mental Disorders (DSM-5) specifically defined trauma as: life-threatening events, serious injury, or *sexual violence*. You can refer back to chapter 4 to review the section about trauma.

Adult victims may experience:

- Depression
- Anxiety

- Nightmares or trouble sleeping
- Suicidal thoughts
- Helplessness
- Guilt, Shame, Fear
- Loss of trust
- Difficulty feeling safe
- Intrusive memories, flashbacks, or thoughts about the trauma

Jennifer's Story (Rape and Abduction)

Jennifer was a graduate student working at a counseling agency. One night she left the building around 8 pm after working late. As she walked to the parking lot, a man grabbed her from behind and forced her into her car at gunpoint. He made her drive to an isolated house where he kept her for many hours and raped her repeatedly. He then left her on a corner in a strange neighborhood and stole her car.

"I went straight to the hospital. I was examined and questioned by the police. I felt like a criminal; they questioned me in a way that implied I had somehow done something to cause this to happen to me. I felt violated again during the physical exam. I couldn't believe that this terrible thing had happened to me and no one seemed to care or understand how hurt and degraded I felt. I guess because I didn't have visible bruises, they couldn't understand. I couldn't go back to the job because it reminded me of what happened. I couldn't concentrate on my studies. I had to quit school. I feel like my dreams of becoming a therapist have been shattered. How could I help anyone else when I had become emotionally unstable? For months I had nightmares and constantly relived the experience in my mind. I became afraid of everything. I couldn't trust anyone, especially strangers, but even people I knew. I felt like my life was no longer in my control because bad things could happen at any moment. No place seemed safe anymore and I started just hiding in my apartment. Sometimes I wonder if my world will ever be the same again. Right now it feels like a scary, unpredictable place."

Sandy's Story (Voyeurism)

38-year-old Sandy was alone in her house in the middle of the night when she got out of bed to go to the bathroom. As she climbed back in bed, she noticed someone outside the window, looking through the blinds, which were open slightly. She became frightened and called police. By the time they got there, he was gone. The police took a report and said they would cruise by during the night, but Sandy couldn't sleep. She checked the locks, and then tossed and turned all night. The next night, the man returned. Sandy saw him through the blinds as she stepped out of the shower wrapped in a towel. He was just watching her. She screamed and called the police again. Again, they reassured her that they would keep an eye out, but couldn't really promise anything. They also told her that even if they arrested the man for trespassing, he would probably be out of jail the next day.

"This went on for weeks. The police couldn't catch the man. They couldn't help me at all. I spent thousands of dollars on an alarm system because I was afraid that the man would break into my house and rape me or kill me. I got a dog, but I couldn't sleep, couldn't eat, became depressed, and eventually couldn't function at my job because I was so exhausted and drained of energy. I was a prisoner in my own home. I was powerless."

Professional Sexual Misconduct

It is devastating to have a person of trust, power and authority take advantage of that position to exploit someone's vulnerability. Of course, this is true in most cases of sexual assault, but an additional harm is caused when the abuser is a person of public trust. It is the violation of this sacred trust that compounds the traumatic effects of sexual trauma. We must all be able to go to church or synagogue, send our children to school, visit a health professional, and seek help from police, with an absolute expectation and confidence that we will not be harmed by those in a position to help.

Clergy

Tyler's Story (CSA by Priest)

Though his memories are somewhat disjointed, and he is unsure of the exact order of events, Tyler believes that the grooming and sexual abuse by the priests at his Catholic boarding school began shortly after his arrival at age 14. One day, Father approached him from behind, rubbed his shoulder, hugged him, nuzzled him, and grabbed his left buttock. It seemed designed to be affectionate, but Tyler said the hug felt "strange." The priest told him "we are your family now" and said he looked forward to getting to know Tyler better.

Over time, this touching progressed to fondling, oral sex, and anal rape. Tyler did not talk to anyone about what was happening and did not know how to escape from the abuse. He did not have the words to explain what was happening, and as a Catholic youngster who had been warned that premarital sex in general, and homosexuality more specifically, were forbidden, he felt like he had sinned. Desperate to escape but unable to tell anyone for fear that he would be disbelieved and punished, he attempted suicide by hanging himself from a tree. His parents were called, and he said they were told only that he had misbehaved and broken rules by going into the woods at night. They were devastated that he had squandered the opportunity of this prestigious education. Tyler's deep shame and self-hate continued through his life. He began abusing drugs and alcohol to escape his feelings. Equally painful was that he lost his faith. "It was like being abused by God," he said.

For more real stories of victim impact of people abused by clergy, see:

Link 5.5.

http://www.snapnetwork.org/stories

You can also watch The Keepers, a docuseries on Netflix. Episode 2, in particular, details the crushing effects of sexual abuse of a teenager by priests teaching at her school.

Researchers interviewed many adults who experienced a sexual encounter with a religious leader.* They found five themes that help us understand the context of how clergy abuse occurs: 1. Lack of response (victims and others were so caught off guard that they doubted what happened or their interpretation of it, so these situations are rarely reported); 2. Culture of niceness (we are expected to be nice to others and not make waves); 3. Lack of accountability (these things occur in private, rarely have witnesses, and there is a reluctance to talk about them publicly); 4. Overlapping and multiple roles (in addition to being a spiritual advisor and/or counselor, clergy are also friends, confidantes,

* Garland, D. R., & Argueta, C. (2010). How clergy sexual misconduct happens: A qualitative study of first-hand accounts. Social Work & Christianity, 37(1), 1-27.

and community members); 5. Trust in the sanctuary (people expect churches and temples to be safe places where they don't expect abuse to occur).

Here are some examples of adult victim experiences:

"In the car on the way home, I wondered what on earth had happened. Because I wasn't able to face that he had made advances, I convinced myself that it was just a mistake after all, that my imagination was running wild, and that a priest wouldn't attempt something sexual with me or anyone—and especially not this priest who was such a good friend." (p. 11-12)

"We both stood up, and he said, "How about a hug?" He pulled me into a full-body embrace, for too long. I was uncomfortable and pulled away, and he said he would be praying for me." (p. 14)

A victim's husband said:

"She told me they [she and the pastor] went skinny dipping [i.e., swimming naked]. I didn't say anything to my wife, but I wondered what was going on. I didn't want to cause friction in the marriage. I was just overwhelmed. I wanted to say, "What are you doing?" I wanted to call my parents. But then it got smoothed over, and the worry went away." (p. 12)

Teachers

In a book called Three Women* author Lisa Taddeo describes the true-life experience of a high school senior, Maggie, who had an "affair" with a 29-year-old married male teacher named Aaron (italics in quotes are excerpts from chapters 4 & 6):

The student and the teacher begin to have long conversations. He doesn't give her advice like other adults do – he just listens and makes her feel like her thoughts and feelings are important. He "gets" her.

When he first hugs her, "he makes it seem like it is no big deal, like it's something that happens every day, it's not a wicked thing, you are not a freak or a slut..."

They begin to exchange hundreds of text message. "He writes, I'm a teacher and you're a student, and we shouldn't be talking like this. And she is like, Okay. On the one hand, Maggie is confused as to why he shouldn't be talking to her. After all she has lots of friends and many of them are boys and she talks to them a lot and it doesn't mean anything. She gets along with boys in a way she doesn't with girls. On the other hand, she knows what he means. He means, Don't make me do this, why are we doing this, we can't do this, I love my wife, my kids. But she feels, already, his hands down her pants. She says okay because he is the authority figure. He's older and smarter and if he says they shouldn't be talking—even though he is the one initiating the conversation—then they probably shouldn't be talking. Maggie is aware of a boundary, unclear though it might be, and she doesn't want to be the one to cross it first. It doesn't even occur to her to cross it. She is a kid; she is not his equal. So for him to say, Hey, we shouldn't be talking, made a part of her feel she had done something wrong even though she was mostly confused. All she'd done was answer his questions."

"... His superpower is that he can make her feel stupid very fast. It's not just that he's older, and her teacher. It's something else, but it's also those things...like any young girl who has a crush on someone older, she doesn't know what she wants to happen."

---

* Taddeo, L. (2019). Three Women. Simon & Shuster Press.

"...Children like rules and Aaron gives Maggie some, the most important of which is that she is not to text first. Under no circumstances may she make the first move. This is important for the preservation of the relationship. Maggie wants to do everything to preserve the relationship. She feels it's up to her. She tries not to tempt him. To remind him of his badness. To remind him she's underage. It is her job to be fun, friendly, happy, and also troubled enough by her parents' alcoholism that he can be a savior—over text or voice, whichever is more manageable that day. The biggest problem Maggie faces, bigger than her parents' drinking, is the roller coaster that Aaron keeps her on. Sometimes he gets spooked and says they shouldn't talk. Within hours he changes his mind. Thank God, he changes his mind."

"She stands there and tries to figure out if she really loves him or if her feelings are utterly reactionary—that they exist only because he wants her. It isn't that she's angry with him. It's the opposite. She feels that he cares more than she does, suddenly, and this freaks her out. It makes her feel sad for him and it makes her feel she will suffocate under the pressure to reciprocate; and this feeling of suffocation in turn begins to lessen her liking of him, so the situation becomes cyclical. What she finally comes up with is that she cannot go back in time. If this were a boy from another school it would be easy to meet him at the bowling alley and say, This is going too fast. We need to slow down. And then wait a few hours to reply to his texts until one day she doesn't reply at all. But she can't do this with Aaron. He's her teacher, and it's simply too late."

In the Epilogue, author Taddeo writes:

"Watching the way so many people reacted to Maggie's story was unsettling for me. Even those who believed Maggie's version of events opined that she had been complicit. What, after all, had Aaron Knodel done? Aaron Knodel is not a rapist, they said. He is a great teacher, with a family. He doesn't deserve to have his life wrecked over this. But what Aaron Knodel was accused of is, arguably, nearly as damaging to a child as a nonconsensual event might have been. Society treats girls, like the one Maggie was, as adults who have the faculty of making good decisions. She was a bright child with some hardship. A brilliant teacher like Aaron Knodel could have been the catalyst that propelled her into a lifetime of confidence and greatness. Instead, he became the opposite. Many people, men and women alike, who otherwise accepted Maggie's truth, said to me, Well, she wanted it. She asked for it. But to me Maggie did not ask for it. She accepted it, the way any child accepts any decoration, any gift. Women have agency, but children do not. Maggie's desire for love, for someone to tell her she was a valuable being in the world, was attacked, in the end, for its impudence.

Health and Medical Providers

When you go to the doctor, dentist, hospital, physical/massage therapist, or see other health care providers, you trust them to treat you respectfully and to help you heal. You expect them to maintain professional boundaries, and to not take advantage of your trust, the power difference between you, and the vulnerability created by illness. Sexual abuse by a medical professional is a serious violation of trust, medical ethics, and the law.

Link 5.6.

https://www.rainn.org/articles/sexual-abuse-medical-professionals

Take a look at Maria's story, from a website (Link 5.7) that tells the true stories of six victims of sexual abuse by doctors. http://doctors.ajc.com/patient_stories_sexual_abuse_doctors/

"I am a domestic violence survivor, so I have a lot of PTSD. I'm trying to be healthy and normal, and he doesn't realize what damage he's done again to me…I function every day, but it's very difficult.

[After] he did this to me, I was waking up at night sweating and seeing his disgusting face. And I consider myself to be a strong person; I've been through a lot. I built myself up from so much. So to have somebody tear you down again, it kills you inside.

I couldn't focus. I run my own cleaning business— literally, I almost lost it. I was home schooling my daughter, and I did no work with her.

I've had people say to me, "Why didn't you push him off? How could you let him do that?" I'm like, 'You don't understand. When you're in the position, you can't even believe it's happening. Plus, I could barely even move. And I was half naked.'

I said, 'Is it because he's a doctor they don't believe me?' I used to drive past there and still see him in practice and still see his sign up, and I said, by the time I'm done with him, I'm going to make sure that the sign is down and he's gone. And that's exactly what I got.

It's been a couple months now. The sign's down, and he is out of there. I wanted to kiss the building. It was joyous. I did a happy dance in my car.

You have to speak out. You can't take this. Because they're doctors we can't let them think that they can get away with this.

It felt so great in court. My shining moment was him standing there, saying he did it for sexual gratification. I got my power back. People know that something really did happen, and he's a liar — not me."

To learn more about the impact of abuse by medical doctors, see this enlightening investigation by journalist from the Atlanta Journal Constitution at:

Link 5.8.

http://doctors.ajc.com/doctors_sex_abuse/

You will find a link to a YouTube video about abuse of patients by doctors at:

Link 5.9.

https://www.youtube.com/watch?v=QV2MKuek_Vw

Workplace Harassment

When you are a boss, supervisor, or someone who holds any kind of power in the workplace, using that position to harass of exploit others is unacceptable. Check back to chapter 2 to refresh your memory about what you learned about sexual harassment in the workplace. The harassment imposed on the victims can be physical, verbal, or emotional. Physical abuse refers to sexual assault and violence on body, while verbal or emotional abuse refers to imposing stress and bullying on someone who is usually in a subordinate position to you (you are their manager or boss or someone in charge). Sexual harassment behaviors can range from sexual comments or innuendos, unwanted sexual advances, comments or insults about someone's looks or body, to outward physical threats, unwanted touches, or forced or coerced sexual activities. Even if you "didn't mean to make them uncomfortable" the result can cause the employee to feel humiliated, isolated, helpless, anxious, and trapped.

Exercise 5.3: Think About Your Professional Misconduct Victim(s). (minor or adult)

Answer The Following Questions.

☑ Why was your victim unable to consent to the abuse?

☑ What makes professional misconduct victims especially vulnerable?

How did you misuse the sacred trust of your position?

☑ How did you groom or manipulate your victim to get sexual contact?

How did you make them feel safe?

Why are strict boundaries so important to avoid a "dual relationship"?

How does the power difference in a professional relationship make someone especially vulnerable and why is this so important to think about?

☑ In what ways do you think that your behavior harmed your victim?

☑ How did you justify your sexual interactions with those who trusted you to help, or lead, or serve?

☑ How did you minimize or rationalize the wrong you were doing?

☑ Knowing what you know now about professional misconduct or sexual harassment, why was this harmful to them?

Exercise 5.4: Read the Stories earlier in this chapter and on the following pages. then answer the following questions:

List 5 reasons why sexual assault is never the victim's fault:
1.
2.
3.
4.
5.
List 5 ways you took advantage of your victims' trust or vulnerability:
1.
2.
3.
4.
5.
List 5 feelings victims have during and after sexual assault:
1.
2.
3.
4.
5.
List 5 ways sexual assault affects the life of a victim: SHORT TERM:
1.
2.
3.
4.
5.
List 5 ways sexual assault affects the life of a victim: LONG TERM:
1.
2.
3.
4.
5.

Jeff's Story (CSA)

Jeff was 4 years old when his uncle began to wrestle with him and fondle him in a sexual way. At first Jeff didn't even notice, but when his uncle began asking him to undress and perform sexual acts with him at age 5, he knew something was wrong. His uncle convinced him that their "little secret" was a special bond between them, and if anyone else knew, they wouldn't understand, and bad things would happen. Jeff liked the attention and treats he got from his uncle, and, after all, the sexual touching felt kind of good in a weird way.

When his mother walked in on them when Jeff was 8 years old, she immediately called the police, took action to protect Jeff by refusing to let the uncle have contact, believed and supported Jeff, and reinforced that what happened wasn't his fault. Jeff testified at the trial, after which his uncle was sent to prison for 20 years.

As an adult, Jeff is extremely unsure about his sexual orientation. He is attracted to women, but finds himself also thinking about men in a sexual way. Although he knows his parents acted appropriately and protectively, he still feels guilty for "sending" his favorite uncle to prison. He has been told that the abuse was not his fault, but he knows, deep down, that the liked the attention and went along with it. He continues to live in fear, waiting for "something bad" to happen, as his uncle promised. As an adult he knows that this is irrational, but he can't help feeling anxious all the time.

Stephanie's Story (CSA)

14-year-old Stephanie was molested by her father, beginning from age 7. Although there was medical evidence of anal trauma, her father denied the allegations and was never arrested. Instead, Stephanie was placed in foster care, forcing her to change schools and lose her friends, and making her feel alienated from her family. It seemed that she was the one being punished.

Stephanie actually had a closer relationship to her father than to her mother. She lost this relationship when she was removed from home. Her mother did not believe that the abuse took place, and believed that she fabricated the allegations in response to an argument with her father about not being allowed to date boys. Her mother frequently states that Stephanie has destroyed the family and subjected them to financial ruin. Her two brothers have been told that Stephanie was removed from the home because she is a liar.

Stephanie, alone and depressed, wishes she had never said anything to anyone. Although she hated being sexually abused, she loves her father and now feels she has lost her entire family.

Kimberly's Story (Indecent Exposure)

Kimberly was at the park with her two children in the car. On a bench in the park was a man sitting and watching the children play. Kimberly noticed he put his hand in his pocket and seemed to be rubbing himself. A few minutes later she saw that his penis was exposed.

Afraid that the man would hurt the children, she quickly rushed them out of the park and drove away. She did not report the incident to the police because she feared that if she were identified as a witness, he would learn her name from the police report, track her down, and retaliate against her. Her children became afraid to go outside to play.

Darby's Story (CSA by Sibling)

12-year-old Darby was fondled on her breasts and kissed by her oldest brother, age 20, several times over a three-month period. Feeling unsure of what to do, she wrote a letter to her godmother explaining the situation. Her godmother discussed it with a friend who worked in a school, and therefore he was required to report the incidents to the local abuse hotline.

Social workers and police investigated. Darby's mother was at first shocked and reluctant to believe what was being alleged, but when she confronted her son, he admitted to the accusations and promised not to do it again. Darby felt relieved that now that her mom was aware of her brother's behavior, the abuse would be over. She didn't want her brother to go to jail, she just wanted the abuse to stop.

Reassured and convinced that her mother would now protect her, when the police returned to question Darby the next day, she stated that the whole thing had been a mistake and that nothing had happened. The police officer made her write a letter of apology to her family and threatened to arrest her for filing a false report. Shocked, shamed, and scared, she knew that if anything ever happened to her again, she could never go to anyone for help.

Janet's Story (Rape by Intoxication)

Janet was 20 when she was raped by a guy in college. She had gone to a frat party and had too much to drink. Because she was drunk, she might have been a little flirtatious. The guy at the party offered to drive her home, and because she knew him and trusted him, she said yes.

He walked her into the dorm and asked if she needed any help. She fell right into bed, feeling dizzy and sick. He took her clothes off, telling her he was just helping her when she protested. He rubbed her back and began kissing her, and she didn't really say anything at all. When he took off his pants she pushed him away and asked him to leave.

After he raped her, he warned her not to tell and said everyone saw her flirting with him at the party. Ashamed, she never told anyone. She stopped socializing, withdrew from all her friends, and her grades began slipping. Eventually she dropped out of school. She still has trouble trusting people who try to help her.

Candice's Story (CSA & Physical Abuse)

Candice was 3 years old the first time her stepfather sexually molested her. The abuse continued for years, and by the time she was 7 he was having frequent anal and vaginal intercourse with her and forcing her to perform oral sex on him. Candice's stepfather was also physically abusive, as was her mother.

When she was 8, after an abusive incident, Candice put a pair of underpants that were wet with her stepfather's semen in the hamper. Candice's mom found them, and when Candice tried to tell her mom what her stepdad had been doing to her, her mother beat her for urinating in her pants and then lying about it.

At age 9, Candice revealed to her health teacher in a sex education class that her stepfather was abusing her. Investigators questioned Candice's stepfather before getting a statement from her. He convinced them that Candice, a rebellious child, had a wild imagination and was just trying to get attention. After investigators left, Candice's stepfather turned on the stove, sat Candice on top of it, and reminded her that she had better not tell anyone about this again.

You can also watch I'll be Gone in the Dark, Episode 2 (HBO) to hear the harrowing stories of survivors who were raped in their own homes by a serial predator who victimized California communities for decades. Over 30 years later, these victims and their family members remain severely traumatized by their experience.

As you do the following exercise, you might find that it is hard to know how your victim was feeling, especially if you have never been sexually abused yourself. If you were sexually abused as a child, think about how you felt to help you understand how your victim felt. If you were not sexually abused, think about some other experience in which you were victimized or felt powerless, such as being physically abused, being the victim of a violent crime, or another experience that happened to you that was out of your control. These are difficult exercises. Take some time to think about them.

Exercise 5.5: Think About Your Own Victim(s).

Answer The Following Questions.

- ☑ Why was your victim unable to consent to the abuse?
  - Can children really make decisions and understand the consequences?
  - How do children know right from wrong?
  - What are children taught about the role of adults?
  - How do children protect themselves?
- ☑ How did you use or manipulate your victim to get sexual contact?
- ☑ In what ways do you think that your behavior harmed or damaged your victim?
- ☑ What would it feel like to anticipate sexual assault?
- ☑ What would it feel like to be molested, raped or flashed?
- ☑ What if the abuser was a person the victim trusted?
- ☑ What would a victim think and feel after the abuse?
- ☑ What would it feel like to tell and not be believed?
- ☑ What is it like to keep secrets?
- ☑ What is it like to not feel safe or protected?
- ☑ Think about how sexual abuse affects victims with regard to the following issues: trust, sexual boundaries, emotional boundaries, power, control, sexuality.
- ☑ How do you think abused children feel about themselves?
- ☑ Based on your understanding of how child abuse affects victims, how do you think sexual assault impacted your victim?
  - How did the abuse change your victims' living arrangements?
  - Did your victims have physical injuries as a result of abuse?
  - What is your victim(s) doing with his/her life now?
  - Does he/she have a job? a relationship? How does he/she achieve in school?
  - Is your victim in therapy?

What problems do you know or think your victim might have now?

More Resources

You can also just google "sexual survivors" and find many books, websites, and YouTube videos to learn more about the impact of sexual crimes. You can listen to survivors of Bill Cosby, Harvey Weinstein, Michael Jackson, Larry Nassar, Jeffrey Epstein, and others in cases with lots of media attention. Of course, there are thousands of other cases that get no attention at all, and do not result in reports, arrests, or convictions. You can find survivor voices on websites and YouTube videos across the Internet. In other chapters in this book, you will also find suggestions for documentaries, videos, articles, and podcasts about victim experiences, grooming, minor attraction, offending, and the healing power of talking about it all.

Choose a few of these podcasts, videos or websites to listen to… you will gain more insight into victims, survivors, the far-reaching impacts and ripple effects of sexual assault, and voices of therapists working with survivors and people who've offended:

Beyond Fear Podcast (Link 5.10)
https://beyondfearpodcast.com/

OneVoice Podcast (Link 5.11)
http://www.iamonevoice.podbean.com/

Vice (HBO) Episode: Consent (Link 5.12)
https://www.youtube.com/watch?v=DhFyGz8wQaY

And hear a brave man reveal his story after hearing the video of Trump admit to grabbing women: "I did it too" (Link 5.13)
http://ididittoo.org/blog/2016/10/20/just-like-trump

To view or listen to some victim / survivor videos see Link 5.14
https://metoomvmt.org/survivor-story-series/

Collateral Damage and Ripple Effects

Sexual Assault hurts many others besides just the victim. You hurt the victim's family, partner, children, and friends. You hurt not only the victim's current relationships, but also future relationships. Sexual assault may affect the victim's ability to have fulfilling relationship for his or her entire life.

Your Family as Victims of Your Crime

You also hurt your own family. Your family may have lost a great deal of money and time helping you fight your legal battle. They have lost trust. If you have your own children, they will almost surely be stigmatized by your behavior. Your family probably feels ashamed, embarrassed, and isolated. They may be humiliated in their community.

Several studies have explored the impact of sex-offender management laws on the families of people who are convicted and required to register. Employment problems for the RSO is the most pressing issue identified by family members, followed by concerns about housing. In states and towns with residence restrictions ordinances, families often face a housing crisis if the home is too close to a school or park. Some face the financial burden of supporting two households if the RSO can't live with the family, or having to move to a different home that is compliant with buffer zones. Others face the stress of having the RSO becomes transient or homeless due to these laws. Housing and employment are sometimes disrupted by limitations imposed by the offender's probation or registration status, resulting in economic hardships for family members. Family members who live with an RSO sometimes experience threats and harassment by neighbors.

Sometimes children in your family (maybe your own kids) are prevented from having relationships with you. The deprives them of family relationships and your active involvement in their lives. It may make them feel like you don't care, especially if they don't know or understand why you can't see their school play, come to their birthday party, or go trick-or-treating with them.

Children of RSOs report adverse consequences; more than half (58%) said they were treated differently by other children or teachers at school, or that their friendships had been impacted in some way (78%). Many children of an RSO had experienced ridicule, teasing, depression, anxiety, fear, or anger. Many family members describe persistent feelings of depression, hopelessness, shame, and stigma due to living with a registrant. Sometimes a family member's decision to remain in contact with you leads to breaks in relationships with other relatives.

Family members report that they are subjected to intense scrutiny, searches, and intrusion by parole or law enforcement agents, and that their right to privacy has been impacted by public registries. Many report feeling overwhelmed and demoralized, struggling to cope on a day-to-day basis. Some have a great deal of mixed feelings, wanting to support the RSO but feeling angry that their life will never be the same as a result of his choices.

You might want to check out this website called Accidentally Brave, the story of one family coping with the arrest, conviction, and registration of the husband/father. On Link 5.15 you will find several articles and links to videos sharing the personal story of this wife and family – their experience is unique, or course, but in many ways is probably similar to what your family has gone through.

http://www.accidentallybrave.com/media/

You can also watch I'll be Gone in the Dark, Episode 6 (HBO) to hear the stories of traumatized relatives who did not know that their loved one was committing brutal home invasion rapes and murders for decades.

Children of Incarcerated Parents

Having a parent arrested, jailed, or imprisoned is considered one of the ten primary adverse childhood experiences (ACEs) identified by the Center for Disease Control (CDC). The incarceration of a parent can cause immediate and long-lasting consequences to a child's development and well-being. Research shows that parental incarceration can cause attachment problems, shame, stigma, poor physical health, mental health disorders, and extreme trauma for kids.

Think about it: A child sees his or her parent be arrested, disappear from their life, talked about in the neighborhood, and maybe the child is even removed from their own home due to authorities thinking he is at risk for abuse. The arrest and imprisonment might have devastating financial impacts on the family. The parent misses important events in the child's life, is unavailable to be a role model, and his absence interferes with their bonding and attachment to each other. The child might be embarrassed or told by family members to keep the incarceration secret. Or, maybe the child does not even know where the parent is! He's just missing… and the child waits and wonders and worries.

The severity of the effects stemming from parental incarceration has been compared to the trauma of divorce, abuse, or death of a parent. Separation from a parent can cause physical and psychological effects, adverse school experiences, and social stigma. The child might wonder, "Why didn't my parent love me enough to avoid offending?" As they get older children are at higher risk for substance abuse and violence or other criminal behavior. Their uncertainty about the future can overwhelm the already compromised coping skills of these kids (Link 5.16).

https://youth.gov/youth-topics/children-of-incarcerated-parents/listening-session

Exercise 5.6: Think About Your Own Family.

ANSWER THE FOLLOWING QUESTIONS.
How did your behavior affect each family member? Emotionally? Financially? Stigma and Shame? What did they lose or have to give up? How did it change their beliefs about you and ability to trust others whom they love? How do they suffer the consequences of your choice?

What Does a Good Apology Look Like?

The following excerpt is from a book called The Apology written by Eve Ensler, a sexual abuse survivor who waited her whole life for an apology from her abuser – her father. After he died, she decided she could no longer wait, so she wrote the words she longed to hear to herself. The book is available on Amazom.com. You can also search her name on YouTube to see various video segments of her talking about her childhood sexual abuse and writing the book.

> *What is an apology? It is a humbling. It is an admission of wrongdoings and a surrender. It is an act of intimacy and connection which requires great self-knowledge and insight… An apology must be thorough and can only be trusted in its veracity and dedication to details… [There are] very strict guidelines: Recognize what I have done as a crime. Face how deeply my actions and violations have impacted and devastated you. See you as a human being. Attempt to experience or feel what it felt like inside you. Feel profound remorse and regret over my actions. And finally, take responsibility for my actions by doing extensive work to understand what made me do what I did. (Ensler p. 10).*

Some thoughts about Apologies…

- Must be victim driven, meaning that contact should be initiated by the victim.
- But you can write a good apology based on what you think your victim needs to hear.
- Apologies speak to lessons learned – Let your victim know what is different about you now, why you won't do this again, and describe how you acknowledge and understand the harms caused by your abuse.
- Harm can't be undone – Remember, whatever you say, and however you've changed, you can't make it go away.
- Forgiveness is a very personal matter for each individual, and you have no right to ask for forgiveness or to expect it (or anything) from your victim. Your victim does not owe you anything.

Exercise 5.7: Using Ensler's Guidelines, Write an Apology Statement Outlining Your Responsibility for Your Offense and the Ways in Which Your Victim(s) Might Have Been Harmed.

1. Name the wrongdoing.
2. Acknowledge the harm caused.
3. Accept responsibility.
4. Talk about what has changed for you (why should the victim believe you won't do it again?)
    - Identify at least three qualities about your victim that you misused and took advantage of. Describe exactly how you were able to manipulate the victim by exploiting these qualities. Speak about each quality separately. For example, trusting, eager to please, obedient.
    - Identify at least three ways in which you harmed the victim. Use "I" statements about how you hurt the victim. Use feeling words to describe the harm. For example, I betrayed your trust, I left you feeling like you did something bad, I made you take care of me instead of me taking care of you, I made you keep a secret, I made you believe that other adults couldn't help you.
    - Why you did it (focus on you, not the victim). For example, the selfishness of the act, the dismissal of the victim's choice and value, your poor boundaries, how you broke the rules, the lack of consent, and how you took away the victim's rights.

Here are some good documentaries to watch that will help you understand grooming, the impact of sexual assault, and why victims often don't tell or aren't believed. You can also find similar TV segments of cases profiled in the media if you check YouTube. Many of them have been featured on 20/20, Dateline, 48 Hours, the morning shows, Nightline, and PBS News Hour, among others.

- Leaving Neverland (HBO)
- Surviving R Kelly (Lifetime; now on Amazon)
- The Keepers (Netflix)
- Unbelievable (Netflix)
- What Haunts Us (Starz, or Amazon)
- Rape on the Night Shift (Frontline)
- I am Evidence (HBO)
- The Hunting Ground (CNN or Amazon)
- Audrie and Daisy (Netflix)
- The Invisible War (Amazon)
- Athlete A (Netflix)
- Filthy Rich (Netflix)
- Untouchable (Hulu – about Harvey Weinstein)
- I'll be Gone in the Dark (HBO)
- On the Record (HBO Max)

In the 2012 book Through the Glass, Shannon Moroney courageously described her horror and journey of healing after discovering that her husband committed brutal rapes (Moroney, 2012). In 2019, a one-woman Broadway show called Accidentally Brave (now an Audible book), written and performed by Maddie Corman, introduced us to the hidden world of the traumatized families behind the headlines (Corman, 2019). You can look both of these women up on google or YouTube to hear more about the impact on wives, partners, and families of people convicted of sexual crimes.

There are some good documentaries to watch that will help you understand/ground the impact of sexual assault and [illegible] victims of a [illegible] don't tell or aren't believed. You can also find similar or stronger [illegible] of cases [illegible] in the media if you check [illegible] of them have been [illegible] 2017 [illegible] #MeToo. The [illegible] [illegible] News [illegible]

- Leaving Neverland (HBO)
- Surviving R. Kelly (Lifetime; now on Amazon)
- The Keepers (Netflix)
- [illegible] (Netflix)
- What Haunts Us (Starz or Amazon)
- [illegible] (Hulu)
- [illegible] (HBO)
- The Hunting Ground (HBO or Amazon)
- [illegible] (Hulu/Netflix)
- The Invisible War (Amazon)
- Athlete A (Netflix)
- [illegible] Rich (Netflix)
- Untouchable (film about Harvey Weinstein)
- [illegible] in the [illegible]
- [illegible] (HBO Max)

[illegible] through the [illegible] journey [illegible] described her [illegible] journey of healing after [illegible] her husband [illegible] (Lindsey, 2017; 2019) [illegible] performed [illegible] when [illegible] (Conant, 2019) [illegible] to [illegible]

CHAPTER 6
RELATIONSHIP AND COMMUNICATION SKILLS

Understanding Relationships

You might have heard the saying, "No man is an island." This saying means that none us can exist alone. Yet it seems that some people who become caught up in self-destructive and compulsive behaviors feel like an "island." They feel isolated, unable to be close to others, unable to be understood by others. Even when they are with somebody—sometimes even when they are married—many people *feel alone*.

The simple fact is that we are all social beings. We have a built-in need to be with other people, to be part of a group, to have a partner. We need to be accepted and valued by others. In earlier sections we discussed our "basic needs." One of those basic needs is for *Love and Belongingness*. All healthy people have this need.

So why then does it often seem that love is a fiction—a cruel joke, something that only happens to other people (or maybe to no one)? The answer frequently has to do with our early experiences. Many people grow up believing they are unlovable because they felt that way in their families. Or they believe other people are untrustworthy and not worth caring about. In Chapter 4 we examined the many ways that children are ignored, made to feel unimportant, belittled, blamed, neglected, or abused. These experiences leave their mark. Negative experiences in childhood often leave children wondering—sometimes all their lives— *"Am I okay? Is there anything good about me? Could anybody love me? Are other people worth trusting?"*

These kinds of feelings make it difficult to freely relate to other people. People who don't know if they are lovable tend to hide from others. Without even being aware of it, they tell themselves, *"If other people really knew me, they wouldn't like me."* Until you become aware that you are influenced by this basic belief, it can undermine every attempt you make to be close to others. If you are afraid that others won't accept the real you, you will try to present yourself as you think you should be or as you think others would want you to be. Or, if you believe other people are not worth loving, you won't see any point in opening up to them. Either way, you'll never feel comfortable around other people. Even when others like you, you might convince yourself that it's only because they don't know you—or because they want something from you.

In this chapter, we will discuss how to improve your relationships – all relationships! Not just romantic relationships, but also relationships with friends, family members, co-workers, and others. Even your group members! As you learned in Chapter 4, early life experiences can shape the way you relate to others. In this chapter you will learn about:

- Recognizing your role in relationship patterns
- Basic beliefs about relationships
- Self-defeating styles of relating to others
- Patterns and Themes that repeat themselves across various types of relationships
- Intimacy
- Conflict resolution

Figure 6.1: How Might Your Patterns Follow You Through Many Types of Relationships? (family, friends, work, parenting)

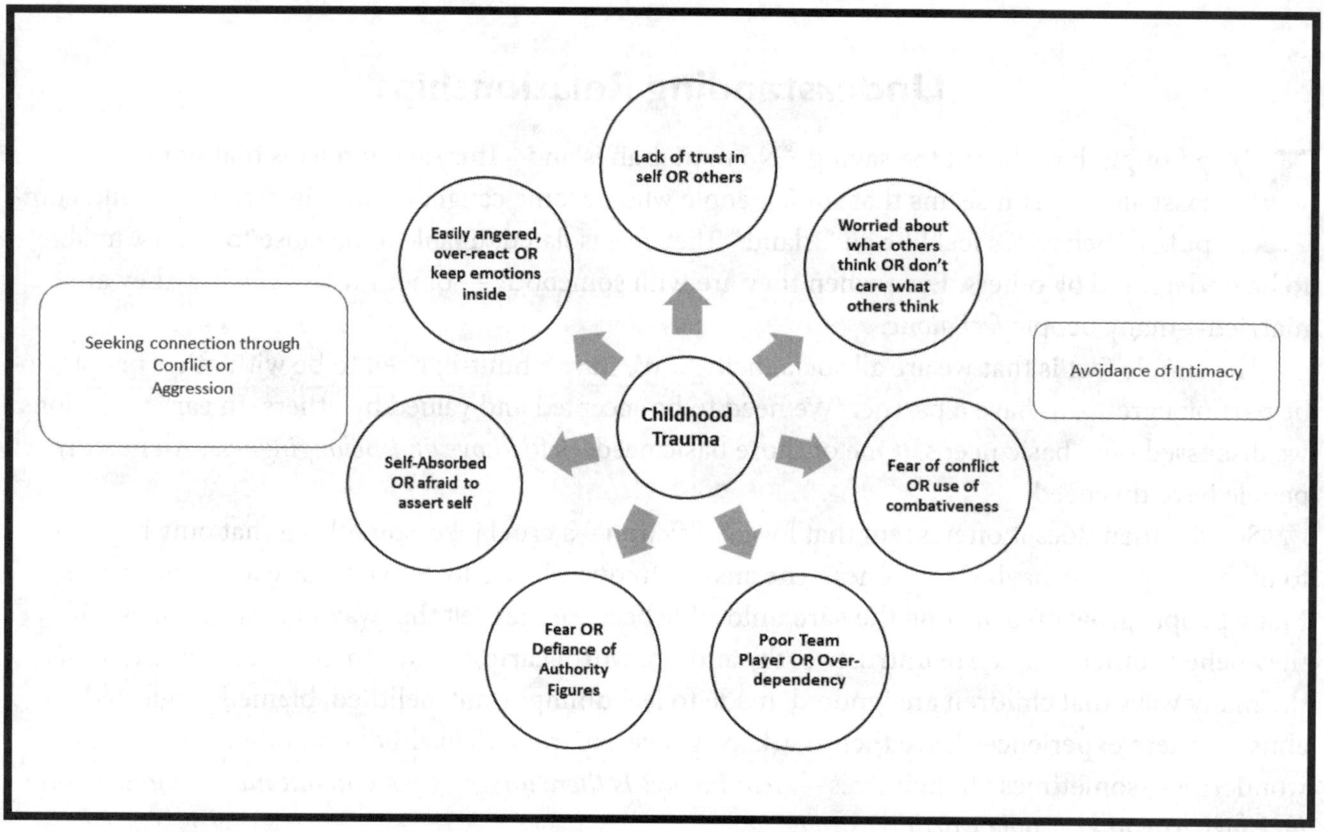

Seems Like I've Spent My Whole Life Hiding from People...

If you have spent your life hiding from other people, this can lead to depression. Hiding from others can lead to loneliness. Worse—it's work to put on a front for people. It takes an enormous amount of energy to not be able to be genuine and authentic with others. When you start being yourself, you free that energy for better purposes. Having a genuine relationship with even one person can free you to be more confident, more open, and more relaxed with everyone.

If you have committed a sex crime, you having a real relationship might be even more uncomfortable because you worry how others will see. If you convince yourself that meeting people or trying to have a real relationship couldn't possibly lead to anything good, you won't even try. You might tell yourself instead that you don't need anyone. But how does that make you feel? Probably pretty empty.

Even within relationships that start off feeling right and seem destined for happiness, men can still struggle with feelings of wanting to withhold parts of themselves. If you are not really comfortable with your own feelings or with who you are, if you're not fully trusting of your partner, these problems can lead to poor communication and bad feelings in the relationship.

As You Take Control of Your Life and Start to Trust Yourself...

One of the things we discussed in the Introduction to this book is learning to differentiate *who* you are from what your problems are. Now that you have learned some important things about who you are, it is time again to remind yourself that you are more than the worst thing you have ever done. Even when the potential to reoffend may exist, as you exercise control, as you start to live a different lifestyle, you will gain greater confidence in yourself. You will start to remember that there is much more to you than just this problem. You will rightly feel that you are gaining the freedom to be who you really were meant to be instead of a slave to destructive and futile attempts to meet your needs.

In time you will face new questions. These questions will be in the form of:

- Is it possible for me to have the things other men have: a partner who loves me? A family?
- Why would anyone love me?
- Why shouldn't somebody love me?
- Why haven't my efforts to create a relationship worked in the past?
- What could I do to improve my chances of having a real relationship?

A lifetime's worth of fear and anger don't go away overnight. Neither does the pain of having been hurt by partners, friends, or family members. But as you have already discovered if you have been participating actively in your group, talking about these feelings does help you to get them out. Everyone has suffered emotional injuries in their lives. As we said earlier, it is never easy to remember sad times and feel the pain they bring up. But it is much harder to spend your whole life hurting from the unfortunate events in your past.

That relationships have not worked for you in the past is not a reason to believe that they never can. The fact that you have been hurt by people in the past is *not* a reason to believe that all people are untrustworthy or will not care about you. These beliefs are examples of what we call distorted thoughts. Sex offending itself is an attempt to get your intimacy needs met in unhealthy ways. Needing other people is normal and healthy. Be honest with yourself about your needs.

Recognizing Your Role in Relationship Problems

Ultimately, you will find that the pain of failed relationships is somewhat easier to deal with when you are able to be honest with yourself about what role you played in the breakdown. You may recognize that, without being aware of it, you brought distorted ideas that you learned in your childhood about yourself and other people into your relationships (as everyone does). You will be able to see the ways you contributed to communication problems and made it difficult for your partner to know you and trust you. As you look honestly at yourself you will also see how you may have isolated yourself when you were hurt or angry instead of openly discussing things with your partner when there were problems.

If in your heart you expect other people not to really accept you or care about you, you might set yourself up for failure by pursuing relationships with people who aren't healthy for you. But if you learn to accept yourself you will believe you have the right to be respected and accepted by others.

You will be selective: you will wait until you find someone who appreciates you and cares about you as much as you care about them. You will not trust someone who hasn't demonstrated trustworthiness. And if you find yourself in a relationship in which you have misjudged a partner—trusted someone who turns around and treats you poorly—you will know that you have other options. You can find another partner. You are only trapped in a relationship when you have trapped yourself. Relationships can only work when they are built on mutual (two-way) respect.

You can begin to improve all your relationships by starting with the following questions:

- What am I doing to contribute to the problem?
- What can I change about the way I think about this problem?
- What role can I play in the solution?

Figure 6.2: Healthy and Unhealthy Relationships

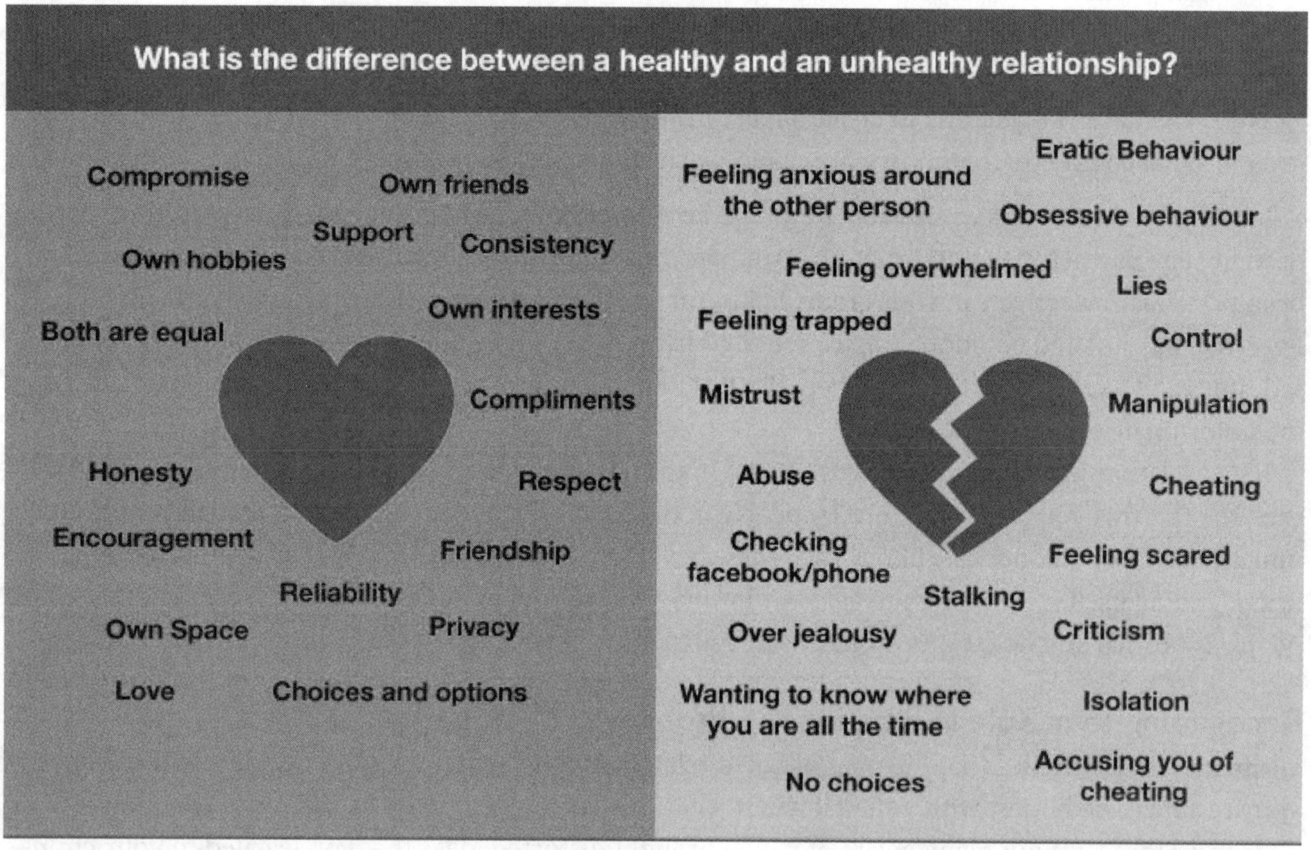

It's important to remember that your spouse, partner, or family members were also harmed by your arrest. You're here, but do you ever talk with your loved one about how your sexual behavior problems affected them? This is a good conversation to have. You might want to start by looking at the website below to get an idea of the thoughts, feelings, and issues that your family members are dealing with when they love a person with sexual behavior problems.

Link 6.1 – Cosa Recovery
https://cosa-recovery.org/

But I Don't Know Where to Start...

Well, here's some good news: you've already started. In fact, you've already come a long way. In your group you have been thinking about and talking about the early experiences that left you feeling unacceptable or that make it hard for you to trust others. You are able now to see where you learned to keep your thoughts and feelings to yourself, to act like things are okay when they're really not, and to avoid conflict and confrontation, or to protect yourself through aggression or manipulation. If speaking your mind as a child only got you punished, it was good sense on your part to keep your mouth shut! You had to survive in your family. And, like everyone, you brought to your adult experiences the lessons you had learned as a child.

The questions that face you now are: Do you have to keep thinking and acting in the same ways that you have in the past? Because your parents or your brothers or sisters or schoolmates didn't understand you or value you, does that mean that you can't value yourself or that someone else can't? If you can't start seeing the good in others will you really be able to be happy? Because you have hidden your true feelings from others in the past, does that mean you must keep doing that? Do you have a right to be yourself and feel good about who you are? Do you have the right to expect the same things from life that other people do?

Exercise 6.1: Identify Feelings About Direct Communication.

What is scary or uncomfortable about talking about how you feel and what you need?

____

____

____

____

How has this discomfort affected your relationships or your ability to succeed at work?

____

____

____

____

Well, if you've been doing the exercises in this book and discussing them in your group sessions, you've probably already made a good start toward changing your patterns from the past. You have been open and honest about yourself. You have let go of your most shameful secrets. You have been your most vulnerable self. You have risked being judged and put down by others. And what has been the result?

For many people in treatment, therapy is the most intimate relationship they've ever had. It's the first time they can talk honestly about their thoughts, feelings, and behaviors without being judged. But it's hard. It's scary. Think about your experiences being in treatment, with your therapist(s) and with your group members.

Exercise 6.2: Feelings About Treatment

1. Describe the feelings you had in your first group sessions. Be honest. Don't spare your therapist's feelings on this one.

2. Describe your expectations of the other group members when you started treatment. Did you expect them to accept you? Did you expect them to try to understand you?

3. Describe your feelings about openly discussing your offenses during group while you were still minimizing and denying them in public.

4. Describe the feelings you had the first time you were honest with the group about your offenses. Don't stop with just one feeling (because you probably had a bunch of them).

5. Describe your feelings about coming to group now. Be honest about the good and the bad feelings.

Exercise 6.3: Discuss Your Communication Patterns.

For many people in treatment, therapy is the most intimate relationship they've ever had. It's the first time they can talk honestly about their thoughts, feelings, and behaviors without being judged. But it's hard. It's scary. Think about your experiences being in treatment, with your therapist(s) and with your group members.

Ways you've expressed your needs & feelings: ______________________________

____

____

____

____

Ways you have attempted to get what you wanted: ______________________________

____

____

____

____

How you have felt about your relationships: ______________________________

____

____

____

____

Factors that might interfere with your ability to have healthy relationships: ______________________________

____

____

____

____

Basic Beliefs That Interfere in Relationships

In this book we have talked a lot about how early experiences stay with us and affect us later in life. This happens in two ways. The first way is that we carry *feelings* with us that were never resolved or expressed. By making ourselves aware of these feelings and where they came from, and by talking about them with others who can understand them and will listen, we have a chance to get them out of us. This is why we use groups for treatment and why we encourage everyone to talk about their feelings in the group.

The other way that our early experiences stay with us and affect us is by influencing the ways we *think* about things. We have described how early experiences create our *basic beliefs,* and how those basic beliefs form a foundation of thoughts about everything. If you grew up in a family where people treated each other poorly and treated you poorly, you probably hold basic beliefs about yourself and about other people that are unrealistically negative. Those beliefs will lead you to have negative thoughts and expectations in your relationships now. When you are unaware of the distorted thoughts you have about relationships, those thoughts can sabotage your relationships. Of course, everyone has their faults, and no doubt your partners have theirs too. But being aware of the attitudes you bring to your relationships can help you understand how you may contribute to the problems as well.

For example, if you have a basic belief that says, *"If someone is nice to me, they probably want to use me for something,"* anytime someone is friendly you will have an automatic tendency to pull away from that person. The other person will think you don't really like them, and will pull away from you. What will be accomplished? You will have defeated yourself by creating exactly what you fear and expect.

Here are two other examples to show how distorted basic beliefs lead to self-defeating automatic thoughts:

1. Basic Belief: "I'm stupid" leads to automatic thoughts like: "I'm lucky to even have this job. I better not ask my boss if I can have a vacation. Even though I'm resentful because other people are going on vacation and I have been here for over a year, I better keep my mouth shut."
2. Basic Belief: "I'm a sex offender so no one will want me" or "I'm unlovable" leads to automatic thoughts like: "Why bother applying for that job? Or asking that person on a date? Forget it."

In the next few sections we will be looking at relationship styles and basic beliefs that interfere with creating good relationships. By looking closely at the beliefs you hold and the ways those beliefs influence your thinking, you can start to exercise more control over your feelings and your behavior. Later you will learn how to recognize distorted thoughts and "restructure" them into realistic and useful ones.

Psychologist Jeffrey Young and his colleagues created a list of what they called "early maladaptive schemas. Schema is just a fancy word for thoughts. So, schemas are flawed patterns of thinking that you got in the habit of believing because of experiences you had growing up. Take a look at the list in Figure 6.3 and think about the ones that apply to you. Then give some examples of the ones that apply to you by writing down some things you believe or say to yourself.

FIGURE 6.3: Early Maladaptive Schemas

Early Maladaptive Schema (EMS)	Brief description
1. Abandonment	The belief that significant others will leave
2. Mistrust/Abuse	The belief that others will lie or take advantage
3. Emotional Deprivation	The feeling that adequate emotional support is not available
4. Defectiveness/Shame	The belief that one is flawed or worthless
5. Social isolation/Alienation	The feeling of separation from others
6. Dependence/Incompetence	The feeling one is unable to take care of oneself
7. Vulnerability to Harm or Illness	The belief that catastrophe is impending
8. Enmeshment/Undeveloped Self	The fusion of identity with a significant other
9. Failure	The belief one is inadequate compared to others
10. Entitlement/Grandiosity	The belief that one is superior to and more deserving than others
11. Insufficient Self-Control/ Self-Discipline	The belief that one cannot restrain emotions or impulses
12. Subjugation	The feeling that one's own needs are less important than those of others
13. Self-Sacrifice	The focus on meeting the needs of others at the expense of one's own
14. Approval-Seeking/ Recognition-Seeking	The heightened need for approval/recognition from others
15. Negativity/Pessimism	The pervasive focus on negative aspects of life
16. Emotional inhibition	The constriction of emotional expression
17. Unrelenting Standards/ Hypercriticalness	The perfectionist drive to achieve
18. Punitiveness	The belief that mistakes warrant punishment

Hawke, L. D., Provencher, M. D., & Arntz, A. (2011). Early Maladaptive Schemas in the risk for bipolar spectrum disorders. *Journal of Affective Disorders*, *133*(3), 428-436. (Table 1).

Young, J. E., Pascal, B., & Cousineau, P. (2005). Young Schema Questionnaire-Short Form 3 (YSQ-S3). *New York, NY: Schema Therapy Institute*.

Exercise 6.4: My Maladaptive Schemas

Early maladaptive schemas that apply to me:	Examples of those thoughts in my own life:

Attachment Styles

Humans need other people in their lives – for survival, for love, and for companionship. We learn about ourselves and others through our earliest relationships with family and parents, and later through our interactions at school with teachers and friends. Our experiences in these early years form the foundation for how we think about relationships and how we interact with others. This is called our "attachment style." There are three types of attachment styles: *secure, anxious, and avoidant.* Trauma in early life, such as neglect, abuse, or parents who were absent or emotionally unavailable, can lead to difficulties in relationships later.

Securely attached people generally had a healthy childhood and are better at having intimate relationships. They expect to love and be loved because they felt safe and secure in early relationships with their parents, caretakers, and others in their lives.

Other people with anxious attachment may struggle to connect with others, because they worry about not being "good enough." They may feel incredibly needy, and afraid of being alone, or feel like they need a partner to make them complete. They may feel jealous or possessive, or need constant reassurance from their partner, and in their desperate attempt to connect with people, they might push people away, creating exactly what they fear.

Those with avoidant attachment may be so afraid of rejection or abandonment, they completely avoid intimate relationships with others. This protects them from being hurt. They expect people to be selfish, critical and rejecting, and they may act the same way. They may wish they could have relationships, but they are also afraid of them. Their relationships are superficial, and they don't usually last. People with avoidant tendencies might connect with others only through conflict, anger, aggression, or superficial sex.

We tend to repeat the same kinds of relationships we were first exposed to, because they seem comfortable and familiar (even if they weren't healthy). If you like yourself and you like other people, you will tend to have healthy relationships. Healthy relationships do not guarantee that you won't be hurt. Everyone suffers heartbreak and loss. Life is just like that: it's full of ups and downs and frustrations and disappointments. But if your basic beliefs about yourself and others are positive, you have a built-in compass that will steer you back toward people who are worthy of your attention and who appreciate you. You won't give up. You will expect good things from people and you will get them.

But what if you don't like yourself? What if you believe you have nothing to offer others? What kind of relationships are you likely to end up in then? What if your basic beliefs are always steering you away from other people? Or what if you see other people only as users? What if your basic beliefs are about protecting yourself from others, or taking advantage of others?

Self-Defeating Styles of Relating to Others*

The kinds of beliefs you have will help you understand how you approach relationships. These have to do with whether you see yourself in a positive or negative way and whether you see others in a positive or negative way. They are:

1. Negative you/Positive others. We'll call this style, ***"Insecure-but-Wanting."***
2. Negative you/Negative others. We'll call this style, ***"Insecure-and-Avoidant."***
3. Positive you/ Negative others. We'll call this one, ***"Cold-Avoidant."***
4. Positive you/Positive others: Secure Attachments and Healthy Relationships.

Look at the descriptions below to see if you fit into one of these styles. Remember, no one ever fits any style completely. But if you recognize parts of yourself in a style (or in more than one style) you can learn important things about yourself.

Insecure-Wanting

This person doesn't like himself much. They know that they need other people. They hate to be alone. They want to be in a relationship. They are romantics who fall in love easily. But they fear rejection terribly. Rejection feels awful because they see it as proof that they are not good enough. Sometimes they avoid rejection by not approaching others, waiting instead for others to approach them. They feel lucky when someone wants them—but it may mean they end up with partners they didn't choose, and who can't really meet their needs.

They may have rocky relationships because they need a lot of attention and approval from their partner. They are always worried that their partner is not satisfied with them, so they want constant reassurance of their love. They seek to please their partner and they may be good at pleasing them in some ways, but they still feel worried because they know they need their partner more than their partner needs them. They may smother a partner with their needs, causing them to feel suffocated. To the Insecure-Wanting person, sex is the main way to feel close to someone, and they may be hurt if their partner doesn't want as much as they do. They may also be jealous and try to control their partner. If their partner doesn't want to be controlled and pulls away, they feel rejected and angry.

* (Adapted from: Ward, T., Hudson, S.M., Marshall, W.L., & Siegert, R. (1995). Attachment style and intimacy deficits in sexual offenders: a theoretical framework. Sexual Abuse: A Journal of Research and Treatment, 7, 317-335).

Some of his distorted basic beliefs might sound like these:

- ☑ I am not someone a partner would love.
- ☑ I can't tolerate being alone.
- ☑ I am not very smart.
- ☑ Without someone smarter than me to tell me what to do, I will be lost.
- ☑ When someone rejects me, it is because there is something wrong with me.
- ☑ If I say something that makes someone angry, they will get rid of me.
- ☑ I don't have anything interesting to say.
- ☑ If I'm not successful, no one will want me.
- ☑ If I don't control others, they will not do what I want.
- ☑ If I fail at something, it means I am a failure.
- ☑ If someone doesn't act friendly to me, it's probably because they can tell what a worthless person I am.
- ☑ Only if I keep people guessing, or make them laugh, or shake them up, will they find me attractive.
- ☑ When I don't have people's attention, I feel like a nobody.

The *Insecure-Wanting* offender may be drawn to minors because they will always look up to him or her and respect him or her in ways that adults won't. They don't have to be afraid of children spotting their weaknesses and criticizing them. They feel in control with minors. They do a lot of grooming with their victims because they want to have a lasting relationship with them and feel close to them. They will sometimes say they "fell in love" with their victim and "forgot" they were a child. Sometimes this is called "emotional congruence with children" (see chapter 2), which means that a person feels like they relate more to children than adults because they don't feel very confident about themselves.

Scott was a twin who grew up in a family of six brothers and four sisters. His parents both drank heavily and what he remembers best about his home-life is that everyone seemed to be fighting all the time. His father, a factory worker, lost a lot of jobs because of his drinking and the family often had to live off welfare. Scott remembers being embarrassed in school because he never had decent clothes and only had his sister's old bikes. Everyone knew he was "poor."

Scott learned that his mother would be nice to him if he helped out around the house and he became what his brothers called "mama's best boy." Still, his mother ignored him a lot, and she always seemed to be worn out.

Scott did a lot of babysitting for his little sisters. He enjoyed being in charge of his sisters and felt close to them. When he was thirteen, he discovered masturbation, and, after seeing some porn, tried to get his 8-year-old sister to fondle him. First, he fondled her for several months until she threatened to tell on him.

Scott was never very good at schoolwork. He was a good athlete when he was young, but no one ever seemed to notice. When he was in the sixth and seventh grade he signed up for little league, but because his mom didn't have a car, he missed practices and the coaches kept him on the bench during games. By the eighth grade he gave up baseball completely. He dropped out of school in the tenth grade.

When he was eighteen, he married a seventeen-year-old girl he had gotten pregnant. He suspected Monica didn't love him but they had good sex and he loved her. Besides, she was excited about having the baby and Scott hoped she would learn to love him when she saw what a good father he was.

By the time his daughter was four Monica was bored being a mother and said she wanted to "live." She started working as a manicurist and going out nights with her girlfriends, leaving Scott to baby-sit Gabrielle. Scott told himself she would settle down in time and tried his best to be a good husband, taking care of the apartment and spending time with his daughter.

A few years later Monica discovered cocaine and things got worse. Suddenly his job as a warehouse worker wasn't good enough—she needed more money. Scott took a second job, but no matter how much he worked Monica was never satisfied. She mocked him in front of her friends, calling him a "little boy in a man's world." Sometimes she stayed out all night now.

Scott felt there must be something wrong with him for her to treat him so badly. He found himself drinking more heavily than he had before. In time he found himself thankful when Monica was gone, and looked forward to his time with Gabrielle, who was now seven. Gabrielle was afraid of her mother and clung to Scott. Scott felt himself "falling in love" with Gabrielle and he treated her like a princess, downloading all the movies she liked and watching them with her for hours on end. He "knew" she wanted to be touched because she hugged him so hard. He molested her from the time she was seven until she was eleven, when Monica was arrested on drug charges and child protection workers investigated the family.

Scott tried to build a relationship on a foundation of not liking himself and not believing he had much to offer a woman. He could see that Monica didn't love him but married her anyway, hoping that sex and having the baby would lead to love—a bad way to start. When Monica distanced herself from him, he felt lonely and helpless to fix their problems. With Gabrielle he felt important. She listened to him and appreciated him. In time he began to see his daughter as a new "partner," someone he could have a "romance" with. He wanted to see her need for affection as something sexual because for him closeness was built around sex. Of course, children aren't thinking about sex at all when they want hugs and kisses, but Scott's emotional needs had overtaken his common sense.

Insecure-Avoidant

Some of these people go for long periods between relationships, which means they get little practice talking to others, which makes them feel even more fearful of relationships. The *Insecure-Avoidant* offender may try to meet intimacy needs through distant, impersonal sex. They may end up spending a lot of money on sex. Prostitutes, hook-up apps, video chats, pornography and strip clubs are appealing because they don't require the risk of letting anyone get close to them or the need to take an interest in another person.

This type of person may be is a loner who is generally comfortable being alone. They might be carrying deep emotional scars and made up their mind a long time ago not to let anyone hurt them again. To make sure no one can, they keep everyone at arm's length. Distance keeps the Insecure-Avoidant offender from being vulnerable or being hurt. This type of person might prefer to meet people online, where the anonymous veil of the Internet allowed them to avoid intimacy and possible rejection (see chapter 2).

They hold basic beliefs that sound like these:

- ☑ People shouldn't be trusted.
- ☑ If I allow myself to care for another person I will be hurt.
- ☑ If I open up to another person, they will use what I say against me.
- ☑ Most people are only out for themselves.
- ☑ Everyone looks down on me.
- ☑ I am not someone a person would love.
- ☑ Other people are always looking for something to criticize.
- ☑ I don't have anything interesting to say.
- ☑ If I'm not successful, no one will want me.
- ☑ If I don't control others, they will control me.
- ☑ If I fail at something, it means I am a failure.

These kinds of beliefs will lead to sexual needs being met only through impersonal sex. Here is an example of what these beliefs can lead to.

Vernon was a twenty-year-old title-examiner who lived at home with his mother. His father had left when Vernon was twelve, and his mother was still angry. Vernon sometimes felt that she took out her anger on him by ignoring him. He had always stuttered and he was used to being laughed at by kids in school. He hated the kids who mocked him and hated himself for stuttering and being such a geek. Masturbation was the only thing he had to look forward to.

He was sexually excited by everything. The beach, the movies, television, the Internet, even the women's magazine covers in the supermarket turned him on. He had one girlfriend in the eleventh grade but that lasted only a month. He longed for sex, but the only sex that didn't involve the risk of rejection was masturbation. He had a large collection of porn magazines and masturbated to them frequently. Sometimes when he was driving, he would become aroused seeing high school girls walking in their sexy outfits. If he became aroused enough, he would masturbate in his car, telling himself he just couldn't wait to get home to do it.

Over time Vernon masturbated more and more frequently while driving or while parked in a parking lot. He discovered that when other people were around his orgasms were more intense. One time when a woman in a parking lot saw him and seemed to be interested in what he was doing his orgasm was especially powerful. He was hooked. He started "flashing—exposing himself to unsuspecting women and girls and masturbating in front of them.

He spent countless hours cruising for just the right victims. He found that teenage girls were his best "audience" because they seemed to be curious and weren't as angry with him as older women. He started looking for school buses because the girls could look down from their high windows and see him masturbating clearly. When someone he flashed had the presence of mind to write down his license plate number, the game was suddenly over. He was arrested and charged with committing a lewd act on a minor.

Vernon got sexual excitement from the idea of being "with" another person, but the reality of actually being with someone was too threatening. So he settled for "long-distance intimacy," a kind of make-believe contact with his victims that didn't involve any risk of their getting close to him. He was in control. He decided who he would flash and when. They had nothing to say. They couldn't reject him. Porn served the same purpose. Vernon was emotionally isolated, but he could steal a few minutes of sexual excitement by flashing.

Other *Insecure-Avoidant* offenders may abuse children because they believe they just don't measure up to other adults. Children are much less threatening, and provide a substitute for real relationships, which this type of person feels they must avoid.

Cold-Avoidant

The *Cold-Avoidant* may like himself but looks down on others. They are very detached from personal connections and see relationships as unnecessary. By paying little attention to what others think and dismissing any criticisms others may have of them, they preserve their positive self-image even when it is undeserved. Others see them as cold and distant, sometimes intimidating, sometimes outright hostile and aggressive or arrogant (see chapter 4 section on entitlement). They may have many sexual partners, but they don't become involved with any of them. They prefer one-night stands. Since they are not planning to see their partner again, they don't have to worry about whether they are accepted or whether the other person is enjoying the sex or not. Instead of grooming one victim for a long-term relationship, this style of offending may involve strangers or online victims, or predatory behavior.

The *Cold-Avoidant* offender may laugh at the idea of marriage as if it were a plot to steal their freedom. They may see potential partners as manipulative users. Actually, they use others, since they want sex but do not offer much in return. They may abuse minors or adults in a hit-and-run fashion. Since they are not interested in maintaining a relationship with their victim, they use only enough grooming to get the victim to go along with them. The Cold-Avoidant is good at picking victims who don't seem to have anyone to talk to, or who are unlikely to report them or to be believed.

If it's necessary, these offenders will use threats or even force. Usually they won't hurt the victims more than necessary to get their cooperation, but any force or threat makes sexual assault even more damaging to an adult or a child.

Their distorted basic beliefs sound like these:

- ☑ Relationships only take away your freedom.
- ☑ Most people are only out for themselves.
- ☑ If someone is nice to me, they just want to use me for something.
- ☑ If I follow rules or take other people's advice, I will lose my sense of identity.
- ☑ Since other people are just out to get what they can from me, I should try to get what I can from them.
- ☑ Most people are so stupid they deserve to be taken advantage of.
- ☑ Rules are for suckers.
- ☑ I'm special and I have the right to take whatever I want.
- ☑ Other people would hurt me if I gave them the chance, so I don't have anything to feel guilty about if I hurt them.
- ☑ Hurt others before they hurt you.

In its extreme form, the *Cold-Avoidant* style can lead to a complete lack of feelings for others. Far from wanting to please sexual partners, the *Cold-Avoidant* may get off on hurting their partners. When they are a flasher, they are hostile to their victims, hoping to shock and frighten them. They may approach them or touch them to scare them. When they are a peeper, they may allow themselves be seen by their victims to frighten them, or even enter a victim's house. When they rape or molest, the *Cold-Avoidant* may use more force than they need to. The object of a rape isn't the sex at all—it's to hurt and humiliate their victim. Sex is merely the method they use to accomplish this end. At their worst, this type can be a sadistic rapist whose main sexual pleasure comes from the pain and suffering they cause their victims.

Carl was a welder who lived for excitement. He worked on large buildings high above the ground and prided himself on his willingness to do work that frightened other men. He especially liked to work high on cocaine and to brag about his drug use to the rest of the construction crew. Even though he made good money he sold cocaine to bring in more, and twice had been arrested. Being on probation didn't slow him down: he continued to use and to sell to co-workers. He was thrown out of his drug treatment program for being disruptive.

Carl's father had deserted the family when Carl was two. Because his mother had emotional problems, he had been raised by an aunt who had four children of her own and little time for Carl. He carried a lot of anger toward his mother who "gave him away." He said he loved his aunt, but he also said he couldn't wait to get out of the house, which he did when he was sixteen. His sister was raised by his grandmother and Carl lost contact with her over the years.

At 37, when he entered treatment, Carl claimed to have had sex with "hundreds" of women. He said he had had "one or two" girlfriends in his twenties, but one was a "skank" who cheated on him and the other wanted to control his every move. He claimed the keys to "intimacy" were having a "pocketful of money" and driving a fancy car. He said he "knew" even as a teenager that he could have any woman he wanted and he had never changed this opinion. He said sometimes women resisted his advances at first, but once they felt him inside them "they changed their minds." He said a woman had falsely accused him of raping her when he was twenty-four, and he was still angry that he had to pay a lawyer to defend him. He said the case had fallen apart when the woman got on the stand and admitted she had willingly gone into his bedroom. After that, he said, he knew that women who went back to his apartment were "his."

When he first entered treatment, he claimed the two rapes he had been convicted for, at ages twenty-nine and thirty-two, were also false accusations. It wasn't until he had been in treatment for almost a year that he started to be honest with himself and the group. He admitted that he started being interested in "rough sex" as a teen. In his twenties, he said, he started raping women anally, knowing that they would feel used and humiliated. He said that he would then make them leave his apartment as soon as the sex was over.

Carl said the first time he hit a woman during sex he realized that this was the most exciting thing he had ever done and that he would do it again. He knew he couldn't take a date to his apartment to beat her up, so he started picking up prostitutes— "I knew no one would care about them or believe them" he said. He said he would drive her to a deserted area and then "punch her face in" before raping her. He said none of the 15-20 prostitutes he had done this to had ever come forward to accuse him.

In his honest moments (which, unfortunately, were not very frequent), Carl admitted that between his conquests he had been a lonely man. He continued to claim that he had no need for a partner, but he admitted that the lifestyle he had created was not bringing him happiness. He fought hard to defend his distorted beliefs—especially his favorite: "Trust no one"—but in the end he recognized that such thinking gave him little to look forward to except offending. He knew that the next time he got caught he would go away for life.

Positive You/Positive Others: Secure Attachments and Healthy Relationships.

People with secure attachments have healthy relationships that have the following qualities:

- They respect the other person and feel respected by them.
- They can assert their opinion, but still "agree to disagree."
- They can tolerate conflict in a relationship because they don't find it threatening or worry that conflict will lead to loss of the relationship.
- They are able to feel close (intimate) with others by being honest and emotionally vulnerable.
- They allow others to be vulnerable with them, and don't take advantage of that or use it to manipulate the person.
- There is an even, mutual, shared balance of power between people.
- When relationships end, they feel a sense of loss but they don't interpret that loss as meaning "I'm not good enough."

Exercise 6.5: Identify Your Distorted Basic Beliefs About Relationships.

Which one of the attachment styles of thinking and acting described above do you see yourself fitting into? Why?
Which of the distorted basic beliefs listed above do you hold? What other beliefs interfere with your relationships?

Achieving Intimacy

Many people use the words "sex" and "intimacy" as if they mean the same things. Actually, sex and intimacy are very different. Sex is only one part of intimacy. And sometimes, sex is not really intimate at all.

- ☑ Sex: physical release and physical gratification.
- ☑ Intimacy: sharing one's thoughts and feelings openly with another; truly knowing another person and being known by them; feeling close and connected or bonded; having a "soulmate" or a companion who cares unconditionally for you.

Almost everyone has sexual needs. What frequently gets overlooked is that everyone also has intimacy needs. Many people, without realizing it, attempt to create intimacy through sex. It seems like a quick and easy way to create closeness. But it creates only the illusion of closeness. Real intimacy is never quick or easy. Intimacy means opening up to someone—and that means taking the risk of being hurt or rejected. For many people, vulnerability feels too threatening. We all need intimacy for our lives to feel complete but sometimes people settle for sex because the risk of opening up with another person is too scary. Sometimes promiscuous sex (having sex with many partners) can be a way of protecting oneself from being hurt. *Having sex with lots of people usually means being close with no one.*

In order for others to feel close to us they must first know us. Frequently a relationship never has a chance to develop because one of the persons in it refuses to allow the other to know him or her. Many people create such barriers without even being aware they are doing so. They may feel frustrated and bewildered at their "bad luck" in relationships, never recognizing that they are the one closing the door to connecting with others. This kind of self-defeating behavior can make relationships seem hopelessly complicated. The more aware you are of your own behavior the better able you are to adjust it and make it work.

Relationships work best when the people in them are able to be intimate. Intimacy is being able to be your genuine self with another person. Not having to pretend. Feeling close. Not playing games. When we think of being close to another person, we think of being able to express who we are and what our deepest feelings are. Intimacy is about truly knowing another person and being known by them.

Intimacy is the basis for true caring. In hard times intimacy leads to support and help. Good times are not as good when there is no one to share them with. Being able to talk with someone who cares about what you have to say and "gets you" is simply part of what it means to be alive. Intimacy is a simple idea, but that doesn't mean it's easy to achieve. It involves believing that you can be yourself and be loved. If you've never felt that way before it's a scary thought.

Developing intimacy is a process. It happens slowly, over time. It starts with the willingness to take a risk. The process is one of opening up with another person and revealing yourself to them. The risk is that they will get to know you—and maybe stop loving you. It takes courage to develop an intimate relationship.

A great website about sex, intimacy, and relationships can be found here:

Link 6.2 – Sex & Relationship Healing

https://sexandrelationshiphealing.com/

Intimacy Begins with Trust

Social work professor and scholar Dr. Brene Brown described the components of trust using the acronym "BRAVING". Think about how you can develop trusting relationships using these ideas. How do you demonstrate (or not) each element? How do you evaluate how others demonstrate each element (or not) when you think about the important relationships in your life?

It is important to remember that trust issues are important not only in romantic relationships, but in all relationships – with family, friends, co-workers, employers, and others you meet and interact with. Intimacy is about closeness and feeling connected with others, not about sex.

FIGURE 6.4: The Anatomy of Trust: BRAVING by Brene Brown

- Boundaries
  - Respect the boundaries of others
- Reliability
  - Do what you say and say what you do.
- Accountability
  - Own your mistakes, apologize, and make amends.
- Vault
  - Respect privacy and hold things in confidence, don't share information that belongs to others
- Integrity
  - Choose what is right, do the right thing, even when it's hard.
- Nonjudgment
  - Listen without judging or shaming others
- Generosity
  - Interpret the motivations, words, and actions of others with a benefit of the doubt.

Brown, B. (2018). Dare to Lead: Brave Work. Tough Conversations. Whole Hearts. Random House.

Watch Brene Brown talk about Trust: https://www.youtube.com/watch?v=G72JWvqdNLA

During the course of our lives sometimes we trust people who end up hurting us. Sometimes we will blame ourselves and realize that we really didn't have a good reason to trust a particular individual, that we really didn't know the other person—we simply wanted to trust them and did so blindly. We learn from these experiences to be selective, and to trust others only when they have earned our trust. We also learn to trust our own instincts—to pay attention to red flags and listen to the voice in our head.

Other times we will trust others who we should be able to trust—family members or close friends or lovers—and they will let us down. From these experiences we learn that there are no guarantees in life and that even when you are selective and have done all you can to protect yourself, any time you place your faith in another there is always a risk of being hurt.

Choosing to Trust

Ultimately, we are faced with two choices about trusting. Neither choice is without cost. We can either choose not to trust others, to isolate and protect ourselves, or to trust others and risk being hurt. Not trusting has its benefits. If we do not trust we will be protected from being hurt. If we place no faith in others we will never allow them to get close enough to us to hurt us. The cost of not trusting, however, is enormous: a life of isolation and loneliness. Trust is the basis of intimacy and ultimately, of the freedom to be yourself. Many people go through periods in their lives when they find themselves unable to trust, but if they can't bring themselves to try again and trust another, they will have no chance to find intimacy.

Choosing to trust is choosing to take risks. Why would we do that? The answer is simple: because if we want a chance to truly be alive and feel alive, we have no choice. Of course when there is a chance of being hurt, we don't want to take more risk than we need to. As we grow, we learn how to minimize our risks. In our relationships that means learning when to trust and how to build trust.

When to Trust

Building genuine trust is a process that takes time. If we find ourselves being asked to trust before there is a good reason to trust—alarm bells should go off in our heads. If we find ourselves disclosing too much too quickly—without receiving genuine self-disclosure in return—alarm bells should go off.

Remember, one-sided relationships are never satisfying and never last. Before you place your trust in someone wait until they have responded in a trustworthy way to you. That means they have shown a willingness to genuinely accept you and a willingness to return your self-disclosure with their own self-disclosure.

We have talked a lot in this book about being honest with yourself. When you are honest with yourself you come to trust yourself, to trust your instincts and your judgment. Trusting others also starts with trusting yourself, your instincts, and your judgment. You will be making judgments about how trustworthy other people are. You need to trust your feelings (your "gut") about others to make these judgments.

Ultimately, trust is about honesty. When you are honest with another you create trust. In a truly intimate relationship, you know that you can trust others because they are honest with you. And the people in your life know they can trust you because you are honest with them.

Like anything in life, trust must be maintained. Trust grows when communication remains open, and withers when communication becomes difficult.

Building Trust

Just as there are two people involved in any relationship there are two dimensions to trust. Both parts are necessary to build trust. They are:

1. **Opening up and giving of yourself:** By revealing yourself to another person, you are giving trust.
2. **Accepting the other person:** By listening to the other person, by trying to understand them, and by accepting them for who they are, you are rewarding them for putting their trust in you. You are being "trustworthy."

There are also two ways to destroy trust:

1. **Not Accepting:** If another person responds to your attempt to be open by not paying attention, changing the subject, laughing at you, making a joke out of what you are saying, criticizing you in a disrespectful way (rather than a way that communicates that they care about you), or telling you they don't want to hear what you have to say, you will find yourself no longer willing to trust that person.
2. **Not Giving:** Even if the other person accepts what you have to say in a supportive way they still must give back—open up about themselves with you—or you will find yourself pulling away from them. Sometimes you will continue to be open for a while in the hopes that they will eventually give back to you. But over time you will find yourself opening up less and less. Trust does not grow in such a one-sided relationship.

Self-Disclosure

We can never control how other people feel about us or how they respond to us. What we can control is our behavior toward them, and our reactions to what they say or do. If we take steps to create positive feelings and closeness, we have done our part to promote a healthy relationship. Of course, not all our attempts at creating relationships will work. Just as we are interested in some people and not in others, some people are going to like us and want to be close to us, and some people are not. This is reality.

How do we take the first steps to creating closeness? By letting others know us. This process is called ***self-disclosure***. In most conversations we have with people we are giving and receiving information. Sometimes this information has nothing to do with who we are as individuals. Self-disclosure, on the other hand, has to do with what you think and what you feel. Self-disclosure is the process of opening up about your values, your feelings and thoughts, your hopes, your fears, what makes you excited and enthusiastic, what makes you angry or depressed. In other words, what makes you who you are. Only by revealing yourself to others can they come to appreciate you and care about you. Friendship, commitment, and trust can only occur when people know each other. This can be scary!

Distorted thought: "If this person doesn't like me, it means there is something wrong with me."

Healthy thought: "Just because one person doesn't seem to like me it doesn't mean I'm unlikable. Not everyone hits it off."

Think about the people you have liked and cared about and you will be thinking of people who have opened up to you and let you into their lives. On the other hand, you can probably also think of people you have known for years whom you have never really cared about. These are people who keep their feelings hidden. You may feel that although you have "known" these people for a long time, you don't really *know* them at all.

Self-Disclosure Must Be A Two-Way Street

Self-disclosure is partly a testing process. At the beginning of a relationship, people talk about safe things: "small talk." Small talk serves a purpose. It lets you test the water to see if the other person is interested in getting to know you. If the response is positive, you try another test: you reveal something about yourself. Not something private, but something safe. You wait and you watch. How does the other person respond? Do they ignore your self-disclosure, or respond to it? Do they ask questions and seem interested in your ideas? These are important messages. If the other person is not responding to you, you can't continue to self-disclose safely. When others respond to you with interest and validation and mutual sharing, this is the go ahead signal to continue.

Meanwhile, the other person is going through the same process with you. Pay attention to what you are hearing. If they tell you something about them but you aren't paying attention or asking questions or you only talk about yourself, they may feel you aren't interested in who they are. They are testing you in exactly the same way you are testing them.

If someone risks an open (personal) remark but you aren't open with them in return, they will pull back. *The process of getting to know another person is slow, and it must work both ways.* When one person gets ahead of the other, problems arise. Relationships can only work when they are mutual, or two-sided.

Knowing Yourself is a First Step

You can't reveal yourself to another person if you don't know yourself. We focus a great deal in this book on understanding yourself. We have put emphasis on your early experiences and how they shaped you. And of course there is much more to you than just the crime that brought you here. You have many sides to you. You are a son, a friend, a neighbor, a lover, an employee, a co-worker, a group member. Maybe you are a father, a brother, an uncle, a husband, a supervisor, a boss. You have special abilities, special interests, values, and beliefs. You have a personality that is always growing and changing, yet in most ways remains the same.

It is important to recognize how many different roles you have taken on in your life and continue to take on. If you focus only on one side of yourself you can lose your sense of who you are. Seeing yourself only as a provider, or a son, or a husband can lead to emptiness—especially if you are not pleased with your performance in these roles. Seeing yourself only as a RSO will surely lead to depression.

Developing a sense of yourself, or a *self-concept,* is a lifelong process. As we said in Chapter Four, your sense of yourself begins to develop early in your life—and it is based on the way other people (mainly, your family) treat you. As a child you take your cues about how important, how smart, and how lovable you are, from your parents, your brothers and sisters, and other people around you.

Later in life, you are more able to look at yourself and form your own judgments about who and what you are. But even as adults, we all still learn a great deal about ourselves from how others respond to us. What this means is that *the very process of revealing yourself to others helps you to know yourself better.* This is another reason why interacting with others and talking about yourself is important: in so doing, you are actually developing and describing your self-concept.

Knowing Yourself Better

There are some simple ways to get to know yourself better.

1. Observing and recording your thoughts and feelings. You could carry around a notebook and write down your thoughts and feelings, or you could text them into your phone if that's easier for you. And guess what? When you actually take the time to notice what you are thinking about and how you are feeling *at the moment these things are happening*—and write them down—you learn a great deal about yourself. You're paying attention to your thoughts and feelings. When you are able to look back over two weeks' worth of notes about what you actually spend your time thinking about and how those thoughts affected you, you are looking at a snapshot of who you are. Sound like too much work? Try it just for one or two days and see if you haven't learned things that you never knew before.
2. Talking to others about yourself and your life actually helps in several ways. Talking about things forces us to organize our thoughts and clarify things in our minds. Hearing yourself say something can actually help you understand it better. When people go into therapy to try to work through difficulties in their lives a large portion of the insight they gain comes just from listening to themselves. A major part to the therapist's job is just to ask questions and encourage the patient to talk. Talking also helps your brain process your thoughts differently when you say them out loud and get feedback from others.
3. When you talk to others they respond to you. We call these responses "feedback." Feedback lets you know several things: how successfully you are putting into words the things you want to say, and what others think about the thoughts and feelings you describe. Of course you don't open up with everybody; only with people you trust to listen to you and try to understand you.
4. Observe what you do. Our actions are the result of our thoughts and feelings. When it is difficult to identify your feelings, you can always work backwards. Look at what you do. Not just for a moment or a day, but over time. It's easy to say something is important to you, but your actions over time tell you what is really important to you.

Your Feelings Are Part of Who You Are

We have already said that recognizing your feelings and allowing yourself to feel them and express them is important for several reasons. We have feelings about things that matter to us. We have talked about how boys are kind of steered away from paying attention to their negative feelings like fear, sorrow, and pain—and discouraged from expressing them. (This is sometimes called toxic masculinity. Google it!) Developing genuine intimacy means you have to be aware of—and be able to talk about—your feelings.

Accepting Yourself

Before you will be willing to open up about yourself you must first accept yourself. If you don't like yourself you will continue to hide. Here's a place to start: understand that everyone has had the experience of looking in the mirror and not liking what they see. In this book we have focused on making important changes in your lifestyle. We know that you can make these changes if you want to and if you work at them. As you make them give yourself the credit you deserve.

Ask yourself if you think it would be possible to *fully* accept yourself. Maybe you have never done that. Maybe now is a perfect time to begin. Start by fully accepting that you have harmed people in the past and that you have the potential within you to do that again. Accept that you may have deviant attractions but that you can and will control your behavior in the future. Accept that you have feelings you don't like: anger, resentment, hostility, fear, sadness, or depression. Accept that you have been confused about how to meet your needs and that—like everyone—there will be times in the future when you will be confused again. *And then accept that you are human, that you have made bad choices, but that you are making changes, and that there are many good sides to you.* Accept all of it. All of it is who you are. Make no mistake: you can accept yourself. If it seems impossible to you, talk about your doubts in group. What thoughts hold you back from accepting yourself? Write them down. Later you will learn how to examine them objectively to see if they are realistic or distorted.

The importance of self-acceptance cannot be overstated. Self-acceptance is the very foundation of mental health.

Fear of Rejection

Everyone is nervous. Everyone is afraid of rejection. Everything in life that allows you to grow and develop makes you nervous. Going to a new school, starting a new job, getting a promotion and having new responsibilities, going to a therapy session—you name it. If it is new, if it is worthwhile, it is going to make you nervous. If you find someone you are attracted to and approach that person, you are going to be nervous. *It's okay to be nervous.* If you start to open up to that person, you will be making yourself somewhat vulnerable. Vulnerability carries with it risk, and risk brings fear. *It's okay to be afraid.* A great psychologist pointed out that courage isn't some magical quality that you either have or don't have. Having courage simply means that you *do courageous things.* Feel the fear and *do it anyway.* Enough said.

Self-Esteem

In Chapter 4 we said that many people come out of their childhood feeling bad about themselves. They think they are dumb or boring or annoying or doomed to failure. We say they have "low self-esteem," meaning they don't value themselves or like themselves. By now you should have an understanding of why this happens.

In doing many of the exercises in this book you will be noting your thoughts. Included in these thoughts, of course, will be many thoughts about yourself. All of the "I'm not smart enough..." statements, all of the "He's not going to listen to what I have to say..." statements, all of the "Why would she want to talk to me..." statements not only make you feel powerless and nervous, they interfere with what you are trying to accomplish—*and often lead to exactly what you are afraid will happen.*

The bottom line on self-esteem is that the longer you allow your thoughts to be dominated by distorted thinking that focuses only on the things you like least about yourself, the longer you will be paralyzed into inaction by these thoughts and the longer you will not be able to accept yourself. If you start to understand how you have limited yourself, you will see that you can try opening up with others. The more you reveal yourself to others, the more they will understand you and like you. The more they like you, the more you like yourself. And so on. Other people can help you like yourself more. But not if you don't let them know you.

Finally, what about your appearance? Your appearance is a statement to the world about how you feel about yourself. (Appearance has nothing to do with money. The poorest person can dress neatly and cleanly and be clean shaven). Do you shower and make sure you smell clean? Do you make sure your clothes are clean and neat? Does your appearance make the statement that you don't care about yourself and don't expect anyone to treat you with respect? Or do you take pride in your appearance and use good hygiene? Other people will see you as you see yourself. When your appearance says, *"I care about myself; I take care of myself"* other people will see that you feel worthy of respect.

Your Partner

Maybe you have had significant or long-lasting relationships but you have a negative view of your partner. If you ask yourself, "what is my partner like?" how would you describe them? Do you think of them as kind, honest, loving, giving, hardworking, trustworthy? Or do you see them as abusive, uncaring, sneaky, selfish, or controlling? Do you think your partner cares about what you need? Do they make as much effort as you'd like? Or do you do all the work? If you feel trapped in a relationship with someone you don't really like or respect, you cannot be intimate with that person.

Are you in a relationship with someone like that now? Have you been in such relationships? Why? Have you been so uncomfortable being alone that you've had partners you didn't really like just to have someone?

What about the times you've met someone who really was good for you? Have you lost interest in such a partner over time because they wouldn't let you control them? Have you found yourself focusing on a partner's faults rather than good qualities until you stopped appreciating them?

All of these patterns are related to the ways that you *think*. Ask yourself what your attitudes toward people are. Do you expect people to be dumb, untrustworthy, uncaring? Do you hold a belief that people are manipulative? Does that apply to all people? Where did you get these beliefs?

Basic beliefs like these can undermine any relationship you have. No one will ever be good enough, and you'll never be happy. Research suggests that men who rape women, in particular, tend to assume negative qualities in female partners and focus on those.

Check your beliefs about partners against those listed below. Do you have other distorted beliefs that could be contributing to your unhappiness? Write them down.

☑ Once someone gets their hooks into you, they start using you.
☑ If you don't control a partner, they will control you.
☑ People are manipulators who shouldn't be trusted.
☑ Most people are only out for themselves.
☑ If I open up to someone, they will use what I say against me.

Autonomy

Some people fear losing their ability to think for themselves and be their own person if they give themselves to a relationship. Some people have had the experience of willingly giving up their own identity to a partner and becoming dependent on that partner. Autonomy means having a sense of independence, a sense of your own individuality even within a relationship. Autonomy is about always keeping your own identity.

How dependent are you on your partner, and how dependent are they on you? Do you feel like you rely on your partner for everything, or that you couldn't survive alone? Or do you feel that you have to control and dominate everything your partner does? Either of these attitudes can poison a relationship, since both people in a healthy relationship need to retain their own sense of themselves, their own identity, and their own ability to make decisions for themselves.

Even within a relationship, it is important for you to have your own interests, your own opinions, and your own accomplishments. It is important for your partner to have these things too. Healthy relationships allow individuals to need each other and support each other while still allowing them to be individuals with their own identity. It is not healthy for a couple to be overly involved in each other's lives.

Expression of Affection

Think about the ways you show affection to your partner. Are you comfortable expressing affection? Can you be loving and affectionate in nonsexual ways? Are you? Listening to your partner speak is showing affection. Supporting them when they need support is showing affection. All the little things people do for each other out of caring and concern can be expressions of affection. Many people who've sexually offended (and many people, in general!) are unsure how to show affection without becoming sexual. Does expressing affection always lead to you wanting to have sex? Do you "sexualize" love, intimacy, or affection? If you do, your partner may sometimes wonder if they mean more to you than just a sexual partner.

Try showing affection to someone you love through verbal expression, cards, gifts, and other thoughtful gestures. Hugging is always nice—it doesn't have to lead to sex. Remember, the idea is to be affectionate without turning it into sex. Pay attention to how you feel when you do these things. Recognize that they bring a good feeling even when no sex is involved.

Sexual Satisfaction

Of course, sexual satisfaction is also important. One part of staying away from harmful sexual behavior is creating intimate and pleasurable healthy sexual relationships with consenting adults. Thinking back on *consenting* relationships you have had with adults; how would you rate your sexual satisfaction? Have you experienced high satisfaction? Have you felt unable to satisfy an adult partner? If so, go online, or to the library or bookstore and look for some books, podcasts, documentaries, or websites about improving sexual satisfaction.

Have you been unsatisfied because you are unable to explain to your partner what you like? If this is the case, you need to become more assertive in helping your partner understand your sexual needs. (Being assertive means speaking directly about your feelings. Communication issues are addressed in the next part of this chapter).

Talking about your sexual needs can be awkward and embarrassing. Maybe you feel like you don't have a right to "demand" anything from your partner. Maybe you are afraid your partner will be hurt. Maybe you feel unattractive or shy about your body. But you and your partner deserve to have a satisfying sexual relationship. Try asking your partner what they like, and that might open up an opportunity for you to explain what you like.

Some people have the opposite problem: they are focused only on their own pleasure and don't think about their partner's feelings or sexual desires. Do you ask your partner what he or she likes? How to touch them in a way that feels good to them? Do you feel like you know how to please your partner?

If you have never had sex with someone you care about, ask yourself why. Is it just bad luck? Probably not. You have probably intentionally chosen people you don't really care about to avoid closeness and intimacy—and all the risks that go along with intimacy. Maybe it's time to explore your thoughts about intimacy and relationships. You're missing out on good sex.

Most often people don't have satisfying sex because they *don't really feel close to each other.* They don't have true intimacy. Although many people try to achieve intimacy through sex, it actually works the other way around. Good sex comes from true intimacy; it is *physical closeness that comes out of emotional closeness.* When a couple fights all the time, doesn't spend time together, and/or doesn't talk to each other about important events or feelings in their lives, that couple becomes emotionally distant. Emotional distance will sap their chance of achieving real sexual satisfaction.

Sharing your feelings with your partner and believing that your partner understands you are the real keys to good sex.

Relationship Commitment

"Commitment" refers to your willingness to make a relationship central in your life. You make a promise to another person that you will stay with them through whatever the future holds. When you are committed to a relationship you cherish it and devote yourself to it. When you believe in a relationship you don't want to risk losing it: you let your partner know that they are the most important thing to you and will go on being important. Commitment goes hand-in-hand with trust and intimacy: people are more trusting and more intimate when they believe in the future of a relationship.

Some people are hesitant to commit themselves to relationships. They are afraid they will get "tied down" or lose their freedom. Or they don't really believe that their partner loves them and will go on loving them. They are convinced that relationships "aren't for them," that they don't have what it takes to hold a partner, or that they don't want to hold a partner. Some have never committed themselves to anyone so they have no way of knowing the satisfaction that comes from having a stable, predictable, loving relationship. The problem with withholding commitment from a partner is that they probably will hold back from committing to you. The result is the same old thing: short, superficial relationships that don't meet anyone's intimacy needs.

Think about how committed you are to your current relationship or the most recent relationship you've been in. Are you giving yourself to the relationship or holding back? Think back over all your relationships. Have you had many "flings" or "encounters" which you view as unimportant in your life? Or do you take relationships seriously? If you have never had a committed relationship, what might that tell you about how you view the possibility of real love and real relationships?

Once again, the things we believe and the things we tell ourselves are all-important. See if you hold some of these beliefs:

- ☑ If I allow myself to care too much for a partner, I will be hurt.
- ☑ Relationships take away your freedom.
- ☑ Marriage is a trap.
- ☑ Commitment opens the door to being taken advantage of.
- ☑ As soon as they know they "have you," everything changes for the worse.

Dealing with Conflict

Communication is what relationships are about. When relationships become cold and distant, it is because the people in them have stopped communicating. Communicating information is not what troubles people. Communicating *feelings* is what is most difficult—but also most important.

We have discussed some of the reasons why people have difficulty being open about their feelings. Tension and conflict make it even more difficult to be open. But everyone who wants to be close to another person must learn to accept tension and conflict as necessary parts of relationships. Communicating effectively even when tension is high is what allows people to successfully *resolve conflicts* and not only hold onto their relationship, but *make it even closer.* We will now focus on the things that make communication difficult and the things that make it work.

Fear of Conflict

Many people believe that conflict is what ruins relationships. They work hard to keep their relationships conflict-free by trying to ignore the things that make them unhappy and swallowing their anger and frustration. Instead of disagreeing with their partner they just close up or try to change the subject. "After all," they tell themselves, "if we start fighting about things, that will just be the beginning of the end. Every relationship has its ups and downs. If I just go along maybe things will get better."

There is some truth to this point of view. Fighting certainly doesn't promote a healthy relationship. But let's look at the underlying assumptions of this position. They might be expressed as:

- ☑ People who care about each other can and should avoid conflicts.
- ☑ Fights start with disagreements.
- ☑ If I disagree my partner will think I'm rejecting them.
- ☑ Disagreement only leads to anger and hostility.
- ☑ I can control my feelings. I will just ignore my unhappiness and frustration.
- ☑ I don't need to make a big deal out of everything. Things will work themselves out.

Actually, **none** of these statements is true. Consider:

1. People who are truly close to each other care deeply about how each other feels about things. It is inevitable that they will have areas where they will disagree, *sometimes strongly.* Only couples who really don't care much about each other or don't really talk to each other can avoid disagreements.

2. Fights start when people are angry with each other. Anger results from feelings of hurt, helplessness, frustration or injustice. Honest disagreement does not cause feelings like these. It is the failure to disagree—which is a form of *dishonesty*—that causes these feelings. Attacking, blaming, sarcasm, selfishly refusing to listen—these tactics lead to anger and to fights. But these are not ways of disagreeing. These are ways of avoiding real communication. Honestly and respectfully expressing your feelings—and listening respectfully when your partner expresses theirs—turns disagreements into understanding.

3. If you *attack* your partner verbally, they will think you are rejecting them. If you express your feelings they will appreciate you. They want and need you to express your feelings. When you withhold your feelings, they feel closed out and rejected. We will discuss how to express negative feelings in a later section.

4. Disagreement respectfully expressed usually leads to increased intimacy and closeness.
5. By now you should understand that by ignoring your feelings you are denying who you are and cutting yourself off from yourself. This is exactly what creates depression. In the short run you can probably live with unhappiness, but in the long run unexpressed frustration and unhappiness lead only to anger and resentment, which come out in the form of bitter attacks and hurtful fights—or worse, deviant fantasizing and acting out. If you want only small talk and fights, ignore your feelings.

Why We're Afraid of Conflict

As with all things, we learn from our experiences. In many families, children who disagree are punished. You speak your mind, you "backtalk," you get smacked. Why? Because many adults don't respect children. Children don't have the right to be heard. They are to be "seen and not heard." If they're smart they learn to keep their mouths shut.

And where does that leave them? As they grow, they bring with them a basic belief that says: *Nothing good comes from disagreeing; disagreeing will only lead to a fight I can't win.* Based on their experience they believe that they must either swallow their feelings and keep their mouth shut or be ready to fight. There is no middle ground. There is no such thing as talking things through and listening to each other and arriving at a new understanding that allows both people to feel okay. In its extreme forms this belief can take children in two opposite directions.

One type of child never does disagree. Instead, he learns how to go *around* people to get what he wants. He keeps his thoughts and feelings to himself, agrees with everyone, and then does what he wants. He trusts no one. He learns to sneak, to make excuses, to lie, to change the subject, to hide. When he's angry, he "gets even." He might break things or set fires or skip school. Sometimes he gets into more serious trouble, partly just to feel like he is somebody, and partly to get back at his parents. If you ask him how he feels about his parents, he will tell you he loves them because that is the correct answer. He always knows the correct answer. But actually he hates his parents because they don't really even know who he is and they don't care.

When he grows up and falls in love, he is lost. He wants desperately to make his partner happy because what he needs most in the world is to feel loved. But to him being loved means he must always agree. He can never be himself. He can never be honest. His partner feels his distance and his dishonesty and protects herself by pulling away. He feels helpless and angry because he has been trying so hard to be agreeable. His anger leads to fights, withdrawal, hopelessness.

The other type of child becomes a fighter. Since speaking his mind is not an option in his mind, he just skips that part and attacks people who are in his way. Everyone is his enemy and he is ready to do battle. He is tough, and he advertises that fact in the way he looks and the way he carries himself. To him, agreeing with anyone means giving up his identity. He makes his life much more difficult than it needs to be because he cannot allow himself to cooperate with anyone even when it is in his best interest. He communicates openly with no one. Even when he falls in love he cannot truly trust and cannot risk giving up any control. No matter how hard his partner tries to please him he never lets down his guard. He is always suspicious and always in control. Eventually, he pushes away all the people that try to reach him....

Even in less extreme forms, the basic belief that disagreement only leads to fights causes great pain and confusion. Out of this belief come other beliefs, such as: "No one really cares what you want because they only care about what they want"; or "Rather than be honest with others, figure out what they want to hear and tell them that"; or "If others knew how you really feel, they would reject you" (which means you can never really be accepted by others for who you are); and "You can never really trust anyone".

What People Really Fight About

No one really needs to fight about matters of fact. If one person believes that toads cause warts and another disagrees, they can always look it up. It often appears that people fight about matters of opinion, but this is not really the case either. People may disagree vehemently on matters of opinion, but they can do so respectfully.

Most often, what you are fighting about is not really about what it seems to be about. It's more about not feeling heard, respected, or valued. People fight about matters of feelings. Feelings come into play when a person's values, or needs, or rights are challenged. It is important to learn to keep differences of opinion from turning into hurt feelings and fights.

Why Disagreements Turn into Fights

It is always interesting to ask couples who come for marital counseling what their last few fights have been about. Most of the time they can't remember what started the fights, or they will say, "Oh, it was just something silly." What they are saying is that the content of what causes their fights and makes them miserable is often unimportant. It is how they disagree that is the problem.

David Burn, M.D., the author of The Feeling Good Handbook, lists what he called "Characteristics of Bad Communication." They are adapted below. As you read them, ask yourself which you have found yourself using.

The Characteristics of Bad Communication

- ☐ **You have the inside story on The Truth:** You are quite sure that you are "right" and the other person is "wrong."
- ☐ **Blame:** You know that the other person is the real cause of the problem.
- ☐ **Put-downs:** Since the other person is clearly wrong but won't admit it (that is so annoying, isn't it?) you are free to let them know they are a loser who doesn't have a clue and "always" or "never" does certain things.
- ☐ **Hopelessness:** You give up because the other person is so exasperating there's no point in even trying to communicate.
- ☐ **Whining:** You insist you're entitled to better treatment, but you don't ask for what you want in a direct, straightforward way.
- ☐ **Denial:** You insist that you don't feel angry, hurt or sad when you really do.
- ☐ **Passive-Aggression:** You pout or withdraw or say nothing. You may storm out of the room or slam doors.
- ☐ **Self-Blame:** Instead of dealing with the problem, you blame yourself. Even when you mean it, this attitude cuts off communication and leaves both people feeling bad and without a solution to the problem. When you don't mean it, it is a manipulation, another form of hopelessness and passive-aggression.

- ☐ **"Helping":** Instead of really hearing how depressed, hurt, or angry the other person feels, you try to "solve the problem" by giving them advice.
- ☐ **Sarcasm:** Your tone of voice is hostile and undercuts whatever communication might be going on.
- ☐ **Scapegoating:** You suggest that the other person is the one with the "problem" and that you are sane, happy and uninvolved in whatever is wrong.
- ☐ **Counter-attacking:** Instead of trying to understand how the other person feels or why they are criticizing you, you criticize them.
- ☐ **Dredging up the Past:** Instead of dealing with how you both feel in the here-and-now, you constantly bring up old hurts or old fights.

When You're Right and The Other Person Is Wrong....

Some of these attitudes and tactics listed above are very common but hard to correct because they seem to make sense. For example, it stands to reason that anyone who is in an argument believes that their position represents the "truth," and the other person's is mistaken. How can you tell someone who "knows" they are right that this attitude will undermine communication?

Consider again what fights are about: feelings. There is no "truth" to feelings. My feelings are as "true" for me as yours are for you. So if the fight appears to be about not taking out the trash, or not paying enough attention to your partner's visiting mother, or one partner criticizing the other for not managing the money, the "truth" of the facts is not as important as the "truth" of the feelings involved. If you are fighting about taking out the trash, it's not about the trash!

Let's look at an example of what we mean:

Ray and Sue fought all the time because Sue felt Ray was more interested in hanging out with his friends than being with her. After all, she said, he is out three nights every week drinking and smoking weed. When he does stay home, he invites his friends over to watch sports together and she gets ignored.

When they first came for marriage counseling, Ray insisted that Sue was exaggerating, as she always did, that he rarely goes out more than one night a week, that he only has a couple of beers, and that he never smokes weed. He said last week she blew up because he had to drive his cousin to driving school and wait for him there even though he didn't want to. He said she nags him constantly, which makes him want to go out with his friends. He thinks Sue is influenced by her mother, who is married to an alcoholic and constantly warns Sue to keep a tight leash on Ray or he will turn into an alcoholic too. Sue and Ray both insisted they were right and that the other one must change for their relationship to survive.

Notice that Sue and Ray appeared to be fighting over where he was and what he was doing. Each counted the nights Ray was out to "prove" they were right and the other was wrong. What they weren't saying out loud was how they both were feeling.

As counseling went on, it became clear that Sue was feeling afraid that Ray was pulling away from her, that she was no longer important or special to him, and she was afraid there was nothing she could do to change that. It scared her to think that he wanted to be drinking a lot, because to her that would mean he was escaping from their relationship. She really needed Ray to understand her fears, not to argue about how many nights he was out or how much he drank.

At first Ray said he was frustrated because he couldn't get Sue to realize how unreasonable she was being. He knew he spent no more time away from home than his friends spent away from their wives, and none of his friends had to account for their time like he did. But he needed to stop "winning" the argument to begin communicating with his wife. When he gave up being "right" and started talking instead about how he felt, the couple started to understand what they were really fighting about.

In one counseling session he said: "I love you and need you. Nothing has changed about my feelings. But I need my friends too. These are the people who have always been there for me. I don't want to lose touch with other people. Sometimes I feel that you don't trust me, but I don't understand why and I feel hurt and angry. Maybe that makes me want to stay out more. But I wish we could try to understand each other better and not be shutting each other out."

As this couple talked about their feelings, it came out that they had been having trouble communicating about sex. Sue talked about how scared and lonely it made her feel that Ray didn't seem as interested as he once had. She felt shut out of his life. She admitted that she did sometimes wonder who he was seeing when he went out. Ray agreed that sex was a problem for him, because he was afraid to talk about what he wanted in bed for fear that he would be rejected. Finally, the couple was able to talk about the things that really were upsetting them.

The point is that "winning" an argument by "proving" that you are "right" might feel good. But going for a "win" with a partner may not be the best thing in the long run. It can increase the tension and hostility and make your partner feel you don't care about them. Even when you do win an argument, you are losing the important goal: keeping your relationship working.

FIGURE 6.5: How do You Handle Conflict?

Passive	Aggressive	Healthy
Ignore	Yell, hit, or threaten	Apologize
Hide feelings	Domination & Control	Compromise
Fail to set boundaries	Curse or call names	Talk it out
Give in	Deny loudly	Find a win/win
Talk behind someone's back	Put others down	Listen and use I statements
Roll eyes, Avoid confrontation	Blame others	Talk about feelings
Stomp around, slam doors	Break things	Talk about alternative solutions

Effective Communication Techniques and Constructive Conflict Resolution

Constructive conflict resolution will only work if both parties genuinely want to resolve the conflict. That means you will be willing to sacrifice winning in order to find a solution that makes both of you feel okay. It is next to impossible to successfully resolve disagreements when either partner insists on winning—which means, necessarily, that the other person is "losing." Anytime you have a "winner" and a "loser" you have bad feelings.

The keys to resolving conflicts peacefully are simple to describe. In the heat of an argument they are difficult to use because all of us have entrenched habits that first need to be recognized and changed. Many of these habits are described above in the section titled *"The Characteristics of Bad Communication."* Any of these styles of communication can undermine your efforts to resolve your conflicts in a way that leaves both parties feeling good. Healthy boundaries and communication require you to see that your needs and the needs of others are equally important. So how do you please yourself without disregarding the needs of others, without giving in to things that leave you feeling resentful?

The Essentials of Successful Conflict Resolution

1. **Figure out the source of the conflict:**
   Is the disagreement about a fact, an opinion or a feeling? If it is about a fact, check it out with some reliable source. If it is about a difference of opinion, know that people's opinions are based on their values and the real source of conflict may be grounded in a difference in values. If the conflict is about values, needs or rights, the feelings of each party must be clearly expressed and understood by the other. Most importantly, they must be respected by each person.
2. **Decide whether this is the right time to deal with the conflict:**
   If one or both people are too upset or if it is not the right place or there is not enough time to work through to a solution, postpone dealing with it. But do not postpone it indefinitely. Agree on a time to deal with the problem.
3. **Describe how you are feeling.**
   Forget about everything else. It is not important who is "right" and who is "wrong." What is important is that you are both feeling misunderstood, frustrated and angry.
4. **Ask, Don't Tell.** When the other person is speaking give your attention to them. Try not to think about your own feelings or what you are going to say next. Be sure you understand the other person. Do not assume you understand what she meant. Check out your assumptions by asking, "Are you saying...?" Once you start making this question a regular part of your discussions, you will be amazed at how often you think you know exactly what the other person is saying, but when you say it back to them you learn that you didn't understand at all.
5. **Search for an agreement together:**
   Consider many solutions and choose one together to try. If it does not work choose another and keep trying until you are both satisfied. Remember, a good relationship is not one without conflict. It is one in which the partners can resolve conflicts so that no one feels hurt or oppressed.

FIGURE 6.6: The VOCAB Strategy for Communication

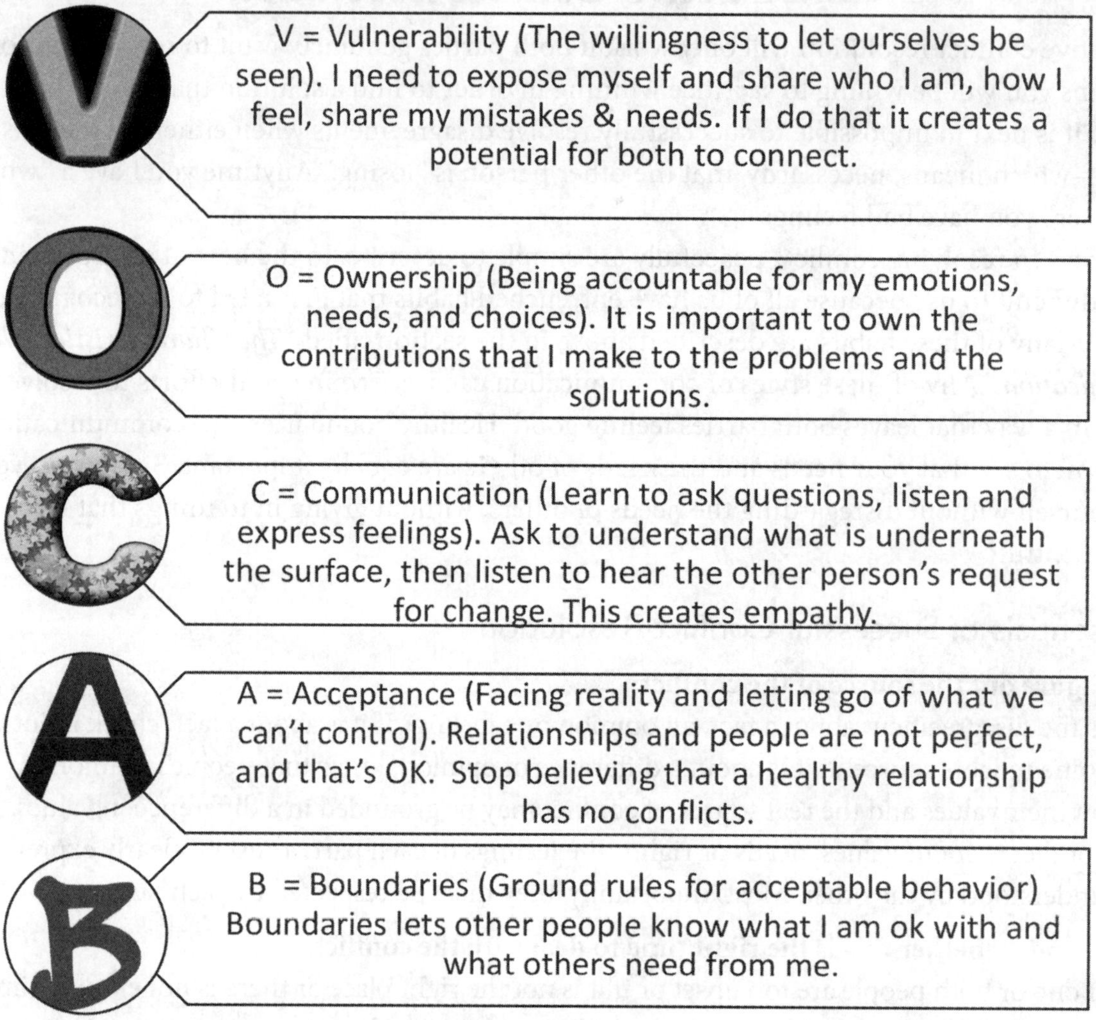

You can search on YouTube for the Ted Talk by Clair Canfield called The Beauty of Conflict, which describes the VOCAB Strategy for Communication.

Exercise 6.6A: Describe a Recent Conflict with Someone Close to You. Then, Identify How You Could Have Used the Vocab Strategy to Change Your Communication in this Case

When You Are Trying To "Help"

Men are natural-born problem solvers. Solving problems is a good way to be in control of your life, and no one would ever suggest that solving problems is a bad thing. So how can we say that helping another person is bad communication?

Problem solving becomes a problem when another person really just wants you to listen to how they feel and try to understand them. It feels uncomfortable to problem solvers to listen to a partner talk about problems that are upsetting her and not offer solutions. It's only natural to offer help, isn't it? You feel like the other person wouldn't be telling you the problem if they weren't looking for advice.

But there's another way to look at the situation. People (and women, in particular) often feel a need to just talk about how they feel. And often, all they need and want is for the other person to understand how they feel. They don't want to hear solutions. By trying to solve their problem you are communicating to them that you aren't interested in understanding how they feel, only in how to get rid of their negative feelings. Your intentions are good, but you are not giving them what they need. They need you to understand and accept their feelings—in other words, to "empathize" with them. They need to know that their feelings make sense to you and that you would probably feel the same way in the same situation.

Here's what it sounds like:

She: I can't believe it! After all I've done for her, she gives the promotion to that new guy! He doesn't have a clue! I'm the one that makes that office run! What is she thinking of?

You: It hurts, all right. It seems like she doesn't appreciate you at all.

She: That's just it. I've been so loyal to this company, and now she just shuts me out! I can't believe it.

You: You feel betrayed. Can you tell me more about how it all went down?

She: I feel like such a fool. Why did I ever trust her? I'm so stupid!

You: You expected to be rewarded for your hard work, then she pulled the rug out from under you.

She: I hate her! All of her phony bullshit! All of her "thank you for staying late," and "I know I can count on you." She just used me.

You: Boy, that hurts. I can understand why you're so angry. You really did give her your all. What do you think you should do now?

Notice: all you are doing is **listening to her feelings** and trying your best to understand them. Then you are **saying them back to her.** *That's it!* No solutions, no suggestions about what to do next. Nothing but listening and reflecting and asking questions so she can sort it out herself. *This is what she needs from you.* This is how you can be close to her and really help her. This technique requires being aware of what your partner needs from you and it requires practice. You can start practicing anytime, and you will immediately notice that you feel closer to your partner, and she feels closer to you.

Later, she may say, "I don't know what to do. What am I going to do next?" Now she is asking for suggestions. You don't have to solve the problem for her, but ask questions that lead her to her own solutions.

Of course, when she is mad at you, that makes it more difficult to refrain from "helping" her understand that what you think she should know. But if you can continue to use the listening and reflecting technique, you will find that you can disarm the angriest person. Simply by saying, *"You're really mad, help me understand why?"* you will find that you can stop a fight in its tracks. She suddenly doesn't need to tell you anymore how mad she is. You've just said you already know. Now she knows that you are listening to her and that you understand how she feels. Her fear that you won't listen to her or respect her feelings is eliminated. The force of her anger is instantly reduced and now you can both focus on the problem and discuss it calmly and rationally.

Talk Less, Listen More

Here's the formula for what is called "Active Listening":

1. Listen: Just let someone talk about what happened or how they feel.
2. Validate feelings: See if you can put a name to the feeling(s) they probably have (see above), which shows that you are listening carefully and reading between the lines to hear the internal experience someone is trying to share with you, and what it means to them.
3. Re-state content: When you paraphrase what somewhat is sharing with you, you repeat it back to them but in your own words. This shows that you are trying to understand the meaning of what was said to you. The other person will either say "Yes! You get it!" or "No, that's not what I was saying…" and then you can ask for clarification.
4. Ask open-ended questions: Open-ended questions don't have a yes or no answer. They allow someone to elaborate.

Closed	**Open**
Did you talk to your boss today?	How did it go with your boss today?
Did he give you the raise?	What happened when you asked for the raise?
Did your mom go to the doctor?	How's your mom doing? I know you were worried about her.
Are you going to do….?	What do you think your options are?

Try it yourself! Change some "closed" questions you might use to an open-ended question.

When you listen with curiosity and compassion, it really helps others open up to you and feel understood. These strategies work really well with children and teenagers too. It can be especially hard for parents to listen, validate feelings, and ask questions without giving advice. But when you use these strategies, you model healthy communication and help your children learn effective skills.

Exercise 6.6B: Talk Less, Listen More

Describe a recent situation in which, looking back, you think you could have listened better. Then, identify how you could have used the Talk Less, Listen More strategy to change your communication in this case.

Shared Power

Sex offending is about taking power and choice away from the other person. Shared power is a set of skills that many people learn in childhood through their families, teachers, and schoolmates. Think about the Shared Power Skills listed below. How did you learn them? How good are you at them? Can you give some examples of times you've used them recently? Or chosen not to? Remember this list of strategies to use in your quest to improve all your relationships – with your friends, family, children, romantic partners, bosses, supervisees, and co-workers. And with your groupmates!

FIGURE 6.7: Shared Power Skills

- **Dialogue**
- **Negotiation**
- **Compromise**
- **Cooperation**
- **Collaboration**
- **Sharing**
- **Taking Turns**

Exercise 6.7: Understanding Shared Power

Did you learn shared power skills as a kid? How? Or how not?

Describe a recent conflict, and identify ways you could have used shared power skills to get a better resolution.

Using "I Statements"

Anytime you are expressing your feelings your sentence has to start with the word "I." Using "I" statements forces you to talk about yourself. There is no single element of constructive communication that is more important than making sure you are using "I" statements. As soon as you start beginning your sentences with the word "you" you are beginning to blame, to accuse, to attack. Anytime you attack another person, you force them to defend themselves and to resist you. How do you respond when someone attacks you? You probably dig in your heels. You feel hurt and even more angry than you did before, and now you can't even concentrate on what the original problem was because you are thinking about defending yourself and counterattacking.

Attacking, blaming, name-calling, threatening and accusing are not forms of communication. They are substitutes for communication that are easier than real communication. They feel better in the short run because they make you feel powerful. In the long run they kill real communication and leave only confusion, humiliation and resentment in their wake. Obviously, this is not the formula for making peace.

FIGURE 6.8: Using I statements

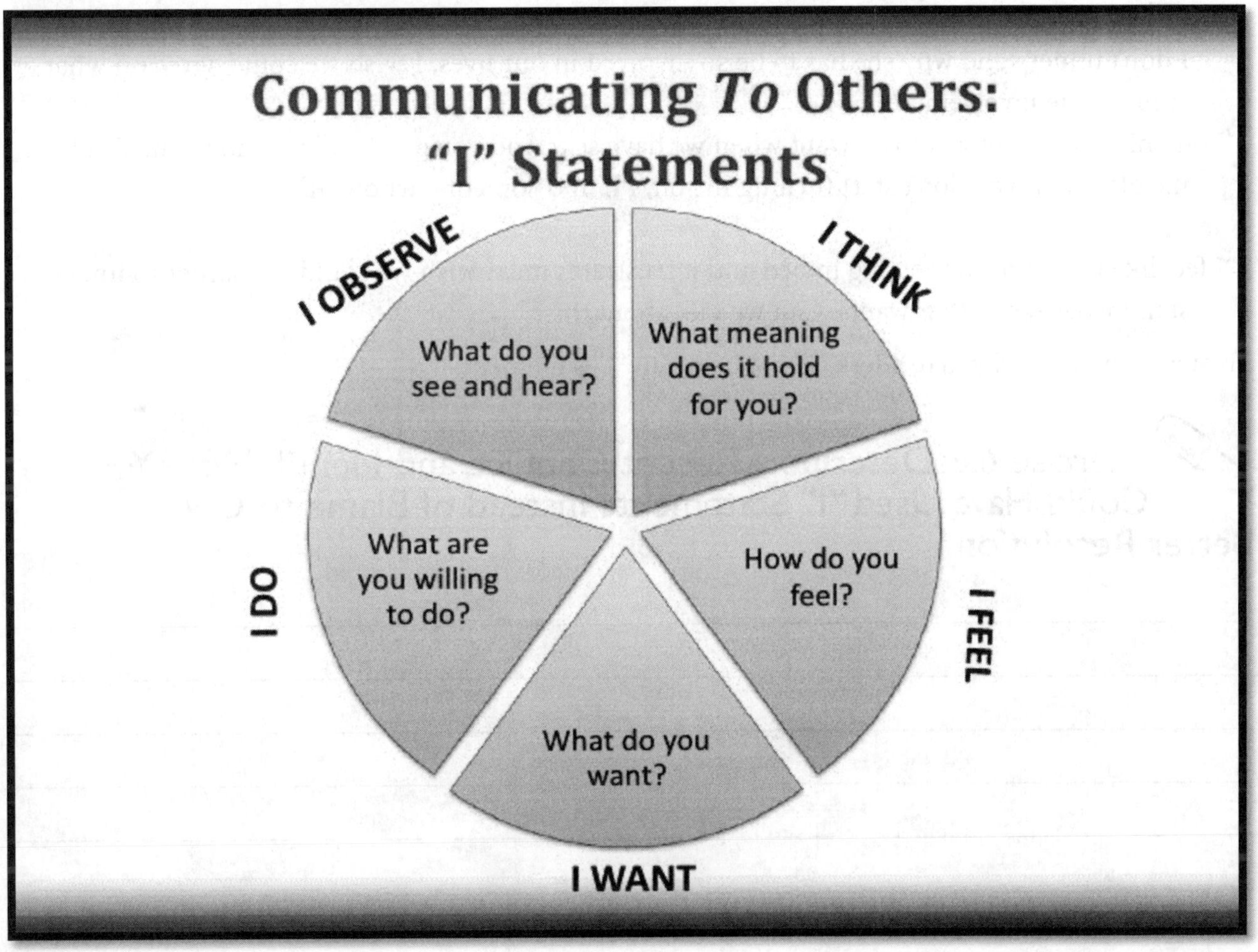

In looking at the statements below, ask yourself which statements are likely to lead to increased communication and which are likely to lead to increased hostility:

"You never listen. You think you're the only one who's important. You're always right."

Or

"I feel left out of your life sometimes. I feel like I can't reach you. I wish we could respect each other's feelings more than we do."

"You've got a problem. You think money grows on trees. You better grow up and do it fast or I'm out of here."

Or

"I feel helpless to catch up with our bills. I feel like we're drowning. I wish we could agree on a budget."

"You care more about your mother than you care about me. I thought you were married to me, but you have to okay everything with her. And she just wants to break us up so she can have you back."

Or

"I'm hurt and I'm mad when I think we've reached an agreement about something and then I have to hear that your mother has second-guessed us. I feel like I can't compete with your mother. I don't understand why she has to be so involved in our lives. I wish we could agree on what's appropriate involvement for her."

"You only care about what you want when we have sex. And you're fat. All you do is eat. You turn me off, and if you don't start turning me on, I'll find someone who will."

Or

"I feel like we're not connecting in bed and it frustrates me. I wish we could try harder to understand what each other wants. Can we talk about this?"

Note: Saying, "I feel you're a jerk" is not using an "I" statement.

Exercise 6.8: Describe a Recent Conflict, and Identify Ways You Could Have Used "I" Statements Instead of Blame to Get a Better Resolution

Some Final Thoughts…

- Stay on the issue. Don't bring up past issues or old disagreements.
- Name-calling, sarcasm, and cursing only raise the level of tension and hostility. If other people in your past have done these things to you, you may automatically do them without even realizing how harmful they are. Think about how you have felt when you were on the receiving end of these behaviors. If you want to communicate with someone and maintain a relationship, accept that hurting your partner won't get someone to feel closer to you.
- Don't raise your voice. In some families the loudest person "wins" arguments simply by intimidating the others. But nothing ever gets resolved this way. Shouting will only cause the other person to shout back. It doesn't make them more willing or more able to understand your point of view. If the other person is not listening, *lower your voice.* Then calmly say, "I feel like you're not listening to what I'm saying." If you are frustrated and angry, say that you are.
- Don't debate. In some families, the only interesting conversation is a good debate. But in a debate, the idea is to prove that you are right and someone else is wrong. Use your shared power skills to find common ground and agree on solutions.

Sometimes it is ok to remove toxic or unhealthy relationships from your life. Sometimes you have to accept that you cannot have a close relationship with that person no matter how much you would like to. Sometimes you simply have different values and ideals, different goals, different personality styles. Sometimes you have to accept that the situation won't change and there's nothing you can do about it.

In summary, in order to communicate effectively in any situation, you need to be able to do four things:

1. Express your feelings using "I" statements in a way which focuses on YOU, not the other person. Talk about what YOU need and what YOU want and what YOU feel without blaming, accusing, demanding, or defending.
2. JUST LISTEN to the other person talking about their feelings. This sounds easy—but for most people *it can actually be much more difficult than jumping in with solutions.* It can make you very uncomfortable to listen to someone who is very upset, especially someone you care about. Many people need to actively restrain themselves from trying to help their distressed partner.
3. You need to reflect to your partner what you are hearing, so that they know you are listening and understanding. By reflect, we mean just what it sounds like: you are a mirror of your partner's feelings. Your job is to ask yourself, "What are they feeling?" as they are speaking, and *just say back to them what you are hearing.* You can do this by naming a feeling and paraphrasing what they are saying in your own words.
4. Ask open-ended questions, to show that you are listening with curiosity and compassion.

Exercise 6.9: Identify Appropriate And Acceptable Methods of Expressing Thoughts and Feelings.

Use three personal examples of ways you handled conflict situations in the past and what you would do differently now.

Exercise 6.10: Identify and Discuss Ways Your Communication Patterns Have Improved.

How has your ability to communicate improved? Describe your current relationships. Are they less conflictual? Do they feel satisfying? How do you feel in relationships now?

Give three examples of recent experiences in which you communicated effectively or accomplished conflict resolution with significant others in your life.

1. In each example, describe the problem and the positions each party took.
2. In each of your examples, identify specifically how you used active listening techniques.
3. In each of your examples, identify specifically how you used conflict resolution techniques.

Exercise 6.11: Demonstrate Communication Techniques in Group Sessions.

Describe and discuss 2 examples of how you have used new tools of communication and conflict resolution in your treatment group.

Apologies

When we've been wronged, most of us want the same thing—an apology. What we really need is an acknowledgement that what was done to us was wrong, that the person who harmed us has taken responsibility, that they are willing to do something to make amends, and some assurance that they won't do it again.

There are many reasons why you should make a sincere apology when you've hurt someone's feelings or have made a mistake. First, an apology allows communication between yourself and the other person. It shows your remorse for your behavior. It acknowledges that what you did was harmful and validates the other person's feelings. Finally, a sincere apology shows that you want to change your behavior so the person you've hurt isn't hurt by you again in the future.

Apologizing is good for the other person because when you acknowledge that what happened was your fault, you validate the reality of the other person. This can begin the healing process, and also helps the person to not blame themself for what happened. Apologizing is good for you because it can help you feel more self-respect and integrity. You can feel like a good person because you did the right thing. Not apologizing can damage relationships and create resentment. It can also make you feel shame inside.

Apologies are important in everyday life, and they are important in sexual assault cases too. People who have experienced sexual abuse often state that their needs include having the harm acknowledged and validated. They often state that an authentic apology from the person who harmed them would help them move on with their lives.

Steps to a genuine apology:

1. Admit responsibility
2. Acknowledge the harm caused
3. Express remorse
4. Make amends
5. Change your thinking and behavior so it does not happen again.

Exercise 6.12: Describe a Recent Time When You Did Something Wrong. Practice What You Would Say to Make a Genuine Apology.

Who got hurt?

How did it happen?

What happened?

How do you think the person felt?

Why was it harmful to the other person?

What can you do to make it better?

How will you make sure it doesn't happen again?

FIGURE 6.9: Apologies

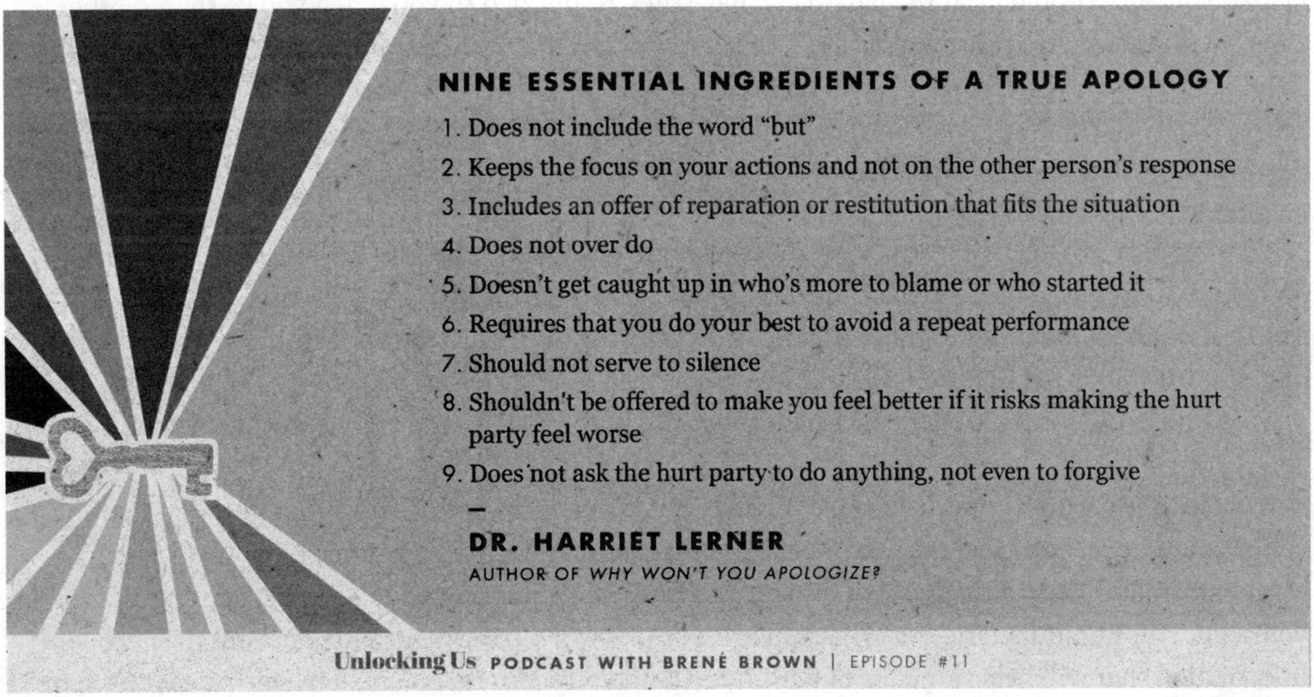

Talking with Others About Your Offense History and Your Sexual Behavior Problems

When it comes to deciding to share your offense history with others, it can feel emotionally risky. There are a number of things to consider as you ponder why you might want to share, who to share with, what exactly to share, how to describe it, when is the best time to disclose, and where to do so. Sharing about past offenses and/or minor-attraction is a personal decision that only you can make, depending on what you hope to achieve, how you think others might respond, and the perceived pros and cons. Here are some ideas that can help you think through your decision-making process.

Why?

What are your motivations for sharing? Of course, healthy and direct communication can make us feel closer and more connected with others. Sharing your private thoughts can create emotional intimacy, decrease isolation, and remove the shame of secrecy. But remember, you can only control your own thoughts, behaviors, and reactions – not those of others. So, you should share only when your expectations are clear, when you are not hoping to alter someone else's perception of you, and when you are prepared to accept and respond to the reactions of others no matter what they are. There might also be reasons that you are not ready to tell: maybe you worry that it would ruin a relationship, or you think sharing would make you unsafe, or you don't trust someone to keep your information private.

Who?

Who are the people in your life you could trust to share with? Is there someone in your life who has helped you with problems in the past? How have they responded to you when you've shared other things with them? Are they supportive? Compassionate? Do they listen and ask questions without judging? How can you choose people that will respond to you in a way that affirms your positive sense of self? Do you want to share with a family member, personal acquaintance, friend, or romantic partner? There are various online forums for MAPs to discuss experiences with disclosure (see chapter 2).

What?

Think about how much is too much or too little. Keep in mind that most people do not share a lot of detail with others about their sexual interests, arousals, fantasies, or behaviors. These are typically private things that bring with them certain personal boundaries. Some people may need to know only about your criminal record, but not the details of your sexual behavior struggles. On the other hand, it may feel important to you that certain people in your life whom you care about know something about your concerns or struggles, so they can understand and support you. Do you want to share some information about the types of minors you find yourself attracted to? Do you want to share your concerns about fantasies, or what you are working on in treatment? Do you want to share some information that will help someone better understand your depression, anxiety, self-perceptions, or relationship patterns?

How?

Discussing sex offenses and/or minor-attraction can be a pretty tricky subject. Unfortunately, people's beliefs about sex offending are often shaped by media stories that can naturally invite negative judgments and false assumptions. Think about what you want to say ahead of time and make some notes. Start by avoiding labels (like pedophile or rapist) and just describe what you did (I sexually abused someone) or what you're concerned about: "I'm attracted to younger kids." Let the person you're telling know what you need from them and how you hope they can help. Share your own human emotions, your struggles with self-acceptance, your commitment not to harm anyone in the future, and your wish to have what every human wants – to live a genuine and authentic life surrounded by people who love and accept you. Be prepared to be interrupted, and to be asked questions. You could be ready to share information to help them make sense of it all, like this website about sex offending and registries:

Link 6.3 – NARSOL
https://narsol.org/

This one about minor-attraction:

Link 6.4 – Stop It Now
https://www.stopitnow.org/help-guidance

or this one, which includes podcast episodes with people who love and care about a minor-attracted persons:

Link 6.5 – The Global Prevention Project
http://theglobalpreventionproject.org/maps.

When?

The timing of a disclosure can be an important consideration. Depending on who you want to share with, think about scheduling a talk with plenty of time to discuss and explore. It may or may not be best to choose a family gathering, for instance, but this depends on your support system and your disclosure goals. Also, you might want to think about when in the course of a relationship is best. For instance, no one shares all their personal and intimate details very early in a relationship; you want to allow time to get to know someone and evaluate their trustworthiness and your ability to depend on them to be supportive, reliable, and non-judgmental. On the other hand, sometimes disclosing after a long time in a relationship could lead to the other person feeling betrayed or deceived, so it can be tricky to balance these. Finally, the most important factor is when is right for YOU?

Where?

The question of where can relate literally to physical space, but also to virtual space. Obviously when discussing personal and intimate things about ourselves, we want to choose settings that are appropriately private and avoid unwanted eavesdropping. Sometimes decisions have to be made about whether to share in-person or by phone. If you disclose using text, email, or chat, remember that anything you share electronically has the potential to be forwarded to others, shared, copied, or captured in a screen-shot and re-posted in a public forum.

A Final Consideration:

Be aware that state laws require professionals (and citizens) to report child abuse so that victims can be protected and get help. Keep this in mind if you are sharing something that has not been previously reported to authorities. Professionals are required to report sexual contact with a minor, and in some states, the use of child pornography (CA, DE, PA and possibly others). You can easily find out about the reporting laws in your state by doing some online research, talking with your therapist, or by calling anonymously to the Stop it Now! Helpline: 1-888-PREVENT.

Exercise 6.13: Disclosure.

Why?	
Who?	
What?	
How?	
When?	
Where?	
Pros & Cons?	
Possible reactions?	
How to handle them or respond?	

Talking with a Partner About Sex

It can be really hard to talk to a partner about sex. It's awkward, embarrassing, and can make us feel vulnerable. But it is important to understand what your partner likes and needs, and for your partner to understand what feels good sexually for you. Communication increases the sense of intimacy (closeness) and also improves the sexual satisfaction for both partners. It can be hard not to be "shy" about talking about these things.

Everyone is different, and each person might feel differently about how often to have sex, what kinds of sexual activities are enjoyable, and where, or when, or how to have sex (morning or night? bedroom or couch? A planned "date night" or spontaneous act? Lights on or off? Top or bottom?). Talking about these things and working together will help you and your partner to find satisfaction.

Once you feel more confident about your sexual relationships with adult consenting peers, you might feel less likely to act out sexually.

Steps to talking about sex with a partner:

1. Find a quiet, private time and a safe space.
2. Acknowledge that you want to have a mutually satisfying sexual relationship.
3. Ask questions about what your partner likes, wants, and needs.
4. Use "I" statements when describing what you like (instead of saying "you don't…)
5. Being willing to try new things, but set boundaries of your own when needed, and respect the boundaries of your partner.

There are some great websites about creating healthy sexuality with a partner:

Link 6.6 – ASHA Sexual Health
http://www.ashasexualhealth.org/sexual-health/talking-about-sex/

Link 6.7 – Sex & Relationship Healing
https://sexandrelationshiphealing.com/

Exercise 6.14: Do You and Your Partner Discuss These Things? Why or Why Not? Practice What You Would Say to Improve Your Sexual Relationship.

How do you like to be touched?

How does your partner like to be touched?

Where, when, and how often do you like sex?

Where, when, and how often does your partner like sex?

What kinds of acts do you and your partner like or not like?

What kinds of sexual boundaries feel right for you or your partner?

Do either of you have sexual trauma in your background? How might that impact your sex life?

Spirituality: Your Relationship with God

For many people, spirituality is an important part of their lives. Yet spirituality is difficult to talk about in mixed groups because it usually comes out of religious beliefs, and everyone has different religious beliefs. If you have wanted to talk about your religious beliefs and your counselor has discouraged you, it's because religious debates are usually not appropriate in treatment group discussions. Everyone has their own personal religious and spiritual beliefs. Religious discussions are discouraged in group because they sometimes lead to moral judgments based on scriptural interpretation. In your church or temple meetings you can explore your religious beliefs from a theological or philosophical point of view. In this program we can only explore how one's unique spirituality contributes to a healthy, meaningful life.

Spirituality is different from religion in that spirituality is about your personal relationship with God, by whatever name you call Him. (We could say "Higher Power"). It is their relationship with God, more than other parts of their religion, that usually offers most people hope and peace of mind. As with all relationships, you can look at what He brings to the relationship and what you bring.

For most people, a healthy spiritual life provides a source of things that are positive: growth, hope, love, morality, meaning, direction. A life that has a higher purpose involves recognizing that values do exist, that life has meaning, and that that meaning can only be achieved by delaying gratification and focusing on long-term goals. For many men, God and spirituality provides the rock of security and stability that allows them to redirect their lives and start building the foundation of a future. It is exactly that foundation of meaning and purpose that is the basis for a healthy, fulfilling lifestyle.

You can change yourself and you will. And you will find that fulfillment comes from the *process* of making small, step-by-step changes. Let God be who He is to you and He will help you become all He meant you to be.

CHAPTER 7

HEALTHY THINKING SKILLS

In this chapter we will help you think about your thinking. As you get better at understanding your ways of thinking and their connection to your feelings and behaviors, you will get better at changing your thinking. In this chapter, you will learn about distorted thinking in general areas of your life, and distorted thinking related to sexual offending.

We will build on the earlier chapters to help you connect some dots about your early family life and childhood experiences, your ways of thinking, and the behaviors that got you into trouble. Get ready to start thinking in different, more healthy ways!

Glossary of Terms

Here are some new terms you will be learning in this chapter. Don't worry if they don't seem clear now; there will be lots of examples:

Cognition or Cognitive: Thoughts. Anything that has to do with thinking, including knowing, believing, deciding, planning, remembering, imagining, fantasizing, picturing things, and especially, saying things to yourself (in your mind).

Cognitive Distortions: Twisted thoughts that allow you to believe what you want to believe. Excuses, justifications, rationalizations, or minimizations to convince yourself that what you are doing is okay. Also, untrue things you say to yourself that make you unhappy.

Fantasies: Thoughts or images, *even momentary,* of something pleasant or desirable. Fantasies can be based on memories or can be imaginary.

Obsessions: Thoughts that take over your mind. Thoughts you feel like you cannot get rid of. Thoughts that are repetitive, over and over in your mind.

If you're going to change your behavior, you first have to understand how behavior occurs. That means breaking behavior down into its nuts and bolts, then seeing how all the pieces fit together. The first step is simply to realize that behavior never just happens. Behaviors are parts of *chains* of thoughts, feelings, and other behaviors. Until you make a point to look at what goes on inside you, you probably won't notice how your behaviors are connected with your thoughts and feelings. What you will soon be seeing in yourself is:

The way you *think* affects the way you feel and behave.
The way you *feel* affects the way you think and behave.
The way that you *behave* affects the way you think and feel.

The second step in learning to control your behavior is to recognize the relationships between your thoughts, feelings, and behaviors. You will be seeing many examples of these connections.

As we have seen in previous chapters, some of our current feelings are a product of old experiences. We have carried these feelings with us. Other feelings are part of our physiology– our body. If we are sick or something is wrong with our body we will feel down, lack energy, and maybe even feel sad. Our body also stores traumatic memories and they can trigger feelings like fear or anxiety or depression. But many of our feelings come directly out of our thoughts.

This is fortunate, because we cannot control or change our old experiences (though we can calm down our body – see chapter 3), but we can control our thinking, and therefore we can control the way that we feel. And when we are in control of our thinking and our feelings, we will be more in control of our behavior. That means the most important part of controlling our behavior is understanding our thoughts and feelings.

Automatic Thoughts & Feelings

In Chapter 4 we said that some of our early experiences stay with us and shape us through conditioning– which means that either (1) you associate a thought or feeling with a person, place, thing, or experience; or (2) you were punished or rewarded for behaving in a certain way, which negatively or positively reinforces the behavior.

In some cases, you were conditioned to associate sexual arousal with non-consenting or abusive behaviors. Your deviant sexual arousal is the single biggest threat to your recovery because it can happen automatically and instantly and throw you into the grip of the PIG before you know what hit you. The covert sensitization exercises of Chapter 3 are designed to help you "undo" the connection between deviant situations and sexual arousal. We said you should do the exercises ahead of time so that you will not automatically be sexually aroused by deviant situations or fantasies in the future. In this chapter and chapter 8, you will be learning that even if you do continue to experience deviant sexual arousal, that does not mean you must give in to the PIG. Yes, automatic feelings can take us by surprise, but it is the thoughts that follow the feelings that determine how we act. You can tune in to these thoughts, and you can change them. That means you have the power to stay in control of your behavior.

Many types of experiences stay with us and shape us. This is not hard to see. We all know, for example, that someone who falls out of a boat as a child and almost drowns may have a hard time ever feeling comfortable in a boat again. That person may not even be able to go near the water without feeling fearful. For such a person, fear is an *automatic feeling* that is associated with boats and water, and it is triggered anytime they go near a boat. It is the thoughts that come out of their automatic feeling that keep their fear alive. Their automatic fear triggers them to think, "Oh, no, it's going to tip over! Don't make me go on it!" These thoughts keep them afraid. But if they think instead, "This is a bigger, safer boat. We were just reckless kids when my accident happened. Now I can swim. The people I'm with now are mature and won't do anything to rock this boat," their fear will start to subside. Then, if they take some successful boat rides, their automatic feelings will begin to fade away. The new, safe experiences in the boat create new thoughts and feelings to replace the thoughts and feelings associated with the old experience.

FIGURE 7.1: Cognitive-behavior chains

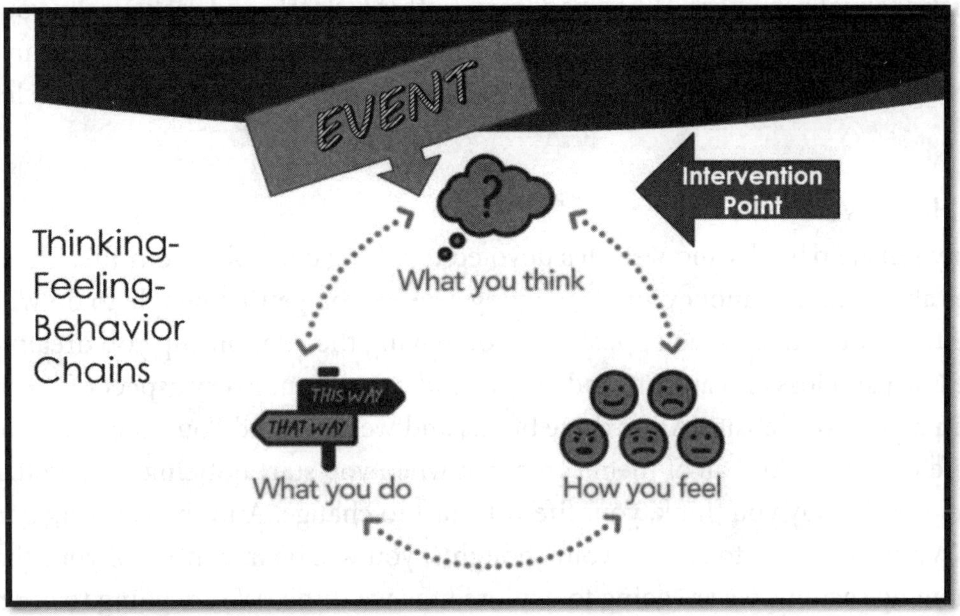

All automatic feelings are not bad feelings, of course. We might feel peaceful and hopeful every time we walk into our church or synagogue. We might feel excited every time we enter a stadium for a sports event. Or we might feel comforted just by picking up the phone and hearing the voice of someone who loves us. We could say that the church triggers feeling of peacefulness, the stadium triggers excitement, the voice of our loved one triggers our feeling of comfort.

Just as many things can trigger feelings in us, those feelings, in turn, can trigger other things inside us—especially thoughts. For example, when we walk into church and automatically feel at peace, that feeling can then trigger the thought "I should come more often."

In the next chapter we will be talking a lot about "triggers" for sex offending and noticing how a feeling can trigger you to start thinking about sex. Depression, frustration, anger and loneliness are some of the feelings that trigger men to think about sex. Or running into someone you hung out with when you were offending might remind you of the "old days" and trigger the same feeling of excitement you got from offending.

The important point for now is simply to notice how your mind works. An automatic feeling can come to you anytime. But automatic feelings don't last. It is the thoughts you have that determines what you do with your automatic feelings. (The person with the fear of boats keeps that fear active by saying to himself, "It could tip over again. Don't make me go on it!") Without thoughts that reinforce the feeling and keep it going, the feeling can fade away. In the next several sections we will be seeing that it is really your thoughts that determine how you feel over time. When you learn to change your thoughts you will be more in control of your life.

In the following sections we are going to explore how we think. We are going to see how the ways that we think control how we feel and the things that we do. You are going to learn to recognize when your thinking is becoming distorted and self-defeating and leading you in dangerous directions. You will understand how your distorted thinking makes you unhappy and angry and hopeless. And you will learn how to change all that—how to *reshape* your thinking and regain control.

Learning to be in control of your thinking will help you in every aspect of your life, including your problematic sexual behaviors. When you learn to think clearly and realistically you will be on the road to a healthier you. The important point for now is simply to notice how our minds work. An automatic feeling can come to you anytime. But you can change your thoughts, which leads to new feelings.

Looking at How We Think

There are many self-help books and websites devoted to taking control of your life. There are also many websites about making money, on developing a career, on getting people to do what you want, on making yourself attractive to the opposite sex, on having the relationship you dream of, on overcoming depression and loss and anxiety and anger...and on and on. Every aspect of life you can think of is covered in a book or website. All of these books and websites and YouTube videos are about creating the life you want. And all of them agree that when you start noticing what you are thinking and start changing the way you think, your life will start to change. And the amazing part is that they're right! When you learn to control your thoughts, you will be in control of your life.

In the following sections we are going to explore how we think. We are going to see how the ways that we think control how we feel and the things that we do. You are going to learn to recognize when your thinking is becoming distorted and self-defeating and leading you in dangerous directions. You will understand how your distorted thinking makes you unhappy and angry and hopeless. And you will learn how to change all that–how to change your thinking and regain control.

Learning to be in control of your thinking will help you in every aspect of your life. Most importantly, it is going to help you stay in control of the urges that have threatened to destroy your life in the past. When you learn to think clearly and realistically you will be on the road to a healthier you.

How Our Self-Statements Influence Our Feelings

At any given moment you are talking to yourself. We all talk to ourselves inside our heads. All the time. (Right now, you may be saying something like, "No I don't," or "How do you know what goes on inside my head?") We call the things we say to ourselves *Self-Statements.* This is the main way we think. Most of the time it's easy for us to hear the things we are saying to ourselves. Sometimes it's not as easy because we think fast–especially when we have thoughts we've had many times before (like, "Tired. Going to bed."). As you go through this section you will be tuning into your self-statements a lot, and you will find that noticing the things you say to yourself is the real key to understanding and *controlling* your feelings and your behaviors.

We said that thoughts, feelings, and behaviors are all connected to each other, meaning they all influence each other. The most important of these connections is how *thoughts* (self-statements) affect *feelings.* Except for our brief, automatic feelings, our feelings are directly related to what we are thinking. It usually appears to us that our feelings come from what is happening outside of us. But as we will see, outside events themselves actually do not determine how we feel. *It is the way that we think about events that can lead to our feelings.*

Let's take an example: Someone cuts you off in traffic. Instantly you are afraid of a crash (automatic feeling). But then your feeling quickly turns to anger. It seems like a simple connection: (a) the person cut you off, (b) you are angry. Clearly, it was the other person's behavior that made you angry. Right?

Well, let's take a closer look at what actually happened, remembering how quickly your mind works and slowing down the playback. In slow motion you will see that (a) the person cut you off, (b) you said to yourself, *"You mother@#$%&^# ass$%@!!"* (c) you felt angry.

Here's the important point: you didn't have to feel angry. Had you said something different to yourself, you would have felt different. For example, you might have said to yourself: "He must be racing to the hospital with an injured passenger" or "Maybe he's having a heart attack and lost control" or "Must be a new driver. Thank God he missed me." Notice that if you had said any of these things to yourself, you would not have felt angry. The point is: it was not actually the driver who made you angry, but what you said to yourself about him that made you angry. This means that it was not him who made you angry but you. *You control the feelings you have through the things you say to yourself.*

Now in real life you probably won't think the driver who cuts you off is racing to the hospital. You'll think he's a jerk, which he is. But that still doesn't mean you have to make yourself angry. Lots of people stay calm in this situation. How? By saying to themselves something like: "Lots of distracted drivers out there! Good thing I'm paying attention and practicing defensive driving. I'm glad I'm safe!" "There's nothing I can do about them except be careful, so they don't get me into an accident."

Let's take another example. Suppose your boss gives you a compliment. Again, it might seem that the chain is simply: (a) Mr. Brown compliments your work, and (b) you feel good. But wait. It's not that simple. There are many ways you might have reacted to the compliment. If you said to yourself, "Oh, God, wait 'til he finds out the job is only half done," you would feel worried. If you thought, "I don't believe it. He's setting me up to make me come in on Saturday!" you would feel angry. And what would you feel if you told yourself, "What a dork. He's trying to suck up to me because I caught him making out with the secretary"?

Notice: the compliment itself (the external event) has no power to make you feel any particular way. Only the way that you think about it does. Only if you say to yourself, "Hey, all right! Somebody recognizes my good work," will you feel good about the compliment. *It is your thought that creates the good feeling.*

Changing Perspective

Think of a situation that seems to disprove what you have just read. In other words, think of something outside you that clearly makes you happy or sad or angry without any need for any thoughts. Write it down and ask yourself if it is possible that the event or situation you have described could make you feel a different way by changing the way you think about it. If it is possible, how would it be possible? If you can't think of any way you could possibly feel other than the way you do, bring the example into the group and describe it.

The Thinking-Feeling Link at Work

The link between thoughts and lasting feelings is important. The next time you notice yourself feeling worried or angry or sad, *ask yourself what you were just thinking.* If you play back (like a recording) the things you were saying to yourself just before the feeling came on, you will see how that connects with the feeling. You can control how you feel (and how you act) by changing the way you think.

FIGURE 7.2: Link between thoughts, feelings, and behaviors

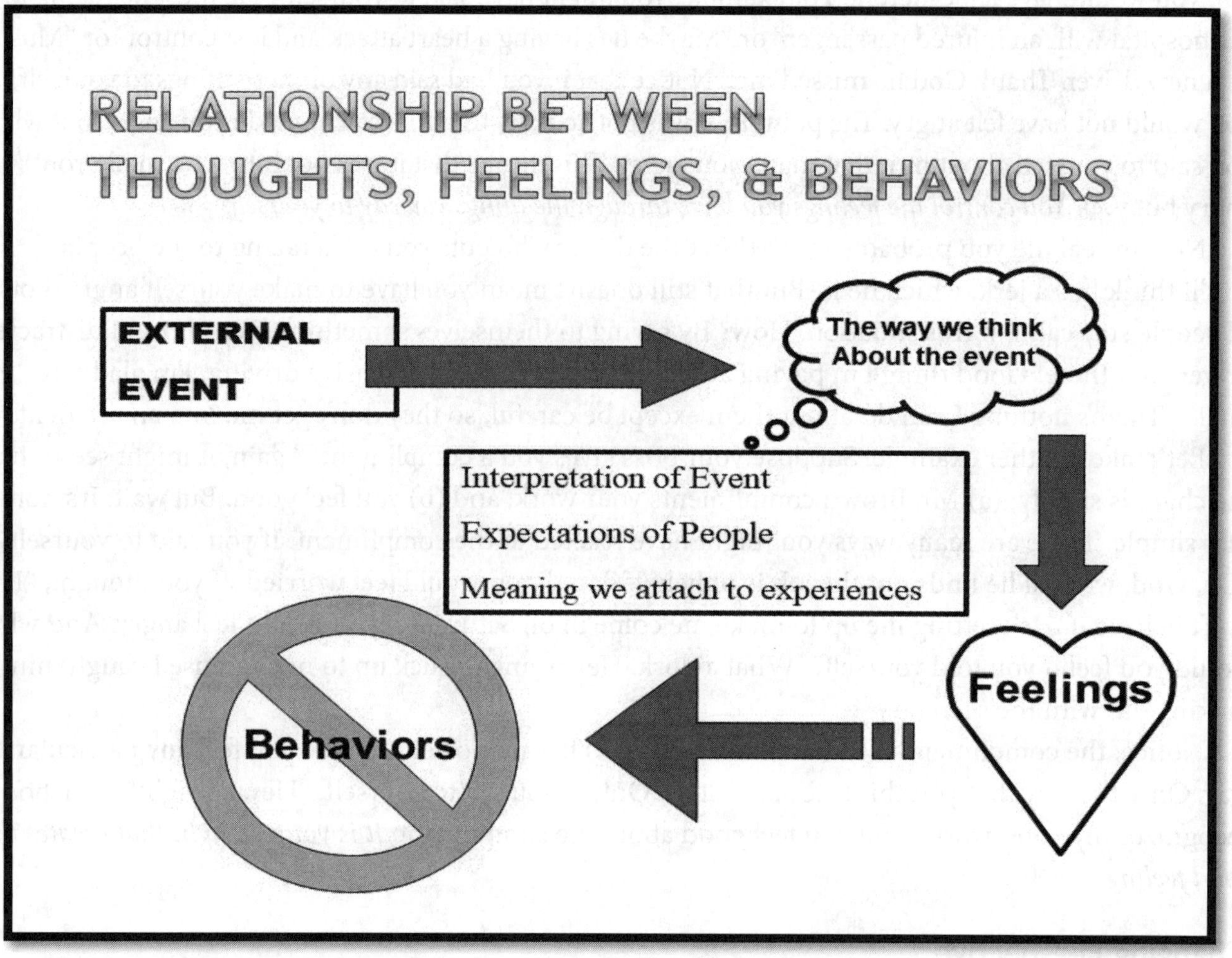

Certain kinds of thoughts lead directly to strong feelings. Below are some of the kinds of thoughts that lead to negative feelings.

Thoughts that lead to...	**Feelings**
Thinking about losses, such as the loss of a loved one or something else that was important to you.	sadness deprivation
Thinking that you've hurt someone; thinking you are bad or worthless; thinking that if others really knew you, they wouldn't like you.	guilt shame
Thinking you are being treated unfairly; thinking someone is trying to take advantage of you; blaming other people for your problems.	anger annoyance resentment
Thinking you are in danger; expecting the worst.	worry fear anxiety nervousness
Comparing yourself to others and believing you are not as good as them.	inferiority inadequacy
Thinking about how you don't get the love you need; thinking about how alone you are; thinking you don't fit in.	loneliness isolation alienation
Telling yourself that your problems will never go away; believing things will never improve; seeing your life as out of control.	hopelessness discouragement

Some questions to ask yourself when you have strong, inappropriate, or upsetting reactions:

- Why do you think you reacted that way?
- If you find yourself blaming others ("they did this...") ask: That's about them, what about me?
- What were you thinking or feeling? Do those thoughts and feelings seem familiar?
- When have you felt that way before? When was the earliest time you can remember feeling that way?
- What did it seem to mean about you (or about them) when that happened?
- Why did you interpret the situation that way? Are there other ways to interpret what happened?
- What were the pros and cons of how you reacted? How might you want to react differently?

Look at the following example and then you will try it yourself.

	Circle one:	Event: My mother asks me to clean up my room and bathroom.	Evaluation & Solutions
T = Thoughts F = Feelings B =Behavior	**T** / F / B	My mom is always telling me what to do and she thinks that I'm a slob.	This thought may be distorted. Does she really always do that? How do you know what she thinks?
	T / F / **B**	I yell at my mom and tell her she's annoying and controlling.	Did you over-react? Is yelling a positive way to solve problems? If you need to set boundaries with your mom, is there a better way to express yourself? What's the feeling between the thought and the behavior?
	T / **F** / B	I feel pissed off! Then I feel a little sorry that I yelled, but also scared that my parents will kick me out.	Did you feel bad because you over-reacted to your mom's request, or because you worry that your behavior could have a negative consequence?
	T / F / B	It's true, I am a loser and I'm trapped here living with my parents because I can't get a job because of that sex crime arrest.	It might be true that it's hard to get a job as a RSO, and it is true that you might feel trapped. But what might not be true about your thought?
	T / F / **B**	I tidy up my room, for real this time, and it looks more organized and clean.	You motivated yourself to behave differently and you succeeded.
	T / **F** / B	I actually feel proud and calmer when things aren't so cluttered.	After the fact, you are in a better position to evaluate your mom's request, your reaction, and your solutions.
	T / F / **B**	I apologize to my mom for yelling.	Taking responsibility for your part of the problem is a mature and healthy behavior!
	T / F / **B**	I share with my mom how bad I feel about myself and how I was triggered by her request because I felt criticized, and that reinforced my own shameful feelings about myself.	Being able to self-analyze, and to have a support person to talk through feelings with, can help you de-escalate your feelings, see things from new perspectives, and connect with others.

Try this exercise with a situation of your own. Describe the precipitating event, then the thoughts, feelings, and behaviors that came from it. Use your evaluation to think of some healthier solutions. (Often under anger are other feelings, like sadness, shame, or fear). Use the questions on the previous page to help you sort through your reactions, thoughts, and feelings, and to figure out where they might have originally come from in your early life (schemas – Figure 6.3).

Exercise 7.1: Thinking About the Thinking-Feeling-Behavior Link

Write about the situation and ask yourself if it is possible that the event you have described could make you feel a different way if you changed the way you think about it?

	Circle one:	**Event:**	**Evaluation & Solutions**
T = Thoughts F = Feelings B =Behavior	T / F / B		
	T / F / B		
	T / F / B		
	T / F / B		
	T / F / B		
	T / F / B		
	T / F / B		
	T / F / B		

Using New Perspectives (Thoughts) to Create New Feelings

You may have met people who seem to have it all together. They seem to take things in stride, to keep things under control, to get the things they want—in short, to enjoy life. You might have told yourself that they're lucky: they were born into money, or born into a good family, or they just "know the right people." Once in a while those things are true. But much more often they're not. Lots of successful and happy people were born into poverty or dysfunctional families. Lots of people who are born into wealthy or well-connected families grow up to be miserable.

So what is different about people who have peace of mind? One thing that's different is that they understand the thinking-feeling connection discussed above. They recognize that they can affect the way they feel by noticing and changing the ways they think about things. It stands to reason that if (a) what is really going on is not that the bad things in our lives make us feel bad, but that (b) the ways that we think about those things is what is making us feel bad, then (c) if we can change the ways we think about things, (d) we won't have to feel bad.

This doesn't mean that there aren't hard times, sadness, hurt, loss, anger, or people who don't treat us well. All of those things are true, and bad thing can happen. Things happen that are out of our control, and of course strong negative feelings exist and are legitimate. But being able to think about things in a way that helps keep perspective, have an open mind, accept things we cannot change, and re-frame things to see them differently at times are all thinking skills that help us cope with challenging times.

But, then, what is it about people who always seem to take things in stride? How can they not let things bother them? Is it that they're just lucky all the time? Maybe no one ever cuts them off in traffic, no one ever ignores them or criticizes them, bad things never happen to them and no one breaks their heart? Could that be the answer? Well, think about the people you know who seem to be at peace with themselves. Are they lucky all the time? Never a hardship, never a loss, never a failure? Probably not.

Here's another question to ponder. Why do we seek out certain people for advice and not others? Think of a friend or minister or uncle you have always turned to for advice when things looked bleak. What is it about that person that brings you to him or her? First, they listen. That's important. What else? Is it that they have a certain way of seeing things that makes the bad things seem not so bad? Do they find a different angle, something you hadn't thought of, that puts things in a different perspective?

Although we all seek the truth and believe it, there are many ways to see the truth. We interpret things differently. How we interpret them affects how we feel about them. If we are in the habit of seeing things in ways that make us feel angry or sad or hopeless, we can find other ways of viewing them. When we change our thoughts, we will change our feelings, and be better prepared to react with healthy and constructive behaviors.

How would you feel if you heard your company is "downsizing" and you were going to lose your job? Many people would feel helpless because they would start with a stream of distorted thoughts. "It's so unfair—I'm always getting screwed!" "I'll never find another job like this." "It doesn't matter what you do, someone's always going to pull the rug out from under you. Life sucks!"

Now that you understand that you are in control of what you think and what you do, you could ask yourself how to think in constructive and healthy ways about this situation. You could think something like, "Well, yes, I am upset and nervous about this and I wish it weren't happening, but that's okay. Shit happens." Then you might recognize that you could look for the positive side and focus on it. You could say, "I'm going to make a plan and turn this crisis into an opportunity."

Distorted Thinking: Making Life Harder Than It Has to Be

Throughout this book we have mentioned different types of distorted thinking, which we also refer to by the fancier term, cognitive distortions. Distorted thinking is unrealistic, unhealthy thinking. Alcoholics Anonymous calls cognitive distortions stinking thinking. Others call them thinking errors. There are different types of cognitive distortions and they serve different purposes. Some cognitive distortions come from experiences learned in childhood. Many people carry these distortions their whole life without ever knowing it. Other distorted thoughts we make up as we go along to justify or explain what we are doing. There are all kinds of cognitive distortions people use to make it okay to offend.

In the next section we will be talking about how to identify distorted thoughts. Once you can spot these sneaky, misleading, and false ways of thinking, the next step is to learn how to change them so they don't control and ruin your life. When you think about your life in more positive and realistic ways you will experience greater self-esteem, productivity, and closeness with others. Being in control of your thoughts means being in control of your behavior and your life.

When something happens, we have a choice about how we want to think about it. When we pay attention to our thoughts, we can then change them, leading to different feelings and behaviors.

FIGURE 7.3: Changing the way we think

That said, sometimes people do act impulsively. You learned about trauma-related self-regulation problems in chapters 2, 3, and 4. When someone has lived in a traumatic environment (like prison, an abusive family, or a violent neighborhood), their brain begins to constantly scan the environment for danger in order to respond quickly to protect oneself (see Figure 4.1). When threatening circumstances are common in your life, your brain becomes ready to take on an automatic movement from threat to action. This is called "hyper-arousal." That's a fancy way to say your brain is always on patrol, and this means that it can misinterpret non-threatening cues in the environment as dangerous. In Exercise 3.8 you learned how to slow down your reactions so that you can act in a more deliberate decision-making process. You will continue to improve skills to think things through so that you will act less impulsively, allowing you to think about your choices, the possible outcomes, and the consequences to yourself and others.

In Chapters 4 and 6 you learned about Schemas (see Figure 6.3). Early Maladaptive Schemas (EMS) are ways we got programmed to think about ourselves, others, and the world around us based on our early experiences and family life. EMS impact the way we think about things that happen to us: how we interpret events, our expectations of other people, and what our experiences seem to mean to us. In chapter 5, you learned about victim impact. In this chapter you will look at how distorted thinking about offending is connected to your ability to have empathy for your victims (or not).

Basic Beliefs – Early Maladaptive Schemas (EMS)

In our childhood we take in an enormous amount of information about the world and the people in it. The ways that people in our families treated each other and treated us shaped our thinking and influenced us throughout our lives. Now we will take the time to really examine the things we learned and question them.

The things we believe about the world we call our "basic beliefs." Like the roots of a tree, they are the source of many of our daily thoughts. Without being aware of it, we are constantly making assumptions about everything based on our basic beliefs.

The problem that can occur with basic beliefs is when we have learned things that seemed true in our childhood—or maybe even were true in our childhood—but that are no longer true in our adult lives. If we hold basic beliefs that aren't true, we might be making assumptions that aren't true. We assume that everyone and everything in the current time will be the same as they were in our early life experiences. Look at some of these basic beliefs that people bring with them out of their childhood:

- ☐ "I am helpless."
- ☐ "If I take a risk, I will get hurt."
- ☐ "I can't believe anyone."
- ☐ "People will hurt you if you disagree with them."
- ☐ "I'm not important."
- ☐ "There's no point in talking. No one ever listens."
- ☐ "No one really cares about anyone but themselves."
- ☐ "The only way to get things is to just take them."
- ☐ "I'm special and rules don't apply to me."
- ☐ "People are stupid and easy to fool."

Each of these beliefs will lead a person to make assumptions later in their lives that will make their lives more difficult and less rewarding. For example, if you believe "People will hurt you *if you disagree*," throughout your life, every time you disagree with someone or even think about disagreeing, you will think something like, "I better keep it to myself..." or "He's going to be mad at me..." or "She's gonna get back at me...." or "I'll go along for now, then do what I want to later..." As a result, you will find yourself automatically agreeing with people thousands of times over the course of your life, when maybe you really disagree.

All of these thoughts will come into your mind so quickly you may not even be aware of them. Because they come automatically, they are called **automatic thoughts.** Distorted automatic thoughts can be extremely destructive because they lead you to make faulty assumptions and decisions without even being aware of it. When you finally become aware of the things you are saying to yourself, you can question whether they are really true or not!

The truth is that some people will be unhappy with you if you disagree with them, but most people will be willing to listen to why you disagree. The truth is that sometimes you need to respectfully disagree if you are going to get your needs met. If you keep all your opinions to yourself you are going to feel angry and resentful, dismissed and unappreciated.

Since everyone develops different basic beliefs early in life, it is not possible for us to list all the possible beliefs that can lead to unrealistic automatic thoughts. It is possible for you to examine your basic beliefs about other people and yourself and question whether they are realistic and useful or whether they needlessly make you feel bad about life. You can start by going back to the experiences you wrote about in chapter 4 and simply ask yourself, "What lesson would I have probably taken from this kind of experience?"

Cognitive Distortions Serve a Function

Other types of distorted thought serve a specific purpose. Distorted thoughts serve many different purposes. For example, if you tell yourself that you're not as good as everyone else, maybe it's because you are afraid to try to better yourself (what's the point—you're going to fail anyway, right?). So even while it makes you miserable, you might be holding on to this thought because trying something new or striving for a goal feels even more scary.

Many cognitive distortions serve the purpose of making it okay to do something you want to do. Identifying cognitive distortions is equally important to see how they allow themselves to do the things they do. We have talked a lot about identifying needs that get met through offending. It is important for people who sexually offended to understand why they do the things they do. At the end of Chapter 4, you wrote about the emotional or psychological needs that you were trying to meet when you were offending.

If you have a need that is not being met you might try to meet those emotional needs through sex offending. But nobody can just go out and do things they know are wrong. First you have to justify it and explain to yourself that it really isn't so bad, and she probably really likes it or else she wouldn't let you do it, or you're just teaching her about sex like any good mentor would do, or you're not going to physically hurt him so what's the harm, and nothing really matters anyway because life stinks, and you deserve some pleasure, and you won't be able to stop thinking about sex until you just do it and get it over with, so why don't you just do it? All right, then, it's settled. Just this once.

You might have distorted thoughts about treatment, too…

When they first come into treatment, most people carry a lot of cognitive distortions with them. All of these distortions serve a purpose. They say, "She seduced me," meaning they don't have to feel guilty because it was the victim's fault. Or, "I couldn't afford a real lawyer and got stuck with a public defender," meaning they could have gotten away with the crime and wouldn't have had to face what it means about them if they had more money. They say, "I've learned my lesson," meaning "Don't make me go through this… I can't talk about the shameful things I think about and do."

Anyone who is trying to change will feel uneasy. Change is always difficult, uncomfortable, and sometimes downright scary. As you think about making real changes in your life, you might find yourself having thoughts about whether you really need this program and whether you really want to change. Taking a close look at these thoughts as they occur to you will be a good way for you to see how your thoughts function to convince you it's okay to do what you want to do.

Putting on a false front and being dishonest with yourself and others can be a way to deal with uncomfortable situation. You will probably find yourself wanting to do those same things as the treatment program starts to call for more change than you want to make. For example, if you tell yourself that you never really needed this treatment in the first place, that will make it easy for you to convince yourself that you just have to "play the game" and get it over with.

Even when you are trying to be honest with yourself and your group, there might still be times when you say things that are designed to protect you from having to change— and that's normal, because that's just the way people are. *We all resist change.* So you be prepared to recognize the new cognitive distortions you might invent to justify *not changing.*

Lots of self-statements are designed to make it easy to not change. They sound like this:

- ☑ "This is stupid. This will never work."
- ☑ "These people don't know what I've been through. They have their fancy schooling, but what do they know about my life and my world?"
- ☑ "So I made a mistake. I've paid for it. They just want me to think I've got a problem so they can make money off me. It's all a scam."

And on and on.... Notice that all of these statements help you justify to yourself why you aren't really putting effort into this program. Remember, even people who have decided to be responsible for dealing with their problem will from time to time have these kinds of thoughts. People who are still busy blaming others for their behavior and its consequences will frequently have thoughts like these about treatment.

Styles of Distorted Thinking

The term 'cognitive distortion' was originally defined by psychologist Aaron Beck in his work on cognitive therapy for depression. Beck defined 'cognitive distortions' as unique thought content that is flawed or unrealistic. Also known as "thinking errors," they are irrational patterns of thinking that can cause you to feel bad or act in self-defeating ways. These include statements made by offenders that allow them to deny, minimize, rationalize or justify their behavior.

Cognitive distortions, whether they come out of distorted basic beliefs or they are serving a function in a person's life, are generally based on a particular style of thinking that a person adopts. The thinking styles listed below are defense mechanisms to help people psychologically deal with realities that are uncomfortable for them to accept. Distorted thinking is a trap that everyone falls into from time to time, but that some people tend to use much of the time. These styles of thinking generate distorted thoughts. Which ones sound familiar to you?

ENTITLEMENT. I believe that if I want something, I am automatically entitled to it. I deserve it and anyone who tries to interfere with my having it is being unfair. Example: I work hard, and I deserve a day off, so I'll call in sick even though I'm not.

CATASTROPHIZING. I automatically expect the worst of situations and people. I make things worse than they really are by focusing all my attention on what can go wrong. Example: If someone doesn't respond to me the way I want them to, I automatically assume they don't like me and think the worst of me. I imagine that they wish me no good, and may even be out to get me. Example: If my boss criticizes me or reprimands me for being late, I start expecting him to fire me. I think about what it will mean to lose my job and not be able to pay my bills, and soon I have worked myself into a panic state.

IMMEDIATE GRATIFICATION. I must get what I want right away or I will feel frustrated and angry. I do not believe I can tolerate feelings of frustration. Example: If I have a sexual urge, I must have an orgasm. I must act immediately on my sexual feeling, even if that means risking hurting someone else or getting myself in trouble.

RATIONALIZATION. I try to explain or excuse behavior or an attitude with logical reasons, even if these are not appropriate or factual. Example: I had a bad day, so I will eat a bag of cookies because I need something to make me feel better.

MINIMIZATION. I try to make my behavior seem less important or harmful by reducing it to the smallest possible amount or degree of value, importance, influence, etc. Example: I did look at child pornography, but at least I didn't molest anyone.

JUSTIFICATION. This thinking provides a way of showing or declaring something to be right or reasonable. Example: I have to use pornography every day in the bathroom at work because my partner does not like to have sex.

DEPRIVATION. This thinking distortion goes along with the felt need for immediate gratification. If I don't get what I want when I want it, I will feel deprived. Being deprived makes me feel empty and angry. Example: I expect that if I don't act on a sexual impulse, but ride it out and let it fade, it will leave me feeling empty and frustrated instead of proud and in control of myself.

OBJECTIFICATION. Objectification is the act of thinking about, or treating a person, like an object or a thing. It dehumanizes others, which means seeing another person as a tool for your enjoyment, gratification, or other benefit. Objectification fails to see someone as a whole and complex person with feelings, thoughts, and a life that exists beyond your needs. It sees someone as not having the right to their own autonomy, sees them as interchangeable or disposable, and views them as not entitled to their own boundaries. Objectifying others treats them as something that you are entitled to. Example: Looking at porn objectifies women (or men, or children) as someone just there to please another sexually, not as a whole person with feelings, who should have an interactive choice in the behavior, the chance to say no, and mutual intimacy needs.

ALL- OR- NOTHING THINKING. I use words like "always" and "never," "everyone" and "no one," "everything" and "nothing." People are either "good" or "bad." If something isn't perfect, it's terrible. If someone doesn't love you, they probably hate you. I see things as black or white, because it seems easier and safer to see them that way than in the shades of gray that most things really come in. Example: Seeing people as human beings who have good qualities and bad, and who are sometimes nice and sometimes not, is too confusing. I need to be able to put a "good" or "bad" label on them. Other Examples: The boss is always unfair; nothing good ever happens to me; no one can be trusted.

FOCUSING ON THE NEGATIVE. I only see the negative in others and in myself. Example: In a group meeting I am annoyed that a new member seems like a know-it-all. I am so focused on my annoyance I refuse to listen to interesting points the new member makes. Example: I have a conversation with a woman I'm interested in. Even though it goes very well and she seems to like me, all I can think about is the part where I got a little nervous and repeated myself. "She must think I'm an idiot," I say to myself.

OVER-GENERALIZING. Another way we simplify life. We take one example of something and tell ourselves this is the rule. All things like that one must be the same. Stereotyping is a form of over-generalizing. "All politicians are corrupt," "All smart people are arrogant," "All sex offenders will reoffend," are things people say because they don't want to be bothered dealing with reality, which is that none of these statements is true. Cynicism is another form of over-generalizing and simplifying. If you tell yourself, "Everyone's just out for the buck," you don't have to try to figure out what really does motivate people. When over-generalizing becomes a habit, especially when you combine it with focusing on the negative, it can make you feel miserable and hopeless. Example: I try to talk to a woman at my company who brushes me off. I tell myself, "Women only want men who can offer status or money. With my average job and pay, I shouldn't even bother to approach a woman." The truth, of course, is that women are all individuals and are all looking for different things.

"SHOULD" STATEMENTS. Telling yourself that things should be a certain way—the way you'd hoped or expected them to be. Must, ought to, and have to have the same meaning. Should-statements about yourself lead to guilt, and should-statements about others lead to anger. Examples: Saying to yourself: "I should never have bought that car. It's been nothing but trouble," will make you feel guilty and incompetent. "My therapist shouldn't expect me to do so much work," will lead to anger and resentment.

MIND READING. When you make assumptions about what others are thinking and don't check it out with them you often find yourself involved in misunderstandings. You can't know what others are thinking without asking! Also, if you expect others to know what you want or need or how you feel—without you telling them—you are setting yourself up for disappointment and frustration. Example: You get mad at your partner for not knowing how to please you sexually even though you've never communicated your needs to them. You believe they should "just know" or follow your body language.

BLAMING OTHERS. Putting the blame for your problems on other people protects you from having to take responsibility for your life. If you always blame others without looking at what you are doing to contribute to your problems, you will not be able to figure out what you can do to change the situation. Blaming others means believing that you have little or no control over your life. Example: Blaming your probation officer for not letting you leave the county, instead of recognizing that must gain back trust after committing a crime. Example: Blaming the police for a "sting" instead of recognizing that the reason you got caught in a sting is because you were doing something inappropriate and unlawful in the first place.

VICTIM BLAMING. Putting the blame for your offense on the victim – for enticing you, telling on you, reporting you, or participating with you – is a way of pretending that you are not responsible for your own behavior. Focusing on what the victim said, did, or did not say or do takes the focus off of your accountability. Example: My adult "victim" went along with having an affair with me, because I was her boss and she wanted a raise.

WISHFUL THINKING. Something will happen because I want it to—not because I've got a plan or because I'm working to make it happen, but just because I want it. Example: "I'm going to win the lottery." Example: "My ten-year-old car is going to make it across the country." We also fool ourselves about things we don't want to happen. Example: "I know smoking causes cancer but that won't happen to me."

Often, styles of distorted thinking go together: Objectification + Justification = Victimization

The "Why Lie"

Sometimes distorted thoughts are deliberate untruths—or lies. Why do people lie?

For many reasons.

1. They want to avoid consequences or getting in trouble.
2. They are ashamed of something they think or something they did.
3. They are trying to make themselves look better in someone else's eyes.
4. They don't want to disappoint someone.
5. The lie reflects something they wish was true.
6. A small fib snowballs into a big lie and it seems too late to admit the truth.
7. They want to avoid hurting someone with the truth, or they want to make someone feel better.
8. They believe what they say is true, because sometimes memory is tricky and facts can be misinterpreted.

Exercise 7.2: Can You Think of Other Reasons You've Lied at Times in Your Life?

THE LIE	THE WHY

The Lie Pie

Lies can happen in three different ways, and they each involve different types of mis-information:

1. Commission: Deliberately saying something untruthful (committing a lie).
2. Omission: Leaving out (omitting) important information that changes the meaning or implication of what you are saying.
3. Distortion: Changing the meaning of something intentionally so it may not be a bold lie but alters the reality of what you are saying.

FIGURE 7.4: The Lie Pie

Thanks to program member RT for this.

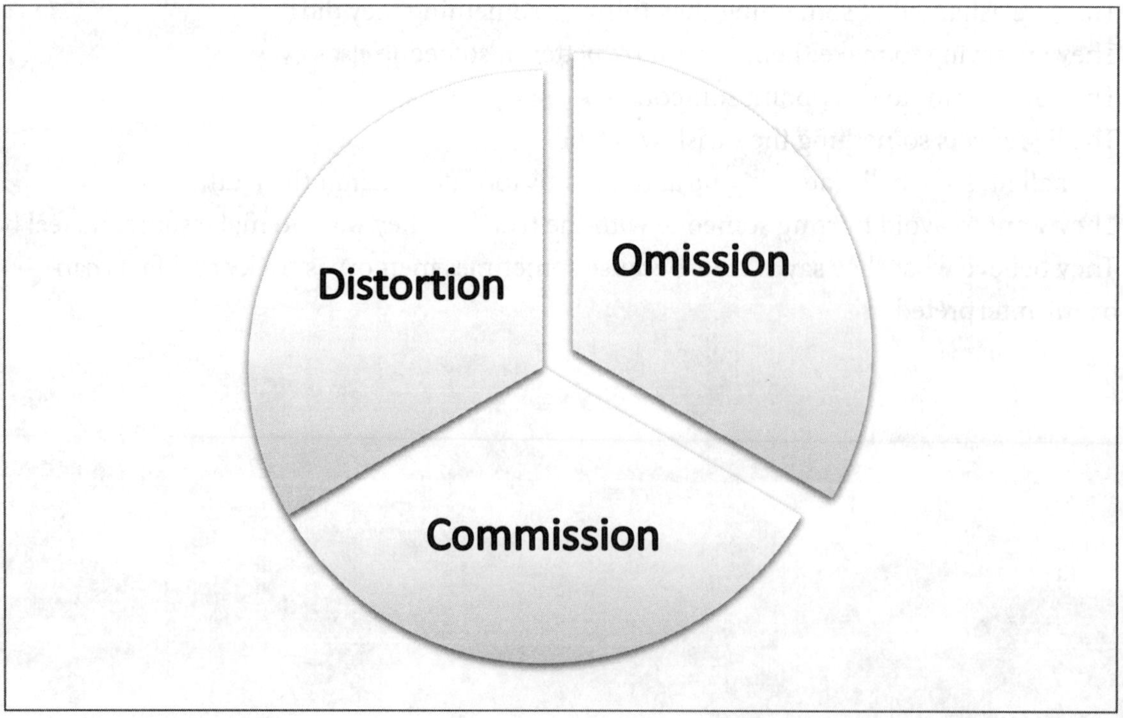

Exercise 7.3: Describe Lies You've Told of Commission, Omission and Distortion

Commission	Omission	Distortion

Restructuring Distorted Thoughts

Cognitive "restructuring" is a way of looking at distorted thoughts and changing them. Remember, the way you choose to look at a situation is something that you can control. For example, once you recognize that the real motivation behind the kinds of thoughts listed above is to protect yourself from uncomfortable truths or to avoid consequences, you can reexamine them to see which parts are true and which are just ways of fooling yourself. Then, by keeping the parts that are true and changing the parts that are not, you can restructure them to be useful to you instead of working against you.

There are four steps in the process of identifying and changing distorted thoughts.

1. **Identify the thought you want to examine:** What exactly are you saying to yourself? Write it down.
2. **See if the thought fits into any of the "Styles of Distorted Thinking" in the previous section:** Go through the list of styles of distorted thinking and compare your thought with the examples of each type of distortion. Write down each distorted style that seems to apply.
3. **Ask yourself "what is true" and "what is not true"** about the thought. Break the thought into parts and examine each part. Separate out the parts of the thought that you identified as distorted in step #2.
4. **Substitute realistic new thought** by keeping the parts that are true from #3, and correcting the distorted style in the other parts.

Let's look at an example to see how the process works. We'll start with an example of distorted thoughts from childhood.

EXAMPLE: *You find yourself in group sessions feeling reluctant to share.*

1. **Identify the thought you want to examine:** *"There's no point in talking. No one ever listens to me."*

2. **See if the thought fits into any of the "Styles of Distorted Thinking" in the previous section:** Go through the list of styles of distorted thinking and compare your thought with the examples of each type of distortion.

   As we go through the list, we see immediately that our thought is an example of both *All or Nothing Thinking and Overgeneralizing.* The reality is that some people are poor listeners. But when we say "no one listens" we are overgeneralizing from some people to all people. And when we say "no one ever listens," we are also making a leap. Even the worst listeners listen some of the time, don't they? Is there really anybody who never listens? Really? And isn't the first part of the statement also an all-or-nothing statement too? Do you really mean that there's never a point in talking? Really? No, not really. Of course you have communicated with people many, many times in your life—and gotten them to listen.

   While we're looking at styles of distorted thinking, let's ask ourselves if our statement also qualifies as *mind-reading.* How do we really know whether another person is listening or not? Sometimes we test them by asking them what we just said, but if we haven't tested them we really don't know if they heard us or not. In that case we're mind-reading if we decide they haven't heard us.

   So we see that our statement, *"There's no point in talking. No one ever listens."* is distorted in three ways. It's *All-or-Nothing Thinking, it's Overgeneralizing,* and it's *Mind Reading.* So let's fix it by keeping whatever is true and getting rid of the distorted parts.

3. **Ask yourself "what is true" and "what is not true"** about the thought.
   Break the thought into parts and examine each part. *Separate out the parts of the thought that are not true.*

   Okay, what's true here? It's true that some people don't listen very well. It's also true that, at one time or another, most people can be poor listeners. It's true that it is annoying when you say something and the other person doesn't seem to get it. It's true that if you say something important to someone you care about and they don't listen or understand, it really hurts. So it is true that sometimes it *feels like* there is no point in talking.

   What's not true? It's not true that talking never helps. It's not true that nobody ever listens. That's a clear exaggeration and distortion.

4. **Substitute a realistic new thought** by keeping the parts that are true from #3 and correcting the distorted style in the other parts. In other words, say the same basic idea you were trying to say but say it in a realistic way. There is no one right way to say anything, of course, so you might try a couple of different ways to say what you want to say. Here, we might say something like: "Sometimes it feels like there is no point in talking to people because they don't seem to be listening. Some people seem to be very poor listeners. But trying to express myself can sometimes lead to feeling heard and understood. That helps me sort through my feelings and make sense of them."

When we put our example in a table so we can look at it, it looks like this:

Exact Thouht	Style of Distorted Thinking	What is True/ Not True	Substitute Realistic Thought
1. There's no point in talking. No one ever listens.	**1. ALL-OR-NOTHING THINKING:** This is an all-or-nothing: "no point" is unrealistic; "no one" and "ever" are both extremes. **2. OVER-GENERALIZING:** Any time you use words like "no one" or "ever" you are probably over-generalizing. **3. MIND READING:** Do you really know when someone is listening? How can you know for sure? How can you test whether someone seems to be listening and under-standing?	**True:** 1. Some people don't listen very well 2. Even people who are good listeners can get distracted or not hear you. 3. It is annoying when you say something to someone and they don't hear you. 4. If you say something important to someone you care about and they act like they didn't get it, that hurts. **Not True:** 1. Nothing is accom-plished by talking to people. 2. Nobody is a good listener. 3. Bad listeners never hear what people say.	Sometimes it feels like there is no point in talking to people because they don't seem to be listening. Some people seem to be very poor listeners, but maybe that's not true of everyone. Maybe I could try sharing in group and see what happens.

If you can change your way of seeing things, things can be seen from a different perspective. Think about sitting in a room. If you get up and move to a different chair, you're in the same room but seeing it from a different angle! Well, that's what we're talking about. Everything can be seen in a different way. When you change your thinking, you can change your feelings and behaviors.

Try it out!

Exercise 7.4: Restructuring Cognitive Distortions

Exact Thouht	Style of Distorted Thinking	What is True/ Not True	Substitute Realistic Thought

Search for Serenity

In 12-step programs (see more in Chapter 3 about 12-Step Programs), they say the "Serenity Prayer" which is brilliant in its simplicity: "Grant me the serenity to accept the things I cannot change, the Courage to change the things I can, And wisdom to know the difference."

The serenity prayer is a great cognitive strategy for remembering what you can control and what you cannot. This can help you avoid spending energy on things you can't control, and focusing your efforts on things you can change about yourself or your situation. Somethings things happen that we can't control, and we can't control other people, but we can control the way we think and react to things.

Exercise 7.5: What I Can and Cannot Control

Look at the examples given, and then write in some examples from your own life.

Things I Cannot Control	Things I Can Control
How my father talks to me or treats me.	How I talk to my father, how I respond with healthy boundaries, and how often I speak with him.
Whether my boss recognizes and values my efforts at work.	Showing up, doing my best job, speaking respectfully to others, and following the boss's directions.
My partner cheated on me.	How I react to my partner, how I express my feelings about what happened, and the boundaries I set about what is healthy for me in a relationship.

Slogans

If you've ever gone to a 12-step meeting, you know they use a lot of "slogans" to help them through tough times. Slogans are actually great cognitive coping strategies. They talk about the Three As: Awareness, Acceptance, Action. Be aware of your thoughts, accept them, and act to change them. Use these slogans to tell yourself something different when you become aware of thoughts that are distorted. Can you think of any other slogans that you say to yourself that are helpful to you?

Slogan	**What it Means:**
Attitude of gratitude	Notice what you have to be grateful for in the moment
Easy does it	Go easy on yourself and others
Fake it till you make it	Act in the way you want to be and it will become true
Fear to fate	Sometimes we create what we expect and fear
First things first	Prioritize and take things one step at a time
Hope is not a plan	Take action
How important is it?	Put things in perspective
If it is to be, it is up to me	I am in control of my life
Nothing changes if nothing changes	If you do the same thing you will get the same results
It works if you work it	Your program only works if you make the effort
It is what it is	Accept reality
Just for today	Stay present in the moment, not the past or the future
Keep an open mind	Be open to new ideas from others
Keep it simple	Don't over think things or make them more complicated
Let it begin with me	When I change, people and situations change in response
Listen and learn	Talk less, listen more
Live and let live	Accept other people and don't try to change them
One day at a time	Stay in today so the future feels less overwhelming
Progress not perfection	You don't have to be perfect!
Stinking thinking	Recognize your distorted thoughts
Use the phone you're not alone	People are out there to help you. Reach out.
This is not my problem	I don't have to solve other people's problems
This is not a problem I can solve today	Stay in the present and don't worry too much about future

LIST YOUR OWN NEW SLOGANS BELOW	

Identifying Distorted Thoughts That Lead to Sex Offenses

(Thanks to program member DL for his contributions to this section)

Most people have used distorted thoughts to justify their offending. Many people in sex-offending treatment don't even recognize or question them. Look through the following list and check off the statements you have said to yourself. Put an extra check next to the ones you still believe. Be honest.

Thoughts About Sexual Contact with Minors:

- ☐ My victim did not experience any major problems because of the abuse.
- ☐ I believe that sex with my victim made him/her feel close to me.
- ☐ Sometimes children don't say no because they enjoy sex.
- ☐ My victims didn't tell because they liked it and weren't bothered by it.
- ☐ Having sexual thoughts and fantasies about a child isn't all that bad because at least it is not really hurting them.
- ☐ If a person does not use force to have sex with a child, it will not harm the child as much.
- ☐ Some people are not "true" sex offenders: I just made a mistake.
- ☐ Fondling a child is not as bad as penetrating a child and probably will not affect the child as much.
- ☐ My relationship with my victim was a lot like an adult relationship.
- ☐ Sexual activity with children can help the child learn about sex.
- ☐ Some people who commit sex crimes get longer sentences than they really should.
- ☐ Kids who get molested by more than one person are probably doing something to attract adults to them.
- ☐ People made a much bigger deal out of my offense than it really was.
- ☐ I suffered and lost more than the child(ren).

- ☐ I did not manipulate my victim.
- ☐ Some minors want to have sex with adults or older people.
- ☐ Most minors who have been sexually involved with an adult will eventually get over it and go on with their lives.
- ☐ Some children act very seductively.
- ☐ Staying away from minors is enough to prevent me from molesting again.
- ☐ My sexual abuse was not planned, it just happened.
- ☐ If I tell myself I won't offend again, I probably won't.
- ☐ Sometimes children initiate sex.
- ☐ Mothers should know better than to dress children in revealing clothing.
- ☐ I think I turned to sex with a child because I was deprived of sex from adults.
- ☐ My victim was much more adult-like than other minors.
- ☐ Children give adults more love and acceptance than other adults.
- ☐ The main thing wrong with sex with minors is that it is against the law.
- ☐ If I hadn't been molested as a child, I would never have offended.
- ☐ If I hadn't been drinking or using drugs, I would not have offended.

Thoughts about sexual assault of adults:

- ☐ People who commit sexual assault probably do it because they are under stress.
- ☐ People who get raped sometimes brought it on themselves.
- ☐ If a person does not strongly resist my sexual advances, then they are probably willing to have sex.
- ☐ Women often falsely accuse men of rape.
- ☐ My victim had sex with a lot of other people and was promiscuous.
- ☐ If a person gets drunk at a party, it is really their own fault if someone takes advantage of them.
- ☐ When women wear tight clothes, short skirts, and no bra or underwear, it looks like they want sex.
- ☐ A lot of people claim they were raped because they changed their mind afterward.
- ☐ My victim was somewhat to blame for what happened.
- ☐ If two people had sex in the past, then it is assumed it's consensual in the future.
- ☐ Fantasizing about forcing someone to have sex isn't all that bad since no one is really getting hurt.
- ☐ A lot of times when people say no they are just playing hard to get, but they really mean yes.
- ☐ Often a woman reports sexual assault after the fact because she gets mad at the man and is trying to get back at him.

- ☐ As long as a man does not hurt a woman in the process, forcing her to have sex is not so bad.
- ☐ People who experience unwanted touching will eventually forget about it and get on with their lives.
- ☐ Sometimes one person "teases" another and makes it seem like they want sex.
- ☐ Men cannot be sexually assaulted by other men.
- ☐ If someone lets another person kiss and touch them sexually, they should be willing to go all the way.
- ☐ When a woman acts like she is too good for a man, most men think about raping her to put her in her place.
- ☐ Society and courts are too tough on people who committed sex crimes.
- ☐ My victim was a slut and got what they wanted.
- ☐ Before police investigate a claim of rape, they should find out what the victim was wearing, if she had been drinking, and what kind of person she is.
- ☐ Rape is not planned, it just happens.
- ☐ If I tell myself I won't offend again, I probably won't.
- ☐ Women say "no" to sex because they don't want to seem too easy.
- ☐ If a person goes home with someone or invites them to their own house, it's usually because they want to have sex.
- ☐ Many people have a secret desire to be forced into having sex.
- ☐ People who rape have stronger sexual urges than other people.
- ☐ People can prevent themselves from being raped if they really want to.

Distorted Thoughts About Illegal Pornography or Interacting with Minors Online
(note: CSAM = child sex abuse material, otherwise known as child pornography)

- ☐ Finding CSAM is not planned, it just happens.
- ☐ Society and courts are too tough on CSAM offenders.
- ☐ I just looked at the stuff, I didn't take the pictures.
- ☐ The kids in the videos seemed like they were enjoying it.
- ☐ I would never really hurt anyone; I just had a few pictures on my computer.
- ☐ You can't victimize someone by just looking.
- ☐ At least I don't have any real victims.
- ☐ Role-playing in a chatroom is not illegal.
- ☐ The cops lied and pretended to be someone else. They set me up!
- ☐ Shouldn't the cops be out looking for real criminals?
- ☐ I never touched anyone.
- ☐ I wasn't even really chatting with anyone underage; it was a sting!
- ☐ I didn't travel to meet a minor, it was a cop!
- ☐ I wouldn't have gotten out of the car, I just wanted to see what he looked like.

- ☐ Since when are thoughts or fantasies illegal?
- ☐ Trading images allowed me to have a community – a community I didn't have in the "real world."
- ☐ I went online to escape the stress of my daily life, not because I was looking for kids.
- ☐ When I searched for "teens" I meant 18 or older.
- ☐ I never planned to look at sexual images of children – I just clicked on the pop ups.
- ☐ It was not really about the minors in the pictures, I love being able to collect and organize things.
- ☐ I never looked at the pictures, I just wanted a large collection.

Common Cognitive Distortions Often Fall into the Following themes:

- ☐ Victim Blaming: "You could tell by the way she was dressed that she wanted it."
- ☐ Minimization of harm: "We were just playing around; I didn't hurt them."
- ☐ Victim's Intentions: "Did you see how they were looking at me? They wanted it."
- ☐ Plausible Deniability "There's no proof of what I've done, it's their word against mine."
- ☐ Offender as Victim: "Maybe they didn't like what I did to them, but what happened to me after the arrest was a lot worse."
- ☐ Offender's Rationalization: "I was teaching them how to be good in bed."
- ☐ Offender's Need for Control: "I can make her do anything I want. She's my girl."
- ☐ Victim harm: "Secretly spying on them getting dressed doesn't hurt them if they don't know I'm doing it"
- ☐ Deflecting responsibility: "It's not my fault, it was the drugs. When I get high, I get super horny."
- ☐ Offender Fantasy: "I would never do what I did online in real life."
- ☐ Offender Fetish/Paraphilia: "Their feet looked so sexy, I had to touch them; I couldn't control myself."
- ☐ Obsession: "Since I first saw them, I felt like I couldn't live without them. They're all I thought about."
- ☐ Acceptable Manipulation: "I told them I would give them drugs and they totally went along with it."
- ☐ Male privilege: "I took her out to dinner at that expensive place; she owed me."
- ☐ Entitlement: "She asked me for a ride home. What did she expect? I'm her boss."
- ☐ Perceived Needs: "All I wanted to do was love them. I really cared about them. They needed real love so badly."
- ☐ Gender Roles: "In my culture, women must do what men tell them to do."
- ☐ Lack of Empathy: "She drank too much and passed out. She didn't care because she didn't even know."

Exercise 7.6: Identifying Your Cognitive Distortions

1. Pick out at least 5 statements from the lists above that seem to apply to you.
2. Give examples of other statements about sex or sexual assault that apply to you.

What other distorted thoughts about offending did you use?

Bloom's taxonomy is an educational theory saying that learning is cumulative, and it builds upon itself. Two layers include the learner's competencies (skills) and application of your skills and knowledge in new real-world circumstances. When we apply our learning and use new skills, we connect different ideas to each other and that can change the way we think and live. It is more than just knowing information that we store up – learning leads to "lightbulb" or "Aha" moments. By applying knowledge in a different way, we use new skills.

In order to change, learning consists of analyzing the world around us, evaluating specific situations, and creating a new, healthier reality. For example, let's say a person in treatment sees their ideal victim. They must **recognize** and **analyze** their reaction to the victim, **evaluate** the positive and negative consequences of their response, and **create** a new course of action based on the knowledge and skills and learned through treatment. By **remembering** this link between thinking, feeling, and behaving later, they **understand** how to **apply** the ideas to new situations.

Try it! Can you analyze these statements and identify the cognitive distortions you find?

- "I'm automatically attracted to beautiful women… I just start kissing them. It's like a magnet."
- "When you're a star, they let you do it. You can do anything. Whatever you want…Grab 'em by the pu**y. You can do anything."

Restructuring Distorted Thinking about Sex Offending

When you read the lists of cognitive distortions about sex offending, you probably recognized some thoughts you had at the time you were offending. By now hopefully you can see that those thoughts were justifications or excuses to do what you wanted.

It's not always easy to tell. After all, our thoughts don't seem distorted to us. If we believe something it's because it seems to make sense to us. The thing about cognitive distortions is that there's usually a little bit of truth to them! So how can we tell if we are really fooling ourselves with a distortion?

Example: "Victims of rape are usually somewhat to blame for what happened."

Exact Thouht	Style of Distorted Thinking	What is True/Not True	Substitute Realistic Thought
Victims of rape are usually somewhat to blame for what happened.	**BLAMING OTHERS:** You imply that by wearing certain clothes or getting in your car or going somewhere to do drugs with you she put the thought in your head that you were going to score. **ENTITLEMENT:** And once *she made you think* you were going to score; you believe you deserved to score. **IMMEDIATE GRATIFICATION:** Once you are sexually aroused, you must have an orgasm. **DEPRIVED:** If you have gotten yourself aroused by telling yourself you're going to get sex, and you don't get sex, that will be unfair.	**True:** The victim may have been interested in you or attracted to you. She may have made the mistake of trusting you. She probably didn't think that she was vulnerable or that you could attack and violate her. She trusted you. **Not True:** A person who shows interest in another person deserves to be taken advantage of and violated by that person. A woman who wants to be attractive to men or dresses in sexy clothes deserves to be attacked and hurt. A woman who isn't always "on guard," watching her every step, distrusting every man she meets, and never being alone with a man, deserves to be scarred for life.	Nothing a woman could do could justify someone violating her sexually. No one owes me anything. I have looked for any excuse to try to blame my victims. I wanted to pretend I didn't really have a problem, that it wasn't even my fault. In reality, I am always solely to blame for my actions. This is a simple fact of life that no amount of lying to myself can change.

Take a look at the following scenarios and identify the distorted thinking that is used to justify the behavior.

Tommy, age 22, was hanging out with his friends at someone's house. "The girls were drinking our beer and smoking our weed. It was all cool and happening, and then my friend was like, let's roofie that chick… She was passed out and everyone was laughing at her, and her own friends even posted the pic of her passed out on Instagram… Those guys took her into the room and did her up, man. I watched but didn't do anything. They told me to take her home and she was all hanging on me… I pulled over and had her suck my dick… she didn't even know; she was so out of it. Everyone did it. These chicks know that if you smoke some dope you gotta pay one way or another…"

Mac, age 50, was attracted to teens but always tried to keep it "barely legal." He went on Jack'd, a meet-up app for gay guys. "The app is for people who are over 18. If you sign up you say you're over 18. How do I know the difference? He might have hinted that he was 16, I don't remember… but what's the difference? He was on that app looking for older guys. He knew exactly what he was doing. He had his mom drive him over to my office for a "job interview." He was looking for it and he got it. Teens have sex all the time. They're totally up for it. Just because his mom found out and wanted to teach HIM a lesson, she had to ruin my life too. Totally unfair."

Now, think about your distorted thinking about offending. Give it a try!

Exercise 7.6: Restructuring My Cognitive Distortions About Offending

Exact Thouht	Style of Distorted Thinking	What is True/ Not True	Substitute Realistic Thought

Now, go back to chapter 1, and review the types of denial. Then identify 5 cognitive distortions that you have used to avoid responsibility for your offense. They might involve minimization, rationalization, justification, victim-blaming, entitlement, or other styles of distorted thinking. Restructure all 5 using the worksheet and the steps outlined above.

Exercise 7.7: Restructuring My Denial Distortions

Exact Thought	Style of Distorted Thinking	What is True/ Not True	Substitute Realistic Thought

Putting it all Together

You have had a chance to think about what you learned about how early life experiences like trauma or family dysfunction can shape your early maladaptive schemas (EMS). You can now try to figure out about how they might connect to your offending patterns. Also, think about the types of distorted thinking about offending that you used to justify, rationalize, minimize, or excuse your behavior and tell yourself it was OK or not so bad.

Here's an example: The Case of Paul. As you think about what might (or might not) be distorted about these statements, consider what we know about Paul's history, and think about his EMS and who they shaped his distorted thinking about sex offending.

Paul described his offenses as being in "relationships" with underage teen victims he met at work in a fast food restaurant. He also abused a few 11-year-old girls he befriended when he was a lifeguard at a pool. He said that he "never hurt them" and that the sex was "entirely consensual."

Paul who is now 32 years old, was the youngest of four children and described himself as the "dumb one" of the family. Paul stated that he was as a 'mistake' – meaning an unplanned pregnancy. He said that his mother didn't want him and that she was only nice to him when he did things for her.

Paul had a good relationship with his father, but his father worked long hours and wasn't at home much. He was sexually abused at age 10 by a teenage female family friend who babysat him, and he said there were positive aspects to this experience. Paul stated that his babysitter gave him attention that no one else did, and he believed she genuinely cared about him. When she taught him "how to love her" he felt special and wanted.

Paul was bullied by his brothers and classmates because he was small, and he describes himself now as a loner with few close friends. Paul adamantly states that he prefers the company of kids because they don't "hurt" him or "let him down" like adults "always do."

Kids make him feel special and important. He insists he would never hurt a child.

Let's take a look at Paul's EMS

EMS about himself	EMS about others and the world
▶ I'm not smart. ▶ I wasn't wanted. ▶ I feel like I'm not good enough. ▶ I expect that peers won't like or respect me. ▶ My needs get ignored. ▶ I'm not really important to others. ▶ I am vulnerable to being hurt by others.	▶ Love is conditional. ▶ People are dangerous. ▶ People meet my needs only when I do things for them. ▶ I am there for others, but I can't depend on others to be there for me. ▶ I expect others to let me down. ▶ Sex is the way to gain human connection. ▶ Sexuality with someone who is nice to me makes me feel cared for.

We can begin to see how Paul came to understand the world the way he does. It makes sense when we hear about his life as a child. For starters, sex between adults and children was normalized. In fact, the sexual abuse by his babysitter was really the most nurturing relationship he had as a child. Paul developed some distorted ideas about sexualized coping (using sex to feel better about himself) and sexualization of intimacy (sex is the only way he knows to connect emotionally with others). His understanding of the appropriate boundaries between adults and children are distorted based on what he "learned" as a child through his own abuse by a trusted caretaker. He feels more comfortable around kids because he feels like he relates better with them than with his peers (check out the section in chapter 2 describing emotional compatibility with children). Kids and teens don't expect things from him like adults do.

Paul has internalized many distorted themes about himself and others:

- Inferiority
- Vulnerability
- Feeling close to others is dangerous and will result in getting hurt
- Children and minors are more likely to be accepting

And these distorted beliefs show up in his behavior patterns:

- Avoidance of peers
- Pursuit of non-threatening partners

Importantly, Paul might also be thinking: *If I acknowledge the harmfulness of the abuse that happened to me, what does that say about me and my abuse of my victims?* (Paul doesn't want to think of himself as someone who hurts others).

Sometimes in his adulthood, Paul's life doesn't feel very different from when he was bullied as a child. Other people have mistreated him throughout his life, and he's been left feeling like he's somehow defective or not good enough. But children don't judge him. (That's why it is always important for group members to communicate with one another in respectful ways, and respond to each other without blaming, criticizing, or belittling). Now, let's take a look at the distorted thoughts about sex offending that Paul might display:

Exact Thouht	Style of Distorted Thinking	What is True/Not True	Substitute Realistic Thought
The "relationships" with minors were consensual He never "hurt" them. They wanted to hang out with me.	Rationalization Justification Minimization Victim Blaming Wishful Thinking	The minors might have wanted to hang out with me, but minors can't consent to sex with an adult because they don't have the maturity to understand all the factors involved in making decisions. At the time, I might not have understood or appreciated why my behavior was sexually abusive; but now I see that kids need to trust adults to know right from wrong and I wasn't a good role model of that. It is true that it seemed consensual, but minors can be easily manipulated into sexual behavior because they want to please an adult and do adult things.	An adult can't have a truly equal relationship with a minor because of the power imbalance. I should try to find some other adults I can relate to and try to connect with them. Healthy relationships feel risky because I'm afraid of rejection, but abusing teens is not an option. I have a lot of good qualities that other adults might like about me, if I give them a chance.

Exercise 7.8: My EMS and how they connect to my sex offense

Go back to chapter 6 (Figure 6.3 and Exercise 6.4), and also to the earlier section in this chapter about where distorted beliefs come from. This is about your own EMS, and how they might show up in your adult relationship and behavioral patterns. How do they connect to the cognitive distortions about sex offending you identified earlier in this chapter?

EMS about yourself:	**EMS about others and the world:**	**Distorted thinking about offending:**

Congratulations! You have made it through a very important part of treatment. You now understand how your thoughts influence your feelings and behaviors to shape everything you do. As we said at the beginning of this chapter, these are the "nuts and bolts" of human behavior. In the next chapter we will be looking at how to prevent problematic behavior from repeating itself. Most of our behaviors occur in patterns, because we all tend to do the same things over and over. We are "creatures of habit," as the saying goes. When you understand your own offense patterns, you are more able to recognize them and stop them.

CHAPTER 8

RELAPSE PREVENTION, SELF-REGULATION & HEALTHY SEXUALITY

"Relapse prevention" is the term we use to describe all the steps that go into staying free of sexual crimes. It is the most important part of your treatment program. The bottom line of treatment is: **Will you stop yourself from reoffending?**

In chapter 1, you addressed your denial and accountability. In chapter 2 you learned to understand your sexual behavior, and in chapter 3 you developed some tools and strategies for managing your emotions and behavior. Chapter 4 helped you look back at your childhood and family dynamics to see how your personality patterns developed, and how you began trying to meet emotional needs through sex. Chapter 5 helped you see things from the victims' perspective, chapter 6 focused on improving your relationship and communication skills, and chapter 7 helped identify distorted thinking about yourself, other people, the world in general, and sex offending more specifically. Now it is time to tie it all together with your relapse prevention plans.

Relapse prevention involves learning how to see an offense coming and how to keep yourself from falling into the same patterns that led to offending in the past. The goal is to help you correct problematic behaviors, avoid re-offending, and improve your own emotional and sexual well-being. Sounds like a good plan, right?!?

Some of the questions you will focus on in this chapter are:

- What kinds of factors outside of you (external) can start your thinking about sexually harmful behavior?
- What are some of the feelings inside you (internal) that start your thinking about sexually harmful behavior?
- What are the patterns of thoughts, feelings, and desires that led you to lose control of your behavior?
- How did you set up your offenses? How did you groom your victims?
- What were you trying to accomplish? What needs were you trying to meet?
- What can you do now to help prevent yourself from returning to your old patterns and reoffending?

GLOSSARY: New Terms You Will Be Learning in This Chapter

You have had a chance to think about what you learned about how early life experiences like trauma or faily dysfunction can shape your thinking. You can now try to figure out about how they might connect to your offending patterns. Also, think about the types of distorted thinking about offending that you used to justify, rationalize, minimize, or excuse your behavior and tell yourself it was OK or not so bad.

Abstinence: Completely avoiding a specific activity. When you stop doing something (like drinking, smoking, sex) you are abstaining from it.

Abstinence Violation Effect (AVE): When a person has lapsed (violated their abstinence plan), sometimes they develop a mindset of thinking that since the lapse or relapse has already occurred, there is no point in stopping the behavior now or trying to keep working their program.

Coping Strategies: Clear alternative behaviors or thoughts that you can use to deal with problems you face or bad feelings or urges to offend.

External Triggers: Situations, people, places, and things outside of you that can lead you to start thinking about offending.

Grooming: The acts you engage in to gain the trust of a victim as you prepare them for sexual assault. Giving special attention, buying things for them, or introducing "innocent" physical touches are examples of grooming.

High Risk Factors: Any trigger, whether internal (thoughts, feelings) or external (situations, places, events, or people) that increases the likelihood of sex offending by threatening your self-control.

Internal Triggers: Feelings or thoughts that lead to the process of planning and carrying out a sex offense.

Lifestyle Risk Factors: All the things you do, or don't do, that prevent you from meeting your emotional needs in healthy ways.

Offense Chain: The string of events, thoughts, and feelings that lead up to your offenses.

Offense Cycle: The string of events, thoughts, and feelings that lead up to your offenses, and then re-occurs over and over again.

Problem of Immediate Gratification (PIG): When a person is fighting an urge to have what they want instantly, feeling they need it and want it and deserve it and can't delay or deny the desire.

Relapse: Committing a new sexual offense.

Relapse Prevention Plan: The plan that you construct and put into place when you have decided that reoffending is not acceptable and that you are going to do whatever it takes to prevent reoffending. The relapse prevention plan identifies all of the components of your offense patterns (such as risk factors, cognitive distortions, and grooming) and strategies that you can use to change your behavior and turn yourself away from offending.

SIDS or SUDS: Seemingly Irrelevant Decisions or Seemingly Unimportant Decisions. Choices you make that increase the likelihood of committing an offense even without your conscious recognition of your intention to do so.

Stimuli: Anything that stimulates or excites your mind or body.

Stressors: Those experiences in your life which contribute to negative feelings like pain, fear, anxiety, pressure, or anger.

Relapse Prevention Planning

Relapse prevention takes commitment. It's not something you can read about and think, "Well, yeah, I guess that makes sense," and then forget about it. It's not something you can do for a couple of weeks and then start letting it slide. It's not something you can do when you happen to think of it. Relapse prevention is a new way of approaching your life. It is a way of thinking and a way of behaving that is different from what you've done before. It involves making sacrifices. It involves being aware of how you are thinking and what you are doing at all times.

Relapse prevention is a commitment—a commitment to yourself that you will do whatever it takes to avoid sexually harming someone in the future. And it's not easy. The plan you make to control your behavior is called your *relapse prevention plan.* There are really two parts to relapse prevention.

The first part of your plan is about the big picture. It's about your *lifestyle.* How will you change your life so you won't be tempted to sexually offend? If you have to deal with temptations to offend every day, if your life becomes a long battle with yourself, you will be miserable and in the end you will lose that battle. Fighting for control of yourself is no way to live. If you learn to create a lifestyle that works for you, that makes you happy and meets your needs, prevention won't be an endless struggle. If you create a life that is fulfilling, you will have less temptation to use sex to meet your needs. Would that be worth working for? It can only happen if you start to work now to create a rewarding, fun lifestyle. Did we say *fun?* You bet. Fun is important. Some adults have completely forgotten how to have fun. What about you?

The second part of the plan is in the details, that is, the day-to-day part: What will you do *at the moment* when you are tempted to give up your self-control and offend? You will need to learn what are called *coping strategies*—things you can do and think that will help you avoid or escape from risk factors that threaten your self-control. You will learn to notice people, places, situations, and things that trigger negative thinking and behaviors. You will make new rules for yourself to keep you from falling back into old patterns of behavior.

When you are ready to graduate you will be able to describe your understanding of the emotional needs you were trying to meet through offending, and the ways in which you have learned to meet your needs in healthy, adaptive ways. These new approaches will lead to lifestyle changes that will alter everything you do in a positive way. In the end, relapse prevention is much less about *avoidance* of triggers, risky situations, and sexual stimuli, and much more about *moving toward* meeting your emotional needs in healthy ways so that you are less prone to seek validation and self-esteem through victimizing others.

Risk Domains & Self-Regulation

Know Your Risk Domains

Back in chapters 2 & 3, you learned about sexual behavior problems and risk factors, and worked on identifying your self-regulation challenges. You learned about three types of self-regulation: General, Emotional, and Sexual. General self-regulation problems can include impulsivity, substance abuse, and other types of boundary-violating behavior like physical & emotional abuse to others. Your emotional self-regulation issues might include difficulties managing your anger, tolerating distress or frustration, and over-reacting to things. You might also feel like you have trouble with depression, anxiety, PTSD, or mood instability. You might want to take this opportunity to go back to chapter 3 and review your work there.

Here we will focus a lot on the third self-regulation area: *sexual regulation*. One way to tell if you have trouble regulating your sexual behavior is this: do you feel shame about something you are doing, or do you engage in secretive sexual behavior?

There are four main areas that create the biggest sets of risk factors that motivate or facilitate sexual re-offending*: Paraphilic interests, hypersexuality, personality traits or other mental health issues, and context factors.

Paraphilic (sexually deviant) Interests: These are sexual interests like attraction to children, teens, nonconsensual sex, exposing your genitals, voyeurism (peeping, watching, photographing or recording others), frotteurism (rubbing up against or touching people in crowded places), or other sexual arousals or attractions that if acted upon would be illegal, harmful, or victimizing to others.

Hypersexuality: This means you have trouble controlling your sexual behavior. You might have a high sex drive, an excessive sexual appetite, or you like to have sex very frequently. You might tend to be preoccupied with thoughts about sex, masturbate a lot, or look at porn on your phone or device all the time – even when you should be doing other things. Your sexual thoughts and behaviors interfere with your life -- they impair your ability to work, go to school, or be productive. You engage in sexual behaviors that are outside your value system, and create risks or problems for you legally, socially, romantically, financially, occupationally. Your sexual behaviors might even create risk for your health and safety. You sometimes want to stop and control your behavior, but you just feel like you can't. You keep doing it even though you try to stop, even when it causes consequences for you in your life or relationship. Sexualized coping is also a problem for some people.

Personality factors: (These come in a lot of different flavors). Maybe you have a general tendency toward criminal thinking and behavior. You think rules don't apply to you, or you don't really care about the impact of your behavior on others. Maybe you've had a lot of arrests or run-ins with the law, and the people you hang out with tend to be involved with crime as well. You might have narcissistic tendencies—you think the world revolves around you. You have a lot of trouble seeing things from the perspectives of others, and you only really care about how something affects you, not others. You can be self-absorbed and self-centered.

Some important examples of these sorts of personality traits are: *criminality* (rule-breaking behavior; rules don't apply to me; engaged in a variety of different types of unlawful behavior),

---

* Seto, M. C. (2019). The motivation-facilitation model of sexual offending. Sexual Abuse, 31(1), p. 3-24.

narcissism (I'm different, better, more deserving than others), being *manipulative* (to get what you want by exploiting others' vulnerabilities), lack of empathy (not concerned about the impact of my actions or words on others), *entitlement* (I deserve whatever I want when I want it regardless of the risk to others or myself) and *objectification* (seeing others as existing to please you or serve your needs—obviously sexual objectification is most relevant here). Also, think about qualities like impulsivity, inability to see things from other perspectives, closed-minded, dismissive of others, resistant to norms, or defensiveness. These qualities can make it more difficult for you to absorb or practice what you've learned in treatment.

Finally, ask yourself: do you have an **"addictive"** personality? (this could be related to hypersexuality as well). Some people with sexual behavior problems also find that they have addictive or compulsive behaviors in other areas.... If so, you should discuss them with your therapist and work on understanding them and changing them too. Often, if someone gives up one addiction or problematic behavior, it can get replaced with another. Maybe you have other types of behaviors (in addition to sex) that also tend to be out of control at times. Do any of these apply to you? The most common are:

- ☐ Drug or alcohol abuse
- ☐ Over-eating (or restricting food intake)
- ☐ Gambling
- ☐ Hoarding (collecting too much stuff, having trouble getting rid of things)
- ☐ Over-exercising
- ☐ Over-spending or buying things

Other behavioral health disorders can also complicate your relapse prevention plan: ADHD or bipolar manic episodes (trouble with impulse control), depression or anxiety (which leads you to "self-medicate" your feelings), or substance abuse (which lowers your inhibitions and impairs your judgment). In the fourth domain, think about peer or cultural influences (contextual factors) that sometimes normalize sexually abusive behavior.

In the next exercise, you will list the examples in each domain that you think apply to you. It might also be helpful to think of these ideas as a Venn diagram, with different and unique degrees of overlap.

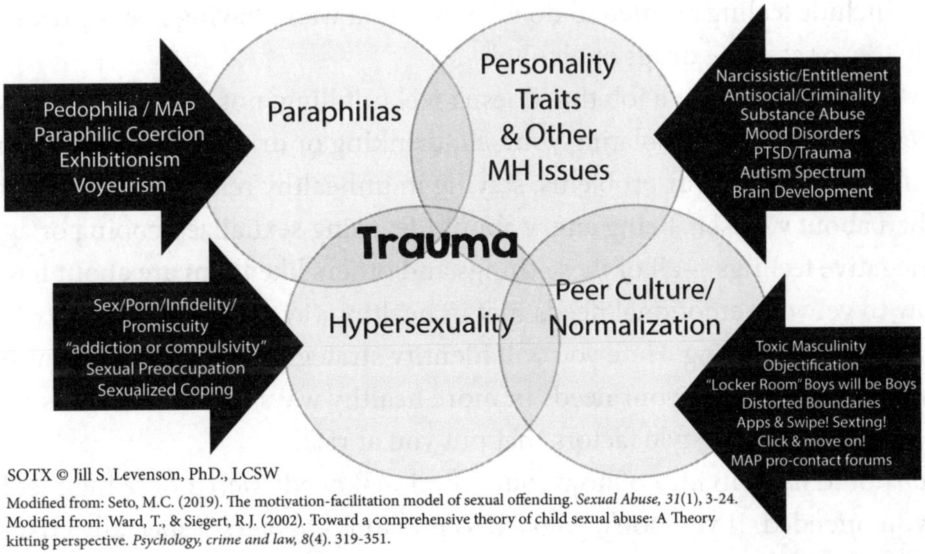

SOTX © Jill S. Levenson, PhD., LCSW

Modified from: Seto, M.C. (2019). The motivation-facilitation model of sexual offending. *Sexual Abuse, 31*(1), 3-24.
Modified from: Ward, T., & Siegert, R.J. (2002). Toward a comprehensive theory of child sexual abuse: A Theory kitting perspective. *Psychology, crime and law, 8*(4). 319-351.

Exercise 8.1: My Risk Domains

Paraphilic Interests	Hypersexuality	Personality & Mental Health	Peer, Culture, Context

In Chapter 3, you also reviewed *dynamic risk factors* – a set of risk factors that are changeable and that you might have been working on here in treatment. Go back to chapter 3, review your dynamic risk factor checklist, and see what you think still applies to you now.

The Big Picture: Changing Your Lifestyle

Lifestyle Risk Factors create risk for doing things that are self-destructive or harmful to others. Some parts of this program are about staying away from dangerous and destructive things. But it's just as important to know what you will be moving toward. What will give you pleasure, satisfaction, and success? What will you look forward to? What might be missing from your life?

In chapter 3 you learned about the "Big 8" risk factors for criminality (see Figure 3.1). These are really about living a lifestyle that isn't healthy or productive. Examples include hanging out with people who think breaking the law is acceptable or who hold attitudes normalizing sexual assault. Risk factors also include feeling entitled to do whatever you want, having a lot of stressors, having a turbulent family life, or abusing drugs or alcohol.

If you find yourself working at a job that doesn't feel fulfilling, not being able to talk to people comfortably, feeling different and isolating yourself, drinking or drugging to numb your sadness and loneliness, blaming others for your problems, staying in unhealthy relationships with people who make you feel bad about yourself, being angry about life, using sexualized coping or aggression whenever you have negative feelings —all of these things and others like them are about having trouble figuring out how to get your emotional needs met in healthy ways. All of them contribute to a lifestyle that puts you at risk for offending. Here you will identify strategies for changing your lifestyle on a permanent basis so you can meet your needs in more healthy ways (instead of by using sex or sexual assault). You'll start with the lifestyle factors that put you at risk.

By now you should have an idea of how your emotional needs were not being met by your overall lifestyle when you offended. If you don't, go back to previous chapters (especially chapter 4), discuss this issue in your group, or ask your counselor for an individual session. Understanding your needs and how to meet them is the central component of a healthy and happy life, not just for people in this program, but for everybody. When you are moving toward meeting your needs in healthy ways, your life will feel balanced, in control and hopeful.

When you start to move toward a new, healthier lifestyle, you will rediscover that life holds many pleasures besides sex. Consider this: some people look forward to getting up in the morning because they enjoy their work and the people around them. These are people who know themselves and have created a lifestyle built around meeting their needs.

Where do you start? Making changes in your life is not something you do all at once. Lifestyle changes start with small steps and they take time to complete. They can be uncomfortable at first. That means you go slow. But once you start to have some success, even small successes, you will know how good that feels and how important it is to keep working at expanding and maintaining the changes you are making.

Earlier you identified some of the needs you might have tried to meet through sex and sexual assault. Let's go back to those needs to start thinking about how you might address them if they are problem areas for you. Step by step, you will reach the same goals other people do. Sexualized coping and sexually abusive behavior may be a way of soothing distress, and/or meeting needs for intimacy, affection, attention, power or control.

Meeting Your Needs in Healthy Ways

Control

Sometimes sex can seem like the only thing within your control. But other things that seem to be beyond your control might really not be – you can find ways to take charge of your life and stop feeling that life just "happens" to you. We saw in Chapter 7 that looking at the ways we think—the things we say to ourselves—determines how we feel about things and what we do about them. Getting rid of distorted thinking styles and replacing them with useful ones is the first step in taking control of your life. When you first came to this program you probably thought that it wasn't fair that you were being forced to come. Because of the way you were thinking, you probably felt resentful. Do you still feel that way, or have you changed your thinking and found a way to be in control by using the program for your own benefit?

Sometimes people use sex to feel a sense of control. You can decide how often, or where to masturbate. You can look at porn and be in control of what you look at and for how long. You can use sex to have something to look forward to. Sex can become like a "self-medication" to make you feel better. If there are lots of things in your life that feel outside of your control, it might seem like sex is something you can control.

It is true that having a criminal record or being registered as RSO can create a lot of obstacles for employment. You might not be able to work in your chosen field. This creates a huge sense of loss if you loved what you did and trained for it and have a passion for it. That sucks! But don't give up. If you find something else to do that you like, you can live a life where you wake up every day and look forward to being productive. If you live a responsible lifestyle and demonstrate your good qualities, someone will give you that second chance!

You can start by focusing on what makes you valuable in the workplace. If you're not sure you like the job you're in, you will get a copy of What Color is Your Parachute by Richard Bolles (available in bookstores or amazon.com) and consider all the possible directions you could go it. In the meantime, you might start putting in applications at other jobs so you don't find yourself in an unemployment crisis. If you find that you have to take a crappy job temporarily just to get by, you might decide that it's time for you to upgrade your skills and make yourself more valuable. In the end, you can turn this crisis into an opportunity and end up with a better job because you know you are in control of how you think and you will steer your thoughts into positive, creative channels.

If you feel trapped in an unhappy marriage, for example, you can examine your thinking to see how you are making yourself feel trapped. Then you will weed out the distorted thoughts and replace them with useful ones. You will recognize that you are completely in control of the choices you make, whether that means choosing to work on making the relationship better or choosing to leave.

By recognizing that you always have choices (although, of course, some choices are more appealing than others), you will be recognizing not only that are you in control of your life now, but that you always have been in control—whether you knew it or not. In the past, when you've chosen to view yourself as helpless, that was your choice. As you change your thinking about all the choices you have and start exercising those choices more deliberately, you will also feel more in control.

I can't control anyone else, but I can control and choose my own:

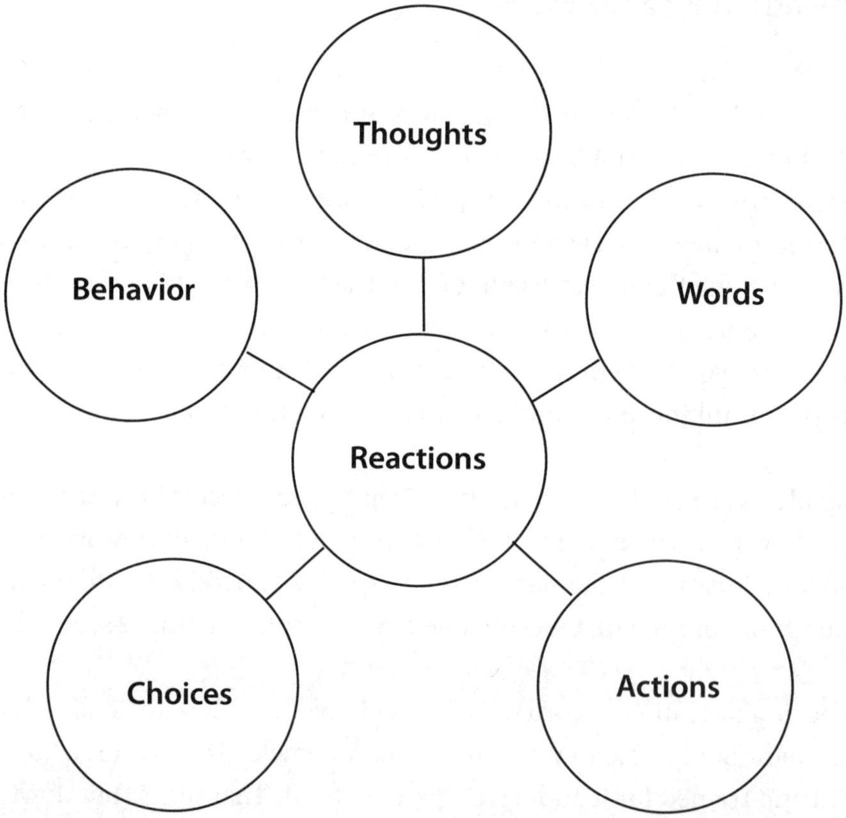

Remember the Serenity Prayer? Its simplicity is brilliant and life-changing:

Grant me
the serenity to accept the things I cannot change,
the courage to change the things I can,
and the wisdom to know the difference.

Situations which feel out of control in my life:	Three things I can do to change the situation:	Things I can change about my own responses:

Power (or Empowerment)

Frequently, people who have felt powerless in their lives carry basic beliefs that other people are not to be trusted. If you believe that other people are only out for themselves, or that they don't care what your needs are, then it makes sense to also believe that the only way to get them to do what you want them to is to force them. Sometimes people who grew up in abusive households or poor communities feel disempowered all their lives. It seems that other people tell them what to do, or deprive them of opportunities. You may grow up feeling like no one is ever again going to make me do anything I don't want to. Sex can be a way of feeling powerful over others.

Prisons are, by design, disempowering places where rules are rigidly forced upon people with little concern for the impact of confinement on inmates. In fact, even being called "Inmate" is de-humanizing and disempowering. After conviction, or after release from jail or prison, notification and registration (SORN) laws create huge barriers to reintegration. The unique stigma of the "sex offender" (RSO) label can foster a profound sense of disempowerment, social isolation, hopelessness, and shame.

As you heal and grow, you can give up familiar and effective survival skills that have protected you from vulnerability and disempowerment. You are learning in treatment to incorporate other tools with which to replace them. For some people, giving up their denial, defensiveness, or cognitive distortions can be extremely difficult as you come face to face with the pain of your own shame and the scorn of society. This initially feels disempowering, but when you see that your group doesn't judge you and that it feels good to share your inner thoughts with others, that become empowering.

The problem with trying to have power over others is it usually doesn't work. If you try to control someone because you don't trust them, you'll only push them away. No one likes to feel controlled. Have other people told you that you are "controlling"? Listen to them. They are trying to tell you something to help you. Ask them for examples of what they mean. You may not see what you do that pushes them away. Being controlling interferes with others being able to feel close to you. Controlling others in relationships can turn into domestic violence, stalking, or child abuse. This can become very self-destructive as well as dangerous to others.

Using sex for power can become a way of changing your feelings when you feel dismissed, unappreciated, deprived, or belittled. In Chapter 7 we identified *"Entitlement"* as another one of the styles of distorted thinking. Entitlement comes out of basic beliefs that say, *"I'm more special than other people. I deserve special treatment. Rules don't apply to me. I can do what I want. I can take what I want."* People who think this way usually don't want therapy because they can't imagine that there is anything they should change. (It's the other people in their lives who need to change). Once again though, this kind of thinking just *doesn't work.* A person who thinks this way will temporarily feel good about the immediate gratification he gets from grabbing pleasure wherever he can find it. But in the long run his life is empty, and he feels resentful that others stay away from him. As with all the styles of distorted thinking, the end result is usually depression—followed by more grabbing for immediate gratification and more emptiness.

Practicing your empathy exercises will help you to put yourself in other people's shoes. You will be forced to admit to yourself that other people have feelings and needs that are just as important to them as yours are to you. Practicing *assertiveness* will help you to feel more able to express yourself and get the respect you deserve. When you feel more in control of yourself you feel less vulnerable to what others may do or think. When you are comfortable with yourself, when you have built your *self-esteem,* and especially when you have learned to control your deviant thoughts and behavior, you will like yourself and respect yourself. When you like yourself, you can more realistically expect some people to like you—and to love you—and you will stop feeling that you have to force them to do anything. When you let people be who they are they are then free to love you.

Empowerment is about how to feel more empowered in your life – without needing to overpower others. (See the section about Shared Power in Chapter 6). The exercises below are just a start. Addressing your power needs in healthy ways will be a process that will take time and effort on your part. You will have to tune in to your feelings, especially when you have an urge to try to intimidate, manipulate or bully someone into something. You will then ask yourself, *"What's making me feel powerless now?"* You will know the answer as soon as you ask the question. If you feel that your boss is pushing you around, you will have to address your problem directly and respectfully with your boss. Can you talk to him or her? Can you ask them to explain what they are displeased with? If they do explain what's wrong, will you listen and try to learn or will you only feel hurt and resentful?

You can also plan to monitor your behavior with others (that is, watching and listening to yourself) and asking family and friends to let you know if you are being controlling. Can you start to look honestly at the role you contribute to conflict or relationship troubles? If you can, you will be on your way to starting to live a healthy lifestyle.

Dom came into group one night wanting to "vent" about a road rage incident in which someone cut past him into a parking lot space he'd been waiting for. Instantly enraged, he got out of the car and approached the other vehicle, yelling and threatening the driver. His mother jumped out of the car, crying, "Dom, stop! You always do this! You ruin everything!"

When asked in group why he reacted so strongly, he shrugged and said "no one cuts me off and gets away with it." Group members pointed out he seemed to be triggered by the fact that someone violated his boundaries, and that his narrow focus on "not letting the guy get away with it" meant that he lost all ability to engage in a decision-making process. He went from emotion to action without thinking about the pros and cons, the possible consequences to himself or others, and the feelings of his own mother and children who were witnessing the frightening encounter.

The therapist challenged him to ask himself "what's the worst that could have happened?" (Someone would "get over on me.") "So, what would that mean?" (The guy's an a-hole). "OK, so the guy was rude and obnoxious for taking your spot. But you aren't going to change him… you are letting someone else's choice ruin your day, and potentially, get you into trouble that would hurt you and your family."

By becoming more aware of how his own trauma history (the emotional and physical abuse by his dad) he could see how counterproductive his responses are when he feels disrespected or disempowered. He realized he learned to be a bully by being bullied by his own father. He was able to explore his anger at his father, and at his mother who did not protect him from his dad, and in fact often blamed Dom for "provoking" his dad. This insight helped the therapist coach Dom through self-regulation and steps for decision making that don't come naturally to him in times of high stress.

Examples of ways I have tried to control other people:	**Three things I can do to change how I react:**

Intimacy

We all have a need to be known intimately by someone. Intimacy is the basis for true caring. In hard times intimacy leads to support and help. Good times are not as good when there is no one to share them with. Being able to talk with someone who cares about what you have to say and "gets you" is simply part of what it means to feel alive.

Intimacy is a simple idea, but that doesn't mean it's easy to achieve. It involves believing that you can be yourself and be loved. If you've never felt that way before it's a scary thought.

Developing intimacy is a *process*. It happens slowly, over time. It starts with the willingness to take a risk. The process is one of opening up with another person and revealing yourself to them. The risk is that they will get to know you—and maybe stop loving you. It takes courage to develop an intimate relationship.

Some people use sex to feel close to others, and some people use sex to avoid intimacy because of fear of being close to people. "Long distance" sex like exposing, voyeurism, sexting, online encounters, and promiscuous sex can be ways of having sex with lots of people without the risk of real relationships. On the other hand, rushing into a sexual relationship might be a way of trying to feel close to someone, but it actually lacks emotional connection.

The bottom line is that intimacy is not really about sex at all, it's about closeness. Sex is about being as physically close as you can be to someone, but intimacy is about being emotionally close, safe, and authentic. That's what makes sex even better. Intimacy is so important that we have already devoted an entire section to learning how to bring it into your life. Refer back to Chapter 6 for more about how to address your need for intimacy.

Adequacy

Everyone needs to feel competent and confident, to be good at something and know it. If you don't feel adequate or "good enough" check out your basic beliefs. Did someone convince you early on that you weren't smart enough, weren't strong enough, weren't talented enough? If they did, does that mean you have to keep saying these distorted, untrue things to yourself all your life? If you had a parent or stepparent who told you, *"You'll never amount to anything"*—what the hell did they know about your future? Should one person's opinion keep you from ever challenging yourself and finding out for yourself what you're capable of?

Actually, many people who feel inadequate are simply blind to the things they do well. Maybe you don't give yourself enough credit. Instead, you only Focus on the Negative. Like all styles of distorted thinking, telling yourself that what you do is never good enough is just plain false. It's totally unrealistic. And it makes you feel bad. Stand back and take a look at yourself. Do you really mean to say that you never do anything well? Of course not. Everyone does something well. So why do you tell yourself that? Ask yourself that question. It might bring up some painful distorted beliefs that have nothing to do with your abilities today, but come out of experiences or messages from long ago.

If you feel that you have never really developed your skills, never pushed yourself to master a trade or a craft or a profession, then maybe it's time to start. *"Oh, no,"* says the automatic voice in your head that won't hear of anything that doesn't focus on the negative. *"It's too late for that. I can't change. I'm too old to learn a new skill. Besides, I have no time for that. I have to spend all my time working at my minimum wage job just to pay my bills. Those people who have the good jobs just know the right people, anyway. Everyone knows it's not what you know but who you know. Life is so unfair...."*

Sometimes people engage in criminal behavior to survive. Sometimes it makes them feel a sense of self-esteem or adequacy. Maybe you feel like you couldn't finish high school (why not?) or go to college, but you did a good job selling drugs. You could take those entrepreneurial skills and put the to work for you in some other way.

Well, yeah, sometimes it just feels easier to stay stuck wherever you are. It's always scary to think of making changes. It's scary to think of trying something new and maybe failing. So there is something comforting about telling yourself that you can't change. But remember – staying stuck is still a choice!

For some people who feel helpless to achieve real success, the problem is that they have never known what direction to move in. The things they'd like to do seem beyond them. The things they think they can do are boring. So how could they make a change if they wanted to? Ultimately, the issue comes down to two simple questions: *What do you like to do? What might you be good at?* Have you ever really stopped to ask yourself either of these questions?

No one can be good at everything, but everyone has a talent. There is something you can excel at if you develop your talent. Find it. Are you artistic? Musical? Handy with fixing things? A good athlete? Feeling good at something gives you good self-esteem. Feel proud of it. Start believing that you can master that area and you will find that you really do have the time and energy for it. When you learn what you are capable of and start making plans to move toward that goal, your whole life changes.

Skills and interests I have or would like to develop:	**What I can do to pursue my skills and interests:**

Recognition, Acknowledgement, Attention, Affection, and Importance

Getting the favorable attention from others that we all want is not easy. And it's not something you can make happen. But it is something that you can influence. Think about the people that you admire, and who you show that admiration to. What are the things that make it easy for you to show your admiration to certain people but not to others?

Some people are just more approachable than others. Some people make you feel important by paying attention to what you say. If that kind of person did something good, you'd want them to know that you noticed, right? What other things can you think of that make you want to give certain people a pat on the back? If you think about it, it's really not so much about how skilled a person is. There are plenty of people who are good at what they do but you'd never tell them—right? You can be terrific at something but still be the biggest jerk in the world. People who are considerate and open, people who have a positive attitude and aren't always complaining, people who are willing to give other people credit for what they do—these are the people who other people want to give recognition to.

If you've never given yourself credit for the things that you do, you may not have even noticed that other people were giving you credit. Do you change the subject or make a joke when someone gives you a compliment? If you do, ask yourself why. Do you have a basic belief that it's wrong to feel proud of yourself? Do you believe that nothing you do is worthy of being noticed? Are you so ashamed of your secret sexual problems that you don't want anyone to look at you? These are all issues that are important to discuss with your group and your counselor. Talking about these attitudes and beliefs can help you see them from different perspectives and *change* them in ways that will help you meet your natural need for recognition and respect from others.

A need for recognition, attention, affection, or importance can contribute to sexual crimes. Exposing your genitals cries "look at me! Notice me!" Flirting with all the women (or guys) you meet might bring attention to you, but why don't you feel like people notice you for other reasons besides sex?

What makes me feel special, valued, recognized, or important?	**How I can get noticed, recognized, or valued in healthy, non-sexual ways?**

Other Needs

Of course, there are lots of other emotional needs people have. Only you know what needs you might have been trying to meet through sex or sexual assault. Don't feel you have to try to fit yourself into some category just because we put them in this book! Discuss your needs, whatever they are, with your group and your counselor. You might be surprised to find that other men share your feelings. The old you might never have been open about your emotional needs in a room full of men, right? How does it feel being honest now? Try taking new chances and you will reap new benefits!

List some of your most important needs below.

Exercise 8.2: What Needs Did You Meet Through Sexual Assault?

Think about ways in which you have used sexual assault to try to meet your needs. Refer back to Chapter 4 and your sexual autobiography. Then identify ways you could meet your emotional and intimacy needs in healthy ways.

Using the Worksheet below, develop strategies for meeting emotional needs in healthy ways.

My most important emotional needs:	**How did I use sex to try to meet my needs?**	**Healthy Ways to get these needs met:**

Protective Factors

We know that living a law-abiding life is most likely to be achieved in the presence of positive factors in your life such as positive interpersonal connections, the pursuit of intimacy and self-efficacy, the development of social supports, and living a purposeful and productive life. We call these protective factors because they protect again reoffending. A researcher named Dr. Michiel de Vries Robbé studied protective factors to find those most important to help people avoid recidivism. Rate how you think each one applies to you, and if you need improvement, what's your plan?

Exercise 8.3: Use This Self-Assessment of Protective Factors to Rate Yourself and Identify Areas for Improvement.

My Protective Factors	Rate on a scale of 1-5: 1 = not much, 5 = a lot!	Plan to improve this protective factor:
1. I feel like I have good common sense and problem-solving skills.	1 2 3 4 5	
2. I feel like I had healthy attachments in childhood.	1 2 3 4 5	
3. I practice empathy with others to understand their perspective.	1 2 3 4 5	
4. I usually do pretty well coping with stress and disappointment.	1 2 3 4 5	
5. I have good internal self-control (sexual, general, emotional regulation)	1 2 3 4 5	
6. I have steady work that makes me feel good about myself.	1 2 3 4 5	
7. I have positive leisure activities or hobbies.	1 2 3 4 5	
8. I am financially responsible with my money.	1 2 3 4 5	
9. I am motivated to learn about myself in treatment.	1 2 3 4 5	
10. I respect authority figures and rules and laws.	1 2 3 4 5	
11. I have positive life goals and believe I can reach them.	1 2 3 4 5	
12. I am willing to seek medical and mental health care when needed.	1 2 3 4 5	
13. I have a positive support system of friends and family.	1 2 3 4 5	
14. I have close relationships with friends and/or a romantic partner.	1 2 3 4 5	
15. If I'm prescribed medication for mental health, I take my meds as prescribed.	1 2 3 4 5	
16. I have a safe and stable living arrangement.	1 2 3 4 5	
17. I have external controls in my life like probation, parole, or other accountability partners.	1 2 3 4 5	

Support Systems: Talking to Your Partner or Loved Ones About Your Offenses

You may never have admitted your sex offenses until you came to treatment. By now, hopefully, you have completely given up your denial. But even now you may still be denying your crimes to the important people in your life.

The reasons for denial are understandable. You may be especially embarrassed and ashamed with the people you are closest to. You may believe that if your partner or family knew the truth they might reject or abandon you. You may rightly fear their anger. You might even fear revenge if your partner or family has a relationship with the victim. Maybe you've been lying to them for so long it seems impossible to change the story now. The problem is that to maintain an offense-free lifestyle, you need to be close to other people, and that means being honest. There is no escaping this simple fact.

If you are still lying to the people you love, you probably find it is hard to feel genuinely close to them. Isolation and loneliness can be key triggers to sexual offending. In order to achieve the kind of relationships that make people really feel loved, one must be honest. But how?

Sometimes being honest means taking the risk of being hurt. If you share your secret with someone you love, you do risk being rejected or judged or misunderstood. This is a frightening thought. The risk seems enormous: losing the relationships you need the most.

On the other hand, you are already living in fear—fear of being found out. You may worry that you may slip and say something to give yourself away. You may worry that someone else will tell your secret. You may find yourself having trouble trusting your partner because you know that you are not being honest with them. If you are lying to your partner, you may wonder, is your partner also lying to you? At the same time, you might wish you could talk to your family or loved ones about what you are learning in treatment. You might want to share your new ideas and process your thoughts.

Ask yourself what your deepest fears are about how your partner might respond. Some of those fears are realistic. Your partner might initially be angry with you for lying and may be disgusted by your behavior. You can't control how someone else will respond, but hopefully they will see the risk you are taking and will know why you are taking it—to be honest, to be healthy, to be real, and to avoid reoffending. If, over time, your partner can't accept you or respect your honesty, you may have to ask yourself, "Do I want to be in a relationship with someone who is not able or willing to try to understand me?"

When you do talk to your partner about your offense, and your partner comes to accept you and respect you (even after some initial anger), you will feel a tremendous sense of relief and freedom. You will feel much closer to your partner because you have finally been truly understood and accepted. You will feel a sense of self-worth and you will feel true intimacy with another human being.

It's important to remember that your bad behavior is not who you are. You are a good person who has done some bad things. You are learning not to hurt others again. You deserve a lot of credit for that. And you deserve to be in a relationship with someone who will support you in your recovery.

When you graduate from this program, you will have accomplished one of the most difficult challenges anyone could take on—more difficult than high school or even college. You have made an enormous commitment to understanding and changing your life. Don't you want to be able to share that accomplishment with the ones you love? Don't you want them to share your pride? Until you are able to risk being honest with your loved ones, you are not really free from your shame. Your secret and your past offenses are still controlling a part of your life.

Talk about your fears in your group. You will find that this is an issue many men have faced. The men who have taken the chance of being honest will tell you what they went through and how they feel now. They will tell you it was not easy and they were very afraid. But in our experience, *most are glad they took the risk.* Most of their partners already knew the truth and what they really wanted and needed was honesty.

Your primary goal in this program is to prevent future victimization. Your partner will help you do this by supporting your relapse prevention plan and by understanding what they can do to help you stay safe. If you abused a minor and are living in a home with children, or if you are planning to reunify with children, or if your partner has children, your partner should attend an educational program specifically designed for parents of sexually abused children and partners of people who committed sex crimes. In such a therapy program, your partner will learn about denial in family members, about the effects of sexual abuse on children, and, most importantly, about how to develop a safety plan for the family. A safety plan, based on your relapse prevention plan, is a list of rules family members will follow in order to help you prevent future abuse. Just as the family of an alcoholic must understand how to help their loved one stay sober; your partner must understand your high-risk situations. Your loved ones become your accountability partners.

Developing Support Systems

Some people in treatment feel they have no one they consider themselves close to. Many have intentionally isolated themselves from other people. Some have few friends or family members. Others are married or in a relationship and have "friends", but they still *feel* lonely. It is difficult for many people to trust others or to open up and let others really know who they are. But everyone needs to feel truly known and accepted by other people. At the same time, opening up to others means taking the risk of *not* being accepted.

In the lingo of psychology, having a "support system" means having several people in your life with whom you can share important things—like feelings—or call on at times of need. Having a support system doesn't mean you tell everyone you meet everything about yourself. It means simply connecting with people enough to count them as "supporters."

Some examples of support systems are:

☑ Your family
☑ Your friends
☑ Your partner
☑ A team you might be on
☑ A club you might belong to
☑ Your neighbors
☑ Your co-workers
☑ The people at your church
☑ Your AA or NA program, or your sponsor
☑ Your therapist
☑ The members of your therapy group
☑ Your clergy
☑ Online resources

Ask yourself: Is there someone you could call at 3:00 am if you needed to talk? Is there someone you could call if your car broke down? If the answer to these questions is no, you are still isolated. What can you do to break out of that isolation? Think of who you could contact now—people you used to know, friends you have fallen out of touch with, family members you have cut off, people you have met in therapy groups—that you could approach to start up a new relationship. In your group talk about why it seems hard to approach people. You will find that some of the men in your group will have the same feelings.

Part of relapse prevention is having several sources of support in your life. You need different things in your life that make you happy, and you need people in your life you can count on.

Exercise 8.4: Develop and Maintain a Support System of at Least 5 Resources.

Name the people in your life who are your support system.

My support system:

Accountability Partners

In addition to a general support system, you need accountability partners who are part of your safety plans. Like a sponsor in AA, accountability partners know the truth about your offense, your goals, your risk factors, and your relapse prevention plans. They let you know when they observe red flags (you doing something that seems unhealthy or risky). They know what to watch for, because you've told them. They aren't afraid to be honest with you when they see something that concerns them, because you've asked them to do so. They won't back down if you become defensive, but they'll do it in a loving and caring way. They agree to be someone you can call on at any time to help you control behavior if needed, and to support you in difficult moments. Some examples might be:

- A family member who puts "parental" controls on the computer and keeps the password.
- A family member who notices what you are watching or recording on TV.
- A friend who notices when you seem to be drinking too much.
- A co-worker who notices your depression, or your distraction at work.
- A friend, therapist, or group member you can call if you feel some problematic sexual attractions, trouble controlling your anger, or difficulty dealing with stressors.
- Someone who checks in to help you make sure you are sticking to your relapse prevention plans.
- Going to AA, NA, SAA, and having a sponsor.

Exercise 8.5: Name at Least 3 Accountability Partners.

Name the people in your life who are your accountability partners.

My Accountability Partners and Their Role in My Relapse Prevention Plan...

In addition to your family and social network, here are some safe, confidential online support services if you have concerns about attractions to minors. Check out these links:

Link 8.1 – B4 U ACT
https://www.b4uact.org/attracted-to-minors/

Link 8.2 – VIRPED
https://www.virped.org/

Link 8.3 – Stop It Now
https://www.stopitnow.org/

Link 8.4 – The Global Prevention Project
http://theglobalpreventionproject.org/

Link 8.5 – CSA Primary Prevention
https://www.csaprimaryprevention.org/i-like-kids.html

Link 8.6 – Help Wanted Prevention
https://www.helpwantedprevention.org/

Link 8.7 – Troubled Desire
https://troubled-desire.com/en/

Link 8.8 – Help Wanted Prevention
https://www.helpwantedprevention.org/

Pay it forward to others by being a mentor or "sponsor" to someone in your treatment group. What would you have liked to get as support from a group member when you first started in the program?

Family Safety Plans

Though protection from sexual abuse or exposure to inappropriate materials is clearly important, it is also in a child's best interest to have both parents actively involved in their life whenever possible. When children feel abandoned by adults they love, the emotional harm of disrupted attachment is very real. So, the risks of abuse and the risks of separation from nurturing caregivers need to be carefully weighed and balanced. The benefits of contact between you and specific minors in your life must be carefully balanced with any potential risk of abuse during visits.

You have to be honest if you have attraction to minors and the risk this creates for kids in your life that you care about. If you are at risk for abusing minors based on everything you've learned in this program, you have to make some hard choices about contact with kids. You should avoid incidental contact with children as much as possible. Stick with what's necessary because it's really in the best interest of the child, and plan for how to maintain that contact with appropriate supervision and safeguards.

Visitation with your own victim(s) should be initiated only by the survivor, and contact requires special considerations that should be thoroughly assessed and determined with help from your therapist and the victim's mental health professionals who are familiar with the dynamic of child sexual abuse. You'll find a worksheet on the next page to develop some plans for safe contact. Resources like the Connections Program for family safety (Levenson & Morin, 2002) can also be helpful. Safety plans for contact with children may not be necessary for everyone. Discuss your family situation and risks with your therapist to make these decisions.

Exercise 8.6: Contact with Children: Family Safety Plans

	Questions	Answers
WHO	Who are the children in my life who want and need contact with me? (Your children, step-children, and close family members who feel attached to you)	
WHAT	Under what circumstances is it safe to have visits or contact with these specified minors? What are appropriate activities to engage in? What activities must be avoided?	
WHY	What are my motivations to have contact with each child? Does the child want contact? What are the risks and benefits to the child?	
HOW	How will the visits be supervised? Who is an appropriate chaperone? How will they observe us at all times? What does the supervisor need to know about me and my history, about grooming and CSA dynamics, in order to supervise properly?	
WHERE	Where should the visits take place? Someone's home (who and why?) or a neutral setting?	
WHEN	When is the best time of the day or week, month or year? How long should visits last?	

Healthy Sexuality and Online Plans

You are now ready to work on your healthy sexuality plan. Unlike when someone stops abusing drugs or alcohol, it is probably unrealistic to try to be abstinent from sex – or at least not forever. So you need to create a healthy sexuality plan.

Remember you started to work on this back in chapter 3? Try it again, and update your exercise in Chapter 3 with anything that has changed based on all you've learned about yourself, sexuality, risk, and healthy thinking. Go back and check out some of the online resources in chapters 2 and 3.

Keep your positive motivations in mind. What are your incentives for maintaining a healthy sexual lifestyle? How can you improve your sexual relationship with your partner? How can you engage in healthy fantasy and masturbation? Use the worksheets on the next pages to detail your healthy sexuality and online plans.

First, read this scenario about Kary, and think about how his treatment progress compares with your own. You could use the questions listed below and the healthy sexuality worksheet to think about Kary's situation and what feedback you'd give him if he were in your treatment group.

Kary has been in treatment for a few years after being arrested for meeting a 16-year old female online when he was 25. He is now 30 years old. He has a good steady job, stable housing, and family support. His recent polygraph confirms that he is not doing anything illegal or sexually abusive, and he isn't breaking any conditions of his probation. He does reveal, however, that he has had 15 sex partners in the past year, all females in their 20s and 30s. He masturbates 2-3 times per day while watching Pornhub on his phone. He has a subscription to an online amateur pornography site. He drinks 5 beers a month and has never had an alcohol problem but attends AA meetings once in a while to meet women. He recently had sex with a partner in his vehicle in a parking garage. He video-records himself having sex with partners (consensually, he says) and sends and receives (by text) photos of his own genitals and those of adult females he knows. He uses dating apps such as Facebook dating and Plenty of Fish. He visits strip clubs several times per year to receive lap dances.

1. What do you think about Kary's lifestyle?
2. Do you see any risk factors? Grooming? Distorted thinking?
3. Do you see dynamic risk factors? Like what?
4. What might he be at risk for doing? Why?
5. Do you think he has a Paraphilia? Hypersexuality?
6. Personality or addictive traits that put him at risk?
7. Does he need accountability partners? Why or why not? Who should they be?
8. What might his healthy sexuality plan look like? Why?
9. Does he have protective factors? Like what? Which protective factors need improvement?
10. Or, do any of these things even matter if he isn't doing anything illegal? (or has he?)

In exercise 3.10, you also explored what you needed to do to keep safe online. Go back to that exercise, and use the worksheets on the next pages to work out your current plan. Even mainstream social media sites can have sexual material that is deviant, unlawful, or illicit, so make sure you include how to stay safe on social media and YouTube.

A healthy online plan starts with being honest about how much you really need to be using the Internet. In reality, it's become a necessary tool for daily life in so many ways. But you can use it in the most minimal way possible to ensure that it remains healthy. It can be so easy for all of us now to get lost down the rabbit hole of the Internet, and our brains get hijacked by swiping and scrolling. So, start with these questions: What are the necessary, legitimate, non-sexual purposes you need to go online for? Make a list. Think about things like: banking, payments, employment seeking, job-related tasks, academic or school-related tasks, email communication, GPS directions, applying for government benefits, medical or insurance-related information and interaction, research (things like bus schedules or informational questions), ordering food, shopping, news, healthy diet or exercise apps, or mindfulness apps. What kinds of communication apps do you need to legitimately communicate with family and friends? What are the risks and benefits of something like Zoom or Facetime when used specifically for communicating directly with someone for family or work purposes, versus using other social media or messenger apps to search for "friends" in a way that might facilitate grooming or inappropriate online sexual behavior?

Exercise 8.7: Healthy Sexuality Worksheet

Healthy Sexuality	**TO DO**	**TO NOT DO**
WHAT		
WHO		
WHERE		
WHEN		
HOW		
HOW OFTEN		
WHY		

Exercise 8.8: Healthy Online Behavior Worksheet

Healthy Online Behaviors	**TO DO**	**TO NOT DO**
WHAT		
WHO		
WHERE		
WHEN		
HOW		
HOW OFTEN		
WHY		

Planning for Situational Escape & Avoidance

Though you are working on identifying and changing your "big picture" lifestyle risk factors, there also may be times when you need to be aware of and respond to immediate situations that challenge your sexual self-control. For those factors, you should be prepared to recognize your offense cycles, chains or patterns, and to respond with escape and avoidance tactics.

Remember the **PIG** – the **Problem of Immediate Gratification?** With the PIG around it is very difficult to distance yourself from a high-risk situation and cope with it. In fact, it's hard to think clearly at all. The problem of immediate gratification means that you feel like you need what you want now, and that you cannot delay the pleasure or do without it. That's why it is important to think ahead and plan for these things ahead of time. It's especially difficult to intervene once you're aroused.

After you have been triggered, but before you have consciously decided to offend, some very peculiar things can happen. Even if you are trying to avoid offending, you might fool yourself with what is called a Seemingly Unimportant Decision (SUD). These decisions that "just happen" seem to be unimportant because as you make these disguised decisions, you are not admitting to yourself what they are really about. They are decisions that seem to be about other things but what they really do is allow you to continue along the path to an offense.

Seemingly unimportant or irrelevant decisions are usually "little" choices, but they can be big ones as well—and they can occur in many areas of your life. You may have made **vocational or occupational decisions** which led you to seek employment in places that would put you in contact with children. Someone might speak of their love for children and their desire to help children, leading them to choose activities like youth leadership, coaching, teaching, or babysitting. Another person may choose a job in a nightclub or strip club, or choose employment which allows him access into peoples' homes. When he takes the job, he is not admitting to himself why he is interested in it. He can't help it if the job just happens to place him in a sexually charged environment or with access to potential victims, can he?

Some people make **relationship decisions** that offer them access to children. They may become involved with women who have children, setting up dating situations that involve "family activities." Or a man may choose a much younger adult partner who looks or behaves like an adolescent. Someone who chooses to hang out with other men who belittle, humiliate, or abuse women is making decisions that will reinforce toxic masculinity or violence against women.

Or you might make **decisions regarding places you go, in real life or online.** Maybe you choose to enter a public restroom just after a boy has gone in. Maybe you sit at the beach just to watch the waves, but you choose to sit right near the shower where the moms rinse off the kids. Maybe you do interactive gaming online, telling yourself you just "like the games." Maybe you go on Tumbler or YouTube and gravitate toward more sexual content. Maybe you use "hookup" apps, and look for partners who are "barely legal."

Decisions to assist or befriend a child who seems to be "in need" is a common SUD. You may convince yourself that you love the child and have his best interest at heart. Or maybe you choose to date or befriend partners who seem needy, dependent, unassertive, and easily controlled.

Abstinence is when you make a personal commitment to stop using drugs or alcohol or engaging in some other unwanted behavior. If an individual has a *lapse,* that means they return to using the drug or behavior again, at least once. The **abstinence violation effect (AVE)** occurs when, after breaking your abstinence, you then begin to think: "I might as well have more," or "I already clicked on that porn site, so I won't pass my polygraph anyway, so I might as well enjoy it for a while." The AVE leads to distorted thinking and more extreme behavior, and a relapse can cause you to become discouraged and pessimistic about your recovery.

Relapse prevention tries to teach people how to minimize the size of the relapse (i.e., to counter the AVE) by directing attention to the factors that triggered the lapse (e.g., high-risk situations, poor coping skills, or SUDs), so that the person can quickly return to their goal of abstinence and not "lose control" even further.

FIGURE 8.1: PIG, SUDS, & AVE

Knowing Your Cycles & Patterns

Below you will see the elements of offenses that often create a repetitive cycle or pattern. Some offenses are a one-time thing, but other people engage in patterns of behavior that, if you look closely, are part of a predictable chain of events. Everyone's offense was different. Some people offended during one time period in their life, committed a one-time only offense, or had a few isolated episodes. Some people have repeated or recurring patterns of sexual offending (which you will learn to identify in this chapter), but for others, an isolated sex offense might have been one part of a larger pattern of impulsivity, entitlement, poor judgment, or hypersexuality. Here are the factors in a pattern or cycle:

Lifestyle risk factors	Factors in your overall lifestyle that put you at risk for crime and sexual offending.
External triggers	People, places and things that you see, hear, and experience around you that can lead to thinking about sexually abusive behavior.
Internal triggers	Feelings and thoughts inside of you. The way you think and feel about things that put you at risk for acting out to make yourself feel better.
Thinking errors	Distorted thoughts, stinking thinking, and styles of thinking that twist the meaning of things.
Offense-specific	Thinking errors specifically about sexual offending that justify, minimize, rationalize, or defend your behavior, allowing yourself to think it's OK or not that bad.
General	Thinking errors about yourself, other people, and the world around you.
Grooming behaviors	The things you did to gain trust of a victim or family, to desensitize someone to your physical touch, and to give you opportunities to abuse.
Choice points to offend	The points along the way where you can interrupt the chain or cycle by thinking or doing something different to stop the progress toward the offense. You can choose to offend or NOT!
Evaluation: Pros & cons	How did you feel after you choose to offend or NOT?

We should note that cycles, chains and patterns do not always create the same predictable sequences. In fact, grooming, choice points, and even thinking errors can happen at any point along the way. The key is to notice them when they happen, as early as possible in the chain of events, because the earlier you intervene, the more likely you are to prevent reoffending.

Your job now is to figure it out how cycles, chains and patterns apply to you, and how to prevent it from happening again.

Some people committed many offenses over a long period of time and have repetitive cycles (see Figure 8.2a). These stories are examples of repeat offenses over long periods of time.

Larry was an Olympic gymnastics team doctor. When the young teen athletes got hurt, they came to him for treatment. He developed a "technique" of therapeutic massage that involved inserting his fingers in girls' private parts, even if the injured muscle was the lower leg! Sometimes the girls' mother was even in the room while he did this. That's how much he had gained the trust of the team, administration, and parents. He led them to believe that inserting his hand in their privates to massage them was a medical treatment for gymnastics injuries! He was convicted of sexual abuse and hundreds of victims testified at his sentencing.

Go online and look up YouTube videos of the story of Dr. Larry Nassar on ABC News 20/20. Or, watch the film *Athlete A* on Netflix. Listen to the survivors and parents discuss the offenses. Then, fill in the cycle (Figure 8.2a) by describing Dr. Larry's offense components.

Harvey was a famous movie producer. He was known for using the "casting couch" when he invited young actresses to "audition" for a role. Then he invited them into his office or hotel room and made unwanted sexual advances, coercing them into sex by promising them stardom and threatening that if they refused, their career would be ruined. He was convicted of sexual assault of two women, but dozens of victims came forward to describe his abusive behavior over three decades.

Go online and look up YouTube videos of the story of Harvey Weinstein (for instance, Harvey Weinstein: The fall of the king of Hollywood or interviews with survivors on ABC News with Diane Sawyer). Then, fill in the cycle (Figure 8.2a) by describing Harvey's offense components.

When one hears the word sex *offender*, there is an automatic assumption by many people that they are all repetitive, predatory individuals like Jeffrey Epstein, Larry Nassar, and Harvey Weinstein. Clearly some RSOs like this exist, and they leave a tragic trail of victims, some of whom never report, and their stories go unheard and unseen. Other RSOs, however, engaged in an isolated episode of poor judgment, low impulse control, and entitlement in an otherwise law-abiding life of good citizenship. The offense was an isolated behavior rather than a pattern that was representative of one's character. Use the offense chain (Figure 8.2.b) to map out the components of the offenses in the events described below.

Rolando was a massage therapist. He was used to seeing bodies nude on the massage table, though professional practices required keeping the private areas covered with a sheet. Rolando noticed that a male client started to get aroused. He found the client attractive and began massaging closer and closer to his groin area. The client didn't seem to resist, although he shifted his position a little bit. Rolando moved closer and began massaging the man's genitals. He felt the guy's muscles stiffen, perhaps in surprise, but he still didn't say anything. So Rolando kept inching closer, eventually fully embracing the man's penis with his hand. The next day, the police showed up at the massage business to arrest him.

*Sammy was 18 years old, hanging out with his boys, selling weed, and loving the life of porn on his phone and hook-up apps. One day he skipped school with a bunch of teen friends. They all got high and then he asked the 15-year-old girl to suck his d*ck because he shared his weed. She reluctantly went along with it while his boys watched and blocked the door, video-recording the incident. That night Sammy laughed as he sent the video to his friends in a group chat. They called it the "act-up challenge" and they'd post videos of themselves in sexual acts. When the girl's mother heard about the video, she called the police, and Sammy was arrested for sexual abuse of a minor and producing child pornography.*

Ronan was in his 40s, an upstanding businessman who had never been in trouble for anything. He and his wife had a busy life working and raising their kids, and he began to feel a little ignored by his wife. He got depressed. His 15-year-old niece would come over to babysit his kids, and he found himself enjoying talking to her. That made him feel less depressed about his marriage, because for the past few years his wife felt more like a nice room-mate than a lover and partner. The niece was funny, and cute, and smart. She was pretty mature for her age, and they had long deep conversations about the meaning of life. She looked up to him and he felt like he was falling in love with her. He just couldn't wait to see her each time. He found himself feeling romantic toward her, and over several months he engaged in what he thought of as an "affair" with her. He felt like he was in love with her. He took her for long rides in the car, took her on dinner dates, and eventually "seduced" her in hotel rooms. When they "ran away" together overnight, her parents called police. He spent 6 years in prison, and to this day can't believe he engaged in such uncharacteristic behavior.

Kevin realized when he was in his late teens that he was attracted to boys who were just starting puberty. He liked the way their developing bodies turned from child to teen over a few years. He was a counselor at a tennis camp when he was 19 years old, and loved hanging out with the 14-year-old campers. They were just going into high school, and Kevin missed those days… in his later teen years he felt so different from everyone because he was gay. He realized that as he got older, he stayed attracted to younger teens. He wished that wasn't true. He hated himself for it. He'd drive the kids home from camp sometimes, and then offered to given them extra tennis lessons. He knew he shouldn't get sexual with them, but he just liked them so much. Sometimes he'd bring some beer to let them drink, or show them some porn sites on his phone. He got one kid high, and then showed him how good it could feel… This went on for a few weeks, and he was shocked when the police showed up to question him after the kid was overheard by a parent telling a friend what happened.

FIGURE 8.2a=Cycles & Patterns

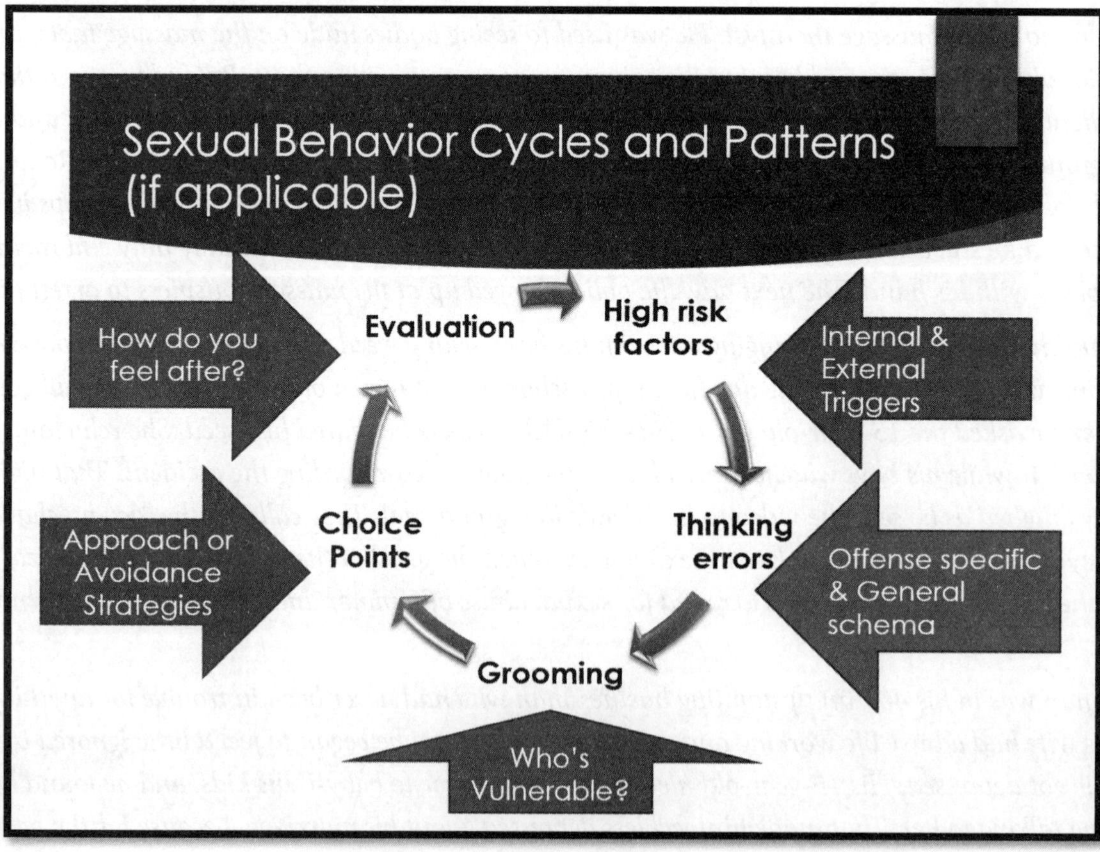

FIGURE 8.2b=Offense Chain

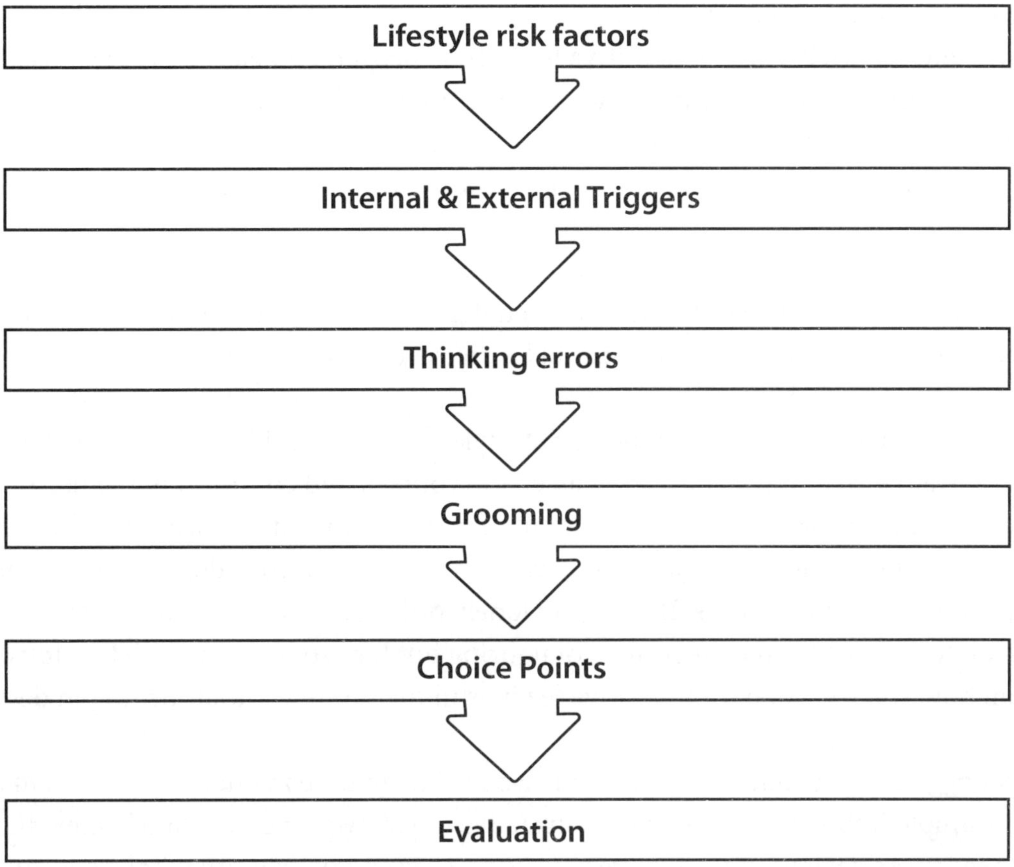

In the next section, you will learn more about each of these components of the offense chain or cycle.

Lifestyle Risk Factors

Not feeling acceptable to people your own age, feeling inadequate, unappreciated, or unimportant, working at a job that doesn't feel fulfilling, not being able to talk to people comfortably, feeling different and isolating yourself, drinking and drugging to numb your sadness and loneliness, blaming others for your problems, staying in unhealthy relationships with people who make you feel unwanted, being angry about life, using sex as a drug—all of these things and others like them are about not knowing how to get your emotional needs met, and all of them contribute to a lifestyle that puts you at risk for offending.

Review your plans from earlier in this chapter for changing your "big picture" lifestyle on a permanent basis so you can meet your needs in more healthy ways (instead of by using sex or sexual assault). List the lifestyle factors that put you at risk.

Triggers

Internal triggers are inside you. Thoughts and feelings are internal triggers. Sometimes it doesn't take anything outside of you to trigger a deviant fantasy. Sometimes, just because of a lifestyle that is unfulfilling, you can have feelings that are just as dangerous as external triggers. Many men identify *anger, loneliness, powerlessness, helplessness, depression and boredom*—among others—as feelings that have triggered them to fantasize about deviant sex.

Sometimes internal triggers can be positive feelings. A peeper who has just won a raise, for example, and feels important for the first time in a long time might want to add to the excitement he feels by cruising through his neighborhood looking to peep in a home. Sometimes boredom seems to be a trigger, when nothing is really happening in your life. Only you can really determine what feelings trigger you.

For some people carry certain feelings around inside them all the time. When you feel these feelings in the future you will recognize them as "red flags" or danger signals. They are a signal that—unless you do something about them—you could be on the path to distorted thinking and bad decisions.

For example, if you see a lot of anger in your lifestyle, for instance, it's clear that you haven't coped with anger in a healthy way. Maybe instead of asserting yourself and confronting the person or situation that made you angry, you took your anger out on your victims. If you see a lot of *depression* in your chains, maybe you turned to sexual assault as a way of escaping your depression instead of finding a way to deal with your pain or losses. If you were lonely or isolated, maybe you sought out younger kids to help you feel close to someone instead of figuring out how to become close to adults. Now it is time to plan how you will cope with negative feelings in the future without turning to destructive behavior.

External triggers are outside of you and can also lead to an urge to offend. An external trigger might be very simple: you see a person who is attractive to you, you spend a lot of time online looking at porn and need more deviant stuff to excite you, or you see an opportunity to take advantage of. You feel excitement at the situation.

For some people, just watching mainstream TV can be a tempting external trigger. One guy talked about randomly seeing *Toddlers and Tiaras, and Dance Moms (*reality shows featuring young girls in beauty contests) while he was channel-surfing. He began pausing the DVR and taking pictures of the screen so that he could look at the little girls in privacy later. By masturbating to the images, he was reinforcing his minor-attraction and pedophilic interests. This puts him at risk for offending.

One guy talked about the instant flash of excitement he felt when he peeped in houses. Just seeing windows on a house could get him excited. He said it made him feel powerful because he was "stealing their privacy." When he was angry, peeping made him feel like he was getting back at someone. Another talked about how drinking made him feel bolder, and he became very flirtatious. Flirting made him feel desirable and wanted. When he knew a woman liked him, and they started being physically affectionate, he'd "persuade" her to go farther sexually than she wanted–often leading to a forced encounter that he convinced himself was consensual. Because at first, it was, until he pushed her to do things she didn't want to do.

Here's an example of an external trigger leading to an internal trigger: a person in treatment for rape watches a neighbor sunning herself in her yard in a bikini and feels resentment at the unfairness of women who seem to flaunt their sexuality. His resentment and entitlement lead him to think about his neighbor in an objectifying and sexualized way.

Thinking Errors (Cognitive Distortions)

Cognitive distortions, remember, are twisted thoughts that allow you to believe what you want to believe, lies you tell yourself to convince yourself that what you are doing is okay. Excuses, rationalizations, and justifications for violating someone sexually are cognitive distortions (the Why Lie). (Refer back to chapter 7 for a full description of cognitive distortions). Now that you are looking at the process of how an offense occurs, it is helpful to look at the particular types of distorted thinking that crop up at each stage along the way.

Early on, cognitive distortions justify moving toward a crime. If you are moving toward a re-offense, you might not even realize it if you are not in tune with your thinking. For example, a flasher thinks, "I just have to get out of the house. A drive will relax me." A rapist thinks, "There's no harm in just looking. I can go to the beach and just look." The incest offender tells himself, "I haven't thought about offending in a long time. Whatever problem I might have had is gone. I don't have to worry about being alone with my stepdaughter now." The pedophile thinks, "I love kids and they love me. As long as I'm careful around kids I'll never do it again. I'm not hurting anyone if I just look."

As someone realizes he is turned on and is deciding what to do about it, new distortions come to mind. The flasher tells himself "I'll just masturbate inside my pants. That way I'll have some fun and no one will even know." The rapist thinks, "Look at these teases just showing it all off." The incest offender says, "She needs me to comfort her. She's so lonely. I can't turn my back on her."

Finally, when he's in position to offend, the offender takes back whatever he had been telling himself about not offending. The flasher tells himself, "Just one more time won't hurt." The incest offender tells himself, "It's too late to stop now. I can't help myself." The rapist thinks, "These bitches are all the same. Playing games." A pedophile thinks, "If he's curious about sex I could teach him what it's about." Or he may justify his behavior by reminding himself how much he "cares" for the victim.

Another distorted thought that helps offenders avoid coming to grips with their responsibility is blaming the victim: "If he didn't want to do it, he wouldn't have come to my house." Or blaming being drunk. Or minimizing: "So I screwed her. She's screwed a lot of guys. I didn't beat her up or anything." All of these types of thoughts will leave the door open for more offenses. They need to be recognized as distortions and restructured into realistic self-statements or they will come up again—automatically—in the future.

Grooming

Grooming is listed as a stage in the Pattern of a Sex Offense but it doesn't necessarily happen at any particular time. Grooming can happen at any time, or, in some cases, all the time. "Grooming" means preparing a victim for sexual contact with you. In many ways grooming is like what we call "courting," which is what people do when they are dating. Courtship is intended to make a partner feel special and loved, to make them like you, to build trust and good feelings. The difference between grooming and courting is that a person who uses grooming knows his intention is to deceive, to manipulate and ultimately to violate his victim. In a dating courtship, there usually isn't a power imbalance, and both people usually have the same goals.

You learned about grooming in previous chapters. Some examples of grooming include:

- ▶ Building Trust & Familiarity
- ▶ Desensitizing victims to physical contact and touch
- ▶ Exposing them to sexual talk or material
- ▶ Gaining their loyalty
- ▶ Creating divides in relationships with others
- ▶ Providing some incentive or reward or gift
- ▶ Creating opportunities to be alone with victim
- ▶ Making victims doubt their own instincts
- ▶ Having a hidden agenda in your relationship with victims and/or their families
- ▶ Testing the boundaries to see what a victim will allow or resist
- ▶ Manipulating victims to do what you want, or manipulating them to trust you
- ▶ Threatening punishment, withdrawal of love, or negative consequences

Grooming of a child involves seducing the child by gaining his or her trust and exploiting the natural willingness of children to go along with adults. It includes gradually becoming closer and more sexual with the child in subtle ways. Playing, hugging, tickling, and wrestling with the child gets a child used to being touched, and at the same time provide an opportunity for the offender to test how comfortable the child is with physical closeness. Grooming also includes providing the victim with favors or special rewards for engaging in sexual acts with you. Grooming also includes the ways you attempted to keep the child from telling on you, whether by threat or by bribes. Grooming is usually a gradual process that can take days, weeks, or even months to complete.

Grooming is about setting up the entire offense pattern. Often, the offender gains the trust not only of a child, but of the child's parent or family. Once trust is established, the offender moves on to creating opportunities to be alone with the child, and then manipulating the child into sexual activity. Grooming also involves keeping the child's loyalty after the offending has begun by making the child feel important and special. Children are easily manipulated by adults because they are eager to please adults, they trust adults, they are taught to obey adults and they depend on adults to take care of them. Perpetrators become skilled at identifying and preying on vulnerable children.

Even as he singles out his future victim for special attention, in his distorted way of thinking, he may deny to himself his attraction or his intention to abuse the child. After an arrest, others may finally recognize how the offender manipulated everyone by giving the victim special attention, special privileges, and buying things for the child. They say, "We thought he was so good, so concerned, so caring." (A good documentary is *Leaving Neverland*, on HBO).

Physical touching begins with play that seems innocent, such as tickling, swimming, hugging, or wrestling. It might even involve legitimate caretaking like bathing or bedtime rituals. The offender trying to see how comfortable the child is with being touched. The child, being sexually naïve, is completely unaware of where the touching is leading. The touching progressively becomes more intimate or sexual (i.e. touching to hugging to kissing to fondling to mutual sexual touching). By the time the child realizes that something is wrong, he or she might have strong feelings of affection for the abuser. And because they naturally enjoyed the abuser's attention and affection, victims often feel they have played a role in their own victimization. Grooming leads the child to blame his/herself for the abuse. This can create enormous guilt and shame. As a result, the child suffers even more from the abuse.

Think about the times you have done any of the things in the list above in order to get a minor or victim to like or trust you. Think also about how you groomed others around you and the victim to trust you and allow your abuse to happen and continue. How did you create circumstances that allowed your abuse or grooming to go unrecognized? Being aware of these behaviors will help you learn what to avoid in the future as you develop your relapse prevention plan.

Grooming happens with teen victims too. Maybe you had deep talks with them about life, and listened respectfully to their in a way that other adults don't always do. Maybe you helped them develop a skill or talent, or helped them work toward academic goals. Maybe you just took an interest and made them feel valued, important, special. Maybe you allowed them to drink alcohol, smoke cigarettes, weed, or vape, or let them watch porn. Maybe you took them places their parents would never approve of – like a gay club – or someplace their family couldn't afford -- like a concert, or theme park.

Troubled youth are especially vulnerable to sexual abuse. First, they may have a traumatized history, and lack positive and nurturing caretakers in their lives. This makes them needy for attention and affection. They may be less likely to be believed if they disclose abuse if they have a history of misbehavior, delinquency, substance abuse, or running away. Finally, because sexual abuse usually occurs in the context of positive interactions between the adult and teen, it can become confusing for kids to distinguish between love and abuse.

If you sexually assaulted an adult victim, you may have engaged in different sorts of grooming. Sometimes exhibitionists engage in conversation with a victim prior to exposing to get the victim's attention (like calling someone over to the car to ask for directions, while your genitals are exposed). People who rape may buy a woman drinks, flirt with her, make her feel safe, gain her trust, offer her a job, do odd jobs in her home, or even date her. You may have gained the trust of someone in your workplace in order to later request sexual favors from them. If you have, you have "groomed" them for abusive purposes.

Examples:

- A doctor sees a patient early outside of regular office hours when medical staff are less likely to be in the office. This allows the doctor to be alone with the patient.
- A teacher hugs a student to offer support during a tough time and begins texting to offer advice.
- A coach tells a parent the young athlete needs extra sessions.
- An older person befriends a teen and becomes a "mentor" – for which the parents are grateful. The older person allows the teen to drink alcohol and watch porn, treating him like he's special while using alcohol to lower inhibitions and porn to allow him to become aroused.
- A guy drives his teen babysitter home, taking "the long way" and asking her personal questions about her friends and dating life.
- A boss takes a worker out to dinner, discussing how impressed he is with her and how he's going to help her become a star in the business.

Critical Choice Points

Now it's time to fine-tune your relapse prevention plans. There are two primary approaches to coping with immediate risk factors. Usually you can use a combination of both.

- ☑ Avoidance and escape measures
- ☑ Cognitive strategies.

The simplest and most obvious ways to deal with high-risk situations are avoidance and escape. Of course, as you become familiar with stimuli and situations that trigger you, your best strategy will be to simply stay away from those temptations. You have to commit yourself to altering your lifestyle to avoid these situations.

Why does it seem difficult? Is it because it involves sacrifices? You've made sacrifices in your life before when you thought there was a good reason. Does it seem difficult because you still don't believe you can be tempted? Even if you don't believe it, what would be the reason for putting yourself in a stimulating situation? To prove to yourself that you don't have a problem? To test yourself? Does that seem a bit foolish to try?

Maybe you don't want to avoid external triggers because they're exciting and you like the excitement. In that case we're not really talking about being tempted by external triggers, we're talking about seeking them out. It can be really hard to give up something you've found pleasurable. But it is necessary. Are you ready to give it up?

Sometimes you really will be taken by surprise and find yourself in a tempting situation unexpectedly. Realistically, though, how often do you think that happens? Isn't it true that most of the times you've told yourself you were surprised it has really been because of a seemingly irrelevant decision you made? Now that you are aware of SIDs, you can notice them and make changes to make your life simpler and safer.

There are some very simple things you can do to avoid dangerous stimuli. Make a list of the situations, people, places, and things that stimulate and trigger you. You know what they are, don't you? Then make the decision to stay away from them. This is a commitment and means making some changes in your life that might be unpleasant. Will you do it? Here are some examples.

> ***Avoidance*** – *Jeremy was arrested for chatting with a minor online -- which turned out to be a police sting when he went to meet him. In treatment, he realized that he tended to befriend older teens and young adults because he liked to help them. He carried around a feeling inside him from childhood that made him think that he had to "earn" people's friendship. It was easiest to do that with younger people on whom he could lavish his financial success. As he recognized this in treatment and dealt with his trauma history that made him feel like he didn't have much to offer, he began to learn how to change those thoughts and meet his needs in healthier ways. He was successful in his work life, so that helped to boost his self-esteem. He also decided to avoid meet-up apps and chatting online with people he didn't know. He began to intentionally find more mature friends through work, and also through joining AA and Gamblers' Anonymous meetings. With his older more responsible friends, he built a strong network of connections and activities didn't revolve around sex, drinking, or gambling. He laughingly referred to his new life as "good, clean fun."*
>
> *Likewise, Max has decided to avoid any video chat application. He was arrested after showing sexually explicit photos of his penis to teen girls, but he had spent years online looking at porn, and using video*

chat sites to engage in cyber-sex. During COVID quarantine in 2020 when his therapist offered online therapy meetings using Zoom, he choose to have regular phone call sessions instead. Even though he is allowed to use the internet, he just did not want to use a chat app like Zoom or FaceTime because he was afraid it would be a risk factor for him by reminding of his old cyber-sex habits.

Escape *– Brad worked in a warehouse where his co-workers would frequently want to show him pictures and videos from Instagram, Tumbler, and Pornhub. They'd be working, and suddenly these guys would want to show him porn. He learned how to walk away, and to be assertive with those work friends. He said bluntly: "Hey man, I don't want to see that. I'm trying to do my work here, and so should you. Don't show it to me, don't tell me about it." When he saw them gathered together, pointing to the phone and laughing, he found a task to complete that he could accomplish by himself.*

John knows that he's attracted to minors. One day when he stopped at his sister's house, she had friends over with their kids to play with his nieces and nephews. When he walked in and saw them, he simply said "hey, hi, I'll come back another time when you're alone."

Some men will find that reading this workbook and hearing the discussions in therapy sessions are stimulating. When thinking and talking about your offenses and the events that led up to them, you might start to feel the same arousal feelings you felt at the time of your offenses. You might even feel aroused by listening to other group members talk about their offenses. Sometimes hearing news stories on TV or online about sexual abuse can be a trigger.

If this happens to you, make sure you talk about it with your therapist. Don't be embarrassed. It doesn't mean there is something wrong with you. It means you are learning to be more aware of what stimulates you and you are accepting that you will need to develop ways to cope with *anything* that excites you in a deviant way. Just bring it up in group, talk about it, and maybe even ask if group members can discuss offense behaviors in less detail.

What about the high-risk situations that take you by surprise? The truth is that it's not difficult to recognize when something is stimulating you and it's not difficult to get yourself away from that stimulation. Risky situations can and must be avoided. You can commit yourself to doing this. As soon as you decide that this is an important thing for you to do you will find that it is almost always possible to avoid or escape risky situations.

When using avoidance or escape as a coping response, your plan will be incomplete unless you also know where you can go and *who* you can talk to and *what* you can do instead. Who do you have in your life that you could tell about an incident that challenges your relapse prevention? (Go back to the exercises earlier in this chapter about accountability partners and support systems). If there is no one, or if you still feel that you wouldn't want to tell anyone, then you haven't created true intimacy in your life. If your group and therapist agree, you might ask to get the phone number of another guy in your group—just as AA uses "sponsors." Keeping yourself away from offending will always be more difficult if you can't get a supportive partner or friend to help you out by listening and understanding your struggle.

Escape and avoidance measures give you some options if you run into a high-risk situation. It is a good idea to think about these strategies ahead of time, so you are prepared if you encounter an external or internal trigger, make a SUD, or enter a risky situation. Avoidance techniques keep you from getting too close to a risk situation in the first place, and escape strategies help you get away before the situation escalates and you engage in a sexually harmful behavior.

Exercise 8.9: Escape and Avoidance

Go back to Exercise 8.1 and review the behaviors in the risk domains that you identified. List the strategies in each domain that you could use to avoid or escape risk.

Paraphilic Interests:	**Hypersexuality:**	**Personality or Addictive Traits:**

Now, make a list of specific 5 situations that you should avoid. Make a list of possible escape plans for each situation that include:

- ☑ What you will say to yourself to convince yourself that it is important to leave?
- ☑ Who you can call to help you?
- ☑ Where you can go instead?
- ☑ What you will say to excuse yourself from the situation?

Thought-Stopping

Cognitive restructuring is used to change unhelpful thoughts (e.g., "I need a chocolate") that lead to unwanted behavior (e.g., overeating) by identifying and replacing problematic thinking with healthier thoughts. Pay attention to your thoughts and

1. Notice the thought and distance yourself from it by just observing the thoughts without feeling like you have to do something about them.
2. Allow the thought to exist without judgement.
3. Choose an adaptive response to the situation by identifying various things you could do instead to respond to the thoughts.

The internal dialogue might sound like this:

1. What am I thinking? What action am I about to take? What need am I meeting through this behavior? How would I feel if someone else did this?
2. Your cognitive reaction is important. But what are the emotions associated with your thoughts? How do those feelings (or needs) interfere with your decision-making?
3. How do you wish you could respond instead of the way you usually tend to respond? How can you change the thinking to become more healthy and consistent with the person you want to be now?

These ideas might be causing a mixed reaction inside of you. It's easier when things are simply one way or the other, and conflicted feelings can be confusing and uncomfortable. But contradictory ideas can co-exist. You can want to offend and want to not offend at the same time. The key is to understand your mixed feelings and the thoughts associated with them, so you can stop, slow down, and go through a process of rational decision-making.

Exercise 8.10: Now, Use This Chart to Plan Out How You Can Use Escape, Avoidance, and Thought-Stopping in a High-Risk Situation You Might Encounter.

High Risk Situations:	Distorted Thoughts:	Healthy Thoughts:	Escape or Avoidance Plan:

The Evaluation

So, how did you do with planning to prevent offense? Did you choose to offend, escape, or avoid? How did that feel? Whenever we do anything, we tend to evaluate it afterwards. We ask how did it go, was it good, how it could have been better, and did we accomplish what we wanted to? Sometimes we also evaluate our performance as it's happening, and you may find yourself evaluating yourself at any time along the way.

Think back to when you were offending. After an offense, what you think will have an important effect on how likely you are to offend again.

After the sexual excitement is over and the PIG releases its grip, did you have to deal with guilt and disgust? Shame? Disappointment in yourself? Did you have some cognitive distortions, like, "I'm hopeless?" Or did you think, "Congrats! I controlled myself and that felt great! It's a relief to not have to worry about getting in trouble or hurting someone!" Not surprisingly, men who hold attitudes that are tolerant of sexual assault feel more positive after committing an offense (due to distorted thinking) and are more likely to continue offending.

You can evaluate yourself at any point along the way. Let's say you catch yourself at the point where you are entering a high-risk situation. Let's say a little voice in your mind asks you, "Hey, what are you doing here? You said you weren't going to do this anymore!" One way to answer that voice is to tell yourself that you can't help yourself. No will power. You can never change. Your urge is too strong and you're too weak.

Or you can tell yourself that you've made some bad decisions (SIDs?) and have given in to some temptations, but you are strong enough to get out. You are still in control and you are still committed to not offending.

If you choose to think of yourself as weak and unable to control your urges you are giving yourself permission to go ahead and offend. But you could also choose to recognize that being in a high-risk situation is just a predictable part of your offense pattern. You chose to put yourself in it and you can choose to get out. You now have an opportunity to look honestly at yourself, your thinking, and your choices.

If you intended all along to offend, you might not have any negative feelings. But if you had been telling yourself you weren't going to do it; you will see what you did as a failure. You will probably feel shame (that you are a bad person), guilt (that you have done a bad thing), or maybe fear (of getting caught) due to your failure. Again, if you blame your failure to control yourself by saying "I'm weak, I'll never be able to stop myself," you are (falsely) telling yourself that you are not in control of your behavior. The same goes for blaming someone (or something) else. If you tell yourself it was the victim's fault or someone else's fault, that is a failure to take responsibility because you made a choice to not stop yourself when you saw what you were doing. When you start to think differently about ways you might have prevented it, and identify your mistakes, you will know that you can control your behavior in the future by using more effective strategies.

We've been looking at patterns of how your offenses happened. Chances are good that your own offenses have followed a pattern. The more you know about what triggers you, how your fantasies work, what types of plans you've used that have led you toward an offense (or haven't worked to keep you away from one), and how you have evaluated yourself, the better prepared you'll be in the future. In the next sections you'll be taking steps to create prevention strategies based on your patterns.

Exercise 8.11: Discovering the Components of Your Own Offense Patterns

You can use this chart to make notes about each component in your case.

	What are my Prevention Strategies?
Lifestyle risk factors:	
External triggers:	
Internal triggers:	
Thinking errors:	
Grooming behaviors:	
Where do I make different Choices?	
Evaluation:	
Pros & cons	

Lapses: Where Can You Intervene to Prevent Sex Offense Relapse?

A lapse is defined as *an accidental or temporary decline or change from a previous standard of behavior: a **lapse** of judgement. a slip or error.*

For our purposes here, a lapse can be a choice, behavior, or decision (maybe a SUD) that brings you closer to a relapse or reoffense. With a sexual lapse, the behavior may not yet be unlawful or victimizing. However, it paves the way for you to move off your healthy and positive path to a dangerous path full of old risk factors or negative coping strategies. How can you intervene early in the cycle or chain?

In some ways, a lapse has to be defined by the person, and it's different for everyone. For instance, if you quit smoking, is taking a drag of someone's cigarette or vape a lapse or a relapse? How about smoking a whole a cigarette? Or buying a pack? If you only smoke a few from the pack, throw it away, and don't resume habitual smoking, is that a lapse or a relapse?

If you are sober from drinking, is a sip of alcohol a lapse or a relapse? How about a whole drink? A glass of champagne once a year at a wedding? In AA, any lapse that involved ingesting alcohol would require a picking up a white chip (a new start date for being sober). How about spending time in a bar? Is that a lapse? Well, it depends on you. Some people can be around others who are drinking, and easily maintain their sobriety. For others, being around people who drink is too much of a risk factor. Bottom line: You have to be really honest with yourself and know yourself.

If you are trying to keep control of sexual behaviors that have been problematic or abusive in the past, you have to be on the lookout for risk factors that might be disguised as "normal" behavior. If you are getting ready to graduate from this program, but you are cheating on your partner, is that in line with your healthy sexuality plan? It's not illegal, but is it healthy? How might secret sexual behavior of any sort be considered a lapse? What about looking at pornography? Once in a while? Daily? What about looking at magazine ads picturing children? What about watching R-rated movies with rape scenes? What about sending or receiving dick pics (consensually)? Sexting? Are these lapses? Relapses? Why or why not?

Remember the **abstinence violation effect** (AVE)? A lapse can be dangerous because it can lead to what has been described as the "F*ck-it" mentality. It's the "I already ate half a box of cookies, so I might as well eat them all" reaction that a person on a diet might have. It's the "I already had a drink tonight, so I might as well keep drinking" thought process that a person trying to maintain alcohol sobriety might engage in.

The AVE helps us look at the difference between a lapse and relapse – it is often an important point between a lapse and a relapse (lapse→AVE→relapse). Some experts would say that a one-time lapse of substance use is not the same as a relapse. Some would define relapse as when someone spirals back into repetitive and compulsive patterns of behavior. In this program, the lapse is usually a return to some type of unhealthy sexual behavior or sexualized coping that is not necessarily illegal or victimizing. A lapse is a big risk factor and puts a person at higher risk to relapse or reoffend. You have a choice as to how you respond to the AVE: Do you give into it or do you quickly change directions to a relapse prevention plan?

Someone struggling with the AVE might relapse and then do one or more of the following:

- Blame the relapse on a personal failure, triggering a sense of guilt, negativity, and defeat
- Blame the relapse on a lack of willpower
- Blame the relapse on not being able to properly cope with stressors "caused by" other people or situations

When one of these occurs, the person who has relapsed enters an unhealthy mindset that says that the process seems uncontrollable, so there is no point in stopping now or trying to correct the path of their recovery.

If you are exclusively minor-attracted, you'll have to be really honest with yourself and cautious about how to experience your sexuality without breaking the law or harming anyone. You should speak to your therapist -- realistically -- about whether thinking about minors in sexualized or objectifying ways might put you at risk in some way.

Your goal is to be in charge of your choices and behavior, right? Whether or not the thoughts or behavior are legal, you have to be able to recognize the choices and distorted thinking that could lead to reoffending or reinforce problematic sexual interests. That means being honest with yourself about what is a lapse. That's your job. Our job is to help you figure out how to figure it out.

Here are some examples of lapses:

Arnold was in treatment for possessing CSAM. He had looked at the illegal material for a short period of time during a cocaine binge and manic episode but acknowledged that he had used pornography and sexualized coping throughout his life. In treatment he described himself as indiscriminately attracted to a range of females from ages 13 to 60. His safety plan required him to abstain from accessing internet porn or other sexually explicit materials / interactions online.

On a polygraph, Arnold noted that he sometimes gets aroused while watching TV. He said he pauses his DVR when he's aroused so he can masturbate to the characters on the screen; all females ranging from teens to older women. He said that he does this about twice per week, and estimated that one out of every four times, the female was a minor. He described watching the sitcom "Modern Family" and masturbating to the teen girl characters. He argued that the actresses were probably older than the characters they portrayed, so it was OK, and said that it happened rarely, so it was better than if it happened more often. He also "borrowed" a family member's phone to watch adult pornography online once in a while. He got defensive in group and didn't understand why everyone was making such a big deal about it.

Or, consider this case:

Denison was a health care professional who was convicted of raping a patient in his medical office. He had established a flirtatious relationship with her, breaching the professional boundaries required between doctors and their patients. He had arranged an early morning visit when the office staff was not there, flirted and "danced" with her in the exam room, and then proceeded to rape her. During treatment he minimized his risk to reoffend, pointing out that he had lost his medical license and no longer worked as a doctor, therefore he could not offend again. The only risk factor he could identify for himself was being unfaithful to his wife. He said that his pattern of objectifying women, and pursuing them as sexual conquests despite being married, could put him in a position of "pushing someone to go further than they were comfortable with."

On a recent polygraph he revealed that he had had 2 sexual partners besides his wife in the past 6 months; both women were in their 20s, though he is in his late 40s. He'd met one at a family picnic, and another at a friend's graduation party. His group told him that this was exactly the type of risk factor he'd identified… he argued that unlike his offense, cheating on his wife is not illegal and that he was breaking no laws.

Or, consider this case:

Benji is a young adult who was arrested for viewing and possessing child sex abuse material (CSAM, otherwise known as child porn). He first noticed being attracted to preteen girls at about age 16. He first found the CSAM on social media by accident, and then began intentionally seeking it out. After his arrest, he began gaining insight into his attraction to minors and was working to improve his self-regulation strategies by masturbating less often. However, since he was on house arrest, and also very isolated due to social distancing during the COVID pandemic, he watched a lot of TV. He found himself looking at the TV guide for shows about teens. He found himself fantasizing and masturbating about these minors, and he was also stimulated by certain commercials and advertisements featuring young girls. He was continuing to masturbate to these thoughts of minor girls.

Exercise 8.12: Evaluating Lapses:

Thinking about the scenarios below, and about your own lapses, complete the charts and discuss them with your group.

Do these behaviors seem to be lapses or relapses? Why?	
What are the risk factors you can identify?	
What are the thinking errors you identify?	
What are the grooming behaviors?	
How could either guy intervene sooner in the chain?	
How would you intervene earlier? Name specific points and strategies.	
What is the AVE here? The PIG?	
What are some alternative coping strategies at each point in the scenarios?	

Can you describe a similar lapse of your own?

Describe a lapse of your own	
Is your behavior a lapse or relapse? Why?	
What are the risk factors you can identify?	
What are the thinking errors you identify?	
What are the grooming behaviors?	
How could you intervene sooner in the chain?	
How would you intervene earlier? Name specific points and strategies.	
What is the AVE here? The PIG?	
What are some alternative coping 'strategies at each point in the scenarios?	

Coping with Stressors: External Events Can Lead to Internal Triggers Unless You Have A Plan

What we call stress and the things we think of as stressful are good examples of the thinking-feeling link in action. Recall that we said the ways we think about things determines how we feel about them. Stressors can be anything that we think of as threatening or overwhelming. When you tell yourself that you cannot deal with a given situation, you make yourself tense or "stressed." Notice that, as with other feelings, you actually create stress through the things you tell yourself.

Think about the different things in your life that you stress yourself about. They could be momentary irritations or long-term problems. Identifying stressors is important because when you are stressed about something it can lead to a breakdown in rational thinking (cognitive distortions), as well as negative feelings *(internal triggers)*.

What stresses you out? Money troubles? Too many bills? Feeling overwhelmed with work? Feeling rejected by a date? Parents on your case? Can't find a job? Got a speeding ticket? Bus was late? Parole officer called? Fighting with your girlfriend? Need to see a doctor but don't have insurance? Miss your kids since you aren't allowed visitation? Worried your family won't accept that you're gay? Big problems and small ones can feel really stressful.

We all have our own issues that we get "hung up" on, that we *catastrophize* about and fret about. You can also see that sometimes the way we think about these events might have been distorted, and that these distortions led to frustration, loneliness, powerlessness or anxiety. These feelings then can lead to acting out to use sex or aggression to meet your needs and fix your feelings.

Remember, stress never causes sexual assault. Offending is always your choice. But staying away from offending will be harder as long as you engage in distorted thinking that makes problems seem overwhelming and then convinces you that sex offending will make you feel better. The new coping skills you've learned in this program help you calm yourself down and deal with stress more effectively (see chapter 3).

What about when you feel really stressed and feel tempted to use sexualized coping or other unhealthy coping (like drugs, alcohol, gambling, violence, spending, etc.)? Now that you know how to restructure your distorted thoughts (chapter 7), you can examine your stressors to see if you can come up with healthier ways to think about them instead of *catastrophizing, focusing on the negative, blaming others or engaging in all-or-nothing thinking* that leads to feeling stress. Write down your thoughts about the things that seem to stress you. Compare them with the styles of distorted thinking in Chapter 7. Then use the "restructuring" process to change your thoughts into realistic, healthy thoughts. Of course, some things will still annoy you or worry you, but you will find that you really don't need to dwell on things or make them worse than they really are.

Stress is not only in your mind. It's in your body, too. When you are feeling stressed, your body gets hyper-aroused. Pay attention to your body when you stress. Do you breathe heavily? Does your heart rate go up? Do you get headaches? Do you feel hungry? Does your mind race? Use mindfulness techniques in chapter 3 to notice where you feel your anxiety in your body, and to calm down your mind and your body.

Make a list of the things in your life that cause you stress. Start with any negative external triggers you've identified. What are the situations that you think of as too difficult, too confusing, or too frustrating? Like everyone, you need to find effective ways to deal with these problems. Persistent feelings of anger, depression, or anxiety often means that you are not dealing with your problems effectively. You can use your self-regulation skills and your cognitive coping skills to approach your problems differently now.

Recall that in the section on Self-Esteem we said that doing something—*anything*—that could lead you toward solving your problems, even in a small way, boosts your self-esteem. When you are doing nothing to solve problems, you feel completely powerless and overwhelmed. Look over your list of stressors. Pick one that seems impossible to deal with. Then challenge yourself to find one small thing you could do that would move you in the direction of finding a solution for the stressor. Often something as simple as talking with someone who has experience with a problem is enough to make you feel better. Who could you talk to? If you don't know someone, you probably know someone who knows someone, right? Or talk about it in your group.

Talk to others about your feelings when you are feeling stressed out or when problems overwhelm you. Talking about your problems, even if it doesn't solve them, still makes you feel better. It shares your burden with others and helps you to remember that others care about you.

Don't be afraid to ask for help when you need it. Isolating yourself from others only reinforces your loneliness and your feelings of being different. Nobody can handle everything themselves. Everybody needs others in their life. If you don't talk to others when you feel burdened and alone. This puts you at risk for sexualized or other unhealthy coping.

The point is, if you decide to, you can find some constructive way to start to deal with your problem. Even if you don't actually solve the problem, but just make some decisions and take some action you will start to feel that you have some control over your life and can lead you toward solving the problem.

Of course, everyone has times when they feel down or disappointed that things aren't going well. Most people have activities in their life that they can turn to for pleasure and satisfaction. Do you? Do you make time in your life just for fun? Having fun is not wasting time: fun is a necessary ingredient of a healthy lifestyle. If you have some things in your life that you enjoy, you can turn to them to regain feelings of joy and pleasure. Playing games, playing sports, watching movies, reading books, listening to music, doing a creative activity, fixing something around the house, playing with your pet, taking walks, meeting with friends or family, and countless other activities focus your time, energy, and concentration on something rewarding and satisfying. When you get away from your stressors for a while through a leisure activity, those worries feel less oppressive and more manageable.

Exercise 8.13: Coping with Stress

Things That Cause Me Stress:	How I Can Deal With This Stress:

As you are learning more about how you tried to get your needs met through sex and sexual assault, you are also learning how to meet your needs in healthy ways that are not harmful to yourself or others. To further help with this goal, it might be useful to explore DBT skills.

A psychologist named Dr. Marsha Linehan developed a program called DBT to teach people to use four core skills to cope with emotional distress in positive, productive ways.

- Mindfulness
- Emotional Regulation
- Distress Tolerance
- Interpersonal Skills

They are described in the following way here:

Link 8.9 – Healthline

https://www.healthline.com/health/dbt#skills

You have learned about these skills in different ways throughout this book. Mindfulness and distress tolerance skills help you work toward accepting your thoughts and behaviors. Emotion regulation and interpersonal effectiveness skills help you work toward changing your thoughts and behaviors.

Mindfulness is about being aware of and accepting what's happening in the present moment. In chapter 3, you learned to notice and accept your thoughts and feelings without judgement. In the context of DBT, mindfulness is broken down into "what" skills and "how" skills.

What you're focusing on, which should be:

- Your body sensations (are you tense? Where in your body? Breathing? Heartrate?)
- Your awareness of emotions and feelings in the present
- Your current thoughts about your current situation
- Separating emotions and body sensations from thoughts

How to be more mindful by:

- Finding rational thoughts to balance your emotions
- Calm your body down by relaxing your body sensations
- Using acceptance to learn to tolerate aspects of yourself (as long as they aren't hurting you or others)
- Taking effective action to use mindfulness skills regularly

Distress tolerance skills help you get through rough moments by using safe and non-destructive coping strategies. For instance, in times of crisis, you might use self-isolating or avoidance, self-harm, sexual coping or sexual offending, substance use, or angry outbursts, all of which are not helpful in the long-run and might even cause harm to you or someone else. These skills can help you tolerate emotional discomfort (check back to chapter 3 for some ideas).

- Distract yourself until you're calm enough to deal with the situation or emotion.
- Self-soothe by relaxing and using your senses to feel more at peace.
- Find ways to have gratitude or enjoy the moment despite the pain or difficulty you are going through.
- Explore coping strategies, choices, and solutions by listing pros and cons.

Interpersonal effectiveness skills help you develop fulfilling connections with other people. Intense emotions and moodiness can sometimes make it challenging to relate to others. These skills combine listening skills, social skills, and assertiveness training (like you learned about in chapter 6) to help you communicate and get along better with others.

- Learning how to ask appropriately for what you want and take steps to get it.
- Working through conflicts and challenges in relationships.
- Gaining greater respect for yourself as you improve your coping and communication skills.

Emotion regulation is something you learned about in chapter 3 to help you deal with emotional reactions before they lead to a chain of consequences for yourself. For example, a primary emotion of anger might lead to guilt, worthlessness, shame, and even depression.

- Emotion regulation skills teach you to:
- Recognize emotions like guilt, shame, anxiety and depression
- Calm yourself down
- Reduce vulnerability
- Increase positive emotions
- Accept your feelings without judging them and without acting on them

If you are interested in learning more about these skills, look them up:

Link 8.10 – DBT Self Help

https://www.dbtselfhelp.com/html/dbt_skills_list.html

Or, you can buy a DBT workbook on Amazon.com, or ask your therapist to help you.

Post-Conviction Traumatic Stress

In chapter 3, you learned about Post-Conviction Traumatic Stress (PCTS), a concept developed by Dr. Danielle Harris and Dr. Jill Levenson which describes the experience of community re-entry following a conviction or incarceration for a sexual crime. Having a criminal record creates a lot of challenges, but the many additional obstacles and restrictions faced by RSOs complicates their experience and creates additional stress. You learned more generally about trauma in chapter 4. Trauma can interfere with emotional and behavioral regulation; you may over-react to things, feel like you have a chip on your shoulder, or become obsessed with worry about the future. Being in jail or prison or civil commitment, or being on probation, parole, or registration can be traumatizing. Your current and past situations can cause symptoms of Post-traumatic Stress Disorder (PTSD) (refer back to chapters 3 & 4 for a fuller description):

(1) Intrusive thoughts or imagery: flashbacks, nightmares, repetitive or intrusive images, thoughts, or memories.

(2) Avoidance of triggers and reminders of people, places, situations or circumstances associated with the crime, victim, arrest, court, jail, police, probation, etc.

(3) Negative thoughts and feelings: Negative moods (anger, fear, depression) or emotional numbness.

(4) Hypervigilance: Feelings of hyperarousal include scanning the environment for perceived danger, exaggerated startle responses, irritability, difficulty concentrating, and sleep problems.

Marvin described the trauma of being on probation. "I live in fear that I will violate a condition of my release without even knowing it. Every time I have to go check in, or my parole officer calls me, I panic. One time I went to a dental clinic at the university. Afterwards, it occurred to me that there are some sort of laws about RSOs being on college campuses. I lived in fear that if my officer found out I'd had my teeth cleaned, he'd arrest me. It's like my whole life is under this cloud of doubt about my own ability to follow my rules. It's exhausting."

Another described this experience: "They came to search my house as part of a routine address verification. Believe me, I follow my rules exactly. I thought I had nothing to worry about. Then they found this old fishing spear stored away in my garage—I haven't used it or thought about it in years—and I was arrested for having a weapon. I spent three weeks in jail waiting for a hearing, and then the judge dropped the case, but it was too late—I lost my job when I didn't show up. Since then, I can't sleep, I've lost 13 pounds, and I can't concentrate. I'm constantly obsessing in my mind to question if there is anything I'm doing that's wrong and against my rules."

Said another parolee, "I've got it all planned out, even though I always do what my conditions say. But my sister has a key to my house so she can take my dog if they arrest me for some violation. She has my car key so she can go get the car if it's parked, say, at the justice center and I'm arrested at my monthly check-in, so it won't get towed. She has my bank account so she can pay my bills if I end up in jail. I'm not doing anything wrong, but there are so many rules with probation and registration and it is so confusing, and sometimes in my counseling group I hear guys talk about restrictions I never even knew about, so I'm expecting at some time I'll be revoked for breaking a rule by accident."

Other triggers to PCTS can include media or news stories, or even being in treatment:

- *After seeing the murder of George Floyd on TV in June 2020 (an unarmed man who was killed by a police officer who placed his knee on George's neck for over 8 minutes during an arrest for a non-violent crime), one group member said he started having flashbacks to his own arrest, which involved a swat team bursting into his home and pointing a gun at him.*
- *Another client said that watching victim empathy videos triggered so much shame and guilt that he found himself unable to sleep. He had obsessive thoughts wondering about the harm he'd caused to his victims.*
- *One man said that his parole officer, as an authority figure who had control over his life, reminded him of his abusive father. He had trouble even talking to his P.O., because it triggered memories of his childhood physical and emotional abuse. He found himself tempted to avoid his check-ins, but obviously he knows that would lead to exactly the punishment he most feared.*
- *Being in jail or prison can cause a person to be "hyper-aroused" – you are always on alert, looking around you for danger. Don't turn around, don't let your guard down, don't even sleep.*

Talk to your therapist about treatment strategies for PCTS / PTSD. Check back to chapters 3 & 4 as well, and review strategies for mindfulness and emotional self-regulation.

Putting It All Together

Congratulations on all the good work you've done. Go back to Figure 1.6 and review the treatment progress checklist. Are you doing well in all those areas? How have you made improvements in your life? It's time now to put it all together and finalize your relapse prevention plans. Use Exercise 8.14 to do so.

Exercise 8.14: Relapse Prevention Worksheets.

The tables below contain a summary of all the major questions you need to answer for your final relapse prevention and healthy life plans.

Internal Risk Factors	
Thoughts	**Feelings & Needs**
What were your distorted thoughts or thinking errors? How did you minimize and excuse your hurtful behavior in the past? How did you convince yourself that somebody or something else was to blame? How did you evaluate your offending after the fact? How have you restructured your thinking errors into appropriate, healthy thoughts?	What are the feelings that tend to trigger deviant thoughts and fantasies? How do you cope with those feelings now? If negative feelings arise from a sense of not having your needs met, how do you now attempt to consistently meet your emotional needs through healthy age-appropriate activities, encounters, and relationships?

External Risk Factors			
Places	**Situations/Events**	**Stimuli**	**Grooming**
Are there places that you should avoid? Where should you not go? Why do you think certain places are safe or unsafe for you in terms of level of risk?	Are there situations in your life that trigger urges to offend? How do you now handle stressors in healthy ways? How do you handle them when they arise unexpectedly? What are the riskiest situations for you? Under what circumstances do you see yourself as able or unable to be around minors or other vulnerable persons?	Who/what are you attracted to? How do these attractions become risky for you? How can you avoid and escape being exposed to risky stimuli? How do you use behavioral or cognitive interventions to control deviant arousal? How might the use of the Internet, other devices, pornography, or apps contribute to risk for you, and what do you do to manage that?	In what ways did you prepare victims for sexual assault? How did you gain their trust? How did you set up the opportunity to sexually offend? How are you avoiding manipulation or exploitation of others' vulnerabilities? What do you do now to stay away from grooming behaviors?

Healthy Life Plans			
Boundaries	**Victim Impact**	**Lifestyle Changes**	**Support Systems**
What have you learned about boundaries, and exactly how are you maintaining healthy and appropriate boundaries: • Physical • Psychological • Professional • Generational • Online / Virtual • Other	What have you learned about the impact of sexual violations on others, and how are you using that knowledge to devise specific strategies to avoid harming others? How so you also avoid physical, psychological, or other harm to others?	What lifestyle risk factors put you at risk for emotional, general, or sexual self-regulation challenges? List them and describe specific changes made to your lifestyle in all the areas that created risk. Include healthy sexuality plans, safety plans, and Internet plans you developed.	Who are your support persons? Name them. Who are your accountability persons, and how exactly do they help you stay accountable? Are there other support networks you have for other purposes in your life? Include healthy social activities.

Having Fun and Rewarding Yourself

Wait! You're not quite done. There is one more important piece to fit into the puzzle. You need to have joy in your life. You deserve to have joy, and fun! Life can be hard, but it should also be fun.

When all is said and done, what all of us most need in our lives is rewards. It's great when others reward us. But it's also important to reward ourselves for our hard work and our accomplishments. Who rewards themselves? All successful people do—that's who. It is important to reward yourself <u>each and every time</u> you successfully use a coping strategy. Every time you successfully avoid falling into traps of anger, deviant fantasies, or high-risk situations, you should immediately find something appealing with which to reward yourself for your good work. It is not enough to think of avoiding punishment as the only reward. You need to give yourself something that makes you feel good too.

Having Fun

When was the last time you had fun? What do you like to do for fun? What do you look forward to? What brings you joy?

Rewarding Yourself

Nobody works for free and you shouldn't either. Preventing relapse might be the hardest job you have ever done. Too often we notice our failings but forget to give credit where credit is due. Get in the habit of giving yourself credit. Make a list of things you will do to reward yourself each time you successfully use a coping strategy.

1. Consciously tell yourself that you are proud of yourself for implementing the coping strategy. Does that sound silly? It's not. It's a necessary and proven part of a fulfilling lifestyle. And it feels good. It's true that you have done something to be proud of. Why shouldn't you notice that and acknowledge it? Practice giving yourself positive reinforcement. Be specific as you remind yourself of exactly what you did to cope. Some examples of these statements might be:

"I did a really good job escaping that situation. I left the mall when I saw that attractive boy and went to amazon.com to pick out some books to read. I am proud of myself and I should be."

"It was good that I told my sister I couldn't baby-sit for her children. I shouldn't be alone with children. I asserted myself with her even though I was afraid she'd be mad. I'm proud I didn't give into my desires or her pressure."

"I made a good decision today not to go online to view porn when I felt depressed. I wanted to but I didn't give in and sure enough, the urge passed. I made a smart choice."

"It was good that I didn't drink at that party. When I drink my boundaries get weird and I get myself in trouble. It was good to stay sober and not have to worry then next day about what I might have done and didn't remember!"

2. Reward yourself with something that you really like and that is important to you. Your reward could be buying yourself something, or engaging in a hobby or non-sexual activity that is enjoyable and that you normally wouldn't do. It could be treating yourself to a favorite food. It could be putting some money away each time to save up to buy something big that you really want. If every time you successfully use a coping strategy you put away $5.00 or whatever you can afford, you will find that soon you have saved a substantial amount of money for that special item. Make sure you identify a specific item—a luxury item, not a necessary one—and begin a "savings account" that you will contribute to each time you use a prevention technique. Do not rob this account for spending money. The reward you are saving for is important for what it symbolizes: the new, smarter, healthier you.
3. Every time you successfully implement a coping strategy, tell your group about it. Your group will be impressed and will give you lots of credit for it. By sharing your coping strategy with the group, you will also be helping others (pay it forward!), which will make you feel good.

Exercise 8.15: Rewarding Yourself

Using the chart below, think of 5 recent examples of when you successfully avoided a lapse or an offense.

1. Make a list of at least 3 positive statements you can tell yourself to praise yourself when you successfully implement a coping strategy.
2. Make a list of at least 3 concrete ways you could reward yourself when you implement a coping strategy.

Situation:	What You Can Tell Yourself	What Brings You Joy And Fun In Life?	The Reward:

FINALLY!

It's been a long road to freedom, but now you're here. You deserve an enormous amount of credit. Celebrate your accomplishment and your new lifestyle. Start enjoying your life to the fullest.

Congratulations on a job well done!

Bibliography

Ackerman, A. R., & Levenson, J. S. (2019). *Healing from sexual violence: The case for vicarious restorative justice.* Brandon, VT: Safer Society Press.

American Psychiatric Association. (2013). *Diagnostic and Statistical manual of Mental Disorders (5th Edition).* Washington, D.C.: Author.

Andrews, D. A., & Bonta, J. (2017). *The psychology of criminal conduct* (4th ed.). Cincinnati, OH: Anderson Publishing.

Bailey, D. J. S. (2017). A Life of Grief: an Exploration of Disenfranchised Grief in Sex Offender Significant Others. *American Journal of Criminal Justice.*

Barnett, G. D., & Mann, R. E. (2012). Cognition, Empathy, and Sexual Offending. *Trauma, Violence, & Abuse, 14*(1), 22-33

Bloom, S. L., & Farragher, B. (2013). *Restoring Sanctuary: A New Operating System for Trauma-informed Systems of Care.* Oxford University Press.

Brown, B. (2018). Dare to Lead: Brave Work. Tough Conversations. Whole Hearts. Random House.

de Vries Robbé, M., de Vogel, V., Koster, K., & Bogaerts, S. (2015). Assessing protective factors for sexually violent offending with the SAPROF. *Sexual Abuse, 27*(1), 51-70.

Fernandez, Y. L. (2002). *In their shoes: Examining the issue of empathy and its place in the treatment of offenders.* Oklahoma City, OK: Wood'N'Barnes.

Garland, D. R., & Argueta, C. (2010). How clergy sexual misconduct happens: A qualitative study of first-hand accounts. *Social Work & Christianity, 37*(1), 1-27.

Gewirtz-Meydan, A., Walsh, W., Wolak, J., & Finkelhor, D. (2018). The complex experience of child pornography survivors. *Child Abuse & Neglect, 80,* 238-248.

Grady, M. D., Levenson, J. S., & Bolder, T. (2016). Linking Adverse Childhood Effects and Attachment A Theory of Etiology for Sexual Offending. *Trauma, Violence, & Abuse, 18*(4), 433-444.

Griffin, E., Moriarity, J., & Delmonico, D. L. (2001). *Cybersex Unhooked: A Workbook for Breaking Free of Compulsive Online Sexual Behavior:* Gentle Path Press.

Hanson, R. K., Bourgon, G., Helmus, L., & Hodgson, S. (2009). The principles of effective correctional treatment also apply to sexual offenders: A Meta-Analysis. *Criminal Justice and Behavior, 36*(9), 865-891.

Hanson, R. K., Harris, A. J. R., Letourneau, E., Helmus, L., & Thornton, D. (2018). Reductions in risk based on time offense free in the community: Once a sexual offender, not always a sexual offender *Psychology, Public Policy, and Law, 24*(1), 48-63.

Harris, D. A., & Levenson, J. S. (2020). Life on "the List" is a Life Lived in Fear: Post-Conviction Traumatic Stress in Men Convicted of Sexual Offenses. *International Journal of Offender Therapy and Comparative Criminology.*

Hawke, L. D., Provencher, M. D., & Arntz, A. (2011). Early Maladaptive Schemas in the risk for bipolar spectrum disorders. *Journal of Affective Disorders, 133*(3), 428-436. (Table 1).

Jung, S. (2017). *RNR Principles in Practice in the Management and Treatment of Sexual Abusers.* Brandon, VT: Safer Society Press.

Lasher, M. P., & McGrath, R. J. (2017). Desistance from sexual and other violent offending among child sexual abusers: Observations using the sex offender treatment intervention and progress scale. *Criminal justice and behavior, 44*(3), 416-431.

Levenson, J. S., & Tewksbury, R. (2009). Collateral damage: Family members of registered sex offenders. *American Journal of Criminal Justice, 34*(1), 54-68.

Levenson, J. S., Willis, G., & Prescott, D. (2017). *Trauma-informed Care: Transforming treatment for people who sexually abuse.* Brandon, VT: Safer Society Press.

Levenson, J. S., & Willis, G. M. (2019). Implementing Trauma-Informed Care in Correctional Treatment and Supervision. *Journal of Aggression, Maltreatment & Trauma, 28(*4), 481-501.

Malone, L. (2014). You're 16. You're a Pedophile. You don't want to hurt anyone. What do you do now? Matter, https://medium.com/matter/youre-16-youre-a-pedophile-you-dont-want-to-hurt-anyone-what-do-you-do-now-e11ce4b88bdb#.uj2ff35j6

Mann, R. E., Hanson, R. K., & Thornton, D. (2010). Assessing risk for sexual recidivism: Some proposals on the nature of psychologically meaningful risk factors. *Sexual Abuse, 22*(2), 191-217.

Marshall, W. L., Marshall, L. E., Serran, G. A., & O'Brien, M. D. (2011). *Rehabilitating sexual offenders: A strength-based approach:* American Psychological Association.

Maslow, A. (1943). A theory of human motivation. *Psychological review, 50*(4), 370-396.

McGrath R.J. (2016) Clinical Strategies for Evaluating Sexual Offenders. In: Phenix A., Hoberman H. (eds) Sexual Offending. Springer, New York, NY.

National Council of State Boards of Nursing (2018). https://www.ncsbn.org/ProfessionalBoundaries_Complete.pdf

National Sexual Violence Research Center https://www.nsvrc.org/

Prescott, D. (2009). *Building motivation for change in sexual offenders.* Safer Society Press.

Prochaska, J. O., & DiClemente, C. C. (1983). Stages and processes of self-change of smoking: toward an integrative model of change. *Journal of Consulting and Clinical Psychology, 51*(3), 390.

SAMHSA. (2014). TIP 57: *Trauma-Informed Care in Behavioral Health Services.* http://store.samhsa.gov/shin/content//SMA14-4816/SMA14-4816.pdf

Sawyer, S., & Jennings, J. L. (2016). *Group therapy with sex offenders: Engaging the full potential of the group experience.* Safer Society Press.

Seto, M. C. (2013). *Internet sex offenders.* American Psychological Association.

Seto, M. C., Stephens, S., Cantor, J. M., & Lalumière, M. L. (2016). The revised Screening Scale for Pedophilic Interests (SSPI-2): Development and criterion-related validation. *Sexual Abuse,* 29, 619-635.

Seto, M. C. (2018). *Pedophilia and sexual offending against children: Theory, assessment, and intervention* (2nd ed.). Washington, DC: American Psychological Association.

Seto, M. C. (2019). The Motivation-Facilitation Model of Sexual Offending. *Sexual Abuse, 31*(1), 3-24.

Skinner-Osei, P., & Levenson, J. S. (2018). Trauma-informed services for children with incarcerated parents. *Journal of Family Social Work, in press.*

Stinson, J. D., & Clark, M. D. (2017). *Motivational Interviewing with Offenders: Engagement, Rehabilitation, and Reentry.* Guilford Publications.

Suler, J. (2004). The online disinhibition effect. *Cyberpsychology & behavior, 7*(3), 321-326.

Trepper, T., & Barrett, M. J. (1989). *Systemic Treatment of Incest. A Therapeutic Handbook.* New York: Brunner Mazel.

Ward, T., & Fortune, C.-A. (2016). The role of dynamic risk factors in the explanation of offending. *Aggression and Violent Behavior, 29,* 79-88.

Ward, T., Hudson, S.M., Marshall, W.L., & Siegert, R. (1995). Attachment style and intimacy deficits in sexual offenders: a theoretical framework. *Sexual Abuse: A Journal of Research and Treatment,* 7, 317-335.

Ward, T., Yates, P. M., & Willis, G. M. (2012). The Good Lives Model and the Risk Need Responsivity Model A Critical Response to Andrews, Bonta, and Wormith (2011). *Criminal Justice and Behavior, 39*(1), 94-110.

Willis, G. M. (2017). Why call someone by what we don't want them to be? The ethics of labeling in forensic/correctional psychology. *Psychology, Crime & Law,* 1-17.

Wilson, R. J., Fernandez, Y., & Prescott, D. S. (2020). Ensuring Responsive Treatment Options for Male Adults Who Have Sexually Offended. *The Wiley Handbook of What Works with Sexual Offenders: Contemporary Perspectives in Theory, Assessment, Treatment, and Prevention,* 201-216.

Yates, P. M., & Prescott, D. (2011). *Building a better life: A good lives and self-regulation workbook.* Brandon, VT: Safer Society Press.

Yates, P. M., Prescott, D., & Ward, T. (2010). *Applying the good lives and self-regulation models to sex offender treatment: A practical guide for clinicians.* Brandon, VT: Safer Society Press

Young, J. E., Pascal, B., & Cousineau, P. (2005). Young Schema Questionnaire-Short Form 3 (YSQ-S3). *New York, NY: Schema Therapy Institute.*

This bibliography reflects many of the most influential sources that informed this book, but may not be exhaustive. We apologize if we missed any. We also thank and acknowledge the sharing of the resources on the following page which also provided research and ideas for this workbook.

https://www.ncsbn.org/ProfessionalBoundaries_Complete.pdf

http://internetbehavior.com/pdf/isst.pdf

RESOURCES FOR MINOR-ATTRACTED PERSONS

Professional

Help Wanted: https://www.helpwantedprevention.org/

Stop it Now! https://www.stopitnow.org/

The Prevention Project: http://theglobalpreventionproject.org/

Troubled Desires: https://troubled-desire.com/en/

Consumer-Driven

B4UAct: https://www.b4uact.org/attracted-to-minors/

Virtuous Pedophiles: https://www.virped.org/

ASAP: https://asapinternational.org/index.html

CSA Primary Prevention: https://www.csaprimaryprevention.org/i-like-kids.html